# THE BRONX

## Lost, Found, and Remembered (1935-1975)

by
Stephen M. Samtur
&
Martin A. Jackson

*In association with* Back in THE BRONX *magazine*

www.backinthebronx.com

Third Printing

Published by
Back In THE BRONX

Library of Congress Catalog Card Number: 98-96858

ISBN 0-9657221-1-2

*Visit our website –* www.backinthebronx.com

Printed in the United States of America

# Acknowledgements

Growing up in The Bronx gave me a feeling of pride and determination that helped shape my life. It is that pride and love of The Bronx that encourages me to keep the dreams of my borough alive for myself and for the millions of others who owe so much to The Bronx. As a result, a seed of an idea began with my magazine, **Back In THE BRONX**. The outpouring of response from my subscribers and the editing and publishing of the magazine, resulted in this book. Our many subscribers, along with some excellent writers, have contributed stories, pictures, slides, and video tapes which gave the book its shape. In fact, Martin Jackson, who collaborated on the book, was introduced to me through a story submission a few years ago.

Martin would like to thank his friends and relatives, who generously shared their deep knowledge of The Bronx with him. Linda Berlinger, Joan Grube, Beatrice Jackson were some who told tales of the Bronx, as did Saul Reichbach and The Bronx Boys who remembered great stories of Pelham Parkway. Our gratitude also to Fred Lane and his poker group, who spent an evening talking about The Bronx of the 1940s. Other Bronxites who happily reminisced about the old days were: Stanley Diamond, Ira Schneider, Robert Diamond, John Mariani, Joel Waldman, Ed Hundert, Larry Snyder, Len Kriegel, Stanley Aronowitz, Vic Ziegel, David Gonzalez and many members of the Bronx Science class of 1958. Jack Shadoian read several chapters and made important suggestions about Bronx movies.

Jonathan (Martin's son) surfed the net to great advantage in the past few years, and his daughter Johanna was a loyal if somewhat bewildered supporter of the project. Most important, though, was Martin's wife Joan who never doubted the outcome and provided the necessary refuge when The Bronx overwhelmed him.

I would like to thank those Bronx restaurants mentioned in the text for giving their precious pictures so graciously, some of which were more than 50 years old. Among them are Alex & Henry's, Charlie's Inn, Joe & Joe's, Louis' Seafood Restaurant, Mario's, Ann and Tony's, Gino's, and the Wedge Inn. The Bronx transportation chapter was a collaboration of the writings of individuals who shared one passion: a love for Bronx mass transit. They gave us pictures, slides, films, videos and most importantly their knowledge of Bronx buses, trolleys and trains. They are Ed Davis, Sr., Gary Grahl, Richard Marks, Steve Goldman, as well as Mrs. Roger Arcara, who gave us access to her late husband Roger's unbeatable collection of pictures and slides.

Pictures for other chapters were contributed by Carl Rosenstein (Art Deco including text), Hank de Cillia (Parkchester including text), Spencer Field (Highbridge), Howie Cohen, Murray Schneider, Jay Becker and Alan Bredberg (Freedomland) and Bob Mangels (Freedomland including text), Scott Mlyn (candy stores), Richard Sklenar from the Theatre Historical Society (movies) and Marvin Scott, whose photography hobby as a Bronx adolescent provided pictures throughout the book. Other pictures came from the N.Y. Historical Society, and the Bronx Historical Society, where Laura Tosi was especially helpful. Mark McKellor of New York Parks and Recreation Department (Van Cortlandt and Pelham Bay) gave valuable help and the researchers at Corbis Picture Archives turned up several excellent photos. A very special thanks to Ken Cobb, the Director of the Municipal Archives in N.Y.C., for his patience and cooperation, and for permitting accessibility to their wonderful Bronx photos.

Lloyd Ultan, a former President of the Bronx Historical Society and a pre-eminent Bronx historian, graciously read early versions of this book, and his suggestions were always valuable. Sandy and Al Zuckerman, and Lily Brandwein generouly gave their time to proof our manuscript. Mike Weiss, a retired teacher, also a DeWitt Clinton '61 classmate and good friend, added a keen insight and perspective as well as thoughtful suggestions. Paul Fargis, of The Stonesong Press, drew upon his three decades of publishing experience and frequently offered his expertise. Bert Neufeld, a talented writer and a Bronx native, gave us the benefit of his advertising experience at several stages along the way. This book would not have been possible without the hard work and technical skill of Barbara Frontera and Diane Huntzicker of Flashback Word Processing.

Finally, I would like to thank my Bronx born wife, Susan, an author of three books herself (none on the Bronx, however) for having the wisdom to marry a Bronxite, and for her patience through the years while I was consumed by this book. I would also like to apologize to our four sons: Adam, Michael, Mark and Stuart, for enduring the dozens of stories about The Bronx and about my youth there, which had little if any relevance to them.

*– Stephen Samtur*

# PREFACE

Photo: UPI/Bettman

**The Grand Concourse looking south in 1946, taken from Louis Morris Apartment Building**. The towers of Manhattan are visible in the distance, as is **Bronx Lebanon Hospital** on the left. The engineers who designed this sweeping boulevard showed striking foresight; by the late 50's and 60's, cars would crowd these same streets that seem so oddly empty in this photo. Parking was easy in the 40's, no need for meters or alternate side rules.

In Catena, Sicily there is a grim and featureless slum area where youth crime is an epidemic and poverty is almost universal. Burnt cars and trash fill the streets; there are few amenities and the housing is flimsy and overcrowded. It is a place for tourists to avoid.

The local inhabitants have named the place "The Bronx."

How this American name was transported across the sea and applied to a nasty neighborhood in a Sicilian port city is a fascinating lesson in media influence, but it also tells us volumes about The Bronx. The citizens of Catena probably aren't especially well versed in American urban history; they would be hard put, we suspect, to name the other four boroughs of New York City. But they do have television in Catena. And they've had American movies for fifty years or so, ever since World War II came to an end. What they know of The Bronx, we can surmise, comes from the media and generally is an unsavory portrait. What Sicilians (and Indians, Japanese and Brazilians too), know of The Bronx is that poor people live there, that crime is out of control, and that ordinary Americans avoid the place like Chernobyl. The image of The Bronx held by countless millions around the world is scary in an exciting sort of way; it exudes an aura of forbidden and mysterious life, the late twentieth century inheritor perhaps of the legend of old Shanghai or the London docks. It appears, in other words, to be a place where civilization has exhausted itself and savagery rules undisturbed.

Around the world, when the media seeks to make concrete the collapse of urban life, the word "Bronx" comes easily to mind. Sadly, The Bronx has probably earned at least a portion of that unwelcome fame — it was, until recently, in fact a place with a high crime rate and substantial problems of poverty, drugs, and poor housing. Not that there weren't untouched pleasant streets and happy people there, but it is hard, nonetheless, to convince people that The Bronx of the 1990s is the ideal urban settlement.

But once the image of The Bronx was very different. There was a time, in the middle of the twentieth century, when The Bronx provided comfort, peace and an island of prosperity for waves of working class people who strove for the American dream with all their might. In The Bronx, to a considerable extent, they found it. This book is about that time, and those people, and that place called The Bronx.

The Bronx barely existed, except for some scattered hamlets and farms, in the nineteenth century. Once a part of Westchester County, it was annexed to New York City in two stages, 1874 and 1895, finally becoming a borough of New York City in 1898. What surprises the student of The Bronx and its people is how quickly that region flourished, and how rapidly it filled with people. The boom began, in earnest, in the first decade of the twentieth century

when the subway lines had finally been extended north from Manhattan, thus making transportation a simple matter for the prospective Bronx settler. Two of the city's subways, the IRT and the IND, built their tracks into the still green fields and meadows of The Bronx, linking up tiny communities such as **West Farms** and **Morrisania** and making them part of the urban network. In a magically short time, the real estate speculators and then the builders had followed the subways, and The Bronx had sprouted a dense forest of buildings. The open spaces available in The Bronx challenged the urban planners and developers of the 1900s, some of whom sketched luxurious apartment houses and planned communities, others who saw the commercial possibilities of a matchless transportation system. The City itself seemed to rise to the moment, providing funds for libraries, schools, parks and, in a fit of truly inspired civic activism, built the magnificent **Grand Boulevard** and **Concourse** to be the grandest thoroughfare in the borough.

Private hands built **Yankee Stadium, New York University,** the **Concourse Plaza Hotel,** and thousands of apartment buildings ranging from dreary, tenement to glorious Art Deco. The stores followed the people, everything from corner groceries to imposing department stores, including the cherished Bronx institution of the candy store. And, of course, there were the movie theaters, men's shops, dress emporiums and the myriad outlets for the 20th century's consumer abundance. The rise of The Bronx, in fact, was concurrent with the economic miracle that was America in the first half of the twentieth century, a time when (despite the Great Depression, of which more later) Americans found themselves with a living standard that had no historical parallel, when impossible dreams of affluence became ordinary lifestyles.

The Bronx was the unwitting beneficiary of the capitalist success following World War I. It was the American dream translated into concrete, populated by the rapidly rising immigrants who, not many years before, had packed the steerage of ships from Europe. What The Bronx represented to these people, the Jews, Italians, Irish and Germans who once dared look no further than Ellis Island, was achievement and personal success. To move from the slums of the Lower East Side or Hell's Kitchen into the fine apartments of The Bronx meant a victory for the immigrant generation. For the children of those immigrants and laborers, The Bronx meant home and what has become, in retrospect, an unreproducible moment in their lives. Looking back, The Bronx meant security, joy and a cultural life remarkably rich in variety. Is this middle-aged nostalgia? Are we veterans of The Bronx at mid-century guilty of overlooking the reality and investing those days and that place with undeserved quality?

Maybe a little. But nostalgia has a basis in fact, too, and what we remember of The Bronx was mostly good, not perfect, but good enough to linger for decades and to still generate an unreasonable passion among those who were there. In this book, we hope to make some part of those days come to life again and to justify, somehow, our memories. Our success will be measured in how often the reader smiles in recognition, and how many long forgotten memories are brought glistening to the surface again.

# Table of Contents

# ART DECO: THE BRONX GOLDEN AGE

**The Fish Building**. 1150 Grand Concourse. Archt. Horace Ginsbern 1937 With its unique aquatic mosaic, and entry doors with overlapping, stainless steel, 3/4 circles which cleverly create piscine shapes, it's no surprise that this is popularly known in Bronx vernacular as the "Fish Building." The textile blocks punctuated with circles (possibly portholes?) surrounding the stainless steel canopy, were borrowed from Frank Lloyd Wright's canon. Also note the wave-like half circles that comprise the entablature.

Everybody who ever walked the **Grand Concourse** remembers the "Fish" building. It has a real name and address, but the thing that stands out is the amazing mosaic on the front of fish swimming through some tropical setting. The building stands (even today) at **McClellan Place** and the **Concourse**, and it is a perfect example of a period in Bronx history when architects and builders made The Bronx a world leader in Art Deco design.

The **Concourse** is the focal point of Art Deco building, but it isn't alone in The Bronx. There are major examples of the style in nearly every neighborhood from **Hunts Point** to **Riverdale**, and the number of buildings decorated in that elegant linear fashion runs into the hundreds. Indeed, The Bronx has achieved a world wide status as a home for Art Deco, rivaled only by South Beach in Miami. Why this should be so, and how these buildings came to be built in the humble streets of The Bronx, is a fascinating story.

In large part, The Bronx was in the right place at the right time. Art Deco was a style of architectural and furniture design that emerged from the Paris Exposition of 1925. It emphasized linear patterns, abstract decorations and was modeled closely on the industrial vision of the factory and laboratory. Art Deco manifested itself in furniture, jewelry, interior decor and especially in such modern products as radios, cameras, locomotives, airplanes and, most dramatically, automobiles. It was viewed as the trademark of the twentieth century, a breakthrough in contemporary art and decor, a true voice of the new times. In Germany, the famous Bauhaus movement helped propagate the new style, and in France, Italy and Russia, the most exciting designers and architects found their voice in the angles and speed of Art Deco. To be fashionable in the late '20s was to buy an Art Deco living room set, or hang an Art Deco mirror, or at least to show familiarity with the latest trend by wearing a piece of Art Deco jewelry.

*Photo: Carl Rosenstein*
**750 Grand Concourse.** Archt. Jacob Felson 1937. The etched palm trees and tropical terrazzo motif give this lobby a Miami Beach feel.

Hollywood, too, was deeply affected by the new fashion from Europe. Look at the movies of the early '30s, to see the height of elegance exemplified by daring white bedrooms and soaring Art Deco interiors. As Jean Harlow and Fred Astaire gracefully lived in these movie dream homes, audiences dreamt of having some part of the style for themselves.

Art Deco was nicely suited to building construction. It was new, it was highly popular, it carried the message of modernity, and best of all, it was not overly expensive. Architects were swept away by the possibilities inherent in the style, with its curving windows and modernistic details. All over Europe in the '30s, and eventually in America, the cutting edge of architectural design was Art Deco. In New York, we can see Art Deco enshrined in two of the major buildings of the early '30s: the Empire State and the Chrysler Building. Both use the Art Deco vocabulary to give concrete reality to the speed, function and science of the twentieth century. They announce their break with tradition by the heavy use of Art Deco details in lobbies, elevators, facades and windows. Other monuments to Art Deco, in

*Photo: Carl Rosenstein*
**The Park Plaza Apartments.** 1005 Jerome Ave. Archt. Horace Ginsbern 1928. This Early Art Deco building is a designated NYC Landmark. It was influenced by the 1925 Exposition Internationales des Art Decoratifs et Industriels Modernes in Paris. It is influenced by Mayan architecture in both its pyramid form and its decorative motifs.

**Art Deco Row.** Grand Concourse between McClellan and 167th Street. This streetscape includes the Fish Building, 1166 Grand Concourse, also by Ginsbern in 1936, and the geometric 1188 Grand Concourse by Jacob Felson, 1937.

Manhattan alone, are the Daily News Building and the McGraw Hill Building (both on 42nd Street as it happens). Other parts of the nation also felt the impact of Art Deco. Los Angeles had a substantial assortment of modern design, spurred notably by the movie industry. Miami Beach was famous, and has become famous again in the 1990s, for its dozens of Art Deco hotels and homes in the South Beach area.

Art Deco was a style that could be essentially pasted on a traditional building, providing an exciting dash and vigor to the stodgy square lines of the office block or the tenement. It involved little in the way of fundamental structural change, but it added a welcome facade to the otherwise ordinary housing plans. Builders, in other words, found Art Deco a congenial and affordable luxury. It sold apartments and stimulated business without requiring expensive new techniques.

Real estate was the growth industry of The Bronx during the first twenty years of the twentieth century. It was the arena in which fortunes were made and neighborhoods created out of thin air. By the end of the 1920s, the glitter had worn off the building boom in The Bronx and savvy developers were casting about for new enticements. The Stock Market Crash of 1929 and the ensuing Depression were, of course, painful to the housing industry all over America, and no less than in The Bronx. One of the solutions to the sluggish

> **A**rt Deco came to define a time and place in Bronx life, and it set the tone for the following few decades in Bronx culture.

**185 Saint George Crescent (a side street between 206th & Van Cortlandt Ave.).** This Art Deco classic has an elegant forecourt and a streamlined entrance.

**1001 Jerome Avenue.** Sugarman & Berger, 1941. The terrazzo floor with its polychromatic Mondrian inspired design is the best in the Bronx. The mural above the fireplace mantel was inspired by the Italian surrealist Giorgio de Chirico.

**2830 Grand Concourse, "The Town Towers."** Archt. Horace Ginsbern 1931. One of the grandest lobbies on the Concourse.

market of the time was an effort to sell amenities. Instead of merely providing apartments at reasonable rents, the builders sold a life style, an ambiance. And it was a very successful campaign, particularly in the West Bronx.

High on the list of amenities offered by anxious landlords were design and style. A three bedroom apartment was fine, but a three bedroom apartment in an Art Deco building, with a smartly decorated lobby, was something else again. And if the landlord could also offer a sunken living room, curved casement windows, a tiled mosaic on the building entrance, some futuristic looking furniture in the lobby along with modern paintings, and top it all off with incised metal entrance doors,

set-backs on the upper floors, and a green area in front, then the apartments would practically sell themselves. On the **Concourse**, with its air of luxury, the prospective tenant might also expect a doorman, elevator service, and parquet floors, not to mention stall showers in the bathroom, an ample entrance foyer to the apartment, and all the latest kitchen appliances. It went without saying that the landlord painted for each new tenant and turned over a spotless, and completely repaired, apartment.

**2155 Grand Concourse.** Archt. Herbert Lillien, 1939. This zig-zag façade was influenced by cubism.

**Tremont Towers.** 333 E. 176th Street. Archt. Jacob Felson, 1937. Detail of terra cotta entrance emblem. The "frozen fountain" was a popular symbol of the Art Deco age popularized by the 1925 Paris Expo.

This was not sheer generosity on the part of the landlords of the '30s. There was a serious glut of apartments in The Bronx, with many buildings standing half empty and others being taken over by the banks for defaulting on loans. Enterprising tenants could manipulate the situation by moving frequently, and taking advantage of the usual one or even two months' rental allowance designed to attract new customers. Many Bronxites can remember moving three or four times a year during the '30s, getting the free rent from the landlord, and then signing on for yet another apartment to start the process all over again. A busy (if slightly immoral) tenant could probably live rent free for most of the year by playing the game of allowances. This changed with World War II, and the landlords got their revenge in spades, when apartments were nearly impossible to find and remained so until well into the 1960s.

In many ways, Art Deco was a style that might have been created for use in The Bronx. It found a home there, thanks to the nature and function of Bronx architecture. In the late 1930s, as many as three hundred recognizably Art Deco apartment buildings were erected in The Bronx, and most of those in the area on or around the **Grand Concourse**. Art Deco came to define a time and place in Bronx life, and it set the tone for the following few decades in Bronx culture. The rise of the Art Deco style happily coincided with a revival in the building industry that occurred in the late 1930s (the New Deal helped in this case) and which continued until the outbreak of World War II in 1941.

The War, with its shortages of labor and material, largely eliminated housing construction and so the Art Deco style

Photo: Carl Rosenstein

**1295 Grand Concourse.** This "Apartments Available" sign with its stylized Deco graphics still instructs you to call the original *Jerome 7* exchange. An elevator apartment was considered a luxury when this building was constructed.

and highly desirable dwelling place, in The Bronx or elsewhere. And often, "pre-war" meant Art Deco.

The Art Deco legacy of The Bronx was, naturally, threatened during the tumult of the '70s. Many fine examples were lost to fire and decay, and many others were razed for newer construction. But there is still an impressive array of these Art Deco monuments to be found in The Bronx, some having been restored, and some never losing their luster. A ride up the **Concourse** from, say, **161st Street** to **170th Street**, will reveal a dozen or more notable Art Deco structures, still beautifully framed by the trees and broad lanes of the **Concourse** and still impressive in their rightness for the urban environment. The edges may be a bit frayed, it is true, but The Bronx Art Deco buildings have survived.

remained a legacy of the Depression era. When peace returned in 1945, the public taste had changed and Art Deco, although hardly ten years old, was viewed as old fashioned and "prewar." What the returning veterans wanted was not found in The Bronx in any event. They were after private homes, not apartment buildings. The energy and innovation that might have once gone into Bronx apartments now (in 1945) went into single family housing in Queens, or Westchester, or most dramatically, Levittown. In coming years, ironically, the term "prewar" would signify a solid, well built

Photo: Carl Rosenstein

**888 Grand Concourse.** A transitional streamlined building with distant meso-american resonance. Emery Roth was a prolific architect with many key commissions in Manhattan, including the St. Moritz on Central Park South and the San Remo Apartment on Central Park West.

# A Day at the Beaches, Pools and Parks in The Bronx

**A crowded day at Orchard Beach.** During the war years, many Bronxites found **Orchard Beach** a cheap, convenient and surprisingly clean recreation site. In the years before foreign travel or even automobiles were widely available, **Orchard Beach** was a haven for the hot Bronx apartment dweller. There wasn't surf to speak of, but the water was always refreshing. The beach was traditionally divided along neighborhood, ethnic and even age lines; everyone knew where to go.

Bronxites, during the post-war years, had a surprisingly large selection of parks, beaches and swimming clubs to occupy their leisure hours. Enlightened city planning in the twentieth century stressed healthful recreation for the urban dweller, and the urbanization of The Bronx, coming late in the history of New York City, benefited from this emphasis. The result was a first-rate assortment of open areas, playgrounds, beaches and otherwise recreational locations that gave The Bronx inhabitant a wide choice of activity. Swimming, for example, was a favorite warm-weather pastime.

Considering that The Bronx was hardly famous as a seaside resort, it contained, within its borders, one of the best municipal bathing facilities in New York City, **Orchard Beach**. Built with the usual vigor and sweeping scale by Robert Moses during the 1930s, **Orchard Beach** replaced an open **Pelham Bay** at the northeast corner of the borough and was a prize demonstration of New Deal money wisely spent. A vast sweep of open space was carved out of the wilderness. Tons of beautiful white sand were trucked in to make a perfect sitting area and beach. Backed up by bold Art Deco bathhouses and cafeterias, **Orchard Beach** was a jewel in the municipal

*Photo: City of New York/Parks & Recreation, Van Cortlandt & Pelham Bay*

**Mass baptism at Orchard Beach.** One of the annual affairs at the beach was a baptismal celebration by local churches. Hundreds of worshippers were welcomed into the faith via the shallow waters off **Orchard Beach**. Note the interracial nature of this group, still not a common sight in the 1940s.

recreation system, and even today remains popular with the newest Bronx residents.

For The Bronx, **Orchard Beach** was a resounding success. Almost from its first day, it became a favorite spot for young people, families and anybody else, of any age, who could manage the tricky commute to the far flung strand. The only real problem with **Orchard Beach** was its location. It simply wasn't easily gotten to from anywhere else. In the '40s and '50s, before automobile ownership was taken for granted, commuting to **Orchard Beach** was a logistical problem worthy of a three star general. The City, of course, made sure there was bus service to the beach, but even the buses weren't convenient for the great bulk of Bronx inhabitants. The best way was certainly by car if a willing father or uncle could be persuaded to transport a few of the neighborhood kids to **Orchard Beach**. Subways wouldn't work. There just weren't any subway lines in that part of The Bronx. This left either buses or bicycles, and it was hard to

carry blankets, coolers, strollers and bags on a bicycle. The bus, therefore, was the favored means of transport and dozens of buses per hour could be

*Photo: City of New York/Parks & Recreation
Van Cortlandt & Pelham Bay*

**Groundskeepers at work at Orchard Beach in the late '40s.** Everything from sand to foliage was carefully planned and imported from elsewhere. There seemed to have been ample labor to keep up appearances.

*Photo: The Bettman Archives*

**Interior of the cafeteria at Orchard Beach.** Men still wore hats, even to the beach, in the '40s and some couples came to stroll on the boardwalk rather than swim. The cafeteria was always a central meeting place at **Orchard Beach**. It could seat several hundred.

*Photo: City of New York/Parks & Recreation Van Cortlandt & Pelham Bay*

**The heart of Orchard Beach.** Ahead lay the cafeteria, the bathhouse an the all important rest rooms. All of this, of course, was free to all comers. There were elaborate rules to follow once on the beach: no pets, no bottles, no running, no bicycles. Most people obeyed out of civic duty.

seen pulling up to the imposing terminal of Orchard Beach on a hot summer day. Still, the bus trip from, say, **University Avenue** or from **Riverdale**, could take an hour or more, and in an un-air conditioned bus at that! It was no picnic. The price was right, though. For most of the time, up until the late '50s, fares on Bronx buses were a nickel. For that five cents (or later ten or fifteen cents) the beachgoer would often have to stand for most of the journey, or at best be packed in with several dozen other people on the lurching ride across **Fordham Road** or down **Westchester Avenue**. Not that these hardships deterred thousands of Bronxites from trekking up to **Pelham Bay Park**, and it was always a great moment when the lumbering bus would finally break free of the streets and enter into the gently curving driveways that heralded the approach of **Orchard Beach**. Many times, the passengers would cheer spontaneously as the sign reading "**Orchard Beach**" came into view. The sign itself became famous for its resounding negative voice. A very large graphic "NO" stood out, followed by a long list of prohibited activities, from running to cooking to bicycle riding, ball playing and fishing. The veteran beachgoer calmly ignored these rules, and so long as truly dangerous actions weren't performed, the police were content to live and let live.

Once unloaded, the eager swimmers headed quickly for their favorite piece of sand. And everybody had a special destination in mind, too. There were patches of beach favored by various age groups, neighborhoods and (let's be honest) by race and ethnic identity, too. The sand looked the same, the water was definitely the same, but for mysterious reasons, some few feet of **Orchard Beach** looked better than other parts. What everyone did share was the sun, the salty air and the amazingly clean sand of this municipal amenity.

Photo: *City of New York/Parks & Recreation, Van Cortlandt & Pelham Bay*
**An aerial view of Orchard Beach.** Robert Moses made his mark on The Bronx with the great municipal beach on **Pelham Bay**. The mid-30's New Deal style is evident, and the bold scale of the project is well illustrated in this panorama. A large number of bathers arrived at **Orchard Beach** by bus, as witnessed by the nearly empty parking lots. The bathhouses on either wing could handle thousands of visitors.

about not swimming after meals. This bit of folk wisdom was deeply engrained in Bronxites, who passed it on from one generation to another. You would drown if you went in the water after eating. Everybody knew that. You would get "cramps", God forbid.

Sunburn was a far less understood result of a day at the beach, at least back in the '50s. A little dose of sunburn was long-viewed as beneficial, a part of a good summer's healthy activity, almost a badge of honor. Little kids delighted in peeling away bits of burnt flesh after a visit to the beach. And it was widely believed that a nice tanned complexion was proof of parental interest and of the availability of fresh air. Anybody who went away to the Catskills, for example, and came home without a tan after a summer's

Lunches would be unpacked, blankets spread on the chosen ground, and the kids let loose to splash in the water. It wasn't really surf, being the calm waters of Long Island Sound as contained by **Pelham Bay**, but it was wet and cold and on a hot day that was all that mattered. The waves were of the smallest variety possible, probably at the specific demand of Bronx mothers who would have been horrified at real surf. And just to make sure, the authorities provided long lines of rope and buoys stretching out from the sand to the deepest water so that uncertain swimmers could always hold on. Swimming at **Orchard Beach** wasn't a daredevil sport. It was more a refreshing dip in the water than a challenge to nature, and that was the way The Bronx preferred it.

Safety was always a paramount concern at the beach. Mothers transported all manner of umbrellas, hats, sunglasses and suntan lotion to make sure the kids weren't too mistreated by the hot sun. And, of course, there were the urgent commands

Photo: *City of New York/Parks & Recreation Van Cortlandt & Pelham Bay*
**The tennis courts at Orchard Beach.** Tennis wasn't a particularly popular game in The Bronx back in the '40s, and even these two lone players are practicing paddleball not tennis. Still, the courts were there, in perfect condition, ready for anyone who cared to indulge. It is clearly wartime; both players are in uniform.

vacation, must surely have done something wrong. Wasting a sunny day inside was an affront to nature, and a red flag to parents in The Bronx. It ranked among medical and health risks with the deadly "running with a pencil" or the even more frightening "eating God-knows-what from the street." Today, the baneful effects of sunburn are more widely known but it is probably too late for a generation of Bronxites (and others

**Shorehaven Salt Water Pool**

from the '50s) whose parents pushed them out of the house into the powerful ultraviolet rays of a mid-day sun.

**Orchard Beach** was only one possible outdoor destination for the apartment dwellers of The Bronx. As automobiles became more common in the '50s, many Bronx families trekked as far as Jones Beach, another Robert Moses project on Long Island's south shore. Or perhaps to Rockaway, Long Beach or south to the Jersey Shore. More accessible by bus was Palisades Amusement Park, just south of the George Washington Bridge on the Jersey Palisades. For Bronxites, Palisades was a relatively short ride away and while it had no real ocean, it did boast the "world's largest salt-water pool." And, of course, Palisades had the lure of rides, games and a carnival atmosphere that was only equalled by Coney Island itself.

Such voyages weren't really necessary, however. Within the borders of The Bronx there were ample spaces to play. **Van Cortlandt Park**, for example, was rich in woods, baseball diamonds, soccer fields

and even golf courses. It was the favorite destination of school outings and competitions, and always hosted a series of Bronx athletic events. In the 1970s, **Van Cortlandt** became the focal point of new games and new Bronxites. Soccer was avidly played by Irish teams and cricket matches drew a big West Indian following to the green lawns in the North Bronx. There was also **Crotona Park**, surrounded by some of the densest populations in the city in the **Tremont** section. There was a major league-sized baseball diamond in **Crotona Park**, along with a boating lake, numerous playgrounds and nicely planted areas for just walking. At the **Tremont Avenue** side of **Crotona Park** was a lavish late-Victorian garden complete with a marble fountain and sweeping staircases leading up to a stately old Borough office building. By the '50s, these amenities had fallen into some disrepair, but they served for the local kids to play in while the WPA of the 1930s had substantially upgraded the walks, fields and boathouses in the rest of the Park. Well into the '60s, it was

Shorehaven Pavilion

as if at the beach, with enough activities to keep everyone busy for days on end. **Castle Hill**, for example, had two Olympic-sized pools, sufficient for hundreds of bathers, not to mention a large wading pool for children. This was in addition to several ball fields, tennis and basketball courts, handball facilities and even a four-wall handball stadium. **Shorehaven** was even larger. It, reputedly, had space for forty thousand people, although that number of people probably never attended at one time. **Castle Hill** seemed more a family situation, while **Shorehaven** had a slightly younger crowd and a reputation for glitzy affairs. At **Shorehaven**, there were dances, live bands and a singles crowd, something like a Catskill resort. **Castle Hill** was famous for its softball tournament, its swimming races and a more sedate social scene. At both clubs, though, dating and matchmaking were a favorite pastime and more than one marriage was initiated at the poolside of **Castle Hill** or on the dance floor at **Shorehaven**.

still possible to rent rowboats on **Indian Lake** in **Crotona Park**, or to fish for little perch and crappies with a bent safety pin. In the 1990s, **Crotona Park**'s facilities were repaired and expanded, including the building of serious tennis courts which today host a professional tournament. Other parks were neighborhood refuges. **St. Mary's, Claremont, Franz Siegal, Poe Park, Soundview,** and **Macombs Dam Park** all had their devotees and allowed for vigorous outdoor activity.

For those still anxious to swim or enjoy water sports, The Bronx offered a number of private beach clubs and swimming pools. Foremost in the memory of many Bronxites were **Shorehaven Beach Club**, and **Castle Hill Pool** both sited in the far east on the edges of Long Island Sound. There were smaller, and older beach clubs, too, such as **Starlight Park** and The **Bronx Bathing Club**, but these were little more than pools with a bare fringe of concrete around them. **Castle Hill** and **Shorehaven**, on the other hand, were extensive resort-like parks where families could sit with chairs and blankets,

*Photo: Judy Piesco*

**Castle Hill Pool, 1944.** The kiddie pool, two feet of warm water for the youngest members.

Being strictly private (and profit making) businesses, **Castle Hill** and **Shorehaven** were selective in their membership. Both required photo IDs for entrance, and there was considerable social distinction in their admission standards. Neither ever admitted a Black person during the '50s and '60s. The membership was heavily Jewish, with a sprinkling of Italian, Irish or other European ethnic groups. In other words, a fairly accurate reflection of The Bronx's population from the '40s through the '60s.

The Bronx, of course, was home to two of the major outdoor attractions in the entire city: The **Bronx Zoo**, and The **New York Botanical Garden**. The **Zoo** drew visitors from all over the city and the country, making it far more than a local Bronx attraction. For kids in The Bronx, though, the **Zoo** was just one more (albeit, more elaborate) park waiting to be explored and utilized for fun. During the '40s and '50s, admission to the **Zoo** was only ten or fifteen cents, and that only on certain days. Many days were free so Bronx youngsters frequently took advantage of the world-class facilities. It just seemed natural, although in retrospect, it was amazing that square in the middle of the urbanized Bronx were elephants, lions, hippopotamuses and wondrous birds, housed in fantastic turn of the century buildings. There was a famous Children's Zoo, coupled with animal rides and boating lakes.

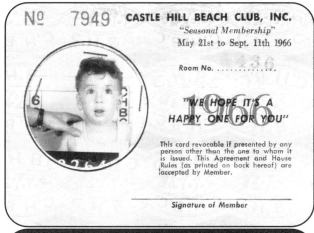

Photo: Judy Piesco
**A pass from Castle Hill Pool.** Sharp eyed guards checked these at the entrance.

Tract train #8 at The Bronx Zoo - Fordham Gate

Running through it all was The **Bronx River**, almost primitive in its unspoiled setting. The **Zoo** was full of surprise turns and winding paths, so that whole days could be spent in exploring and watching the exhibits. On Sundays, in good weather, the **Zoo** would be packed to capacity with families on outings, peering over the elephant moats and giggling at the chimpanzees, all in surprising peace and cleanliness.

The **Zoo** thoughtfully provided a cafeteria, numerous refreshment stands, and even tables where families could bring their picnic lunches. Food was an important item for the animals, too. Feeding the elephants and the monkeys was a widely practiced entertainment.

**The Bronx Zoo in the '40s.** One of the highpoints of any visit was the sea lion pool, especially at feeding times. Note the number of neckties worn and other Sunday attire among these avid viewers. Some families would spend an entire day at the zoo followed by dinner, perhaps on **Arthur Avenue** just a few blocks away.

Again the **Zoo** provided. There were dispensing machines set up around the Park, where, for a nickel, a packet of proper animal food could be purchased. Otherwise, the animals got whatever was left over from the lunch bag, despite the signs warning against feeding the animals anything but approved food. Best of all was watching the keepers feed the animals, and they usually made a show out of the event. Lions and other carnivores were, of course, fed meat and it was always a thrill to see the powerful jaws go to work on a leg of beef. The most entertaining show was at the sea lion pool, a concrete replica of an ice floe where a family of sea lions and seals cavorted for the visitors. The keepers became very adept at tossing fish to the seals, pitching herring out of a bucket towards the wait-

ing seals who then caught them in mid-air. The audience never failed to applaud each graceful catch, and somehow the seals never missed.

Another thrill at the **Zoo**, of a very different kind, was housed in the snake house, or the serpentorium. Inside was a dark and slightly eerie atmosphere, perfect for viewing the (presumably) deadly snakes and lizards. There were, in fact, cobras, rattlers and other harmful specimens behind the thick glass, but most of the displays were of peacefully snoozing snakes. Everybody tried to rouse the cobras, usually to no avail, and there was never a moment when a girl or mother wasn't squealing with delighted fright at the sight of the long evil-looking reptiles. The boys and men, naturally, put on a stern and confident face and maybe even knocked on the window to show

**One of the favorite stops in any Bronx Zoo visit was the famous Children's Zoo situated directly across from the elephants.** In this little bit of early Disneyland, a fantasy of arks, castles and duck ponds enchanted the youngest zoo visitors. For Bronx kids, the chance to pet a goat or a pony was something special and few parents could resist the lure of the pastel colored structures of the Children's Zoo. It was also one of the best photo ops ever created, and the number of pictures taken of tykes feeding a duck or petting a burro probably number in the millions. There was a small admission charge, and adults were admitted at a lower price, but only in the company of a child.

their courage. What would have happened without the glass to protect them is anybody's guess, and this thought was never left unexpressed by someone in the crowd.

The snake house also had the most fascinating of all the **Zoo's** exhibits — the ants. Right at the entrance to the snake exhibit (for some taxonomic reason) there was a case housing a colony of leaf cutter ants. Endlessly and tirelessly, these ants scurried over a wooden bridge to a pile of leaves, cut them into little pieces, and carried the bits back to the nest. A detailed poster gave the visitor a full history and description of the ants and their habits, but just watching the little creatures was an education. Right across the room from the ants was

*Photo: Julian A. Belin*

**Another attraction at the Zoo was this pleasant stretch of The Bronx River where rowboats and paddleboats were rented by the hour.** This summer scene in the 1940s captures the peaceful atmosphere of the park.

**Bronx Botanical Gardens Main Conservatory in 1946.** This remarkable piece of Victorian artistry still graces the grounds at **Botanical Gardens** located at the junction of **Mosholu Parkway North** and **Webster Avenue** between **Fordham Road** and **Gun Hill Road**. On Sundays, the Conservatory and greenhouse were filled with visiting families who delighted in the unmatched collection of flowers and trees from around the world.

a display of electric eels, including one specimen hibernating in a kind of mud cocoon. The idea here was to touch the tank holding the eel and wait for an electric shock. It never came of course.

Alongside the elephant house, in the **Zoo's** central mall, there were animal rides for the kids. Camels and ponies were the beasts of choice here, taking the children a hundred yards or so down the dusty path and back again to the waiting parents. There weren't many Bronx families of the era who failed to have a picture of the children riding a camel, petting a sheep or smiling in front of the elephant.

Even more picturesque than the **Zoo**, if possible, was the adjacent **Botanical Garden**. By some miracle

of municipal planning and urban beautification, The Bronx also hosted a world-class **Botanical Garden**, just across **Pelham Parkway** from the **Zoo**. It was usually too exhausting to cover both **Zoo** and **Botanical Garden** in one day, but in good weather both parks would be fully attended. The Botanical Garden, it is true, held less fascination for the younger visitors. One can only get so much excitement from flowers and trees, after all. But for adults and for tourists to New York City, the **Botanical Garden** was magnificent in its concept and scale. The overwhelming presence in the **Botanical Garden** was the greenhouse, a vast glass enclosure built in late nineteenth century style, filled with thousands of plants. It still stands proudly, magically with windows intact, and many

One of The Bronx's premier attractions, at least according to the official guide books, the Hall of Fame still stands on the University Heights campus of Bronx Community College. It was originally **New York University** until the '60s, when **NYU** sold it to **Bronx Community College**. The **Hall of Fame** was a renowned part of Bronx culture for many years, luring visitors from around the world and an especially popular podium for political speeches. For Bronxites it wasn't particularly exciting. After all, there is only so much entertainment in looking at bronze busts.

*Photo: Marvin Scott*

**The Hall of Fame at the uptown campus of NYU.** Teenagers may have found the bronze busts unexciting but they always appreciated the cool and breezy feeling of solitude in this much publicized Bronx landmark. The **Hall of Fame** also offered spectacular views of the Harlem River and further south one could see the George Washington Bridge and the vistas of the Palisades.

thousands remember with fondness their visits to the steamy interior of the greenhouse. Inside it was like a desert, jungle, or temperate forest, depending on the specimens on display. An otherworldly atmosphere prevailed inside the greenhouse, compounded of the gravel paths and the intense heat and humidity. All in all, journey to a very different world.

Aside from these large-scale parks and beaches, The Bronx was again the beneficiary of considerable civic construction during the 1930s. The work of the WPA and other New Deal agencies gave The Bronx dozens of excellent smaller parks, playgrounds and ball fields, most of which were avidly used. Baseball was, naturally, the premier sport of the day and some highly competent amateur teams took the fields at **Crotona Park** or **Macombs Dam Park** near **Yankee Stadium**. The smaller playgrounds drew crowds of children, carefully observed by mothers who never stopped worrying about the monkey

**At the north end of the aptly name Poe Park, on the Concourse near Fordham Road. Poe Cottage** was at the center of Bronx life. Not that many Bronxites were Poe fans, but the park itself was the scene of weekly dances, political rallies, child walking and generally enjoying the fresh air. Inside the Cottage was a modest exhibit of Poe's work and the desk upon which he worked in his declining years. The City Fathers avidly promoted Poe, and **Poe Cottage**, as a tourist destination but, in reality, the appeal was minimal. Much more interesting to Bronx folks were the dances at the **Poe Park** bandstand, sometimes with live bands, and always with a large crowd.

bars or seesaws as potential causes of facial injury. Still, the concrete covered playgrounds were heavily utilized by a few generations of Bronx children. The prevailing theory (or so it appeared) was that playgrounds and play equipment existed for the convenience of the maintenance crews. Safety and enjoyment were clearly secondary concerns for the Parks Department in the '40s and '50s. The resulting play areas were, therefore, cast in concrete, with the various devices made of sturdy metal and chain for long life. Never mind that the kids might prefer softer, more colorful, play things. These cookie-cutter parks obeyed the strict regulations of the City and so were identical. With it all, though, the playgrounds provided endless hours of amusement and adventure for Bronx children. Swings could become airplanes, and monkey bars could be made into castles, while concrete was pretty good for roller skating. The number of skinned knees and bruised limbs was

**A small memorial plaza at the foot of the Washington Bridge on The Bronx side off of Ogden Avenue.** This very popular location was frequented by mothers with baby carriages. It was also frequented by those waiting for Bus #37 which went to **Yankee Stadium** via **Ogden Avenue** or Bus #11 that went over the Washington Bridge. Bus #11 took Bronxites to shopping in Washington Heights in stores like Wertheimers or W.T. Grants, and a movie at the RKO Coliseum or for lunch at Bickfords.

probably higher than necessary, but such injuries were usually considered normal for a day's play and City playgrounds managed to keep their customers. Some playgrounds had pools or sprinklers in hot weather, while others might even have organized activities, such as checker tournaments or basketball games. The overall supervision of the playground was in the hand of the brown uniformed Park Department personnel, usually silent men, who picked up trash, swept the concrete, watched the bathrooms and got the inevitable name of "parkies." They were very far from being youth workers or recreation specialists, more in the line of police, actually, who were there to enforce the many and complicated rules that governed the playgrounds.

The most popular recreation areas, by far, were the schoolyards of The Bronx. By some inverse law of behavior, the more distasteful the regular school hours, the more popular seemed the after-hours schoolyard. Precisely those students who had to be dragged into classrooms would flock, eagerly, to the basketball courts of the schoolyard immediately after three o'clock. Basketball was the sport of choice in the schoolyard, since most had a hoop (or even several hoops). These hoops rarely had nets but that was easily forgotten so long as a backboard remained intact and the concrete flooring wasn't too badly broken or littered with glass. A big enough schoolyard could simultaneously host a few basketball games, a pick up game of softball, some jump-rope activities and assorted

**Yankee Stadium under reconstruction in the 1970s.** View from the Woodlawn-Jerome Avenue train on the southbound IRT station at 161st Street & River Avenue.

**Yankee Stadium - 1950.** Crowds exited the stadium by walking across the ball field.

small scale events depending on the age of the participants and the tolerance of the older kids who ruled the roost. Schoolyards came with cozy nooks and isolated corners where cigarettes could be smoked, cards played, or just plain bullsessions carried on well out of the eyesight and earshot of parents. That most school yards were officially locked after school closed, and encased by chain link fences was hardly a consideration for the neighborhood kids. Fences were easily scaled or holes opened up, and no Bronx schoolyard ever remained empty for more than a few minutes after the last teacher or custodian left for the day.

*Photo: Scott Mlyn*

**Bronxites relaxing in Poe Park.** For older folks this was their recreation. In the background is the familiar clock tower above the Dollar Savings bank.

If parks, playgrounds, schoolyards and swimming pools didn't satisfy The Bronxite seeking recreation, there were myriad informal play areas. Rooftops were always good (e.g., secluded), while empty lots offered rich possibilities for play, adventure and trouble. Stoops were a world in themselves, where kids could pass hours in games and conversation, and the same for staircases in apartment buildings and the running boards of '40s style cars. There were backyards, alleys, gardens and porches, and always the street itself for playing fields. More exotic sports were available, too, such as horseback riding in **Pelham Bay Park** and boating off **City Island**. With the possible exceptions of ice boating and log rolling, most sports were available somewhere in The Bronx, and at any skill level. Nobody had to be bored in The Bronx.

*Photo: Scott Mlyn*

**Another view of Poe Park and the gazebo where evenings dances were popular in the '50s.**

Bronxites who came of age before the Second World War will remember the considerable pleasures of **Starlight Park**. Although it closed during the Depression of the 1930s, **Starlight Park** was for two decades a magnet for families and young people who relished the vast swimming pool, the roller coaster and the overall carnival atmosphere.

Located on the banks of the **Bronx River**, just off **West Farms Square**, **Starlight Park**, welcomed thousands on a warm summer day. Trolleys and elevated trains were conveniently available from nearly any part of the Bronx and for those with cars, parking was easily found. A submarine (non-working) was a big attraction, as were the many rides and games that made **Starlight** a kind of Bronx version of Coney Island. It was built adjacent to the even older **Bronx Coliseum**, where bike races and concerts were among the attractions. Despite their location, **Starlight Park** and the **Coliseum** were separate entities and one needed two different tickets to enjoy both. During World War II, Starlight Park was demolished and the **Coliseum** became a truck depot, until it, too, fell to the road builder's machines in the 1950s.

**Starlight Park Gyroplane.**    *Photo: Roger Arcara*

**Starlight Park Pool 1938.**    *Photo: Roger Arcara*

**Current aerial view of former site of Starlight Park**

*Photo: Roger Arcara*

**Starlight Park – children's play area.**

**Starlight Park Pool.**                    *Photo: Roger Arcara*

**Honeymoon Express.**                    *Photo: Roger Arcara*

**Kiddie Park.**                    *Photo: Roger Arcara*

**Kiddie Park – Tug of War.**                    *Photo: Roger Arcara*

**Roller Coaster.**                    *Photo: Roger Arcara*

# BRONX STREET GAMES

**The street provides. A good example of kids using the smooth blacktop of a Bronx street, with some chalk to create a playground for themselves.** There are games of Skelly, War and just plain doodling in evidence here. Cars and their running boards provide just the right seating, until the car's owners arrive.

Recreation in The Bronx of the '40s and '50s was largely a self-generated activity; a thing that people did for and by themselves. There were organized sports, and a variety of YMHAs, YMCAs, PAL centers and school teams, but in most neighborhoods, games were the property of the young people, learned from older siblings or just absorbed on the street, and they meant (usually) no adult supervision. Every block and individual building had recognized play areas where youngsters could be safely turned out by their parents and where they could be found if needed. Courtyards in apartment buildings were popular, as were hallways, staircases and basements. In many areas there were empty patches of ground invariably called "the lots." These were undeveloped bits of

**A classic Johnny-on-the-Pony contest.** The game could be played with six or eight on a side, with each taking turns jumping on the backs of the opposing team. The "pillow" stands at the fence and serves as a safety back-stop. The object was to break the "pony" by weight or by well placed knees and elbows.

*Photo: Arthur Leipzig*

**An intense game of marbles underway along an open piece of street.** It's springtime and the marble season has officially opened; this competitor is trying to hit one of the target marbles ranged at the curb. Depending on the size of the target, and the distance, he might win two or five marbles with a good strike. The roles of game operator and contestant changed constantly throughout the day.

real estate, left fallow for some reason or abandoned by the local builders in the Depression, but of great value to the neighborhood kids. Lots were wonderful for fires. For instance, Christmas trees were heaped and burned as soon as they became available after the holiday. Lots were good, too, for firecrackers on the Fourth of July, and for just plain fires on a chilly night. Nobody much minded these uses, since the lots were nothing if not fireproof.

The lot was also a fine place for war games, rock fights, snowball battles and sleigh riding if there was a hill involved. Overall, the lots were for rough games. Generations of young Bronxites remember getting bloody noses and skinned knees in some lot or another, or learning a lesson in courage by standing up to some bigger kid in a lot.

Photo: Martha Cooper/City Lore

**Fishing the subway grates.** A good way to pick up coins and sometimes a ring, but it was dirty work. A long string, some wax or tar at the end of a fishing weight, and a disregard for clean hands was the way to gather riches.

A nearly endless list of other games were situated on the sidewalks. *Off the stoop* (or *stoopball* in some blocks), *captain* and *hit the penny* were some of the ball games alone, and then there were running games like *kick the can* and *ring-a-leevio*, along with old favorites such as *hide-n-seek, tag, statues or Simon Says*. Boys and girls divided carefully along recreation lines: girls played *potzie, jacks* and with dolls, while boys handled the various ball games as a rule. Occasionally gender lines might blur, as in *tag* or *hide-n-seek*, but for the most part, the sexes stuck to their own games. A strenuously male game was *johnny on the pony*, a dangerous sport that resulted in piles of bodies and a fair amount of showing off. The smaller children were content with *tag, hide-n-seek* or *statues*, older ones played *stickball* or *football*. Most times the age groups carried on simultaneously — *stickball* in the gutter, *jacks* or *captain on the sidewalk* and maybe *potzie* in front of the house. Not that playgrounds were absent, but most Bronxites found them unnecessary; the street, as always, provided.

Another game locale was, of course, the sidewalk. Bronx children (like city children around the world) made use of the unique properties of cement, brick and asphalt to develop a wide variety of street games. *Skelly* was a city game very popular in The Bronx involving bottle caps and a chalk drawn grid, which required a successful navigation of the course to win. *Skelly* was always played in the gutter, where the white chalk made good playing grids and where the bottle caps could slide nicely. It might be called *skells* in some neighborhoods, or even *skully* but the rules were the same: one had to lay prone on the street and flick the bottle cap with thumb and forefinger, aiming at suitably numbered boxes. Advanced skelly players filled their bottle caps with wax to give added weight and stability and enable them to knock out their opponents. A good skelly piece was a prized possession.

Games or sports often followed a strict calendar. There was a football season, a marble season, and obviously a baseball season, and it was highly irregular to take out the football in July, or to play marbles in the Fall. There were no official announcements of the change of season, but somehow everybody knew when the day had come; perhaps it was the weather or the opening

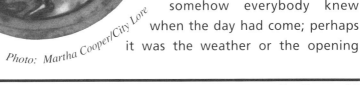

*Skelly bottle cap.* Photo: Martha Cooper/City Lore

and closing of school that signaled certain activities. One day there would be energetic touch football; the next day, by silent agreement, out would come the gloves and bats for baseball. Roller skates were OK pretty much year around, save for the snow days when, of course, sleds were the fashion. Autumn, when school reopened and the summer mood changed, was a particularly busy game period. Skating was at its height and the demand for skate keys zoomed in the corner candy store. With enough clever scrounging, skate boxes, the product of old roller skate wheels and a two-by-four piece of wood, topped by a wooden orange crate, could be manufactured. The final work was a scooter-like affair that could move pretty well downhill and allowed for artistic designs on the crate. A creative kid might tack on bottle caps, mirrors or badges, and rig up a nice

pair of handlebars so that the skate box rolling down an alleyway or a steep street would be a colorful bit of folk art. Guns were also made from old boxes. A pretty impressive rubber-band powered weapon, shooting bits of old linoleum could emerge from an old cantaloupe crate. Fruit baskets might be transformed into basketball hoops and any number of club houses, doll houses and just dark secret places could be made from cartons and crates found on the street. A large empty carton on a rainy day could be magical for a group of youngsters.

*Photo: Martha Cooper/City Lore*

**Schoolyard basketball.** These games went on until dark.

*Photo: Hank de Cillia*

*Photo: Arthur Leipzig*

**Basketball with a brick wall as a backboard.** The mysterious "Post No Bills" sign was encountered all over The Bronx and for the most part, it was obeyed. The age of graffitti hadn't arrived yet and walls remained amazingly untouched. Walls like this were perfect for handball, johnny-on-the-pony and pitching pennies, and half a dozen other street games.

The schoolyard, of course, was natural locale for many sports. Basketball was avidly followed and played in The Bronx, and that naturally called for a regulation hoop (although fire escape ladders might serve in a pinch). School yards were good, too, for real baseball games, or to be more precise, softball. In The Bronx of the '40s and '50s, genuine hardball wasn't common. The Bronx wasn't a hotbed of organized Little

League teams or sandlot baseball, and most boys found themselves in softball competition. This may seem strange in the home turf of the Yankees, and in an era when professional baseball was a religion in New York City, but to many parents baseball seemed a dangerous sport. That unyielding ball could put out an eye, while softball was (or at least sounded) safer. Even more common was stickball, an archetypal city street game that used a ball and bat, but made adjustments to the demands of urban life. Stickball was played city wide, and in The Bronx, it could be found on virtually every block. The basic equipment was a cut-off broomstick and a Spaldeen. The rest was luxury, including gloves, bases or sneakers, which were never really required. Stickball fields were measured by the width of the street, minus parked cars, and the length of the strongest hitters, counted in sewers. A really powerhouse slugger might hit "three sewers", but these were unverified legends; the average home run went "two sewers" or caught a few lucky bounces off a building. Sometimes the game used a pitcher, but generally the batter just tossed the ball in the air himself and took a swing. Top players could toss, swing and connect with the ball before it hit the ground. Pitch-in was more difficult and dependent upon the skill of the pitcher; a crafty pitcher could put a monstrous spin on the ball, or inflict all kinds of bounces, curves and wicked jumps by squeezing the Spaldeen in the proper way. It took a very good batter to get a hit in pitch-in stickball, and scores were consequently much lower in that variation. Even more devilish was a variant of

**A skelly grid.** This one is painted on the blacktop and pretty big.

Stickball was a very popular Bronx street game in the '40s and '50s.

broom handle. The object of their interest was the bat, nothing else. Into the back of the patrol car would go another good stick. What they did with them, who knows? Was there a central depository of stickball bats somewhere in police headquarters, or some paperwork that was filled out to report the seizure of yet another deadly mop handle? Nobody was arrested for the crime of stickballing, and it was understood that the game would resume immediately upon the departure of the car, but the scenario was replayed hundreds of times every summer and spring, all over The Bronx. Occasionally, a sharp-eyed player might spot the cops before they would arrive, and the bat was tossed under a car or down a sewer. The police would find eight or ten boys standing around in exaggerated attitudes of innocence, looking very studious and not the stickball playing types at all.

The more immediate danger to stickball games were the neighbors, or even worse, parents. In the

stickball that used half a Spaldeen: the split ball wouldn't travel as far when hit, thus preserving neighborhood windows, but it could be pitched with wicked skill and it was a high form of art indeed to hit a fast-moving halfball.

A pretty good substitute for *stickball* was *punchball,* where the Spaldeen was hit with a clenched fist. A good solid "thwack" with a knuckle could send the rubber ball soaring, and punchball was suitable for backyards and enclosed spaces. Stickball was the more serious pastime, by far, but it had its dangers or drawbacks. For one, it seemed to be illegal in the eyes of the New York City Police Department. Whether or not there was an actual statute on the books pertaining to stick ball is hard to know, but cops in every precinct took the job seriously enough. They were perfectly friendly about football or basketball, and I don't think the police ever interrupted a game of *pitch the penny*, but stickball was a red flag to the patrol car. Somehow the roving car would sneak up silently behind the batter, just as he was in full view with the evidence (the bat) and the two officers would emerge from the car, grim and awe-inspiring, to seize the offending

*Photo: John Forzaglia*

Bassford Avenue & E. 182nd Street. Stickball.

days when adults were a breed apart, and generally feared, the watchful eyes of the neighborhood could dampen down a hot game of ball very quickly, especially if windows or someone's eyes were in danger. Somehow, ground floor apartments seemed to be occupied exclusively by old ladies, and grumpy old ladies at that. Perhaps they were driven to grumpiness by the endless games of *stickball, captain, basketball* and general noise outside their windows, but these guardians of the street had assumed the task of watchdogs. Pity the kid whose ball accidentally knocked one of the windows, or who yelled too loudly for the elderly neighbor — there were warnings and, in the extreme case, a word to the parents. Neighborhoods being fragile social constructs, a strain on any part caused by children was serious business and the mother involved acted quickly. The offending bat might be confiscated (it probably came from someone's mother anyway), the game dispersed and the guilty party marched upstairs to public disgrace and embarrassment. Automobile owners were equally

> ## "...get out and play in the sun, don't sit in here reading!"

possessive and watchful, so that sitting on the fender or getting too close to a car with a bat were serious infractions.

Mothers were more relaxed when the kids played quiet games: *cards, Monopoly* or something that didn't involve running and loud noises. Stoops were ideally suited for board games and just sitting, and so were backyards, roofs and stairway landings. Lots of kids played *checkers, rummy, jacks,* traded stamps, built airplanes or read comic books on the stoops or in the hallways, or on any flat surface that offered a shaded niche. Rainy days or snow might drive the youngsters indoors, but this was a last resort that didn't please many parents. The deeply rooted belief in those pre-environmental days was that sunshine was necessary for good health; hence, the command "get out and play in the sun, don't sit in here reading!" How many future melenomas were generated by this folk wisdom can't be counted, but it was universally accepted that a good tan and plenty of fresh air marked a healthy child.

An exception might be made for the library, which was somehow connected with school, education and future careers. Going to the library was a familiar ritual around The Bronx. Some public libraries, such as the one on **Washington Avenue** off **Tremont**, were famous in later years as incubators for a whole generation of achievers. Every neighborhood though, had its public library, and getting a library card of one's own was a notable event in the child's life. The youngest kids were restricted to the children's room, where the usual collection of picture books, encyclopedias and "good" literature was available. Upon reaching sixth grade or so, the child graduated to

**Dueling with rubber-band guns.** Only certain fruit boxes made good guns. Rubber bands and linoleum had to be scrounged.

the adult section which meant access to the whole world of literature, history and science not to mention the tantalizing "hot" novels and occasional illustrated medical book. For some reason, Friday afternoons were designated for library visits, and all over The Bronx there might be glimpsed children or teenagers in twos or threes carrying their books to the library, and then walking back home again with another week's worth.

A considerably lower form of literature was comic books, but they were even more widely read and coveted. Candy stores were the source of comic books. Tempting racks were displayed near the front counter (where the owner could keep a sharp eye on the customers). Comic books were considered one of life's necessities for the pre-teen group, carefully collected and sharply traded. The then-current price of ten cents was within the range of most

**Girls playing Hopscotch or Potzie, 1949.** This pastime involved hopping, bending, accurate tossing, and sometimes memorizing slogans or magic words. A skate key was a familiar throwing item (you had to throw it into the box without touching the line) but anything could serve in a pinch. In some neighborhoods, this was strictly a female activity.

young customers (although a dime was serious money in the '40s and '50s) and it was the rare adolescent who did not own at least a few choice comic books. <u>Superman</u>, <u>Captain Marvel</u>, <u>Batman</u> and various other superheroes were popular titles, but there was always a big demand for <u>Archie</u>, <u>Donald Duck</u> and lighter fare. The favorite gift of grandparents were <u>Classic Comics</u>, a loose adaptation of famous books in comic form that provided the illusion of serious reading and even education.

In the '50s, a daring new kind of comic book made its appearance: the horror and science fiction books published by EC Comics. These were the bane of teachers and worried parents throughout The Bronx, and even nationwide opposition was stirred by these gruesome (although exciting) pulp productions. EC comics often found their way into the deepest recesses of the dresser drawers, or under beds where parents were unlikely to look, but, to the true comic aficionado, there was nothing better than a grisly <u>Tales From The Crypt</u> or a bloody <u>War</u> comic from EC.

*Photo: Scott Mlyn*
**Zimmerman's Candy Store – Allterton & Holland Avenue.**

In later years, of course, these ECs and other comics of the period were recognized as true American art forms and now command a dizzying price among collectors. Nearly everyone who lived in The Bronx has a tale of woe that goes "I used to have all of those comics, but my mother threw them out. You know what they'd be worth today?" And they're right. And the same sorry story applies to baseball cards, another prized collectible of the l990s that were common in The Bronx thirty or forty years ago. Baseball cards were dispensed inside packages of gum, a rectangle of sickly pink chewing gum along with five cards, all for a nickel. The cards were liberally covered with gum powder when they were unwrapped and the taste of that gum was horrible. The routine sight outside candy stores (in card season, of course) was of kids with their cheeks distended, chewing glumly, while they sorted the latest batch of cards, hoping for that one prized player or tradable face. Local teams were the most sought-after cards, but some out of town favorites commanded a high value, too: Hank Greenberg was always popular (being Jewish and a Bronx native) but so, too were Dom DiMaggio, Bob Feller, Stan Musial and a few other major stars of the diamond.

Baseball cards weren't just collected, of course. There were contests and games based on the cardboard rectangles, and these games were widespread. Most familiar, probably, was simple flipping. The object was to match the opponent's head or tails by skillfully letting the cards tumble from the hand onto the sidewalk. For some, the cards just floated lazily down, others used a flourish and gave the cards little wrist movements, or sweeping arm motions. Variations included off the wall, where the card was held shoulder high against a wall and allowed to tumble downward. One could also pitch

the cards against a wall (in the fashion of pitching pennies), or perhaps aim at a target — a coin served well for this type of event. Trading, too, was a standard transaction for the card collector. The stars or hard-to-find numbers could bring four or five lesser cards, and there was a constant market for doubles or unwanted cards. All in all, baseball cards (and other kinds, too, such as war or cowboy cards) were a universal currency among The Bronx adolescents.

Other collectibles included marbles, stamps, tropical fish, and coins. The first two items were the most familiar, and there was a distinct marble season to go along with the other seasonal activities. In The Bronx, marble playing took the usual forms of pitching, knuckling or dropping the immies to win and, therefore, accumulate an even larger collection. The rules of marble playing were arcane and fluctuated wildly by neighborhood. Sometimes they called for circles drawn in the dirt (the lots were good here) or lines scratched into the macadam of the street. A Bronx specialty was a kind of casino game, based on a cigar box and marbles. The casino operator, i.e. the kid who found a cigar box and was brave enough to risk his whole collection, cut little slots in the box and invited the neighborhood to roll immies in. A successful pass through the slot might win two, five or ten marbles, depending on the size of the slot and the distance involved. A run of bad luck might bankrupt the cigar box entrepreneur, but a bunch of friends with bad aim could seriously enrich him, too. Some sneaky kids deliberately cut the slots too narrow — the game was rigged in other words. This was a dangerous gambit, both professionally and physically. Some took their crooked cigar box on the road, to another block, risking life and

Photo: Martha Cooper, City Lore

**Not all games were for children.** Jewish women playing Mah-jong. Adults had their own activities and this was one of the most popular: Mah-jong. Bronx ladies formed long-lasting groups who met weekly, to indulge in their passion. Coffee and cake was always served and the neighborhoood news passed around...but Mah-jong was serious business even if played for pennies.

games. The marbles were sold in candy stores or toy stores, twenty or so in a mesh bag, for a dime. Other rarities like stainless steel marbles showed up mysteriously via older brothers or fathers; they were, of course, ball bearings but worked perfectly as marbles under the right circumstances.

Bicycles weren't all that common, as they were relatively expensive, but roller skates served the need for wheels. In the first instance, skates were used for, well, skating. The tough iron wheels were clamped onto one's shoes, with the aid of the skate key to tighten the clamps around the sole of the shoe. Skates also came with ankle straps, but these were flimsey contraptions, more for confidence than the really practical task of keeping the skates on. Skates were hell on shoes, and were the perennial despair of parents who saw expensive new shoes being rubbed into oblivion by the combined force of skate and concrete. Some neighborhoods featured skate hockey, but the more familiar activity was just skating along in a free form exercise. Arms flailing, hair flying, and knees bloody from falls, kids all over The Bronx practiced until too dark to see, and some of them became pretty good. Another level of skating expertise might be achieved in the rinks, using real wooden wheeled skates on a polished wood floor. Skating rinks were a very popular pastime in the '40s and '50s, and The Bronx had at least one famous rink on **Jerome Avenue**, called, naturally, the **Fordham Rink**. (It was near **Fordham Road**, it's true). There were other rinks around the city, so that the true skate fan could indulge on a regular circuit.

marbles. He might come home with a broken box and a nasty purple bruise on his arm. Another scam was to put a tiny bit of dirt or glass in front of each slot, making entry impossible for the player. This, too, was highly discouraged, but not uncommon. One had to be alert in the marble game. But with all the pitfalls and risks, marbles were a popular pastime in The Bronx. On a fine summer day on, say, Elsmere Place off Prospect, thirty or forty kids might gather in a round robin of games, gambles and trading activities. Part of the appeal was the sheer attractiveness of the marbles. They ranged from pedestrian clear-glass immies to fine Chinese marbles with rich multicolored surfaces. There were oversize marbles and tiny marbles, too. Each had its special appeal and prescribed uses in the

**Skelly players waiting for their next moves.** The intricate playing grids were chalked up fresh each day but everybody had his own favorite token, usually a bottle cap. Good index finger control was essential, as was a willingness to lay prone in the street to get good shots. A Skelly game could go on for some time but was clearly a summer sport.

Also in the realm of professional games, or at least games using real equipment, were bowling and pool. These two often cohabited in the same establishment, so that if one bowled, one usually played pool as well. Pool rooms in the '40s and '50s still reeked of a vaguely criminal past. Parents were aghast when they learned their kids (boys, of course) were visiting the local poolroom. The law in New York City specified l6 years old as the minimum age for entering a pool hall, no doubt to cut down on the criminal underclass, but this was a rule universally disregarded at least in The Bronx. **Nat's Pool Hall** and **Bowling Alley**, for example, on **Burnside Avenue**, nourished a couple of generations of future professionals and businessmen in the most unpromising of conditions. It was below ground, a perfectly dank and dark basement (underneath **Flaum's** catering hall) where the only light came from the bright overheads above the tables, or from the endless matches used to light endless cigarettes. On hot summer days, **Nat's** was delightfully cool thanks to its subterranean site, but like a Las Vegas casino, there was no night or day down there. There was, in fact, a Nat, who dispensed racks of balls and kept order

among the customers, and who might be persuaded to fish out a cold soda from the mushy ice bath near the cash register. No liquor was served (New York City statute again) but you could get Pepsi, cream sodas and bags of pretzels. There was a man called Leroy, the table "boy" who used to sweep off the green baize in return for tips, and who generally made himself useful. Leroy, of course, was a grown Black man, a veteran of World War II with an interesting combat record, who somehow found himself in reduced circumstances. To be honest, he may have had a drinking problem.

Aside from the dozen or so pool tables and a few billiard tables, **Nat's** featured a bowling alley. Not much of an alley, but still, it served in a pinch. Even in the mid-'50s, **Nat's** bowling equipment was hopelessly old-fashioned. More accurately, there was no equipment save for the alley itself and a ragged collection of balls. **Nat's** had never upgraded to automatic pinspoting machines, such as were the rage in more expensive lanes, and so there was the charming old tradition of the pin boy. The pin boy would perch at the far end of the alley behind the pins and in front of the rushing bowling ball, and his job was to sweep away the dead wood and set up the pins for the next shot. It was dangerous and noisy, and more than a few of **Nat's** pinspotters were conked on the head by flying pins. The bowling balls in **Nat's** (and most other Bronx alleys

of the time) were pitted, off-center rejects that only dimly resembled real balls. The professionals carried their own bowling balls and shoes, so that only the low ranking keglers would rent. Shoes were available for rental and, if that sounds unsanitary, it was, at least in **Nat's**.

There was a **Nat's** in every neighborhood in The Bronx. Sometimes they were upstairs, over movie theatres or restaurants, and sometimes in freestanding buildings with parking lots around them. The slightly dangerous atmosphere of a pool hall was one of the main attractions, of course, and parents were in constant despair over their sons wasted hours in some dark billiard academy. Nothing much ever happened, though, in these raffish places. One could learn some new obscene words, to be sure, and experiment with cigarettes, but real crime wasn't a problem. The shadiest thing about **Nat's**, for example, was a fellow who offered very cheap (i.e. stolen) LP records for sale. Real bowling alleys were available, with all the latest mechanized equipment. Several were to be found along **Jerome Avenue**, and the sport of bowling drew thousands of devoted fans from The Bronx.

Games and sports were a vital part of Bronx life. The streets were commonly the arena for ballgames and contests of every sort, so that organized activities weren't always necessary. Schools had their regular gym periods and teams, but The Bronx was not obsessed with school sports. How important, after all, could the fate of **Roosevelt's** football team or **Evander's** baseball be in a city where the Giants, Dodgers and above all, the Yankees, were available for the taking. Bronxites naturally supported their high school teams and the occasion of a **Clinton-Evander** football game would generally raise the temperature around The Bronx. But there wasn't the fanatic devotion to organized school sports in The Bronx that characterizes some parts of the

country; amateur ball playing was decidedly in second place to the real thing. Sports however could certainly confer status and celebrity upon the individual. The star athlete from the neighborhood YMCA or high school, or from one of the numerous amateur teams, was a very big deal indeed. Athletic skill was highly prized, as was general physical strength and the always impressive fighting skill. Tough guys weren't necessarily popular or even admired, but they were usually well known and developed a kind of notorious celebrity. Every block and neighborhood had its champion, sometimes a psychotic madman and sometimes just a kid who learned to box and who wasn't afraid to get his nose bloodied.

> In a city where sports were a passion, and for good reason, too, the gaming instinct was well developed.

In a city where sports was a passion, and for good reason, too, the gaming instinct was well developed. It had its own urban character and took on some unique Bronx colorations, but it was the rare Bronxite who grew up without some exposure to sports and games.

**Fishing, Bronx Style ...a popular pastime for kids.** Instructions: Attach a string to a pole and at the end of the string place a piece of perfectly chewed bubble gum to allow proper sticking properties. Lower the pole down a sewer through its grating and "fish" for coins. Carefully lift coin and use to buy more bubble gum.

# EATING IN AND EATING OUT IN THE BRONX

*UPI/Bettman Newsphotos*

**On a rainy night on Fordham Road in mid-'40s, trolleys and taxicabs crowded the streets.** The well-lit Brighton Cafeteria was a Bronx institution for many years as well as the United Cigar Store at far right. At least three theatres offered entertainment (Concourse, RKO Fordham and Valentine). Further east on **Kingsbridge Road** one could see live performances at the Windsor theater. Oldtimers might recall burlesque there, as well.

Everyone's childhood memories has a very large compartment labeled "food". Those who grew up in The Bronx are no different in this regard, and their recollections of foods eaten, prepared and bought are central themes in their histories. Home cooking was, of course, the most important element in one's eating life, but The Bronx was also a place where outside food played a memorable role. For many one-time-Bronxites, the foods they ate away from the dining room table (and mama's careful eye) are the fondest part of their memories. How could a home kitchen, for instance, match the incredible thrill of a jelly apple or a knish bought with hoarded pennies from a rickety push cart on the street, and eaten on the stoop? Mama may have been a good cook, but

the ambiance of the street or the school yard was impossible to duplicate in the home dining room. And how could the family mealtime be remotely as exciting as a massive ice cream creation in **Jahn's** or a frank at **Yankee Stadium**?

Being an urban environment with a varied ethnic composition, The Bronx was a natural locale for a rich assortment of foods and cooking styles. There were candy stores, luncheonettes, ice cream stores, Chinese restaurants and pizza stands in every neighborhood in The Bronx. Not to mention the catering halls, diners, fancy restaurants (they had tablecloths) and cafeterias that stood ready to feed the hungry Bronxite. And most alluring were the countless street vendors, who peddled everything from franks to fruit. The tinkle of the Bungalow Bar truck in the summer, with its promise of ice cream pops, sundaes in a cup and creamsicles, was a Pavlovian stimulus to kids on every street.

The most attractive smell, though, came from delicatessens. The local deli was as familiar as the candy store, and served a similar function, although to a different crowd. While candy stores attracted the kids and teenagers in large numbers, delicatessens lured families. A regular treat for many Bronxites was a periodic visit to the deli. It wasn't quite so fancy or expensive as a traditional restaurant, yet it was eat-

ing out. Delis were local businesses, the kind of place where father might stop for a quick sandwich after work or on Saturday, or where the kids might be given some change for an after-school frankfurter. Dress wasn't required, since the deli was almost an extension of the living room. But the main draw to the corner deli was the heavy aromatic Jewish food. Ambiance, service and price were secondary concerns for most; what counted was the quality of the sliced pastrami, the creaminess of the coleslaw or the crisp-

*Hopkins Studios*

**Entrance to the El station at 138th Street and Willis Avenue in the late '40s.** A familiar scene on a summer evening where a date might mean coffee and a sandwich and a subway ride home. Very few young men at this time had their own car, although they all dreamed of having one in the future.

**Fordham Road looking east at the intersection of Valentine Avenue is a popular hangout for pedestrians looking for a frankfurter and soft drink. Gorman's** was a Bronx version of Nathan's Coney Island in a more compact setting. Shoppers from **Alexander's** and the surrounding area could get a frank or two and a soft drink for under a dollar in the early sixties.

Daniel Epstein of Epstein's Deli preparing a platter in 1954.

ness of the french fries. No thought about cholesterol or fat content worried the consumer of the '50s, who gleefully dug into a massive pastrami sandwich, washed down with a bottle of Hoffman's Cream Soda. In retrospect this kind of eating was deadly, and we may congratulate ourselves in the '90s on our more enlightened view of nutrition. But that smell of the deli still lingers for many who were there. A good deli would announce its presence at least a block

**Waldorf Cafeteria, 140 East 170th Street in the 1950s.** For the most part cafeterias lined the major shopping streets and was more of a hangout for older crowds.

away, by the irresistible aroma of grilling franks and steaming pastrami. On top of the basic meat aromas there was the overtone of beer, and cigar smoke, and maybe mustard. All in all, the deli scent stayed for a lifetime. Once smelled, it was never forgotten.

Inside the average deli, the visual delights followed the olfactory ones. Some delis became famous throughout the borough, transcending their neighborhood origins. **Schweller's** and **Epstein Bros.** on Jerome Avenue, for example, grew huge by virtue of its hearty Yiddish menu. **Mos Kov's** on **Mount Eden Avenue** ranked high in the deli heaven, and there was, too, on **Mount Eden Avenue**, the **Mount Eden Deli**, a well remembered temple of cholesterol. There was the **167th Street Deli**, favored by many who might then stop at the **167th Street Cafeteria** for dessert, i.e., a corn beef on club followed by coffee and cake. **Tremont Avenue**, hosted a number of heavy eating establishments and on **West Burnside Avenue** there was **Fried's**. Some of these neighborhood successes went on to bigger things, sometimes becoming catering halls where weddings and bar mitzvahs were gloriously staged, and fed. And there were dozens more, of local fame, that fed the needs of The Bronx's hard working population. And not all the customers were Jewish. Like pizza and chinese food, the deli became a cross cultural phenomenon. In the local deli, one might find Irish cops, Italian

**Spiegel's Hungarian Restaurant.** Located at **45 East 167th Street** in the 1950s, this restaurant was one of dozens of Bronx restaurants serving Kosher food. This type of restaurant was more up-scale than the local delicatessens and, therefore, used for important family events.

carpenters and Jewish garment workers, all sharing the same tables and wolfing down the East European cuisine as if they had been born to it. In The Bronx, corn beef and cole slaw were universal favorites and everyone loved knishes.

Delis also worked well as take-out centers. A quick mid-week meal could always be collected at the deli counter and carried home in still warm brown bags. Franks, for example, might be sold in strings and served with some of the deli's own potato salad, coleslaw or knishes. A critical part of the deli package, though, was the mustard. Spicy brown mustard was a requirement for real deli food and the good deli made sure the customers had the right stuff. In the case of mustard, the right stuff came in hand-wrapped waxpaper cones that were squeezed (carefully) onto the sandwich or frank. Uncountable numbers of Bronx refrigerators held half-used mustard cones, waiting for some future use, but never, ever, thrown out. Beans were a popular accompaniment to deli meats, but the hands-down brand leader in The Bronx (and in most of New York) was Heinz's Vegetarian Baked Beans, in comfortable green and black labeled cans. Who knows why Heinz came to dominate the market, but it did. The other beans just didn't taste right. The proper deli order also came with pickles, sliced and wrapped alongside the sand-

wich or frank. This counted as the vegetable in the meal. It was green, wasn't it?

Every ethnic group had its own food preferences and traditions, of course. Italians in The Bronx (and elsewhere) put food right at the center of their cultural life, and the result was a major influence on the eating habits of every Bronxite. Pizza was only the most visible and widespread of the Italian influences. There were also scores of Italian restaurants, ranging from the little neighborhood cafe with six tables, to the grand catering halls in the North Bronx. The physical center of The Bronx's Italian life was **Arthur Avenue** in the Belmont section off **Fordham Road**. Into this few square blocks of ordinary tenements and private homes, not very different from the rest of The Bronx in appearance, came generations of Italian immigrants and their foods. What is most surprising about **Arthur Avenue** is not that it existed once, but that it is still there, even in the 1990s. Nearly all the other ethnic enclaves have long since vanished or been transformed since the '50s, but **Arthur Avenue** soldiers on, avidly holding on to its special flavor.

The **Arthur Avenue** market, as it is called, has lured visitors and fine food devotees for decades. It has been the background of at least two of the best films about The Bronx, <u>Marty</u> and <u>A Bronx Tale</u>, both of which made use of the "typically" Bronx street atmosphere of the neighborhood. The New York City Tourist Board knows that **Arthur Avenue** can be a prime destination for foreign guests to the city; it is not unusual to see large tour buses rumbling along **Arthur Avenue** as French, German or Japanese travelers look out in fascination.

Inside the **Arthur Avenue** market, a New Deal structure which was erected to bring order to the push carts and sidewalk vendors of the 1930s, the piles of Italian edibles are stunning in their variety and quality. The same atmosphere existed in the '40s and '50s, too. Families came from far away on Sundays to shop and see relatives, or to stock up on hard-to-find Italian items. The little bakeries and bread shops offered products dear to the taste buds of old neighborhood residents, from two foot long breads to outrageously rich canollis and cheese cakes.

Zsa Zsa Gabor and Rocky Graziano and friends dine at Anna & Tony's Italian Restaurant located on Arthur Avenue in the late 50s.

Gino's Cafe, located on Allerton Avenue and Boston Post Road, was founded the year this picture was taken in 1957. This era featured a family trattoria with a classic Italian cuisine. The seating capacity was limited to 40. In 1964, seating was expanded to 70 and remained so until 1982. Gino and his son Dominic added three dining rooms. In 1968, a dining room was added on the lower level as well as a banquet room that could comfortably seat 120 guests. In 1992, the most recent expansion took place with the addition of two dining rooms, and the grand ballroom was then expanded to its present capacity of 250.

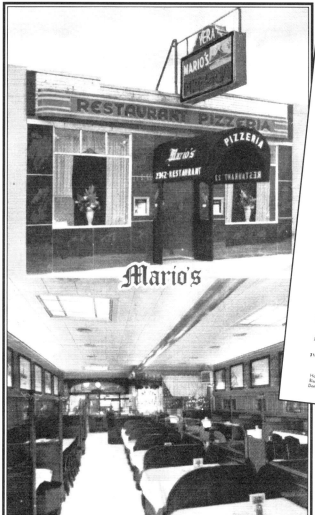

Mario's Menu

## MENU

ALL FOOD COOKED TO ORDER — PLEASE BE PATIENT!

### APPETIZERS

| | |
|---|---|
| Special Antipasto a la Mario | 1.00 |
| Tomato Juice | .15 |
| Clams on Half Shell | |
| Italian Antipasto | .65 |
| Half Order of Clams Oreganate | .65 |
| Shrimp Cocktail | .75 |
| Pimentos and Anchovies | .75 |

### SOUPS

| | |
|---|---|
| Stracciatella a la Romana | .50 |
| Beef Broth with Escarole | .50 |
| Italian Minestrone | .50 |

### MACARONI

| | |
|---|---|
| Spaghetti with Tomato Sauce | .65 |
| Spaghetti with Meat Sauce | .70 |
| Spaghetti a la Mario | 1.00 |
| Spaghetti a la Marinara | .75 |
| Spaghetti Oil and Garlic | .75 |
| Spaghetti Mushroom Sauce | 1.00 |
| Spaghetti a la Caruso | 1.40 |
| Spaghetti with Sausages | 1.10 |
| Spaghetti and Meat Balls | .90 |
| Spaghetti Red Clam Sauce | 1.00 |
| Spaghetti White Clam Sauce | 1.00 |
| Linguine a la Marinara | .80 |
| Ziti with Meat Sauce | .90 |
| Ziti a la Sorrentina | 1.00 |
| Ravioli with Meat or Cheese | .80 |

We Specialize in Home Made

| | |
|---|---|
| Manicotti | 1.00 |
| Lasagna | .90 |

### ENTREES

| | |
|---|---|
| Veal Cutlet a la Milanese, French Fried Pot. and Veg. | 1.15 |
| Veal Cutlet a la Parmigiana, French Fried Pot. and Veg. | 1.50 |
| Veal Cutlet Parmigiana with Spaghetti | 1.60 |
| Veal Cutlet a la Mario | 1.75 |
| Veal Scaloppine a la Pizziola | 1.40 |
| Veal Scaloppine with Mushrooms | 1.60 |
| Veal Scaloppine Al Marsala | 1.75 |
| Veal Scaloppine a la Mario | 1.75 |
| Veal and Peppers | 1.25 |
| Chicken a la Cacciatore | 1.25 |
| Veal Rollatine a la Margherita | |
| Veal Rollatine Al Marsala with Mushrooms | |
| Broiled Sausages a la Pizziaola | 1.90 |
| Italian Sausages with Peppers or Mushrooms | 2.00 |
| Calf's Liver Broiled with 2 Vegetables | 1.50 |
| Tripe a la Livornese | 1.60 |
| Calf's Brains Au Gratin | 1.75 |
| Italian Braciola with Spaghetti or Peppers | 1.25 |
| Breast of Chicken a la Parmigiana | 1.00 |
| | 1.75 |
| | 1.75 |

### STEAKS and CHOPS

| | |
|---|---|
| Broiled Steak with French Fried Pot. and Veg. | 3.25 |
| Broiled Steak with Potato Croquette and Mushrooms | 3.50 |
| Steak a la Pizzaiole | 3.50 |
| Broiled Filet Mignon on Toast with Mushrooms | 3.75 |
| Broiled Lamb Chops, French Fried Pot. and Veg. | 2.00 |
| Broiled (Double Cut) Lamb Chops | |
| Pork Chops, Pizzaiola | |
| Broiled Veal Chops with Vegetables | 3.00 |
| Broiled Half Spring Chicken with 2 Vegetables | 1.75 |
| Broiled Pork Chops with French Fried Pot. and Veg. | 1.75 |
| | 1.60 |
| | 1.75 |

### FISH (SEA FOOD)

| | |
|---|---|
| Shrimps a la Mario | 1.75 |
| Shrimps a la Fra Diavolo | 1.50 |
| Fried Scallops, Tartar Sauce | 1.40 |
| Calamari Luciana Style | 1.00 |
| Shrimps a la Marinara | 1.40 |
| Shrimps Oreganate or Luciana | 1.40 |
| Clam Oreganate (Our Specialty) | 1.40 |
| Calamari in Cassuola | 1.25 |
| Lobster Fra Diavolo, Broiled or Oreganate | |
| Price According to Size | |

### VEGETABLES

| | |
|---|---|
| Broccoli Saute or with Lemon | .75 |
| String Beans Saute | .65 |
| Fresh Mushrooms Saute | 1.00 |
| Escarole Saute | |
| String Beans Marinara | .65 |
| Potato Croquettes (6) | .75 |
| | .75 |
| Spedini a la Romana | 1.40 |
| Egg Plant a la Parmigiana | 1.00 |
| Mozzarella in Carrozza | 1.25 |

### SALADS

| | |
|---|---|
| Lettuce and Tomato | .60 |
| Celery and Olives | .75 |

### CHEESE

| | |
|---|---|
| Italian Provolone | .75 |
| Italian Ham (Prosciutto) | 1.00 |
| Combination | .75 |
| Salami and Olives | .75 |

### DESSERTS

| | |
|---|---|
| Home Made Italian Cheese Cake | .30 |
| Biscuit Tortoni | .25 |
| Demitasse | .10 |
| Coffee with Cream | .15 |
| Italian Spumoni | .25 |
| Assorted Italian Pastry | .25 |
| Tea with Lemon or Milk | .10 |
| Italian Spumoni | .25 |
| Assorted Italian Pastry | .25 |
| Milk | .15 |

**Mario's Restaurant & Pizzeria, 2343 Arthur Avenue.** One of the best Italian restaurants in The Bronx. Mario's menu from the 1940s on the right reflects the great prices of the times.

The famous restaurants of **Arthur Avenue** were themselves tourist destinations, and they managed to survive for many years in the same locale. The **Half-Moon** (renowned for its brick oven pizza), **Mario's**, **Dellavinari's** and the noisy but beloved **Dominick's**, all these were landmarks in the **Arthur Avenue** neighborhood, and throughout the City.

The Jewish equivalent of **Arthur Avenue** was **Bathgate Avenue**, a strip of several blocks off **Tremont** in the **Crotona Park** district. Unlike **Arthur Avenue**, though, the **Bathgate Avenue** markets have gone the way of the trolleys and the <u>Daily Mirror</u>. **Bathgate Avenue** is now widely advertised as an industrial park, a symbol of the renewed Bronx in the l990s, but it isn't the old **Bathgate Avenue** that drew

thousands for its food. Crowded, loud, cheap and colorful, **Bathgate Avenue** offered all the attractions that first generation immigrants could desire. The food was familiar, from the pickle barrels to the challahs on Friday night, everything spoke of home and tradition. Butchers offered any kind of meat, so long as it was kosher. And kosher chicken meant fresh killed, like before your eyes, a practice that continues to give nightmares to a whole generation who accompanied their grandmothers to the kosher butchers. After the slaughter, which was done according to ritual, the finished product (a dead chicken) was packed in a brown bag where it remained sickeningly warm for a long time afterwards. A particularly fascinating part of the procedure was the plucking, which might be done by hand by a specialist who sat surrounded by flying feathers and squawking birds, and who plucked all day long. A more modern butcher might own a chicken plucking machine, a big drum with pointed spikes that ripped the feathers off the chicken's body as it was held against the rotating surface. Both methods were smelly and gruesome, but it did produce chickens of extraordinary quality. Luckily for the squeamish, meat wasn't processed on the spot, so that we didn't have to watch a cow in its final moments. Beef products were vividly displayed in the refrigerator case. Large hunks of bloody meat and parts like tongue were offered for sale and discussion by the customers. And discuss they did. Nobody would think of buying a prewrapped steak or chuck roast on Bathgate Avenue. It had to be negotiated first. Was the meat fresh? "Let me see the scale." "I need it trimmed nice, no fat please." The butcher pretended to be insulted by the questions, but offered assurances and small talk to divert attention from the price. Both parties felt a sense of accomplishment at the conclusion of a sale, satisfied they had followed the honored traditions of the marketplace.

**Bathgate Avenue** offered far more than just food. It was also a center for inexpensive clothing, household goods and just about any other item a Bronx family could conceivably need. Shoppers came from far away to take advantage of the bargains on **Bathgate Avenue**, or (more likely) to bask in the atmosphere. To the younger generation, **Bathgate Avenue** became a symbol of all that they hoped to overcome. It became a term of approbation for the better educated and upwardly mobile who longed to escape the label of "Bathgate Avenue Jews."

Supermarkets weren't yet common in the '40s and '50s, but The Bronx nonetheless was familiar with some chain stores. There were many **A&P** markets and most can remember a visit to the **Daitch Dairy Store. Daitch's** were not restricted to The Bronx, but they seemed an important part of the food experience to many Bronxites. A city-wide chain, **Daitch** was famous for its butter, cream cheese and fresh cottage cheese. The familiar green front of the **Daitch Dairy** was part of many neighborhoods and many youngsters made their first shopping foray to the local **Daitch** dairy counter asking for "a half pound of sweet butter please." The butter wasn't packaged at **Daitch**, instead, it was lopped off a massive block of yellow butter kept behind the sliding doors of the refrigerator, and it was famous for its taste and quality. **Daitch's** butter was sweet butter, since Jewish people rarely bought salt butter, although they were very fond of salted smoked salmon (called by its Bronx name, "belly lox.") Salted butter was a novelty to Jewish homes, something found in restaurants and gentile families.

**Daitch's** also stocked the usual grocery goods and packaged products, so that Bronxites were well aware of the trend to convenience foods and easy cooking. In an era when most cooking meant the mother standing at the stove, the usual relief was a trip to a restaurant. Going out to eat was a popular pastime for New Yorkers in general, and, certainly, for many in The Bronx, a weekly treat at a restaurant was part of life's routine. Not that the variety of eating establishments was impressive in The Bronx. Adventurous eating wasn't yet a hobby for the well-off or the young. Food was

**Bathgate Avenue, a major shopping thoroughfare street in the East Bronx for low-priced clothing but especially noted for its ethnic foods.** The open-air stands on the left were typical of the street as was the live poultry market on the far right. At center is **Moisha's Appetizing and Supermarket** at **1579 Bathgate Avenue. Moisha's** sold familiar Jewish delicacies such as lox, white fish, fresh butter and a wide range of dairy products. **Moisha's** was familiar throughout The Bronx in the '50s with locations on **Featherbed Lane, Jerome Avenue, Lydig Avenue, Westchester Avenue** and **East 165th Street.**

**The Daitch Dairy on Kingsbridge Road in 1946.** Even though this picture was taken about six months after the end of World War II, butter was still being rationed. Bronxites quietly waited their turn for some of **Daitch's** famous sweet butter. It was always cut from a huge block. Later, when 'packaged' butter replaced their 'block' butter, people would recall that the taste and quality was never as good.

expected to be solid, predictable and affordable. The age of the restaurant as entertainment hadn't yet dawned in The Bronx of the '40s and '50s.

Ask a Bronxite about his or her first restaurant experience, and chances are very good they will talk about Chinese food. The height of exotic cuisine in the mid-'50s was Chinese, and none of the latest division by province or style. It was simply Chinese and that meant chow mein, egg rolls and fried rice. Just what the connection is between Jewish people and Chinese restaurants is a minor sociological mystery, but it was well illustrated in The Bronx of the '40s and '50s. Perhaps because The Bronx was so heavily populated with European ethnics, Italians, Irish, Germans and such, it wasn't considered very adventurous to eat in one of those establishments. Going to an Italian restaurant was like eating in a neighbor's house, after all. Fancy "American" restaurants were something reserved for the special visit to Manhattan, or for a trip out of town where they served such oddities as white bread and country gravy. But for hometown dining, it was the Chinese restaurant that held first place in Bronxites' hearts. Hardly a neighborhood existed without its local Chinese eatery, called with unthinking bigotry the "chinks." No one harbored any deep dislike of Chinese people, and it took another generation for the real meaning of that

word to sink in, and be discarded. Where these Chinese cooks and waiters lived isn't clear, but not many lived in The Bronx. Presumably they traveled every day by subway from Chinatown or other enclaves, but they mingled little with local residents. But Chinese food was well known and appreciated, at least a version of Chinese food. It was hardly the kind of Chinese cuisine that would appeal to modern gourmands or sophisticated palates, but in the days of Eisenhower, a dish of shrimp with lobster sauce, mixed sloppily with fried rice and some crispy noodles, was viewed as stylish dining. Nobody would ever try the truly exotic dishes on the menu. Hot spices, sea creatures or various poultry parts were there

**Hom & Hom Restaurant located at 36 W. Fordham Road in the 1960s.** This restaurant was one of several Chinese restaurants serving the Fordham Road shopping district.

for show, and probably would have thrown the kitchen into a frenzy had anyone actually ordered one of them.

The standard request at a Chinese restaurant was for chow mein, probably as part of a combination dish that included soup, egg roll, rice and a dessert (ice cream.) This might be varied with chop suey, spare ribs or some noodle combination, but nothing very spicy please and none of those "funny" meats. As for the kosher question, which might have deterred some Jewish customers, it was somehow negated in the case of Chinese food. True orthodox Jews, of course, never ate in a restaurant, Chinese or otherwise, but for the second generation inhabitants of The Bronx, whose orthodoxy was fast fading, the dietary infractions were of small consequence. Not that these families would ever serve ham or pork at home, but eating a spare rib or a dish of pork fried rice, or shrimp for that matter, in a Chinese restaurant wasn't quite a violation, or so it seemed.

The Bronx did have other restaurants. There were a few steak houses such as **Archies, Alex & Henry's** that drew steady customers for red meat, big portions and a handful of diners that appealed

to the casual diner. **The Post Road Casino**, an aspiring night club on **Boston Road**, offered live music, dancing and the atmosphere of a real downtown locale along with spaghetti dinners. In the 40's, you could get dinner, featured dancing and a variety show for $2.50. There were **Howard Johnson** restaurants, the nearby (Yonkers) attraction of **Patricia Murphy's**, and in later years, a growing number of Puerto Rican dining spots. Many young people enjoyed the food at **White Castle**, a New York tradition that served up tiny, but delicious, hamburgers for a few cents each, along with watery (but wonderful) orange drinks and greasy french fries. **White Castle** had the added attraction of car service in the '40s and '50s. A uniformed waitress would emerge from the faux castle, take your order and deliver it to the driver's window on a little tray, so that the whole crowd would never have to leave the car. Somehow the burgers and onion rings tasted a lot better when consumed in the back seat of a 1953 Pontiac, with the radio on, of course. There were **White Castles** on **Fordham Road, Westchester Avenue, Bruckner Boulevard** and **Allerton Avenue**. On summer nights the parking lots were packed

The Pelham Heath was a well-known Bronx inn located on Pelham Parkway and Eastchester Road. In addition to the $2.50 dinner, it also featured dancing and a variety show. In the '40s, the Pelham Heath also had a driving range towards the back. The neighborhood still showed its rural origins, as noted by the scarcity of cars and surrounding buildings.

White Castle located at the intersection of Allerton Avenue and Boston Post Road.

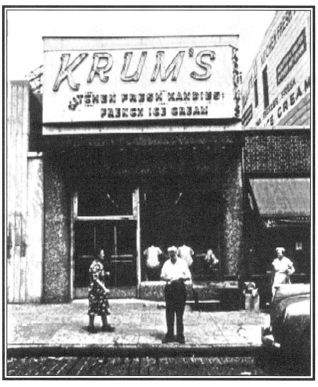

Krum's in the 1940s was located on the eastern side of Concourse, between E. 189th Street & Fordham Road.

solid, teenagers shouting back and forth, or mingling on the street, and all the while devouring the luscious "sliders" at twelve cents apiece. A unique section of The Bronx also famous for its food was **City Island**. An appendage off the eastern edge of the borough, **City Island** had (and retains) an odd small-town feel, as if a New England fishing village had somehow been grafted onto the body of urban New York. It is wildly out of place with its fishing boats, white cottages and rustic streets, but **City Island** is well stocked with seafood restaurants. Many Bronxites took advantage of the proximity of **City Island** eateries to indulge their taste for seafood. These restaurants were busy in warm weather as normally landbound Bronxites sat by the oceanside (Long Island Sound) and enjoyed their shrimp, lobster and clams. **City Island** abutted the popular **Orchard Beach**, so that many families finished their day in the sun by dining on **City Island**. For the younger swimmers, **City Island** was within walking distance and it was routine to leave the sand of **Orchard Beach**, walk over the little bridge and buy shrimp or lobster rolls at one of the **City Island** fish stands.

Still, eating out was a treat. To a generation still recovering from the

**Interior of Krums - At the counter neighborhood businessmen often stopped in for lunch.** The menu included much more than ice cream and the prices were always reasonable. The proximity of **Alexander's** to **Krum's** assured a steady stream of customers throughout the day. Evenings drew strollers and movie-goers from the **Paradise, RKO Fordham** and **Valentine** theatres, all well within walking distance.

Depression without very much excess income, restaurants weren't a regular habit. Real food was made at home and was bought in the neighborhood. The local stores and markets were the foundation for true Bronx cuisine, and every neighborhood had its share of meat markets, dairy stores, fruit stands and bakeries. To describe one battery of local stores is really to describe them all, for they repeated themselves all over The Bronx, differing only in the names and street addresses. Along **Tremont Avenue**, for instance, between **Prospect** and **Southern Boulevard**, the number and variety of food suppliers was impressive and still memorable after forty years. On the corner of **Prospect** there was the **Red Bagel**, a bustling diner/restaurant which served all the standard East European dishes mixed, whenever useful, with more American fare. The **Red Bagel** could provide, for example, borscht with a boiled potato, but also a western omelet or apple pie and vanilla ice cream. It wasn't kosher, but it was decidedly Jewish in taste and a great favorite with cab drivers, local merchants and single people who were unlucky enough to have nobody cooking for them at home. Adjacent to the **Red Bagel** was a singular New York institution, the

Krum's – a candy-lover's dream.        *Photo: Municipal Archives*

Krum's.

Krum's window.

Krum's interior.

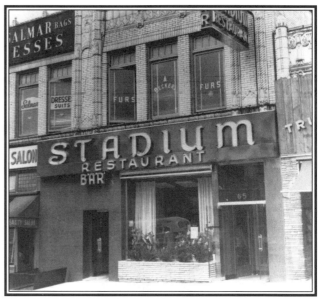

**Stadium Restaurant, 65 E. 161st Street conveniently located one block from Yankee Stadium**. This was a very popular hangout especially during night games at Yankee Stadium.

appetizing store. This, too, was shaped by its Jewish East European clientele and offered a range of fish, dairy and prepared foods. The key product in any appetizing store was its smoked fish department, especially the lox. All appetizing stores had a long, white, refrigerated counter in which was kept the lox, white fish, sable, and herring, all temptingly displayed. By natural affinity, the counter also harbored big vats of cream cheese, cottage cheese, olives, chopped salads, and, perhaps, desserts like rice pudding. The appetizing store naturally sold bread to go along with all this fish, making sure that rye, pumpernickel, bagels and bialys were always available. This inventory continued, however, for appetizing stores were eclectic in their tastes, just as their customers were. Candy was somehow an appetizing item, as were dried fruits, jellies, and the famous halvah. All this, in some mysterious fashion, belonged together. It was "appetizing", and nobody expected to buy meat or vegetables in an appetizing store.

Vegetables were sold in their own venue. The **Tremont Avenue** example was **Murray's**, a cavernous space with heaps of vegetables at front and

*Photo: Howard Rosenberg*
**Schack's Appetizing Store, located on West 183rd Street, between Davidson Avenue and Grand Avenue.**Here one could find delicious lox, smoked fish, bagels and candies like "Hopjes".

a counter for fresh fish in the rear. Why fish and vegetables were sold in the same store is difficult to explain, but there it was. The fish was very fresh indeed. It was alive and swimming in a big glass and metal tank. The local shopper would point to the proper carp or pickerel and one of **Murray's** helpers would scoop out the specimen with a big net. What happened after that is hard to say, but, within minutes, the customer got a paper bag with the once swimming fish, nicely gutted, scaled and wrapped. However, it could still produce an eerie movement.

The vegetables weren't very exotic in those days. Potatoes, tomatoes and apples were the routine, along with the usual onions and a few greens. Nobody in The Bronx had ever heard of radicchio (at least, not outside **Arthur Avenue**) and the idea of "gourmet" food shops wasn't yet on the horizon. Food was for eating, not for display or status, and places like **Murray's** sold it by the

Photo: Municipal Archives

**Cushman's Bakery. This store was located at the corner of E. 149th St. & Third Avenue.** The 1931 Bronx Yellow Pages listed more than 40 Cushman's Bakeries throughout the Bronx.

**White Plains Road near Lydig Avenue bears a standard row of stores in the early '50s, running the gamut from a dance studio to a toy store. The Snowflake Bakery** was admired for the high quality of its cakes and pastries. Dinner guests often arrived carrying the pink **Snowflake** cakebox.

pound and at the lowest prices. The amazing thing about Murray (or whoever it was who manned the vegetable counter) was his skill at picking, packing and then weighing a bewildering assortment of vegetables, at lightening speed, and then calculating to the penny how much to charge the impatient housewife. The only aide was a big hanging scale, with only the roughest gradations. Murray would toss the bag on the scale, glance at the reading while the arm was still vibrating, and then announce: forty-two cents. Not forty cents, or forty-five cents, but forty-two cents! How he did was hard to figure out.

Aside from the food suppliers, there were clothing stores, hardware stores, shoe stores and a famous toy store (Dollingers') that had one of the great window displays in retail history. Restaurants, too, lined **Tremont Avenue** from the large **Shanghai** near **Southern Boulevard** to the more restrained **Pine Tree Pizza** restaurant at **Prospect**. Bakeries were necessities, of course, and every few blocks there was another selling fresh rye bread and all the cakes, cookies and danish one could ever need. Banks, stationary stores, appliance outlets, furriers, ice cream parlors and, of course, candy stores filled in the empty spaces along shopping streets like **Tremont**. These were the places where Bronxites shopped and where they expected to find all the goods and services needed for a normal household. And for the most part, they did.

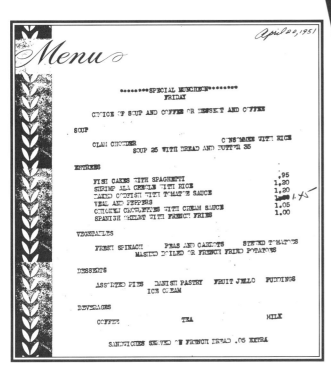

Crosstown Restaurant Menu

*Featuring America's Favorite Dessert*

# JAHN'S *Ice Cream*

## SUNDAES, MONDAES, SHMUNDAES!
*What's the difference? Try one and see!*

| | |
|---|---|
| The Kitchen Sink | 6.50 |
| *Everything else but — serves four to six* | |
| Super Duper For Two | 2.25 |
| *Too much for one — for two it'll do* | |
| A Shissel | 1.85 |
| *If you can't eat it, use it for washing* | |
| The Bombshell | 1.70 |
| *Blow yourself up* | |
| Tall In The Saddle | 1.60 |
| *Hi Ho Silver — Away* | |
| Flaming Desire | 1.40 |
| *A slow burn with a fast finish* | |
| The Thing | 1.20 |
| *We dare you to open it* | |
| Boiler Maker and Helper | 1.20 |
| *Finish this and you'll have muscles so big* | |
| Nosher's Nightmare | 1.10 |
| *Burp!!!!* | |
| Wha Hoppened | 1.00 |
| *Don't ask us* | |
| Brooklyn Kibitzer | 1.00 |
| *Shut up and eat* | |
| Fer a 2¢ Plain | .02 |
| (#"&'$?/) Special | 1.00 |
| *Some people groan after this one, maybe you won't* | |
| Screwball's Delight | .90 |
| *Drive you nuts and plenty of them* | |
| Jahn's Special | .90 |
| *Made especially for you* | |
| The Tree | .90 |
| *This one grows in Jahn's, not Brooklyn* | |
| Rainbow Mountain | .75 |
| *Looks so purty* | |
| Suicide A La Mode | .80 |
| *Why not end it all here, it's cheaper* | |
| Pink Elephant | .75 |
| *This is not the kind you see on the walls* | |

| Ice Cream | .35 per plate |
|---|---|
| Vanilla   Chocolate   Strawberry   Coffee   Lemon | |
| Cherry Vanilla   Black Raspberry   Pistachio | |
| Walnut   Banana   Butter Pecan | |
| Sundaes (any flavor) | .50 |
| Double Sundaes | .70 |
| Triple Sundaes | .95 |
| Ice Cream Sodas | .35 |
| Twosday | .75 |
| *Two Sundaes and a Soda* | |
| Double Wallop (Any Flavor) | .75 |
| *What a Soda! (Nuf Said)* | |

### A SHAKERFUL OF

| | | | |
|---|---|---|---|
| Malted | .60 | Malted Float | .75 |
| Milk Shake | .55 | Milk Shake Float | .70 |
| Frosted | .70 | Frosted Float | .85 |

*Served To You In The Shaker*
*We Mix 'Em In*

### DAIRY RICH DRINKS

| | | | |
|---|---|---|---|
| Malted | .35 | Malted Float | .50 |
| Milk Shake | .30 | Milk Shake Float | .45 |
| Frosted (No Malt) | .40 | Frosted Float | .50 |
| Extra Heavy Frosted | | | .75 |
| *(You'll need a spoon for this one)* | | | |

### COOLERIZERS

| | |
|---|---|
| Iced Drinks — Lemonade, Orangeade, Limeade | .25 |
| Grapeade, .25   Plain Sodas, .15   Pink Lady, .30 | |
| Grape-Lemonade, .30   Grape-Orangeade, .30 | |
| Coca-Cola, .15   Cherry Smash, .15 | |
| Root Beer, .15   Moxie, .15 | |
| Fresh Orange and Raspberry Sherberts | .30 |
| Sherbert Sodas and Frosteds | .35 |
| Shaker Full of Frosted Sherberts | .50 |

*Cover illustration is reproduced from original oil painting by Frank Jahn*

## BANANA SPLITS 65¢
SPECIALTY OF THE HOUSE

*Have you a yen for something real gooey?*
*Tell us what it is — we'll make it!*

| | |
|---|---|
| Finger Bowl | .90 |
| *Fingers in — Nose out* | |
| Pistachio Di La Festa | .80 |
| *Per Te Paison* | |
| Chocolate Pecan Shortie | .80 |
| *Harold Teen takes the blame* | |
| Joe Sent Me | .70 |
| *Joe musta liked us — Thank him for us* | |
| Delaware Square | .85 |
| *You get no run around, it's all square and a yard high* | |
| Buster Brown | .65 |
| *An old favorite made better* | |
| Pineapple Temptation | .50 |
| *For small fry, dowagers and sissies* | |
| Cherry Delight | .50 |
| *Like cherries and good vanilla cream?* | |
| Peach Melba | .50 |
| *Peaches and cream for those on a diet* | |
| Chocolate Sprinkle | .50 |
| *You can get them anywhere, but not like this* | |
| Nut Special | .50 |
| *Toothpicks will be served upon request* | |
| Fruit Salad Sundae | .50 |
| *What's the use — It's good tho!* | |
| Hot Maplenut Fudge | .50 |
| *A Vermont and Texas Combo* | |
| Hot Coffee Fudge | .50 |
| *An Eye-Opener* | |
| Pistachio Marshmallow | .50 |
| *Green with envy* | |
| Hot Chocolate Fudge | .50 |
| *Papa Jahn's original candy recipe* | |
| Hot Butterscotch | .50 |
| *We're not Scotch with it* | |
| Marshmallow Nut Sundae | .50 |
| *As you like it* | |

*printed by WILBERN COMPANY*

Jahn's Ice Cream Parlor and Ice Cream menu, circa 1950.

# FREEDOMLAND

FREEDOM LAND U.S.A.
The World's Largest Entertainment Center

FREEDOMLAND U.S.A.
"The World's Largest Entertainment Center"
June 1960 - September 1964
*By Bob Mangels.*

In 1995, the Walt Disney Company, announced that it was withdrawing its plans to build a theme park based on the history of the United States, because of local opposition in Virginia. Those of us who grew up in The Bronx, in the early 1960's, and millions of our neighbors at that time can easily say; "We already had such a place in the North Bronx, FREEDOMLAND U.S.A.!".

The magnitude of this great theme park has perhaps been lost due to its five season operation, but FREEDOMLAND, was not only one of the best parks of its time, but would easily out distance many of today's theme parks. To say that the park was ahead of it's time would be an understatement. This chapter will outline what FREEDOMLAND, U.S.A. offered for those who never had the opportunity to visit the park, and perhaps rekindle the fun and excitement for those that experienced the "East Coast's answer to Disneyland".

On May 25, 1959, a news conference was held at the Empire State Building, announcing that the world's largest entertainment center would be built in the Baychester area of The Bronx. Not only would the park be 85 acres in size but it would be shaped

This view of Freedomland shows Fort Cavalry.   You could actually eat in the chuck wagons.    *Bettman Archives*

like a map of the United States, and its exhibits and rides would depict American History. At the news conference C.V. Wood Jr., president of the Marco Engineering Company of Los Angeles, announced the project. Mr. Wood had been General Manager of Disneyland from 1954 thru 1956, and was very much involved with the planning of that park. The cost was estimated to be $16 million dollars and would be operated by the International Recreation Corporation. The total announced acreage to be used for FREEDOMLAND, and for parking was 205 acres out of the 400 available acres, leased from Webb & Knapp, a firm owned by William Zeckendorf, well known in real estate circles for the Zeckendorf hotel chain. Webb and Knapp also confirmed the planning of a 600 room Freedomland Inn hotel to be built on the remaining 195 acres, as well as housing on the northerly sector of the property. C.V. Wood's idea for this park he said, had been on his mind for sometime. He convinced many of Disneyland's planners and experts to join him in this project including Van France, who founded the Disney

University, which trained workers on how to be friendly and helpful to the patrons. Van France recalls," At FREEDOMLAND, the theme was to be a "FRIENDLY FREEDOMLANDER", with a smiling Indian on the cover of a training book".

Since France also worked well with getting traffic information for Disneyland, he had the same job at FREEDOMLAND.  When he arrived in New York, C.V. Wood, showed him a check for 13 million dollars, putting to rest any thoughts that the project might not happen. On August 26, 1959, another news conference and press release announced that "construction starts today on the now $65 million dollar project, FREEDOMLAND, U.S.A.,". C.V. Wood explained a few years later that the extra cost was figured on the alleged value of the 205 acres of land. The land, it should be pointed out was a swamp and had been landfill at one time. Since the announcement that FREEDOMLAND was being built some of the major elected officials like Mayor Wagner, Governor Rockefeller, and Bronx Borough President James Lyons, all spoke of their high regard

**FREEDOM LAND U.S.A.**
The World's Largest Entertainment Center

*The World's Largest Outdoor Family Entertainment Center featuring these exciting attractions*

**HORSELESS CARRIAGE:** Drive a 1909 Model Cadillac through scenic New England
**HARBOR TUG BOATS:** Sail through The Great Lakes on a real steam tugboat
**HORSE DRAWN STREETCAR:** Travel New York to Chicago on an old fashioned horse-car
**HORSE DRAWN SURREY:** The "Surrey with the fringe on top" takes you to Chicago
**POLITICAL PEP RALLY:** A taming speech of the 1890s, A German Band suffragettes

## CHICAGO: 1871

**THE CHICAGO FIRE:** See Chicago ablaze – and help fight the great fire
**GREAT LAKES CRUISE:** Sail around the Lakes on an authentic sternwheeler
**CHIPPEWA WAR CANOES:** Paddle an Indian war canoe through the Great Lakes
**INDIAN VILLAGE:** See real American Indians at home in their tepees
**SANTA FE RAILROAD:** Ride the Iron Horse through Freedomland to San Francisco

## SATELLITE CITY: THE FUTURE

**SATELLITE CITY TURNPIKE:** Drive a modern sports car over the road of the future
**SPACE ROVER:** A round-the-Americas cruise through stratospheric space
**BLAST-OFF:** See authentic Cape Canaveral space rocket launching
**MOVING LAKE WALK:** Cross Satellite City Lake on a traveling sidewalk
**SPECIAL EXHIBITS:** see the wonders of modern science and modern Industry

## NEW ORLEANS: MARDI GRAS

**CIVIL WAR:** Ride through cross-fire on authentic battlefields
**BUCCANEERS:** Take part in thrilling pirate adventure
**DANNY THE DRAGON:** A fantastic ride on the dragon's back
**KANDY KANE LANE:** Youngsters can see toys galore, children's rides
**TORNADO ADVENTURE:** Whirl in the eye of a wild tornado
**CRYSTAL MAZE:** A baffling glass house of mirrors
**Spin-A-Top:** You spin in tops that turn on spinning tables

## GREAT PLAINS: 1803-1900

**FORT CAVALRY:** Cavalry stockade of Indian-Fighting day in the west
**PONY EXPRESS:** Swift riders carry your letters to the old southwest
**FORT CAVALRY STAGE LINE:** The western stage coach takes you past buffaloes and bad men
**CAVALRY RIFLES:** Frontier shooting-gallery for marksmen of all ages
**BORDEN'S FARM:** See horses, sheep, pigs, poultry, growing corn - and Elsie the Cow
**HORSE DRAWN STATION WAGONS:** An old-fashioned ride around Fort Cavalry and Bordon's Farm
**MULE-GO-ROUND:** Ride the merry-go-round drawn by western mules

## THE OLD SOUTHWEST: 1890

**OPERA HOUSE AND SALOON:** Soft drinks at the bar, western revue on stage
**BURRO TRAIL:** Western mules carry you across desert trails
**TUCSON MINING COMPANY:** Ride high over Freedomland in an overhead ore bucket
**MINE CAVERNS:** See the mysterious world under the earth
**CASA LOCA:** The house where everything stands on its head
**GUNFIGHT:** A gunslinger's ambush in Billy the Kid country
**TEXAS LONGHORNS:** See live Texas steers and the western wranglers

## SAN FRANCISCO: 1906

**NORTHWEST FUR TRAPPER:** Board a Trapper's built boat for a thrill packed river ride
**CHINATOWN:** A corner of the Far east in America's far west
**BARBARY COAST:** San Francisco glittering entertainment district
**SEAL POOL:** Watch the pacific seals at play in "Frisco Bay"
**SAN FRANCISCO EARTHQUAKE:** See the spectacular "Frisco Quake" and Fire of 1906
**RAILROAD STATION:** The Santa Fe railroad from Chicago stops here
**HORSE DRAWN SURREYS:** Take a leisurely drive to the Old Southwest

**River Ride in the Old West/Frontier Town** - Note that the moose was actually shot in Alaska for Freedomland at a cost of $10,000.

**River Ride in the Old West/Frontier Town** - A view of an Indian Village.

*for the planned park. FREEDOMLAND was scheduled to open July 1, 1960, however a decision was made to open early even though the park was not fully completed. On June 18, 1960, FREEDOMLAND U.S.A., was dedicated with 5,000 in attendance, many of them children who were treated to a parade and a public preview of the wonders being built in the Bronx. The opening ceremonies and preview benefited Boys Harbor, the Children's Village Interfaith Chapel and the Sheltering Arms Childrens Services. Mayor Wagner, hailed the park as " a great means of education for young and old". Wagner, was introduced by William Zeckendorf while Milton T. Raynor, the president, said of the park, "it would have a policy of cleanliness and wholesomeness," and it should be noted that during FREEDOMLAND's life it did. The big day came for the grand opening on June 19, 1960. Crowds started to arrive at 7:30 A.M. for the scheduled opening at 10 A.M. Singer Pat Boone, with his wife and children cut the ribbon to open the park at 8:30 A.M., and about 6,000 were allowed in early for the ceremony. The opening was pushed ahead because by 10 A.M. traffic on the Hutchinson River Parkway and the New England Thruway was jammed, with cars traveling at 4 m.p.h. When it became apparent that early arrivals were not leaving*

*New York City radio stations advised listeners to stay away from the area. Police blocked off exits from the highways, some parked at Gun Hill Road, a great distance away and walked to the park. Ticket sales were halted at 2 P.M., as 40,000 jammed the park, and the people still came. The park was supposed to close at midnight, but for safety reasons it closed at 9 P.M., with the official attendance listed at 61,500!*

*Ed Sullivan's show that evening showed highlights of Freedomland demonstrating to the rest of the country that Disneyland had its equal on the East Coast. There were some problems on opening day just as Disneyland had on its opening day in 1955, but for some reason we heard a bit more about it. Some of Satellite City was not completed and some attractions were not fully open, but for the most part many of us could not wait to get to the place that beckoned a "Walt Disney" experience in The Bronx. "Mommy and Daddy Take My Hand Take Me Out To FREEDOMLAND....", that phrase put to music was the basis for the T.V. and radio spots with film clips of the attractions. Johnny Horton the singer, who had such hits like, "The Battle of New Orleans", "Sink the Bismark", and "North to Alaska", recorded Freedomland's theme "Johnny Freedom"; it is still played today on the 4th of July, with a liner note that says*

*Photo: Murray Schneider*

*Photo: Murray Schneider*

"Freedomland". Columbia Records put out an album (CL1484), entitled FREEDOMLAND U.S.A. featuring this song plus others composed by Jule Styne with lyrics by George Weiss. Charley Weaver even recorded "Danny The Dragon" a song about a Dragon that passengers rode in the New Orleans areas of the park through beautiful flowers and storybook characters. Music on the album by Frank Devol was featured as was his band at the park. Other songs on the album were: "Little Old New York," "The Jalopy Song," "Pine Country," "On the Showboat," "San Francisco Fran," "The Chicago Fire" and "So Long Ma". These all depicted actual and fictional events representing Americana at FREEDOMLAND.

I still remember very well the anticipation of my first trip to this mecca of amusement parks. Despite some hesitation from my mother, she took me and my brother one summer morning in July of 1960. My

*Photo: Murray Schneider*
**Freedomland First Aid Station in Old Chicago.**

mother's hesitation was based on stories that a trip to" Disneyland" in The Bronx, would require much gold dust, so she decided we wouldn't tell my dad who was at work. Since we didn't have a car and couldn't use one of the eight thousand parking spots, we took the Third Avenue "EL" to **Gun Hill Road,** then the Surface Transit bus with a hand-written paper sign on the window that said "FREEDOMLAND". As we made the trek down the hill of **Baychester Avenue** all I could do was look from the bus window with eager anticipation and see the smokestacks of the two sternwheeler riverboats and faintly hear a train whistle. We had finally arrived!!!

After the admission ($2.00 for adults $1.50 for kids), you could buy additional tickets for the rides or coupon books which offered some discounts. There were seven rides for a dime, and five ten-cent rides for adults; rides cost 50 cents each for adults, no ride cost more than 35 cents for kids. The first of the themed areas was "Little Old New York: 1850-1900." It was just like Disneyland's Main Street, but even better as it had more buildings and all built to true scale, with costumed performers as police, political rally participants, German oompah bands and more. The buildings, including Macy's Department Store were filled with great things to look at and buy. The old Apothecary Shop sponsored by Shering gave out free Coriciden. At the F.& M. Schaefer Brewing Co., you could see how beer was made and the little animated life-like elves or gnomes told the story. You could also ride horse drawn streetcars pulled by two horses to take you through New York and into Chicago, or you could take a ride in one of the forty 1909 Cadillac horseless carriages specially designed and assembled for FREEDOMLAND. The car, which seated up to 5 passengers with a gas engine and Klaxon horn, operated for a half mile tour of a New England countryside, past streams and vineyards. In those days there was no middle track or rail, but a wooden guide rail on each side to keep you on the road, but you could steer the car and apply the gas and had a great time. Two Harbor tug boats left New York Harbor, and entered the Great Lakes and returned to New York.

Photo: Murray Schneider
**A typical family enjoys a day at Freedomland in "Little Old New York"**

After spending time in Little Old New York, you entered Chicago by walking under one of the train trestles, or by horse drawn street car. Freedomland's Chicago featured the Chicago fire that burned with real flames every 20 minutes, and later during the park's operation every half hour. Firemen would have guests help pump to put out the fire, and those who helped received certificates. I wonder if some of these certificates exist today, forgotten amongst other childhood remembrances. In Chicago, the Great Lakes Cruise took you around Freedomland's man-made waterways. Passengers would sail through all five of the lakes, on one of two 110 foot, 400 passenger sternwheelers. At that time they were the last sternwheel steamers to be built in the United States,

Photo: Alan Fredberg
**Space City in Satellite City - Sponsored by Braniff**

and built by the Todd Shipyards for Freedomland. The ships were named "The American", and "Canadian". Cliff Walker, the Director of Operations for 4 years, recently told me the depth of the Great Lakes at Freedomland was 7 feet. Another way to get around the lakes was in a real Chippewa Indian War canoe, piloted by Indian guides. Guests would paddle the canoes and visit an Indian Village. Boarding the Sante Fe Railroad at Chicago's train station was not only fun but a great way to take you to San Francisco's attractions, or stay on board to return. The trains at Freedomland were leased from the Eddaville Railroad in South Carver Massachusetts and included two complete sets. These trains were the narrow 2 foot gauge, featuring enclosed coaches and outdoor observation cars.

The amazing aspect of this lease agreement is that the trains were placed on a flat bed truck with rails and transported down from Massachusetts each Spring and returned in the Fall. Several trips had to be made each of the five seasons.

The Great Plains 1803-1900, featured Fort Cavalry, a log-by log replica of an army stockade along with a Frontier Trading Post of the period and a Chuck Wagon wagon train for people to sit and eat. The Pony Express was a place where guests could mail a letter to be picked up by a Pony Express rider and the letter would be available in Tombstone in the Old Southwest. The Fort Cavalry Stage Line, sponsored by American Express, would take visitors through the Rockies, and to see real buffalo transported from Oklahoma each year; a hold-up was also part of the trip. The stages also had provisions to ride inside the coach and topside on the roof to ride "shotgun". A "unique" mule-go-round was also featured in the Great Plains: this was a merry-go-round pulled by Western mules.

Elsie the Cow lived at Freedomland and seeing the real Elsie and her calves at the Borden's Farm was a

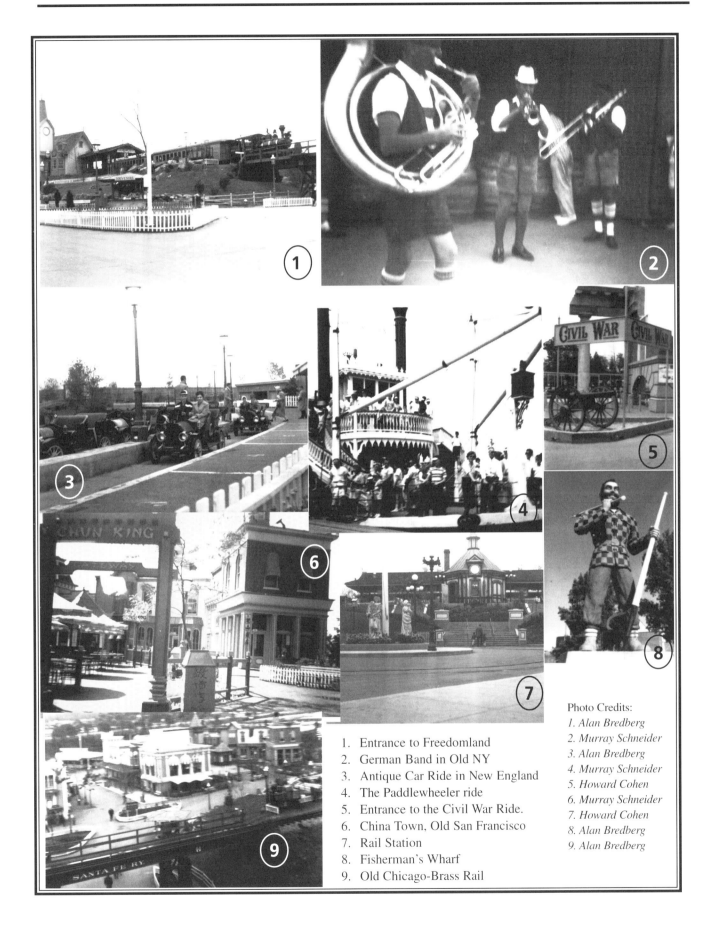

1. Entrance to Freedomland
2. German Band in Old NY
3. Antique Car Ride in New England
4. The Paddlewheeler ride
5. Entrance to the Civil War Ride.
6. China Town, Old San Francisco
7. Rail Station
8. Fisherman's Wharf
9. Old Chicago-Brass Rail

Photo Credits:
1. Alan Bredberg
2. Murray Schneider
3. Alan Bredberg
4. Murray Schneider
5. Howard Cohen
6. Murray Schneider
7. Howard Cohen
8. Alan Bredberg
9. Alan Bredberg

*Photo: Murray Schneider*

**Elsie's Farm. Elsie and her calf were inside the barn!**

*Photo: Howard Cohen*

**A view from a Northwest Fur Trappers boat ride.**

treat that I still fondly remember. But seeing Elsie in a bed and her calves in cribs was just too much! The farm was a real working farm with animals, corn fields, a duck pond and more, plus (what else?) a milk bar to quench your thirst. At the San Francisco area set in 1906, the San Francisco Earthquake ride brought guests back to April 18, 1906 when the ground fell from under San Francisco's feet. The ride had guests in horseless carriages on a track. One would see people dancing before the quake, then watch the buildings collapse, and the ground crumble; it was well done. Freedomland also featured Chinatown with markets and a large Chun King Shangri La Restaurant. The Barbary coast was also represented, as was Fisherman's Wharf, with a seal pool and real Pacific harbor seals. Cliff Walker, Director of Operations said that, since the seals lived there all year, in the winter he had to check the heaters in the pool and when ice formed they had to hire someone to break the ice. The Northwest Fur Trapper's ride was a favorite; it featured a number of "BullBoats" that plied the Snake river in the Pacific Northwest. The passenger ships carried about 30 visitors and the pilot would warn children, "Son, don't put your hand in the water, snakes have been known to be just waiting to bite." On this ride you would see beavers building a dam, cutting down trees, an old bridge would fall just missing the boat, a bear would be frightened off by the guide by firing his gun. Then you were attacked by Indians firing rifles at the boat, a cougar almost jumping into the boat, and, at the end, you would sail past a ghost town with skeletons going about their day including skeleton horses!

At a visit to the Old Southwest 1890, you could take what is now known as the sky ride, that Freedomland called 'ore buckets' because one boarded them at the Tuscon Mining Company. They were unique because Freedomland was the only park that had a total of four aerial cables with two sets running in opposite directions. To this day these sky rides are known as the "ore bucket ride." These ore buckets carried you over the Rockies and the desert, so you could almost see "coast to coast". In old New Mexico, the Frito company had a Mexican Restaurant where I remember wanting a hot tamale and finding out it wasn't very hot. A great indoor ride was the Mine Cavern: a mine box car carried passengers into the underground. With giant bats and beetles, the ride at points was elevated in the dark and you would see lava pits. There was a surprise finale too: but I was prepared for it because the Sunday Daily News had highlighted the ending.

*Photos: Howard Cohen*

**On the left is a picture of the parking lot entrance to Freedomland. On the right is the Bucanneer's Ride in New Orleans.**

Photo: Howard Cohen

**Entrance to Freedomland.**

Photo: Murray Schneider

**Fort Cavalry**

*Just as your mine car was about to exit, another car would come screeching at you; in the car were two lifelike passengers... the car would stop just in time. There were many western buildings, an opera house with shows, gunfights and old fashioned stores. And the Casa Loco house where visitors would walk in and see water run uphill, rooms turn upside down, former tenants come popping out of the wall, and a can rolling uphill out the window. The Burro Trail, featured live burros for passengers to travel through the desert and an opportunity to interact with live animals.*

*Moving next to New Orleans, there was the celebration of Mardi Gras, with the unique King Rex Carousel, a classic merry-go round that featured hand carved animals along with the traditional horses. The animals from this carousel were sold in the early 90's by the Great Escape amusement park, in Glens Falls N.Y., and netted one and a quarter million dollars. Prior to the sale the carousel was operated by Charles Wood, who operated Gaslight Village in Lake George after Freedomland closed. In New Orleans, the Buccaneers was an enclosed dark ride in which passengers rode in a long boat past two ships doing battle, through a town captured by pirates, and next to a giant squid. At the end, a pirate hanging was featured with an over stretched neck. This ride came 5 years prior to Disneyland's "Pirates of the Carribean" but they are amazingly similar. This ride still delights passengers at Cedar Point in Sandusky, Ohio. C.V. Wood, Freedomland's creator told me that his favorite ride was the Tornado, which was a dark ride where passengers in cars saw the swirling tornado bearing*

Photo: Murray Schneider

**Frank Devol's Band at Freedomland.**

*down on them, a real Louisiana twister or "cyclone"and the destruction that it caused. Also in New Orleans, was Danny the Dragon, a 74-foot outdoor train-like ride that passengers rode through beautiful flowers and landscaping along with storybook characters. Charley Weaver recorded the song "Danny the Dragon". Danny and about two thirds of the Tornado ride are still in operation today at The Great Escape.*

*In the New Orleans section of the park was another favorite, "The Civil War Ride". Passengers would board a wagon complete with white flag pulled by a team of mules through the battle ruins of the South, mortar shells and water exploding around you, and mechanical blue and grey soldiers firing. At the end, there was the Court House where Lee surrendered to Grant with both men standing on the porch. Recently I saw the same Court House shown on the PBS series on the Civil War and I realized how accurate it had been duplicated at Freedomland. Still in New Orleans, the baffling Crystal Maze was featured, the world's only transparent walled house of mirrors. While Disneyland had Tomorrowland, Freedomland had Satellite City, where you would step into the future. The feature here was a large flying saucer seating 250* that would simulate a blast off into space for a tour of the Western Hemisphere, covering 10,000 miles in 6 minutes. It was a great simulator ride that has now resurfaced at theme parks in the 90's! You could also drive sports cars on the Satellite City turnpike. The moving sidewalk would take you across a lake, part of which was covered in the second year and became the Moon Bowl. The Moon Bowl was Freedomland's showcase area for big name performers like Bobby Darin, Paul Anka, Benny Goodman, the Lennon Sisters, Diana Ross and The Supremes (who appeared in jeans!) There were many exhibits for science and industry all sponsored by major corporations.

Everything about Freedomland was high quality including the souvenirs. The guide books were well done and gave complete details about the attractions, and were made of high quality embossed paper. Fireworks were displayed each night lasting 20 minutes. Another attraction of Freedomland was the Dancing Waters, on display in the evening at the Hollywood arena.

To this day many people who have fond memories of Freedomland ask this question: Why did this great place ever close? The answer given in late 1964 was bankruptcy. The real reasons are a bit more complicated. First, the 1964 season, Freedomland's last year of operation, was not the same as the original four seasons. The Chicago Fire no longer operated, just the ruins of the city existed with the hand pumped fire engines; also the whole San Francisco area was closed, and that meant the Fur Trappers ride was not operating. The Civil War ride now featured some of the horseless carriage cars that no longer had the same impact for the visitors. Although some thrill rides like the Scrambler were added, Elsie the Cow was no longer at the park... a sign said Elsie was at the World's Fair and would be back in 1966. Schaefer Brewing Company had a similar sign, but of course neither one ever returned. Despite the diluting of the park in the 1964 season it still was fun going there. Having gone to

the park several times during the last season, I remember that a few days before closing late in the afternoon every souvenir had a reduced price of just a quarter. My parents thought that this may have been done every year just before the park would close for the season to reduce inventory.. little did we know.

Since the park's destruction I've always been of the opinion that Freedomland's demise may have been planned, possibly as a step in the construction of Co-Op City. Recently my suspicions were proven correct from several sources which all pointed to the same conclusion. New York City's codes prohibited high rise buildings on land fills and swamp. Test footings and soundings had to be in place for 20 years UNLESS there were existing structures on the land for 5 years. A variance could be granted, in that case, and FREEDOMLAND EXISTED FOR 5 YEARS!! Interestingly, **Co-op City** was not built on Freedomland, but on the parking lot (so much for the variance if someone was watching). The original operator William Zeckendorf, became a creditor, so that the United Housing Development Corporation could apply for the $16 million loan for Co-op City. Ironically, the United Housing Development Corporation would go out of business, with the taxpayers of New York State picking up the bill and may have just finished.

The sad end to **Freedomland** indirectly displaced many Bronxites. People bought into **Co-Op City**, vacating their apartments throughout the Bronx and moving into these high rise structures. The Bronx they left behind, on the **Grand Concourse** and other neighborhoods throughout the borough, would change dramatically. Still, **Freedomland** will always be the yardstick to me when I visit other "theme parks" today. I think how lucky I was to have lived in the early 1960's and visited "The World's Largest Entertainment Center", and I remain in awe of the attractions and of a park way ahead of its time.

THE PARK THAT'S FUN FOR EVERYONE IN THE FAMILY

FREEDOMLAND

Kids! ages 1-2-3 FREE!

OPEN EVERY DAY 10 A.M. TILL MIDNIGHT

$2.50 KIDS 12 YEARS AND UNDER
And For Everyone After 6 P.M.
$3.50 plus tax From 10 A.M.-6 P.M.
For Everyone Over 12
COME EARLY—STAY TILL MIDNIGHT

"MISS BRONX" FINALS SEPT. 2

200 SHOWS FREE

OVER 45 RIDES

In the Bronx 30 minutes from Times Square, where the Hutchinson River Parkway meets the New England Thruway. By IRT subway: West Side Ave. Line in Gun Hill Rd. Lex Ave. Line to Pelham Bay Pk. Buses direct to Freedomland from both stations. Scheduled buses from Port Authority Terminal, 41st St and 8th Ave and Gray Line Bus, 245 West 50th St. $1.20 round-trip. New Rochelle, Sun Haven Drive. Buses from Jamaica LIRR Sta. Flushing LIRR Sta $1.00 round trip New Rochelle. For group rates and bus info. call TUlip 1-0600, or write Freedomland, Bronx 69, N.Y.

# Bronx Street Scenes: Then and Now

*Then*

## Mario's Restaurant & Pizzeria

**Located on Arthur Avenue in the heart of Belmont, Mario's is one of the cornerstone restaurants of the Bronx.** At the same location for more than a half-century it has expanded over the years and presently displays a more modern image to the street. Inside, however, is the old Mario's where families come for Sunday dinners and the homemade tomato sauce and other Italian specialties are still offered in abundance.

*Now*

*Photo: Spencer Field*

The restaurant business is notoriously fickle: hot new places come and go with the seasons. A restaurant that survives in Manhattan for more than a decade is nearly a miracle. In The Bronx, local restaurants aren't immune from this law of the food jungle and there have been plenty of casualties among Bronx eateries over the years. But for a select few dining spots, The Bronx has been a hospitable locale; there are a handful of restaurants in The Bronx that have been operating for more than fifty years. Those pictured here have reached a remarkable longevity, becoming neighborhood landmarks and irresistible

## The Wedge Inn

**Below is the Wedge Inn today. Above is a 1960s picture.** The Wedge Inn is located at **4300 Boston Post Road** and was built in 1940. It was famous for serving great food twenty-two hours a day, and for being the gathering place of late-night drag racers who routinely blockaded the **Hutchinson River Parkway.** Horseback riders from a nearby stable tied their horses to the hitching post next to a parking lot crowded with tractor-trailers. The original Wedge Inn has withstood the test of time in the same location for over a half-century.

lures for generations of Bronxites who continue to patronize the good old tables.

Just why this has happened is a bit of a mystery. A good guess is that restaurants like **Mario's** on **Arthur Avenue**, or **Gino's** up on **Allerton Avenue** have developed a formula that continues to work to their advantage and the owners are smart enough not to tamper with success. The fierce loyalty of Bronxites for their borough and their neighborhoods may be part of the answer too. The Belmont section and its tradition of good food brings back children and grandchildren so that **Dominick's** and the others around **Arthur Avenue** continue to thrive. It might be quite simple really. Give people good food at good prices and you have, magically built a successful restaurant. Not that it always works, of course. A long list of Bronx restaurants have succumbed to changing times and new populations. The famous Jewish delicatessens are almost all gone, and places as beloved as the **167th Street Cafeteria** long ago closed their door. But The **Wedge Inn** on **Boston Post Road**, and **Louie's Seafood** on **East Tremont Avenue**

## Alex & Henry's

Alex & Henry's on Courtlandt Avenue
has withstood the test of time as a
restaurant and catering hall.  Above,
the restaurant in the 1950s.

*Now*

are doing a fine business, even after the passage of decades. **Charlie's Inn** is another long-time survivor, on **Harding Avenue**, and prides itself on being the last of a breed, the beer garden. Originally German in flavor, Charlie's has adapted with the changes in The Bronx and now offers a more "continental" menu, i.e., more Italian dishes. But the key to Charlie's remains its family orientation and the restaurant's welcoming atmosphere. Weddings alternate with retirement parties, and a graduation may follow a christening...sometimes on the same day. It was , and still is, a place where ordinary people (who may come from the tri-state area today) still find a comfortable and affordable meal.

There is **Alex & Henry's** place on **Courtlandt Avenue**, not far from **Yankee Stadium**. Offering a hearty steak-and-potatoes sort of menu (with some health items for today's taste) Alex and Henry's has been host to Joe DiMaggio and Mickey Mantle, and for a generation or two of anonymous Yankee fans. They can handle an Irish wedding, a Latin graduation dance or a business dinner for fifty, and are especially good at Sweet Sixteen parties. In short, **Alex & Henry's** give the people of The Bronx what they need in the way of a restaurant...good food, good prices and a clean well lit place. There are restaurants that have become part of the life of the neighborhood, like **Joe & Joe's** on **Castle Hill**

## Gino's Cafe

**Located on Allerton Avenue and Boston Post Road, it was founded the year this picture was taken in 1957.** This era featured a family trattoria with a classic Italian cuisine.

## Now

*Photo: Spencer Field*

**Avenue. Joe's** sponsors the little league team, caters for big and small affairs and will cook what you need in their historic (1849) dining room, just as they have since Franklin Roosevelt was the President.

Bronxites are fond of their restaurants and slow to give them up. The Bronx was a place where eating out was a major form of recreation, especially to families of the 40s and 50s who discovered the pleasures of restaurant eating and who, for the very first time perhaps, had the money to indulge. Not that Bronx dining was particularly fancy or expensive. Usually

the favorite restaurant was a neighborhood institution where prices matched the budgets of the local people. Coming out of the Depression, in the postwar years, Bronx families were pleasantly surprised at their newfound prosperity, and they counted a weekly dinner in a real restaurant as one of life's important pleasures. For the really big adventures and special events, a birthday or a wedding anniversary, Manhattan was the natural lure. And, of course, you paid for the location and the glamour of a worldfamous restaurant. But eating at **Gino's** wasn't

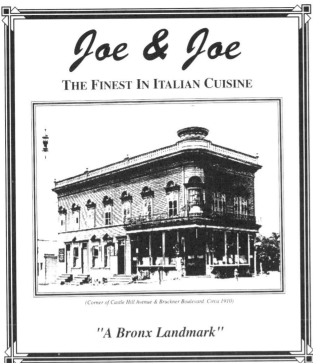

## Joe & Joe

### THE FINEST IN ITALIAN CUISINE

*(Corner of Castle Hill Avenue & Bruckner Boulevard. Circa 1910)*

*"A Bronx Landmark"*

*Then*

## Joe & Joe

**Joe & Joe Restaurant located at 1001 Castle Hill Avenue since 1940.** It occupies an even older site, dating to 1850 when it was known as Bailer's Hotel. It was a recruiting station during the Civil War and was acquired by the Longobardo family in 1940. From 1932-1939, it was known as The Eastern Boulevard Tavern. It is now a third generation business and remains popular among past and present Bronxites.

Now

beyond the means of many Bronx families, and there was always the Chinese eatery where the cost was minimal, or the deli where sandwiches and a soda didn't break the bank.

The comfort and availability of Bronx dining rooms was hard to match at the fancy downtown locales. One could walk to the local eatery, and be recognized by the waiter or the owner, who was quite willing to make the dishes just the way you wanted, In some sense, eating in a neighborhood restaurant was like eating at home, or with an extended family. They knew your name and how you liked your steak. It wasn't so surprising, therefore, that these unassuming Italian, Jewish or German restaurants carried on for generations and some (amazing as it seems) are still there, doing business at the same old spot.

*Then*

*Bettman Archives*

## Concourse Plaza

**The Concourse Plaza still towers over the Grand Concourse and 161st St and has been through some hard times but retains a degree of elegance that it had back in the mid-50s when Presidents came to speak and Yankee stars roomed there during homestands.** The Concourse Plaza Hotel in 1955 was The Bronx's social and political heart. Presidential candidates made a point of speaking here on their campaign trail. Truman, Eisenhower, and Kennedy all addressed Bronx audiences here. The hotel often hosted important weddings and bar mitzvahs and a wide variety of other functions, even fencing matches.

*Now*

*Photo: Spencer Field*

## Macombs Road &
## West 170th Street

**Located at this corner was the Santini Brothers Storage and Moving Warehouse.** This neighborhood, then and today, remains a used car and auto repair center. West of **Jerome** on **170th Street** and further down on **Inwood Avenue**, cab drivers could lease their

*Photo: Spencer Field*

**Now**

taxi for an eight hour shift. For some reason, during the 50s, when tropical fish collecting was a popular hobby, **Macombs Road** housed several aquarium shops. The Town Tavern, as its name suggests, was a place for meeting, eating and imbibing. The atmosphere was always inviting and, at any given time, the locals would be seated at the square wooden tables and chair enjoying the fare. It has now been replaced by the Equator Lounge. Santini Brothers have moved out and the graffiti artists have moved in.

*Then*

*Then*

**Now**

## Ogden Avenue &
## W. 167th Street

**These views of Ogden Avenue and West 167th Street are separated by nearly 50 years.** The Trans-lux Theatre shortly thereafter became the **Crest.** The cobblestone pavement has been covered by familiar asphalt as the trolleys were replaced by buses. The lot and the movie house have now been replaced by a highrise building.

Photo: UPI/Bettman

## Now

## Then

## New York Coliseum & Starlight Park

**Devoe Avenue off West Farms in the mid-30s where the entrance to the popular Starlight Park and the New York Coliseum were located.** Today the scene is dramatically different. Highrise housing projects and the **Sheridan Expressway** in the background are only part of the sweeping changes that affected this neighborhood in the past 50 years.

## Then

Photo: Julian A. Belin

## Now

## E. 161st Street & River Avenue

**The Earl Theatre opened in 1936 and The Bronx County Courthouse at the top of the hill was built in 1933.** For just one nickel you could ride the trolley which was very important because it easily connected the East and West Bronx. By the late '30s and early '40s pedestrian and car traffic started to dramatically increase. Today, the scene is much the same although the Earl Theatre has since been replaced by a coffee shop

*Photo: Michael Bobkoff*

## Bobkoff's - East Fordham Road & Marion Avenue

**In the 50s Bobkoff's sold blue jeans and sneakers to an eager market.** Interestingly, in 1998, the site is occupied by a similar store. In between, a bank was a tenant.

# Now

## Fordham Road & Jerome Avenue

This '60s picture on the left, taken from the Woodlawn-Jerome Avenue IRT, shows the art deco marquee of the Lido Theatre on East Fordham Road. Continuing eastbound, you might stop at **Davega's** for sporting goods and walking westward young ladies would be attracted to **Loehmann's Department Store**. The changes in 30 years are modest with the absence of the Lido being most apparent. **Fordham Road** still remains a bustling shopping district.

## Now

*Then*

*Then*

## Now

## Fordham Road & the Concourse

**This will always be a familiar sight. For over 40 years Alexander's towered over this busy intersection.** The photo on the left in the 60s includes the #12 Bus made famous in the film <u>A Bronx Tale</u>, driven by Bronx-born actor, Robert DeNiro who portrayed an Italian bus driver from **Arthur Avenue**. Bus #12 was the necessary public transport for West Bronx residents looking to get to the sands of **Orchard Beach** and the nautical neighborhood of **City Island**. In the more recent photo on the right, Caldors replaces **Alexander's** and the #12 Bus now goes to **Bartow Avenue** in **Co-op City.**

*The New York Historical Society*

## East Kingsbridge Road & Fordham Road

**A major intersection in The Bronx, where Kingsbridge Road swept down and joined Fordham Road.** This summer day in 1930 shows little of the usual activity of this major shopping street. It is probably Sunday. The New York Telephone Company building, in neo-Georgian lines, is at left and the **Windsor Theater** that presented legitimate plays stands closed for the season. In the 1950s, **Jahn's Ice Cream Parlor** would occupy a space next to the phone company. The above 1998 photo shows modern day **East Kingsbridge Road**. Notice that the **Windsor** has been replaced by a fabric store.

## Now

*Photo: Roger Arcara*

## Ogden Avenue & Jerome Avenue

**This 1947 photo shows both a trolley and a bus on cobblestone streets.** Today the cobblestone are smoothed over and some of the buildings on **Ogden Ave** have been demolished although the small park on the right remains.

## Now

*Photo: Spencer Field*

*Photo: Harold A. Smith*

## East Fordham Road and Webster Avenue

**This intersection was famous for Rogers Department Store.** Today, Sears has replaced **Rogers** and the area has undergone a major renewal including **Fordham Plaza.**

Now

*Photo: Spencer Field*

*Photo: Municipal Archives*

## Gerard Avenue and W. 161st Street

**Yankee fans should remember this popular intersection when they travelled to the Stadium (or registered for the draft).** In the 1950s this street between River Avenue and Gerard Avenue had four famous eating establishments. Remember them? They were Nedick's, Stadium Restaurant, Addie Vallins, and the Roxy Delicatessen.

*Then*

## W. Tremont & University Ave.

**This 1946 photo shows the usual assortment of small stores and shops.** The trolley tracks and overhead wires turn onto **University Avenue**. Five decades later, the apartment building looks virtually the same.

Now

*Photo: Spencer Field*

*Photo: Roger Arcara*

## West Farms

**In 1939, West Farms was a monumentally busy transportation hub for trolleys and elevated train lines. In 1998, buses served the area along with the elevated trains.**

Now

*Photo: Spencer Field*

# Yankee Stadium

**This Yankee Stadium photo taken in the mid-50s when the pennant seemed to have a permanent home here.** The picture below was taken in 1998. In the mid-70s, a major renovation altered the appearance with new lighting and seating patterns as well as a revamped facade.

*Photo: Clem Barry*

Now

By winning the 1999 World Series, and in the process tying their own record of 12 consecutive World Series victories, The Yankees have closed out the century with an unprecedented 25 championships.

*Then*

Now

1961 - New York Yankee fans camp out at the stadium the night before tickets go on sale for a game.

This 1998 picture of the same Bleacher Entrance shows a much different facade.

*N.Y. Transit Museum*

## Grand Concourse at Mosholu Parkway

**This view is facing Jerome Avenue in 1920s**. The scene hasn't changed substantially in seven decades. The green open spaces remain appealing and the **Jerome Avenue** subway continues to serve new generations of Bronxites.

## Now

*Then*

## University Avenue between West Burnside and 179th Street

**This was an important thoroughfare in the University Heights section. P.S. 26** is the large building in the left background and further north was the **Bronx campus of New York University**. Above shows the classic diversity of store ranging from the **A&P Supermarket** to the left, to the usual bakeries, meat market, vegetable store, cleaners, and one of the **Firestone** stores that sold an amazing variety of tools and automotive supplies.

Now

## Then

## East Tremont Avenue between Clinton and Prospect Avenue.

**This was the heart of the East Tremont commercial strip running from Third Avenue eastbound to the major intersection at Southern Boulevard. Tremont Avenue** was a major crosstown thoroughfare with #40 Bus running through this densely populated neighborhood. This row of small buildings was typical and reflected the neighborhood's varied needs. Just a block away was the **Loew's Fairmont Theatre** and further west was the second run but very popular **Deluxe Theatre**, famous for its Saturdays kid matinees.

## Then

● ● ● ● ● ● ● ● ● ● ● ● ● ● ● ● ● ● ● ● ● ● ● ● ● ● ● ●

## East Tremont Avenue, Looking toward 3rd Avenue

**The El shaded Third Avenue and was a friendly land-mark for this part of the east Bronx in the 1940's when this picture was taken.** Back then trolleys had right of way in the center of the street while passengers waited at designated trolley stops in the middle island. On the left, at **La Fontaine Avenue**, was the northern edge of **Crotona Park**. Today **Crotona Park** has been maintained and even improved. The trolley cars are only memories and even the mighty steel pillars of the **3rd Avenue** El fell victim to urban renewal.

*Photo: Roger Arcara*

*Then*

Photo: Roger Arcara

**Looking eastward on a snowy day in the late 1940's you can see the elevated tracks of the Third Avenue Line at E. 190th St.** On the left, hidden by the bad weather, is the campus of **Fordham University** and its Gothic buildings, while **Theodore Roosevelt HS** is barely visible in the background. At the extreme right is **Roger's Department Store**, a Bronx landmark for decades. The slush on **Fordham Road** suggest treacherous driving conditions as cars drove uphill towards the **Grand Concourse**.

## Intersection of Fordham Road & Webster Avenue

Now

Photo: Spencer Field

**This intersection has been radically changed in the last 50 years and is now a showcase for the rebirth of The Bronx.** On the right is the sweeping contemporary building known as **Fordham Plaza** and on the left is **Fordham University**'s striking modern library building, part of a huge campus expansion. The building housing **Sears Department Store** in 1998 (formerly **Roger's Department Store**) is almost unchanged although the neighborhood around it has undergone wholesale renovation.

*Photo: Roger Arcara*

**In 1936 this intersection, taken at the foot of Echo Park (looking east) was crowded with trolley cars from three lines, the 180th Street (at left), the Tremont Avenue line (center) and Webster Avenue line (at right).** In the background, the **Fox's Crotona Theatre** which presented vaudeville along with its first run movies is highly visible and an important part of this neighborhood.

## Webster Avenue at East Tremont Avenue

Now

**The same intersection in 1998 reveals the absence of cobblestone as well as trolley cars, and an effort at beautification.** The **Crotona Theatre** has been closed for three decades, however, the three storied building (formerly housing the **Tremont Tavern**) seems to have survived and even prospered.

*Photo: Roger Arcara*

**This picture, in the 1940's, shows the crosstown trolley car and in the background the Ace Theatre located at 554 Southern Boulevard.** There are the usual neighborhood shops including at least one catering to the growing Spanish-speaking population, largely from Puerto Rico, coming to the South Bronx. Generations of students from this neighborhood attended **Samuel Gompers H.S.** just a few blocks south on **Southern Boulevard.**

# Intersection of Prospect Avenue & Southern Boulevard at East 149th Street

## Now

**The buildings are remarkably intact after 50 years despite changing populations.** The cobblestones and trolleys no longer exist and the **Ace Theatre** has fallen victim to changing times. The large pharmacy in the corner building (right) has taken the name Congress from the original name of the theatre...it was the **Congress Theatre** until 1940 when it was renamed the **Ace Theatre.**

*Photo: Roger Arcara*

**This 1948 picture shows the 167th Street crosstown convertible trolley rumbling eastward down Boscobel Avenue towards Jerome Avenue.** In the background is **University Avenue** and the approaches of the **Washington Bridge** linking Manhattan to the Bronx over the Harlem River. A few years later the **Sedgwick Houses** occupied several blocks near the bridge. Today the **Sedgwick Houses** still remain, although the surrounding blocks have been severely altered to make room for the **Cross-Bronx Expressway** and the new **Alexander Hamilton Bridge.**

# Boscobel Avenue (E.L. Grant Highway)

## Now

**Tremont and Southern Boulevard in the early '60s was a busy intersection not far from the Zoo and the West Farms Road transportation hub.** Here one could pick up the #36 Bus and travel towards **Webster Avenue** and the **Concourse** or as far west as **University Avenue**. The usual candy store is on the corner and a few doors down on **Tremont** was **Fu Manchu's Chinese Restaurant.**

# East Tremont & Southern Boulevard

## Now

The oldest movie studio in America was built by Thomas Edison in 1905 and was located at 2826 Decatur Avenue at the corner of Oliver Place.

*Photo: Museum of Modern Art*

## Decatur Avenue & Oliver Place

Now

*Photo: Roger Arcara*

**Along Fordham Road in the mid-40s, the trolley still ran past the Fordham and Concourse movies houses on the north side.** The ornate **RKO Fordham** was a first-run house and continued in business until the 1970s, while the smaller **Concourse** disappeared shortly after this photo was taken. As usual, the space above theatres was rented to a variety of offices and businesses.

## Fordham Road

## Now

The street is still a major shopping district and traffic continues as heavy as ever, but the appearance of the Fordham Road is sharply altered in 1998. No trace remains of the two movie houses and only long-time Bronxites would remember their locations. All the buildings along **Fordham Road** have been refaced and renovated, and, in the case of the **Fordham Theatre** structure, with considerable loss of eye-appeal.

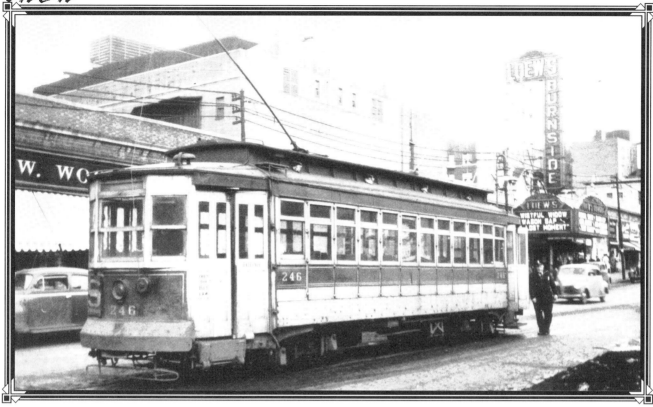

Photo: Roger Arcara

**Burnside Avenue in 1946, as the trolley rolls toward Jerome Avenue to the left.** Just visible behind the trolley is a **Woolworth** store, one of many around the Bronx, that lured kids with its matchless toy department and a well stocked candy counter. At right is the **Loew's Burnside**, a second run Bronx house that served this neighborhood for decades.

## Burnside Avenue

# Now

**The huge structure that housed the Burnside Theatre still looms over the scene but no longer serving as a movie theatre.** Today, it is a pharmacy and discount store, while **Woolworth** has closed its doors too, being replaced by shoe stores and clothing shops. **Burnside Avenue** still holds its status as a key shopping street in the west Bronx.

*Photo: Roger Arcara*

**Chugging its way east along Kingsbridge Road, this trolley emerges from one of the underpasses at the Grand Concourse in 1945.**
A row of familiar neighborhood stores occupy the tax-payer building at right, offering everything from watch repairs to bakery goods to the people of **Kingsbridge**.

## Kingsbridge Road

# Now

**The Concourse and its underpass seem stable, but Kingsbridge Road has undergone radical revision.** Most noticeable is the large structure that replaced the local stores: it is the Bronx headquarters of the **Church of Latter Day Saints**, the Mormons, who conduct a vigorous outreach program in New York. The large apartment building has been preserved and the underpass has had some help in recent years.

# HIGHBRIDGE

**Manhattan seen from Highbridge in The Bronx.**

*Photo: Spencer Field*

The Bronx, like most of New York City, is really made up of neighborhoods. People lived in **Mott Haven,** or **Silver Beach** or **Riverdale** and thought of themselves in local terms. Each neighborhood was, of course, unique with its own special feel, and people formed deep attachments to those few square blocks. In this chapter, we look at **Highbridge,** just one of the many locales that made up the whole borough.

Highbridge sits on the banks of the Harlem River, looking out at Manhattan. It includes the area north of **Yankee Stadium** and west of **Jerome Avenue** and is named for the beautiful 19th century span over the river. Full of hills and rocky outcrops, **Highbridge** wasn't the most convenient spot for mass transit but wonderful for the young people who relished the rugged terrain. There were the standard public schools, movies, candy stores and shopping streets, of course, plus the cool breeze in summertime and the excellent sledding in the winter… and the views were spectacular. It was neither rich nor poor, and in many ways **Highbridge** mirrored the population and pastimes of the rest of the Bronx in those days.

Looking east across the Harlem River towards Highbridge one can see an imposing Macombs Dam Bridge and aqueduct built in 1864. It carried water from the Catskill Reservoir to New York City. It was a Bronx landmark and it was altered to allow for larger ships and barges on the Harlem River. The nice looking but strenuous steps accommodated pedestrian traffic in part from the **Highbridge** (169th Street) stop on the New York Central.

*Photo: Spencer Field*

**Miller Toy Mart located on Ogden Avenue and West 164th Street**. This store sold carriages, strollers, bicycles and baby furniture to young families in the **Highbridge** neighborhood. The popularity of this store was based on low prices and superior service. The adjoining stores helped make **Ogden Avenue** a busy shopping district.

*Photo: Spencer Field*

*Photo: Spencer Field*

**Shakespeare Avenue looking south above Jerome Avenue**. One can see **P.S. 114** at the bottom of **Shakespeare Avenue**. This street is surfaced with interlocking pavers and provided excellent sleigh riding in the winter. There were private homes mingled with the apartments.

*Photo: Spencer Field*

**Crown Drug was located at the corner of Ogden and 168th Street**. This large drug store offered lower prices and catered to the large number of families in nearby **Noonan Plaza** apartments.

*Photo: Spencer Field*

**West 170th Street between Nelson and Shakespeare Avenues looking east towards Edward L. Grant Highway** (once known as Boscobel Avenue).

*Photo: Spencer Field*

**This intersection on West 169th Street & Ogden Avenue shows The Bronx Beacon Laundry located at 1315 Ogden Avenue.**

Photo: Spencer Field

Photo: Spencer Field

**By the late '60s the Crest Theatre had seen its better days.** In the '40s and '50s, the **Crest** was a well-run family movie house showing second run features. Many movie goers would remember the sunken candy counter off the main lobby. Many a youngster would sneak in a hero sandwich from **Rossi's Sandwich Shop.**

**Ogden Avenue in the '60s looking north past West 166th Street.** This was a busy location because of its close proximity to the **Crest Theatre** and the famous **Rossi's Heros Sandwich Shop.** In 1965 a memorable meatball hero cost 50¢ and add another 15¢ for a Pepsi and your meal was complete.

Photo: Spencer Field

Photo: Spencer Field

**These steps are one of seventy step streets unique to The Bronx.** This particular street runs from **Shakespeare Avenue** (top) down to **Edward L. Grant Highway (Boscobel Avenue).** Steps like this were repaired due to the hilly terrain of The Bronx. In spite of its incline, Bronxites found these steps to be very useful shortcuts.

**Public School 73 located on Anderson Avenue and 164th Street was the Highbridge neighborhood junior high school.**

*Photo: Spencer Field*

This P.S. 11 Schoolyard is similar to many around The Bronx, and was very popular for after-school activities. Punchball was one game that was well suited to this schoolyard provided you had a spaldeen.

. . . . . . . . . . . . . . . . .

*Photo: Spencer Field*

Higbridge Play Center located in Manhattan was a short walk over the Harlem River connected by the Highbridge 'walking bridge'. On a hot day, Bronx children were drawn to the pool and the heavy smell of chlorine there still lingers in the memories of many.

**Standing on the Bronx side of the Harlem river, beneath the Highbridge.**

*Photo: Spencer Field*

**Loew's Paradise Theatre**

It was the place of dreams fulfilled, the object of affection for countless Bronx natives, a wonderland on the **Grand Concourse**. The place was, of course, the **Paradise**, and Paradise it was to many thousands of movie goers for forty years. A grandiose movie palace done in the Hollywood Baroque style so favored in the late '20s, the **Loew's Paradise** was the premier venue for The Bronx. It wasn't just a theatre. Nobody went only to watch the movie. Going to the **Paradise** was an event, a signal that the evening's date was more than routine. It was a place to be seen in and a transient bit of elegance that lingered in the memory long after the film itself had been forgotten.

The **Paradise** was erected a few hundred feet south of **Fordham Road**, on the **Grand Concourse**, in 1929. At the tail end of the prosperous twenties (a period even more prosperous for The Bronx than for the rest of America) the Loew's organization was following an industry-wide trend in building bigger and bigger theatres. The movie industry was a fountain of riches for the studios, stars and theatre owners, and Loew's was reaping the full benefit of the boom times. The **Paradise** was designed to be the showplace of The Bronx, a place to entrance the audience and proclaim the splendor of the film industry. Nothing was spared in the design and execution of this showplace. Marble, tapestries, fine woods and the highest technology for sound and projection were available to the builders. The crowning touch was the famous starry ceiling. Legend is that Marcus Loew himself was immortalized in the **Paradise's** ceiling, by setting the stars and constellations in the precise alignment of Loew's birthday.

What Marcus Loew understood was that movie attendance was more than the act of watching a screenplay. To the middle class audience of The Bronx, a journey to the **Paradise** was a transport to another realm. In the **Paradise**, there were superbly trained corps of ushers, dressed in smart uniforms and standing stiffly at attention, waiting to escort the paying customer to his or her seat. The lobby itself was a foretaste of delights to come: towering marble pillars and a magical fountain complete with swimming goldfish. The staircases were clad in deep carpets, the

*Theatre Historical Society of America, Michael R. Miller Collection*

**This photo, from the 1940s, showed the Paradise at its peak, and in previous years it hosted live vaudeville shows with headliners like Jolson and Cantor.** The ultimate movie-going experience in The Bronx. For decades, young men brought their "special" dates to the celestial balcony to watch the clouds pass overhead.

*Photo: Richard DeCesare*

**From this vantage point (looking west) one can see the majestic sight of this movie theatre in all its splendor.**

**The inner lobby of the Paradise**. In the 1950s, all this could be yours for $1.25. There were real goldfish in the fountain on the right and the ornate armchairs suggested a royal atmosphere. For Bronxites, the price of admission fulfilled their fantasies and their egos.

walls hung with tapestry and adorned with statuary. Along the walls were wrought iron benches and throne-like chairs for the weary, or for the nearly delirious children to sit briefly. In the restrooms were more uniformed attendants, dispensing towels, perfume and a sense of wealth to those utterly without such prior experiences. Consider the impact upon a family of, say, garment workers or municipal employees, who struggled through the Depression in a four story walk-up off the **Concourse**. In the days before television or habitual automobile ownership, an evening at the **Paradise** was a fantasy come true. Affordable by even the most constrained Bronxites, the **Paradise** demonstrated anew the wonders of American life and wrote itself indelibly in the memories of two generations.

What everyone remembers best are the stars. The ceiling of the **Paradise** was somehow magically bedecked with stars, stars that twinkled in the dark,

and clouds that seemed to sweep by as if driven by a breeze. Nobody much asked how these effects were produced; it didn't matter much, after all. What mattered was the impact on the senses for all those who craned their necks upward at the famous ceiling, and were transfixed by stars glittering over the walls of some mythical villa garden in Italy.

To the young people of The Bronx, the **Paradise** was the premier dating spot. On Saturday, the sidewalks along the Concourse would be crowded with couples, strolling in the anticipation of an evening at the **Paradise**. In the mid-'50s, admission to the **Paradise** was still under two dollars, and less for matinee shows. Such rates meant that even highschoolers, or working folks, could afford the **Paradise** experience on a regular basis. The balcony, of course, was the preferred destination for the dating crowd and it was the place where smoking was permitted. Downstairs, in the sprawling orchestra, the families

**The balcony of the Paradise**. Along with the clouds and the stars overhead was a fantastic skyline from the architect's imagination. When the lights were lowered the theater-goer was transported to a Moorish castle complete with bubbling fountains and towering pine trees. As in most theatres, smoking was permitted only in the balcony.

••••••••••••••••••••••••••••••••••••••••••••••••••••••••••••••••••••••••••

and seniors found their seats well padded and clean. Ushers, of course, manned the doors; on Saturday matinees, the children's section was patrolled by matrons in starched white uniforms.

After the movie, the **Concourse** was a convenient place for a snack. On the other (eastern) side of the **Grand Concourse** from the **Paradise** was the lure of **Krum's Ice Cream Parlor. Krum's** was a major league soda shop, with its own candy counter and dozens of booths stretching into the next block. But one needn't be limited. Directly next door to the **Paradise** was a perfectly nice ice cream parlor, smaller than **Krum's**, but alluring nonetheless. And within blocks in either direction were candy stores, luncheonettes and restaurants.

In the earliest days of the '30s, the **Paradise** also featured live stage performances. The biggest names in American theatre and vaudeville played on the **Grand Concourse**, and in other parts of The Bronx,

too, for that matter. The **RKO Keith** on **Prospect Avenue** was a top-rated vaudeville locale, and several other of the larger movie houses hosted live stage shows, too. But the **Paradise** was always the top of the line. Eddie Cantor, Al Jolsen, and other headliners brought their acts to the stage of the **Paradise**. Later on the **Paradise** went to a strictly film program, although always a first run location. In the days of Cinerama and VistaVision, when television was ruining the movie industry, the **Paradise** could play the biggest screen, biggest color hits, and it was there that the generation of the '50s and '60s saw such productions as The Ten Commandments, and Bridge On The River Kwai, and every other major release of the time. The **Paradise** also served a civic function. It was the graduation auditorium for several high schools including **Bronx Science**, which was around the corner.

In the '70s, the **Paradise** shared much of the same fate as the rest of The Bronx. It lost its audience to the

**A panorama of the Paradise Auditorium.** The theatre was big enough for 4,000 and was host to high school graduations over the years. If you went to **DeWitt Clinton** or the **Bronx High School of Science** and others, you may remember getting your diploma in this imposing theatre.

suburbs and to television, and ultimately became a multiplex locale. The glorious auditorium was subdivided into four austere little theatres, showing actions and splatter films as often as first run features, and instantly declining to the status of a Long Island mall drive-in. Audiences deserted it in droves. And with good reason. By 1993, the **Paradise** was closed. The encouraging news is that in 1994 a campaign began to restore and revitalize the **Paradise** with considerable political support from Bronx leaders. A realization that this theatre was more than just a movie house led to its exterior being declared a New York City Landmark in 1997, although as of this writing, plans for the rebirth of the **Paradise** were still uncertain and the **Paradise** remains closed.

Closed, but standing. The scheme to divide up the great space for mini-theatres were misguided and happily came to nothing.

The revival of The Bronx in the 1990s has given hope to many partisans of the **Paradise** that the old showcase might yet survive. By accident or divine intervention, the magnificent building itself has survived the fires, slum clearances and urban renewal programs, and it awaits another generation of movie-goers. The grandchildren of the old **Paradise** audience might yet have the thrill of watching those stars move in their stately rotation across the ceiling.

*Theatre Historical Society of America, Michael R. Miller Collection*

**The Franklin, located on 161st Street and Prospect**. The Bronx was a stop on the Keith vaudeville circuit, and some of the great names in show business appeared here. When vaudeville declined, the Franklin became purely a movie house. The RKO theatre was one of the largest of The Bronx theatres when it opened its doors in 1920.

● ● ● ● ● ● ● ● ● ● ● ● ● ● ● ● ● ● ● ● ● ● ● ● ● ● ● ● ● ● ● ● ● ● ● ● ● ●

The Bronx hasn't got the visual appeal of, say, Paris or Monument Valley, but it has nonetheless been the setting for a number of movies over the years. In the '30s and '40s, the golden days of the Hollywood studio system, most movies were made on the sound stages in California. An occasional bold pioneer might take the cameras and other bulky equipment out into the real world, but the controlled environment of a Hollywood back lot was usually preferred. Still, The Bronx occasionally found itself a film location, even when such

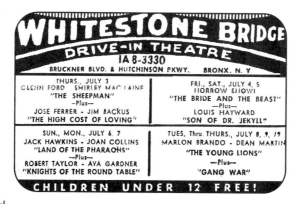

location work was unusual. One of the earliest films with a specifically Bronx locale was Bronx Morning a documentary shot in 1935. Made in the prevailing social realist form of those Depression years by Jay Leyda, Bronx Morning is about the common man, the working stiffs who make up the blood and bone of any great city. There are shots of milkmen in the early dawn, window washers, taxi drivers and shopkeepers and others who calmly and with determination go to their jobs and make the borough work on a beautiful summer day in the '30s. Viewed some six decades later, <u>Bronx Morning</u> has a nostalgic appeal that Leyda probably never intended, but it preserves on film a time in The Bronx that was rarely recorded.

Actually, filmmaking in The Bronx might be traced back to the earliest days of the industry, in the l900s. New York was one of the first centers of film production in the United States, long before Hollywood was discovered. Edison himself had a studio on **Oliver Place** near **Bedford Park Boulevard** where, among long-forgotten actors in long lost films, D.W. Griffith had his first job in the movie industry: as an actor in <u>Rescued From The Eagle's Nest</u>. A young actor who also travelled to The Bronx, to learn from Edison's establishment, was Cecil DeMille: he later did well as a director. On **l76th Street** near **Prospect Avenue** were the **Biograph Studios**, where, among others Chaplin, Griffith and Pickford made movie history before World War I. A huge single purpose building, very advanced for its time (about l9l6), the **Biograph Studios** reflected both the prosperity of the film business and the attractiveness of The Bronx as a locale for cinema artists. Other locations in The Bronx included **Fort Schuyler** on Long Island Sound, where Griffith shot a Revolutionary War movie, and **City Island**, as well as **Van Cortlandt Park**, assorted streets, rooftops and farms. The **Biograph Studios** remained standing until the l970s, and, even in the l960s, were used for television productions.

Filmmakers were, not surprisingly, more attracted by the sights of Manhattan than The Bronx, but there is a select list of movies that owe their special qualities to a Bronx location. Probably best known is <u>Marty</u>, made in l955 by Delbert Mann from Paddy Chayefsky's television drama. This still-affecting story of The Bronx butcher and his struggle to find happiness captured an authentic feel of the Italian neighborhood around **Arthur Avenue**, and made Ernest Borgnine an unlikely star. In <u>Marty</u>, The Bronx was a working class place, full of colorful characters and generally pleasant if not very luxurious. Indeed, it is Marty's greedy cousin, bent on moving away from The Bronx to a "better" suburb, who is portrayed in critical terms. Marty, who has both feet dug into the sidewalks of his native Bronx, emerges as the far better person. Another complimentary, if perhaps exaggerated view of The Bronx, came in <u>Mollie</u> (1949), the movie based on the popular Molly Goldberg radio series. Mollie's family, who lived at **1048 E. Tremont Avenue**, had their heartwarming

*Theatre Historical Society of America, Michael R. Miller Collection*
**The Lido was located at 15 East Fordham Road, across the street from the Army & Navy clothing shops and just a few hundred feet west of Davega's Sporting Goods and close to Vim's.** One of the smallest theatres in The Bronx, the **Lido** barely held 600 movie goers. The **Lido** attracted more of its patrons from the thriving **Fordham** shopping area than from the local area neighborhood. The price to see a movie there was right for the thrifty shopper. Even if the movie playing wasn't current, at least you got to see it before it was too old. In the 1970s, the **Lido** changed its appeal by showing X-rated films.

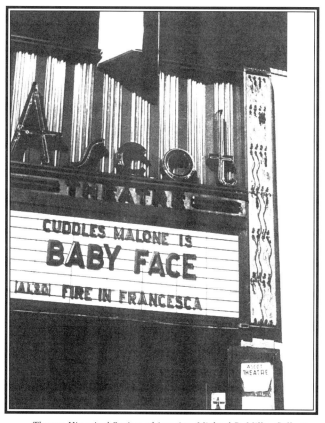

and psychotic drug addicts. Nor did Wolfen, also in 1981 help change the unfortunate impression. In Wolfen, The Bronx was depicted as an urban desert, a rubble strewn wasteland where bands of supernatural wolves ate the homeless. It was a place of nightmares.

A few pictures, too, such as the police action/thriller The Seven Ups, used the streets of The Bronx for their story settings. More directly tied to The Bronx was Philip Kaufman's The Wanderers, (1979) a bitter-sweet tale of life in the '50s taken from Richard Price's novel. The Wanderers featured the mythical Fordham Baldies, the gang that haunted the dreams of many Bronx kids in the 50s but who probably never existed, at least not in the shaved head form of the movie. Martin Scorsese's brilliant Raging Bull in 1983, followed the career of Bronx born Jake LaMotta and it, too, was filmed on the streets of The Bronx.

encounters with everyday life and everybody who lived in The Bronx could recognize the style if not the exact apartment where Molly, Sam, Uncle David and Rosalie lived their lives. Another ethnic story of The Bronx was The Subject Was Roses, 1968, based on Frank Gilroy's prize winning play. This story of Irish Americans, Bronxites, of course, who struggle with personal and social problems, was critically acclaimed in the late '60s. Here, too, The Bronx is a generally benign environment. Problems come from personal crises and sweeping historical forces, not from the streets outside which are still nurturing.

The image of The Bronx began to suffer erosion in the 1970s, and movies reflected the new perceptions. In 1981 there was Fort Apache: The Bronx, which helped establish the unfortunate national awareness of The Bronx as an urban wasteland with its tale of corrupt police

*Theatre Historical Society of America, Michael R. Miller Collection*

**The Ascot Theatre, two blocks south of the Paradise on the Concourse.**

*Theatre Historical Society of America, Michael R. Miller Collection*

**The Loew's Spooner**. Located at **163rd Street** and **Southern Boulevard**, the **Spooner** was part of a densely populated neighborhood. The Loew's chain was interested in real estate as well as movies. Here again, they have built an office building over their theatre and discovered a profitable use for unused space.

*Collection of The New-York Historical Society*

**The Windsor Theatre at 315 East Fordham Road was perhaps the leading Bronx Vaudeville house.** In the late '40s, it exclusively became a movie theatre. Among those vaudevillian who took the stage at the Windsor was Jimmy Durante, Cab Calloway, Bob Crosby, Phil Silvers, Joey Faye, and Ina Ray Hutton's All-Girl Orchestra and many others. One could see a vaudeville show and movie in the '30s for sixty-five cents.

*Theatre Historical Society of America, Michael R. Miller Collection*

**The Loew's Fairmount.** Placed thoughtfully on the main shopping street of **Tremont Avenue**, the **Fairmount** was a lavish movie palace. The building overhead housed a strange variety of dance studios, lawyers' offices, stamp dealers and accountants. The building stands, but the theatre has long since shuttered.

*Theatre Historical Society of America, Michael R. Miller Collection*

**The Freeman, located on Southern Boulevard and Freeman Street.** The **Freeman** reflected the changing neighborhood starting in the early '70s. Many Hispanics chose to move into this section of the East Bronx. The films revealed the change as well as the adjacent shops.

**The Loew's Burnside.** Located on the north side of **Burnside** between the **Concourse** and **Jerome** at the intersection of Walton Avenue. This theatre was part of the Loew's chain. The **Burnside** took movies after their runs in the major theatres. Typical of the class, the **Burnside** was less expensive, and was comfortable and convenient, the place for a family visit or to pass a few hours in the air conditioning.

Robert DeNiro gave life to Jake LaMotta in the film, but The Bronx was a very real presence in every frame. In 1993, Robert DeNiro returned to The Bronx, as the director of A Bronx Tale, a movie that took its story line and atmosphere from The Bronx of the '50s. In reality, A Bronx Tale was mostly shot in the borough of Queens, but probably only native Bronxites could have caught the error. Queens does look a lot like parts of The Bronx.

A greater liberty was taken in 1995, when the martial arts star Jackie Chan directed and starred in Rumble In The Bronx. Once again, The Bronx in the title didn't mean the real Bronx. Rumble was filmed

**The RKO Fordham.** Many theatres in The Bronx hosted live shows and vaudeville acts and some even presented legitimate theatre. The **RKO Fordham**, built in 1920, was one of the larger theatres in The Bronx with a capacity approaching 2500. This bill from the 1930s seems to have been a popular attraction. After the theatre, the **Jonas Candy Store** was available for sodas and ice cream. For those in the '40s and '50s, **Jahn's** and **Krum's** filled that role. Across the street was the famous **Brighton Cafeteria**.

**The Valentine Theatre - built in the 1920's was part of Fox chain of movies and then later became part of the Skouras chain and held about 1500 patrons.** It showed current films, some of them were independently produced, and were usually not shown by the RKO Fordham and Loew's chain. The **Valentine** was located on **Fordham** and **Valentine Avenue** across the street from **Gorman's Frankfurter** stand.

**The Loew's American Theatre, located in the sprawling new housing called Parkchester**. Built in 1940, the **Loew's American** was a striking example of Art Deco design. Fully air-conditioned, of course, the American played first run movies and was a neighborhood landmark for many years.

**The Castle Hill Theatre**. Theatres in the 30's were objects of fanciful design. The **Castle Hill**, for example, built in 1927, has the turrets and half-timbers of the Elizabethian castle. The picture changed every Saturday, although this was a second (or third run) movie house. It offered bingo and was used as a local assembly hall.

**The Fleetwood Theatre was located on 163rd** and **Morris Avenue**. It was built in 1925 and was part of the Consolidated chain. It was a medium-sized theatre holding about 1600. Many movie goers would affectionately refer to it as the "flea bag".

entirely in Vancouver, British Columbia. The result was a mysterious land called The Bronx, where gangs and violence were epidemic, but which had towering mountains in the background and a beautiful harbor. To Bronxites, Jackie Chan's Bronx was laughable, but it probably helped sell the movie

around the world which, aside from its misappropriation of The Bronx name, wasn't bad. In 1995 there was I Like It Like That, an independent film about Hispanic families in The Bronx which alternated between comedy and tragedy in its story. I Like It Like That had a raucous charm and energy that reflected life, its good and bad aspects, in the contemporary neighborhoods of The Bronx. It used the streets of The Bronx for authentic locales and did a good job in capturing the drama of real life.

At the moment, New York City is enjoying a renaissance of filmmaking. Hollywood has been reminded that the streets of New York, including The Bronx, aren't easy to duplicate in California. The practical result is that film trucks and crowds of technicians are ever-present around the City, and The Bronx has claimed its share. A good sign is that The Bronx is no longer a synonym for slum, crime, and gang war. Filmmakers are discovering that The Bronx might also stand for family, neighborhood and good times.

*Theatre Historical Society of America, Michael R. Miller Collection*

**RKO Chester.** Located at the intersection of **Boston Road, East Tremont Avenue and West Farms Road,** the **RKO Chester** achieved nationwide fame in 1955 as a background for the Oscar-winning film <u>Marty</u>. Who could forget the famous dialogue, "I dunno Marty, what do you wanna do tonight?"

*Theatre Historical Society of America, Michael R. Miller Collection*

**The Ritz Theatre located at 1014 East 180th Street.** The **Ritz** started its life as a legitimate theatre and later returned to its roots and became the Yiddish Art Theatre. In between, it showed movies and apparently worked hard at drawing an audience even to the point of holding contests on weekends.

*Theatre Historical Society of America, Michael R. Miller Collection*

**The Loew's Avalon.** This theatre was part of the Consolidated Theatre chain of movies. In the 1930s, one could get in for ten and fifteen cents during the day and twenty-five cents in the evening. Mid-week nights would offer keno during intermission. The name Avalon was popular in the 1920s, and there are scores of theatres, buildings, parks and housing developments with the title. This Bronx example was on **Burnside Avenue** and may have been too large for its surroundings, especially in the dreary days of the Depression when this photo was taken.

**The Park Plaza at 1746 University Avenue, was situated on a busy intersection of University Avenue and West Tremont Avenue**. This theatre drew a loyal neighborhood following. The building in the background is **Macombs Junior High School, (P.S. 82)**. The theatre building also housed dance studios, shops and, of course, the luncheonette for after-movie ice cream. The **China Star** restaurant was across the street on **University Avenue** as was **Rushmeyer's Ice Cream Parlor** which later was named **Luhrs** in the mid-sixties.

**The Royal, located at 423 Westchester Avenue**. The **Royal** was part of the RKO chain which had many branches throughout The Bronx. This photo was taken in the early '30s. Note the large banner for Dracula, a Bela Lugosi sensation of 1931. Also note that the Royal offered a stage show along with the films.

**The Surrey Theatre on Mt. Eden Avenue, built in 1935, was part of the Consolidated and Brandt movie chain of theatres and was a very popular theatre for those students attending William Howard Taft H.S., Wade Junior High and youngsters from P.S. 64** on **Walton Ave**. It was one of the many second-run, smaller, cheaper, but just as well remembered. **Mos Kov's Delicatessen** was just a block away where one could fill their stomach in the 1950s with a frankfurter with mustard and sauerkraut for just fifteen cents.

Theatre Historical Society of America, Michael R. Miller Collection

**The Loew's Grand - Around the corner from Loehmann's.** A very lovely theatre with a huge balcony. It held close to 2500 patrons and it was the largest movie theatre until the **Paradise** opened two years later in 1929. If you had the patience to wait, the **Grand** was where you saw films that were still being talked about.

Theatre Historical Society of America, Michael R. Miller Collection

**The Luxor was built in 1923 and named in honor of King Tut's Tomb found in Luxor, Egypt a few years earlier.** This smallish Consolidated chain theatre featured second and even third run movies. If you couldn't afford the **Paradise** or the **RKO Fordham**, or even the **RKO 167th Street**, you waited until it came to the **Luxor**.

**Pelham Parkway and White Plains Road was the hub for Pelham Parkway residents.** The **Globe Theatre** was a familiar neighborhood sight especially for kids on Saturday morning where they would line up for a day of cartoons and a movie. Students from **Columbus High School** found instruments and records at Concourse Music. In the early fifties, television was becoming popular and Dumont was one of the earliest brands available.

Photo: John Forzaglia

Theatre Historical Society of America, Michael R. Miller Collection

**The Elsmere, located at 1926 Crotona Parkway, was one of the oldest Bronx movies theatres. An imposing classical building that was somewhat small and cozy.** The **Elsmere** not only showed movies but hosted live performances, as well. The titles of the movies date this photo from the late '40s, and reflect some of the Cold War tensions of the era.

# Parkchester: The Grand Old Neighborhood

Parkchester Oval in the East Quadrant with the playgrounds in the foreground.

*By Hank de Cillia*
**(St. Raymond's Grammar School, Graduating Class of 1957)**

*I'll never forget picking up the Sunday New York Times in 1980 and reading an article in the real estate section about **Parkchester**. My wife Pat and I, both*

*born and raised there, had been living in Massachusetts since the late sixties and lost contact with the place. The Times article began "Located on 110 acres in the southeast Bronx, **Parkchester** is..." I couldn't believe my eyes! Only 110 acres? In 1972, together with two other couples (also from Parkchester) we almost purchased a 135 acre parcel of land in western Massachusetts to build homes on*

Photo: Hank de Cillia

North Quadrant ballfield before paving in the 1950's.

Photo: Hank de Cillia

North ballfield after it was paved (roller skating to music)

'collectively' (You remember those days, don't you?) It immediately dawned on me that just 3 families might have lived on a piece of property in Massachusetts that was 25 acres larger than 12,500 families who lived on it in the Bronx Parkchester!

Yes, that's right. When it was completed in 1941 by the Metropolitan Life Insurance Company, **Parkchester** had 12,000 apartments, making it the largest housing 'project' in the world at the time. Just as amazingly, over 52,000 people lived in those apart-

ments, during its peak population period from the late forties to the mid sixties.

I lived in **Parkchester** from birth in 1944 (actually, Pat and I didn't get there until we were a week old, since we were born two days apart in nearby **Westchester Square Hospital**) until 1966 when she and I got married in **St. Raymond's Church** and immediately moved to Westchester County (that other 'chester up north... no relation or similarity).

My parents, Kay and Harry, moved into **Parkchester** in 1941 from Isham Street in northern Manhattan. My mother was then a clerk at Met Life, which apparently helped them get in. I'm told it was very difficult to get 'accepted' for **Parkchester**... you had to fill out long applications and even provide photos. (Unfortunately, this latter requirement enabled them to keep people of color out..a common housing practice at the time, and the only blemish on **Parkchester's** record that I can remember.)

Kay and Harry were overjoyed to get into **Parkchester**, but very anxious about their standing in the new community. For example, after my father died, my mother told me this story. At the time they moved in, Harry was working in the South Bronx as a steel fabricator... not a white or even a blue collar job. To get to work, he would walk from our apartment over to **Hugh Grant Circle** and take the subway. He was so concerned about 'fitting in' that he bought two suits and a briefcase just to wear to work. Every day, he would put on his suit, put his lunch in his briefcase and set out for the subway station with the other

*Photo: Hank de Cillia*

One of the many Parkchester street signs...decorated for most holidays.

*Photo: Hank de Cillia*

A basketball team coached by John Murray(on left). Don Cafero (on right) headed up the Parkchester "Rec" program.

*Photo: Hank de Cillia*

Duncan Yo-Yo champs, including Jim Cafero (on right), son of Dom Cafero.

*Photo: Hank de Cillia*

The "famous" Kiwanis Team including John Dearie and Dave Slattery with many future "All Stars"

*Photo: Hank de Cillia*

Roller skating behind the North Quadrant Playground

*Photo: Hank de Cillia*

Square dancing in the East Quadrant playground.

'executives' heading for work. Upon arriving at the shop, he would change into his real work clothes. Mom told me he did this for over a year, until he realized they wouldn't get thrown out for dressing inappropriately.

*Parkchester* was so large it took almost four years to complete. It was literally a "town within a city", as described in a New York Times Magazine feature article in 1941. In describing the place back then, the author John Stanton noted, "Parkchester has a staff of 500 employees. The staff includes gardeners to take care of the parks and recreation directors to coach teams that flourish on its playfields... Parkchester has its own police department and a large staff of 'servicemen' to keep everything working."

Every *Parkchester* playground had a 'Rec Office' in the nearest apartment building on the ground floor, where 'Rec Teachers' supervised all activities. Most parents would let their kids go down to the playground after school or for the whole day on weekends and in the summer, coming home only for lunch and dinner. We also had our own movie theatre, the **Loew's American**, inside *Parkchester* and three others on the perimeter...the **Palace** on **Unionport Road**, the **Circle** on **Hugh Grant Circle** and the **RKO Castle Hill**. There was so much to do that most kids don't remember ever leaving *Parkchester* until they went to High School.

*Parkchester* had its own stores of all types...drug stores, deli's, newspaper stores, supermarkets and

*Photo: Hank de Cillia*
Swings in the East playground.

even three bars: the **Manor House**, the **Park House** and the **Chester House**. The biggest store was Macy's, where my mother worked in Toys, Records and Sporting Goods for 15 years after she left Met Life. My collection of 45's was the envy of all my friends, and whenever I wanted some game or sporting item, my mother would have it "put in the window" and then buy it at a marked down price as a display item the next day. Talk about spoiled.

Here's a unique *Parkchester* Christmas story. On the Northern boundary of the project, along **East Tremont Avenue**, ran the train tracks. It was some kind of depot area and there must have been eight sets of tracks running side by side. Every year, in early December, an entire train with 40-50 railroad cars would pull up to the tracks closest to **East Tremont Avenue**, completely filled with Christmas trees. I'm told over 8,000 trees were on board. They would open the car doors and sell trees right on the tracks for the next three weeks to all the *Parkchester* families who would walk them home to their apartments. It was a major production for everyone in the family to be involved in picking out their tree. After Christmas, the trees would be placed in huge piles on the island along the center of **Metropolitan Avenue**, to be picked up by garbage men. We sure had a great time building tree forts before they arrived.

*Parkchester* consisted exclusively of 7 story buildings with one elevator and 12 story buildings with

*Photo: Hank de Cillia*
"Pool" in the East playground closed after the Polio scare in the early 50s.

*Photo: Hank de Cillia*

"Pool" in the East Quadrant.

that unique place. Although I have lost contact, I've heard it continues to work for families living there today, ironically now mostly people of color.

As a member of the first generation of children born and raised in **Parkchester**, I cannot conceive of a more ideal environment to grow up in. Having said this, I can't explain why all of us desperately wanted to move out the moment we got a job, got married or both. I'd like to think it's because living there gave us a glimpse of how much more we could achieve, but I'm not sure. Later, Pat and I raised our daughter Amy in a nice private home in a small Massachusetts town with a great school system, but we often wish she had the same experience as we did growing up in a wonderful place like **Parkchester**.

They say you can't go back, but we certainly took something enormously valuable from that life experience, something worth revisiting.

two. The apartments had one, two or three bedrooms, but just one bathroom regardless of size.

In grammar school, all my friends lived in my building (building buddies) and we played right outside on the stoop, or in the East playground. On rainy days, the elevator and staircases in our building were perfect for hide and seek. We learned how to stop the elevator between floors during our games, which really endeared us to the grown-ups on their way home from work. The staircases were also ideal for playing cards later as teenagers... in our case, however, we played bridge for money because poker was too boring.

**Parkchester** was a monumental social experiment...and it worked. Virtually all of the lower middle class families who moved there between 1940 and 1965 bettered themselves, as a result of living in

*Photo: Hank de Cillia*

**Several winning basketball teams sponsored by the Parkchester Merchants Association.**

*Photo: Hank de Cillia*

A scene from the famous "Indian Pageants" held every year in the North ballfield.

# Images of Parkchester

...watching the retired men play shuffleboard near the Purdy Street playground...

...roller-skating down Machine Gun and Suicide Hills in the North at breakneck speed...

...spending Saturday mornings in the Palace Theatre watching cartoons and serials...

...playing punchball on Maple Drive with Spaldeens...25 cents chips...

...shooting marbles at the East Quadrant flagpole...hot scramble!...

...watching those huge goldfish swimming in the Metropolitan Oval pool...

...filing into St. Raymond's Church with my class every Sunday for the 8am Mass...

...buying baseball cards with chewing gum from Mrs. Tyler at Parkchester News...

...getting my 'name taken' by the Parkchester Cops for 'running on the grass'...

...watching the girls dance at the Indian Pageant in the Ballfield every year...

...buying 7 cent ices from the Good Humor man outside the North Playground...

...riding the "Twenty" bus down East Tremont Avenue over to Manhattan Prep...

...walking up Castle Hill Avenue to Lambiase's for Italian ices on really hot days...

...playing in the Toy department at Macy's Parkchester just before Christmas...

...bowling at the Playdrome off Unionport Road every Saturday morning...

...having chocolate egg creams at Bunny's on Starling Avenue...

...going to the St. Helena's Dance every Friday night...'leave room for the Holy Ghost!'...

...drinking ice cold sodas at the NQ (North Quadrant) club picnic...

...buying cherry lime rickeys in a wing ding cup at Oval Drug...to go...

...buying 25 cents worth of potato salad at Arfstein's Deli after playing basketball...

...playing on the 'climbing signs' at Starling and Castle Hill Avenues...

...watching the PAL band on Met Avenue in the St. Helena's Parade..trumpets and drums...

...buying Hardy Boys books and Duncan Yo-Yo's at Wormraths...

...shooting pool at the St. Ray's K of C Hall over by Rota's with my father...

# POLITICS, BRONX STYLE

**Joyce Kilmer Park opposite the Concourse Plaza looking north.** The occasion is a rally in support of Israeli statehood during the time of British rule in Palestine. The large crowds reflect the substantial Jewish population of The Bronx which strongly supported the creation of a new state. In quieter moments, this park was ideal for kite flying, strollers and baby carriages.

For the period between the Great Depression and the Great Society, the politics of The Bronx can be easily described: straight Democratic. That is Democratic with a big "D", as in the party of Roosevelt, Truman and Kennedy and in the sense of the machine politics of men such as Flynn, Buckley and their loyal street workers and functionaries who made The Bronx a Democratic preserve for thirty years and more.

With a population very distinctly, and proudly, working class, The Bronx of the mid-twentieth century reflected most of the trends of national affairs, but with a special flavor. The migration of

Jewish garment workers, Italian laborers and Irish civil servants northward into the welcoming streets of The Bronx during the 1920s marked the birth of a Bronx political environment. Older families, who predated the boom of the '20s, might have favored a more genteel politics and may have voted for Franklin's cousin Teddy rather than for the Democratic Roosevelt, but that was a different time and a vastly different population. The subways that brought the ethnic groups into The Bronx and carried them daily to their jobs around the greater city, also carried a bustling, noisy and joyously New York kind of political organization to The Bronx. The

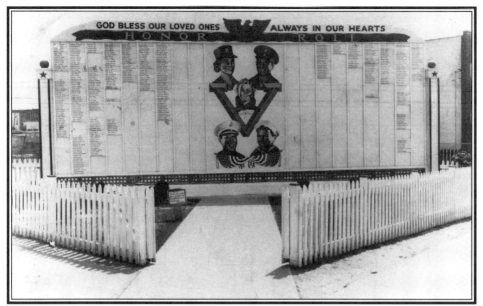

Photo: John Pfeiffer

**Honor Roll Memorial on Tremont Avenue on West Farms.**

many organized efforts to bring inhabitants to the borough. Subway lines were promoted, roads lobbied for and, in general, an infrastructure for an expanding community was assembled by skillful policies and persuasion. Still, the organized politics of The Bronx was left to local ward and neighborhood professionals, with the resulting variety on a borough-wide basis. All this changed with Ed Flynn, the young Irishman from **Mott Haven** who entered Democratic

established New York political system, in the form of **Tammany Hall,** ran The Bronx as it ran the other boroughs in those days with rigid control and centralized authority. Charles Murphy was Tammany's man in The Bronx, but his death in 1922 left the field open for newcomers, among them a young lawyer named Edward J. Flynn. Flynn had served as a state assemblyman and a loyal Democrat, but when opportunity beckoned in 1922, he acted. Moving up from the post of Sheriff of Bronx County (an honorific, if lucrative, post) Flynn became one of three co-rulers of The Bronx organization. In remarkably short time, Flynn ascended to singular rule, and by 1923 he was the youngest county leader in America. He was thirty one years old.

Eager young politicians like Edward J. Flynn didn't take long to understand how The Bronx of the 1920s was going to differ from the bucolic place they had known before World War I. In those days, the political power resided in the trade organizations and boosters clubs that promoted Bronx business. The Bronx Board of Trade, for instance, was a notable force in the development of The Bronx as a residential and commercial center in the twentieth century and had a strong voice with New York political parties. Real estate, especially, was a favorite Bronx industry even in the 1900s, and there were

political activity just after World War I and rapidly grasped the essential fact of Bronx life: the people there needed, and wanted, creative leadership. There was no fear of too much government or hesitation about using the power of the state to affect worthwhile change. The newcomers who crowded the voting lists after the War demanded government services. What they wanted were schools, roads, parks, hospitals and libraries and a local government that understood (and responded) to their unique lifestyle.

Flynn solidified his base by traditional New York City methods. He listened to his constituents and delivered. When civil service jobs were sought or a library was in need of repairs, Flynn and his minions were available and could usually be counted upon to make good their promises. The Jewish newcomers to The Bronx, emerging from the Lower East Side or the slums of Brooklyn, were not strangers to liberal (even radical) politics; and the Irish, Italian, German and other ethnics also welcomed an activist kind of politician. The '20s were economically volatile and a generation that had fought a World War was pressing the old line organizations for their rewards. New York, with its huge immigrant population and its habit of ward politics, was a place in which reform programs and government experiments were familiar and often applauded, nowhere more so than in The Bronx. Home to thousands of trade union members and rising first-generation entrepreneurs, The Bronx often seemed like an open air experiment in social welfare and government programs. It was this legacy of government activism that shaped The Bronx, and which came to full flower in the generation of the '40s and '50s. Schools, parks, libraries and health care were, in The Bronx at least, freely provided by the Democratic and liberal office holders in the first half of the twentieth century.

Maybe it was the wide open spaces of The Bronx, the sense of innovation and starting anew that promoted this political atmosphere. Not accidentally did the socialist and cooperative sponsors of non-profit housing pick The Bronx for their bold experiment, the famous **Coops** on **Allerton Avenue.** The **Coops** were a socialist dream come true. Houses were owned and run by the workers for their own benefit. The system survived until the 1950s and left a vivid impression upon those who lived there. The **Coops** still stand in the 1990s, rentals now and long past their radical origins but with a sense of history still surrounding them. Further north, near **Jerome Park Reservoir,** another experiment in cooperative housing were the **Amalgamated Houses,** an even larger complex built by the Amalgamated Clothing Workers and constructed in 1927. The **Amalgamated Houses** continue in their co-operative fashion until this day. Much later, in the 1960s, The Bronx would again be home to a bold experiment in housing known as **Co-op City.** Located in the far northeast section, alongside the New York State Thruway north of **Orchard Beach, Co-op City** was (and remains) the nation's largest cooperative housing project. It contains more than 15,000 apartments on 300 acres of Bronx real estate. When it opened its doors in the late 1960s, **Co-op City** seemed another example of progressive Bronx social planning, in the tradition of the **Coops** and the **Amalgamated.** The impact of **Co-op City,** however, was questionable. It helped drain the long-time Jewish and Italian residents of the West Bronx from their neighborhoods and paved the way for massive property decline in the '70s.

An important part of The Bronx's forward-looking programs and its notable capital investment during

**The Allerton Avenue Cooperative Housing, or known to those who lived there, simply as the Coops.** This development was created by political activists in the late '20s as an example of enlightened social planning. In its early years, the **Coops** were famous for its left-wing atmosphere. As time passed, the political mood changed. After World War II, the **Coops** took on a mainstream feeling. Throughout its history, the **Coops** fostered a vigorous community feeling. The Coops were a short and pleasant walk to the **Bronx Zoo** and **Botanical Garden,** or a Sunday stroll along **Pelham Parkway. Christopher Columbus** was the local High School.

the 1920s had to do with the governor of New York State in the '20s: Franklin Delano Roosevelt. FDR was a Bronx favorite even before attaining national fame and he appreciated the loyalty of Bronx voters. The Bronx's boosterism and its growing political strength as expressed in voting lists brought significant rewards during the '20s. Not only did FDR funnel state funds to The Bronx, but his predecessor, the colorful Al Smith, was grateful to the solid Bronx Democratic organization, too. Grateful, too, was the famously decadent Jimmy Walker, who was elected Mayor of New York City in 1926, with solid Bronx support. By 1931, for instance, there were one hundred and sixty municipal buildings in The Bronx, including schools, fire stations and offices. The imposing **Bronx County Courthouse** on **161st Street** and the **Concourse,** the seat of Bronx government, was completed in 1933. Ten libraries served the avid readers of The Bronx, and 57 theatres provided films and live performances. For spiritual needs, The Bronx offered more than 200 churches and synagogues. And for more secular concerns, the borough boasted 29 banks. All this in a place that ten years before was lightly settled and widely forested. Where dairy farms once worked, by 1931 there were shopping streets and boulevards.

Hard times came to The Bronx, as to all America, with the Stock Market Crash of 1929. But The Bronx did more than simply survive the Depression. In a paradoxical way, it actually prospered. The explanation was in the nature of national politics and The Bronx's undeviating loyalty to the Democratic Party and the New Deal. One of FDR's earliest and staunchest supporters was the Democratic boss of The Bronx, Edward J.Flynn. As far back as Roosevelt's vice-presidential campaign of 1920, Flynn was a hard worker and a loyal vote getter. And more than just a political alliance joined these two men. They were personal friends and intimates, whose bonds were deeply rooted despite their widely variant backgrounds. Roosevelt, the patrician from the Hudson Valley, and Flynn, the street politico from The Bronx, found a common cause in lively conversation, politics, and in a shared vision of government. This friendship

Marching for Israeli statehood in 1947 in front of Concourse Plaza.

and political partnership would have profound meaning for The Bronx during the ascendancy of the New Deal and for years afterwards. Flynn's cordial relationship with FDR was translated (not surprisingly) into a steady stream of grants, projects, loans and New Deal activities that made The Bronx a showcase of Federal programs. The Triborough Bridge, **Orchard Beach** and dozens of parks, playgrounds, schools, offices and roads were the concrete expression of FDR's warm feeling toward Flynn and his unshakable Bronx machine. Flynn's payment was in the form of votes on election day. The Bronx never wavered from 1932 to 1944. In every election where FDR stood as candidate, The Bronx went solidly Democratic. It was never really a question or a contest in The Bronx. One simply pulled the Democratic lever in the booth or marked the ballot. That Republicans might also be running was hardly considered along the **Grand Concourse** or on **Tremont Avenue.** Parties other than the Democratic and candidates other than Roosevelt were irrelevant in The Bronx. Even the minor parties,

The first court of The Bronx Park East Coops filled with tenants at a 1945 memorial rally in honor of President Roosevelt, whose black-trimmed photo hangs on the Honor Roll of Coop and Allerton service men.

such as the Liberal or the American Labor Party, were essentially creatures of the larger Democratic organization and rarely opposed the New Deal ticket. In The Bronx during the '30s and '40s, as someone observed, "you just voted for Roosevelt and went home."

The Depression brought forth other kinds of political tensions in The Bronx. In the Irish Catholic neighborhoods of the South Bronx, a visible and vocal minority came to support Father Coughlin, the famous Radio Priest of the '30s, who preached an anti-Roosevelt, anti-Semitic message. Many Jewish citizens of The Bronx remember seeing the salesmen for *Social Justice,* the Coughlanite newspaper, along **Willis Avenue** or **Southern Boulevard.** More than one young man got, or gave, a bloody nose in fist fights between Jews and members of the Christian Front. Other Catholics, Protestants and Jews in the South Bronx organized an opposition to the bigoted message of Coughlin and other such groups (The German-American Bund, for example). Jews, for their part, might be active in the various anti-Nazi movements, helping to boycott German goods or bringing refugees from Europe to safety in America. Zionism, too, was a vigorous presence among The Bronx's Jewish population, and there were any number of splinter groups to chose from, ranging from religious to ultra militant movements. Jewish homes frequently displayed a blue and white tin box, known in Yiddish

A victory celebration, possibly V-J Day, on Davidson Avenue. A Bronx street welcomes home the returning veterans of WWII. Banners have been hung and the neighborhood is sparkling clean in anticipation of a parade. The elaborate banner is evidence that on **Davidson Avenue,** at least, there was intense community spirit and organization.

as a *pushkie,* to collect nickels and dimes for Palestine or for another charity.

The public forum for Bronx politics during these years was the luxurious **Concourse Plaza Hotel** on **16lst Street.** It was in the Plaza that candidates came to speak to the faithful and to make their pleas for Flynn's support. Roosevelt came, as did Truman, Stevenson and Kennedy, too, along with innumerable lesser names seeking lesser offices. The annual Ladies' Luncheon at the **Plaza** was a political requirement for the serious candidate who hoped to win Democratic nomination in The Bronx, the equivalent of election in other cities. Nearly as important was The Bronx Borough Day Parade, an

This impressive structure was the heart of Bronx civic government for many decades. It was finally superceded by the County Building on the Concourse during the 1930s. But for many years the **Borough Hall** continued to be the place for marriage licenses, deeds and other documents of Bronx life including draft registration during two wars. The grand staircase at the right lead onto **Third Avenue,** and **Tremont Avenue** is on the left. In the background is **Crotona Park.** This building fell into disuse in the 1960s and was finally demolished. Only the staircase remains.

War, in the humble streets of The Bronx, quickly became icons for the Democratic Party faithful.

During World War II, The Bronx joined the rest of America in active and unswerving support of the war effort. There were scrap drives and victory gardens, air raids and bond sales, and the sight of thousands of young Bronxites lining up at draft boards for their Selective Service registration. Bronx kids took part, as best they could, by blacking out lights during air raid drills or by growing Swiss chard in the lots relabeled Victory Gardens for the duration. A frequent mission was collecting tin foil, somehow a priceless part of the war machine according to popular legend. The procedure was to scan the sidewalks and gutters for old cigarette packs or gum wrappers, remove the tin foil, and accumulate a ball of the stuff. What happened to it after that is unclear, but the simple act of collecting something gave a sense of participation. In the schools, there were air raid drills and war savings plans, and, outside, the war news was avidly followed. Later, during the 1950s, the Cold War generated another kind of participation among Bronx school kids. With the nuclear threat hovering over the **Grand Concourse,** Bronx schools took their responsibilities seriously and taught civil defense. For that post-War generation of Bronx students, civil defense meant one thing — hiding under the desk. The theory was that the next war would be nuclear, and, therefore, the only safe haven was under a wooden desk with head covered by hands and facing away from the window. How this would save lives in a twenty megaton blast was never really explored fully, but it was taken as an article of faith

annual tradition that brought thousands out on the **Grand Concourse** to celebrate the borough's achievements, and to make the politicians visible to the people. From the reviewing stand in front of **The Bronx County Courthouse** or at one of the major intersections, the reigning politicians, congressmen and borough officials viewed the parade floats and marching bands in a grand spirit of Bronx patriotism. It is noteworthy that the tradition of The Bronx Day parade has been revived in the 1990s, with the **Concourse** still the scene of the celebration.

Franklin Roosevelt was the unquestioned idol of The Bronx during his tenure in office. His death in 1945 was a cataclysm in The Bronx, still spoken of in hushed tones by those who remembered that April day. During his life, Roosevelt was not simply admired, he was worshiped. The predominately Jewish voters of The Bronx ranked FDR just below Moses and Abraham in their pantheon, and when the man himself toured The Bronx in 1944, the visit was a triumphal procession. Many still alive today remember with real emotion the rainy day in 1944 when Roosevelt traveled the East Bronx in an open car, waving to the packed sidewalks and ignoring the demands of his aides to stop the parade. Pictures of the President, campaigning in the midst of a World

*Photo: Marvin Scott*

**Ohio Field on the campus of New York University.**

work at the New York Telephone Company or Con Edison. So much was by common understanding. On the other hand, a school, such as **Bronx Science**, was 95% Jewish during the '40s and '50s, as if Gentiles or Blacks could not be found to fill those seats. There were Italian blocks (**Arthur Avenue** was famous in this regard) and Irish neighborhoods where outsiders were unwelcome, unappreciated and frequently roughed up.

But there were other neighborhoods and institutions where a striking kind of ethnic integration was practiced. **Orchard Beach** for example, was open to all, and used by all. On the beach in July there were skin tones from darkest ebony to whitest ivory, and less trouble over mixing than many had imagined. The stands at **Yankee Stadium** were a model of integrated enjoyment, especially after Jackie Robinson broke the color line in 1947 and black faces began to appear on the Yankee bench in the '50s. Sports, in general, were a source of multiethnic and multiracial activity in The Bronx. School yards

> During World War II, The Bronx joined the rest of America in active and unswerving support of the war

and ball fields really did fulfill the American Dream of an open society where only skill counted.

The civil rights revolution was seen by many in The Bronx as something suitable for Mississippi, but not for **Melrose** or **Mott Haven.** Of course, in the following decades this attitude was challenged, and challenged strongly, by Black leaders and marchers.

The problems of the wider world did, however, make their presence known in The Bronx. The Cold War and the Korean conflict of the '50s era generated a Red scare that deeply scarred The Bronx and many of its people. Former Communists, socialists and radicals of all stripes found themselves targeted by school administrations and

by the New York City Board of Education. To the students, it was a light hearted break in routine, something like the familiar fire drills. The culmination of civil defense readiness came in the early '50s, with the issuing of dog tags to school children. Here, too, the idea was that nuclear war would be made less catastrophic if the charred bodies of school kids could be identified after the blast, a dubious proposition at best, but it gave thousands of kids a really neat set of dog tags to play with. They probably still languish in dresser drawers and trunks across the nation.

Other issues of the 1950s made scant impact in The Bronx. It was the time of the Eisenhower prosperity (mostly) when life improved for many, and besides, political dissent was discouraged. The Civil Rights movement, for example, was a distant thunder to most White Bronxites in the '50s and '60s. Schools, after all, had always been integrated in The Bronx, and the outward signs of segregation had long passed from memory. There was, nobody ever doubted, an informal housing segregation which kept Black and Hispanic families from moving into certain neighborhoods. Familiar, too, was a low level kind of bigotry directed towards many other groups. Jews, for example, despite their preponderance in The Bronx, could not find employers during the '50s. The McCarthy assault against Communism was in full swing and The Bronx, with its long tradition of left wing politics, was an easy target. And there was a left wing vote in The Bronx, without question. In 1948, for instance, Henry Wallace and the Progressive Party did surprisingly well in The Bronx, and most notably in the Jewish East Bronx. Some of the vote in 1948 was a protest over Harry Truman's wavering over Palestine and some was a deeper desire for change after decades of Democratic machine control. But for whatever subtle reasons, The Bronx often voted liberal, if not more than liberal. As the Cold War intensified, however, and especially after the outbreak of fighting in Korea, the

**Joseph Brutto in front of the Honor Roll Memorial.**

left wing mood changed. Bronxites who once might have voted for Norman Thomas, or even for the Communist candidate, withheld their support and switched to safer mainstream parties.

The connection to the Democratic Party continued well in the 1960s. The Bronx gave Harry Truman a majority in the election of 1948, and went with Stevenson in both elections of 1952 and 1956. In 1960, with a Republican Ike in the White House and a changing mood since the New Deal, The Bronx remained true to its traditions. Helped substantially by the pressure from Charles Buckley, who had succeeded Flynn as Democratic leader, The Bronx threw its weight behind John F. Kennedy in the 1960 campaign, and he carried that borough handily. Buckley, indeed, was among the first

**Rally in front of Charlie's Inn.**

national figures who courted Kennedy prior to 1960, and he was instrumental in convincing the young Senator to stand for nomination in the primaries. Kennedy, in return, endorsed Buckley for reelection in 1961, a political IOU that did not add luster to the President's name.

The decades after FDR's death were less exciting times for Bronx politics. The fervor of the war years, and the intense engagement of the Depression era, were absent in the late '40s and '50s. Instead, The Bronx coasted along (as did much of America) on a wave of prosperity and political quiescence. Even the popular mayor of the '30s was gone. Fiorello LaGuardia, the Little Flower, who had many fans in The Bronx, was replaced by the colorless William O'Dwyer and later by Vincent Impellittari, an even more taciturn public figure and an unlikely winner in a tangled election. Politics in The Bronx became, more than ever, local clubhouse intrigue during the '50s. The monolithic power of the Democratic machine was beginning to falter a bit after World War II. In 1948, for example, a third party candidate beat the regular Democrat for a congressional seat, and raised eyebrows across America. True, the winner was Leo Isacson, a Jewish lawyer representing The American Labor Party (and he was handily replaced by a regular in the general election of 1948), but it scared national Democrats and infuriated Charlie Buckley.

Even the major issue affecting The Bronx in those years, the **Cross Bronx Expressway,** generated remarkably little political heat. The awesome power of Robert Moses may have dissuaded Bronxites from the struggle against the **Cross Bronx Expressway,** or perhaps it was the tenor of the times. The l950s were a period when strong political statements were suspect. It was the age of McCarthy and the label of Red or Radical was always available to discredit the opponents of major projects like the **Expressway**. Once-loud voices for local action or progressive causes were restrained during the '50s, and it took even more courage than usual to stand up to Robert Moses when he dreamed one of his imperial plans. For whatever reason, the once contentious Bronx was oddly quiet and Moses rolled across whole neighborhoods with his bulldozers. Some voices, it was true, were raised against Moses and his machines, but they found little support. There was a resigned acceptance of the plan by most Bronxites, even those most directly affected by the **Expressway**. A melancholy kind of mood spread in the late '50s, a sense that great events were afoot that would change The Bronx forever. In truth, a good number of people were looking for ways out. Many of the young had already planned to leave their parents' home, and the mood of American society in the '50s favored an upwardly bound career oriented decision, and that kind of decision rarely included remaining in The Bronx. Even the oldtimers, who had lived and raised families in The Bronx for years, aspired to different (or better) circumstances. The lure of the suburbs was very powerful as the '60s opened.

*Bronx County Historical Society*
**Edward Flynn, Democratic Leader of The Bronx County**.

Everyone had friends and neighbors who had already made the move to Queens, or Westchester, or New Jersey. Staying in The Bronx appeared an odd choice by the mid-'50s, and so Robert Moses' sweeping plan for the Central Bronx coincided with a mood that favored change. Borough President Leonard Lyons was resigned to the **Cross Bronx Expressway,** or at least to Robert Moses' unstoppable vision, and so little was done to prevent the ruthless demolition of whole neighborhoods in the late '50s.

Great national issues, like presidential elections and the Korean War, could still stir up Bronx emotions, however. When Eisenhower ran for the White House in l952, he succeeded in winning many Bronx votes despite his Republican label. Stevenson might have been the sentimental favorite, but even in the old working class and trade union neighborhoods Ike was a well-liked figure. In most other regards, of course, The Bronx remained staunchly Democratic. It helped elect Averill Harriman for Governor, Robert Wagner for Mayor, and any number of loyal congressmen, councilmen and assembly members who were solidly tied to the Democratic Party. The notable exception to all this was Jacob Javits, a Republican of liberal leanings, who could count pretty regularly on The Bronx's vote. But, then, Javits was Jewish and a maverick among his GOP colleagues, both qualities that made him popular in The Bronx.

The demise of the old Bronx machine began in earnest in l961, with the election of Robert Wagner

**James J. Lyons welcomes Harry S. Truman at the Concourse Plaza circa 1948.**

as Mayor. Wagner, once a loyal Democrat who gladly took support from Charles Buckley, had become a reformer by 1961 and ran on a ticket opposing the old line bosses. With Wagner came a crop of new-style Democrats, younger and less inclined to follow clubhouse orders. The unimaginable happened in The Bronx. A Republican won the borough Presidency in 1961 following the retirement of James Lyons after 34 years. Joseph Periconi was a very moderate Republican, and also had the backing of the Liberal Party in his campaign, but the symbolism was hardly lost on anyone who remembered Flynn's unshakable control of the borough's politics. The political revolution was completed in 1965, when Charles Buckley himself went down to defeat at the hands of an insurgent, Jonathan Bingham. By the end of the 1960s, the once-solid Democratic Bronx had followed the path of other boroughs and cities and had entered a period of flexible voting and uncertain attachments. The age of the Democratic machine was over.

In the decade of the 1970s, The Bronx went through its political and social Dark Ages. As populations shifted and the whole economic structure of New York City underwent a catastrophic loss, The Bronx felt the impact severely. Nobody, it seemed, could stem the tide of abandoned houses, job losses, school turmoil and most visibly, the spread of crime and drugs. The virtual bankruptcy of the City in 1975 meant that even the minimal services still available were cut, and The Bronx continued its rapid fall. When it was announced that "The Bronx is burning" in the 1970s, there was considerable truth to the remark, for many buildings were torched for their insurance money or by sheer vandalism. Despite some noble exceptions, the political leadership of The Bronx failed miserably in the '60s and '70s to cope with these conditions or to inspire any alternative choices. They deserve a polite silence.

Improvement came in the '80s, with new visions and a far better economic atmosphere for the entire city. Some long promised rebuilding was actually begun, even on famous **Charlotte Street** where both Presidents Jimmy Carter and Ronald Reagan had stood and vowed action.

There was an exciting crop of scandal and indictments in the '80s, but when the smoke cleared, The Bronx seemed firmly engaged in a real reconstruction. Today, some of the most depressing ruins of the '70s have been rebuilt or replaced by other housing. It seems strange to have garden apartments, complete with picket fences, in the heart of the South Bronx, but there they are and they seem viable. The **Concourse** has undergone a major improvement in its housing conditions and the notorious fake windows (meant to cover up empty buildings) have been eliminated in favor of real windows housing very real tenants. The Bronx may not be what some remember from their childhood, but it is a very long way from the *Fort Apache* days of the 1970s.

# GOING TO SCHOOL IN THE BRONX

**P.S. 11, located on Ogden Avenue and built in 1888, was one of the oldest public schools in The Bronx.** Even in the '50s, this school represented an earlier age and was always fascinating for those who attended it. Schools like this would often have separate entrances for boys and girls.

The Bronx may have been divided in many ways, economically, ethnically, racially and by religion, but the great unifying experience was school. Everybody went to school, without exception. Some went to parochial school, a form of education that attracted a large following in the Catholic community. As for private schools, the concept probably existed in some parts of New York City in the '40s and '50s, but only as theory. Aside from the religious schools and the rare private education, school in The Bronx meant "public."

One of the glories of Bronx municipal government was its school system, begun even before annexation to New York City in the nineteenth century. State laws of the nineteenth century mandated public education and The Bronx complied with enthusiasm, going even beyond the required grammar schools to free public high schools. **Morris High School**, for example, opened its doors in 1897 and was considered quite a radical educational departure. During the teens and '20s, as The Bronx filled with new buildings and a new

Taft High School — 172nd Street and Sheridan Avenue.

still stood and functioned; sometimes the only erect structure in a sea of rubble, but still doing their jobs.

The law, of course, mandated attendance and most children started in kindergarten when they were five years old. The local school was the natural magnet. It was rare to send children outside of their neighborhood and none expected anything else. Schools in The Bronx (as in the rest of New York City) were operated on the latest educational theories, meaning that age groups were thoughtfully separated on the theory that different ages required different methods. Elementary school went to the sixth grade (about twelve years old) and then the child was enrolled in junior high, a recognition that the adolescent years were special — and tough. After the ninth grade, the usual route led to high school although here there was an element of choice. While there were large regional high schools (**DeWitt Clinton, Taft, Roosevelt, Evander Childs, Monroe,** etc.), there were some borough-wide high schools that were open to The Bronx student. The most famous was The **Bronx High School of Science,** a highly competitive institution that was founded in the late '30s and designed to give talented students an enriched science curriculum. Bronx residents, however, were also eligible to test for Brooklyn Tech, Stuyvesant and Music and Art High School, all with competitive entrance exams.

population, the school system expanded to meet the explosive demand. By World War II, the elementary, junior high and high schools of The Bronx were neighborhood landmarks, staffed by experienced teachers and well attended. Part of the vast New York City educational plant that had molded immigrants and newcomers for decades, The Bronx public school network was more than textbooks or classrooms. The school was the defining government service in most neighborhoods. They affected every family and certainly were central in the lives of every child. In its other forms, government was a distant, and frequently unwelcome, entity. Government could mean papers, taxes, laws that cost money in some way or, worst of all, the police. But schools were different. The solid brick buildings that housed the neighborhood school was an anchor of stability, a refuge from disorder. Schools, in other words, mattered, and most Bronxites took them seriously. It is noteworthy that during the grim 1970s, when whole neighborhoods were leveled, the school buildings

Photo: Spencer Field

**Public School #73 located on Anderson Avenue and 164th Street was the Highbridge neighborhood junior high school.**

one, but still a code. Blue jeans, for example, were prohibited in school as were sneakers, polo shirts and odd garments in general. Girls could not use makeup (even a hint of lipstick) until high school. The properly dressed male student in The Bronx of the '40s and '50s carried a handkerchief, wore shined shoes, and dress shirts. Girls were expected to wear skirts and blouses, modest jewelry (if any) and never, never, slacks. On assembly day, once a week, the school required ties for the boys and proper white blouses for the girls. School assemblies were solemn events in the elementary years. Classes filed into the auditorium in strict silence, sat at attention under the penetrating eye of the teacher or assistant principal, and waited for the program of the day. On special occasions (Christmas perhaps, or the first day of school) that distant personage, the principal, would appear and speak to the assembled students. Otherwise it was the assistant principal who handled the assemblies, aided by individual teachers who played pianos, had dramatic ability or read nicely from the Bible. It is odd to reflect that in The Bronx of the post-war era, in a public school population overwhelmingly Jewish, that weekly Bible readings were normal and caused no comment. There might be some avant garde principal who read poetry (Carl Sandburg was popular as was the <u>Spoon River Anthology</u>). Others commented upon the news of the day or offered inspirational speeches. The routine of school assemblies went from group singing to guest speakers, or to the classes doing some dramatic performance. Class plays were the delight of the audience — you got to ridicule your friends and giggle in the dark. However, they were the terror of the poor teachers who had to organize and direct these amateur theatricals. There are thousands of middle aged men and women who look back with a mixture of

These aside, most Bronxites went to their local schools. Perhaps because they were local, and under close scrutiny by parents and neighbors, schools in the '40s and '50s reflected community standards of behavior and dress. It was understood that a child reflected the parent, and so in school, the parents reputation rose and fell according to the academic success of the child, and that included good behavior. Getting an "E" in conduct on the quarterly report card was expected, taken for granted by almost all families, and anything less (God forbid a "U") was cause for deep worry. Students, even in elementary schools were expected to follow a dress code — a mild

*Photo: Municipal Archives*

**P.S. 42** This school was opened in 1902 and is located at the corner of **Claremont Parkways** and **Washington Avenue**. In the '30s, '40s and '50s it was a feeder school for William Howard Taft H.S.

amusement and embarrassment as they recall playing an elf, or a talking flower, or a Pilgrim, in one of the required school plays.

School, naturally, meant learning and the serious work of the school was in the classroom. Penmanship was still stressed in those years, and every class in elementary school spent hours practicing the correct form of cursive script. Reading counted heavily and it was taught in a traditional way out of standardized textbooks — yes, there really was a Dick and Jane, two kids with absolutely zero relevance in The Bronx — as did mathematics, which seemed to rely largely on memorization. In fact, memory was a very useful tool in The Bronx schools of the '50s. The multiplication tables, spelling words, and the capitals of the states were all required knowledge for young Bronxites. We also got social studies, in

junior high a science curriculum, and eventually we read the classics, such as <u>Silas Marner</u> and <u>Macbeth</u>. Junior high school also introduced a foreign language to the course of study. Students could pick French or Spanish, although some rare schools might offer German or even Italian. The classic languages of Latin and Greek did not appear until college, unless you went to a Catholic school, where Latin was stressed. All in all, the education was traditional and offered only a limited number of choices. The notion of multi-culturalism had not yet penetrated the school system in the '50s and '60s, so most of the reading, music, art and history was taken from the standard Western Civilization canon. It was the rare teacher who introduced Asian or non-European literature or studies to the classroom. Still, the students who passed through the system in the '40s, '50s and '60s were exposed to a fair sampling of the world's knowledge, and most came away with their basic skills enhanced.

There were lighter moments, too, in school. Modern educational theory stressed sound body as well as sound mind, so that everyone had to take gym class. This was frequently the bane of Bronx students and everyone had his or her gym-based traumatic experience. Often the trouble was the gym teachers, a hardy band of men and women who somehow found themselves with a whistle and a gym full of rambunctious students. Sometimes they were skilled, but, more often, the gym teacher was a drill sergeant, who confused parade ground discipline with physical enrichment. We did get to play basketball, softball, and sometimes swim but for most, the gym class was a time of embarrassment, wet socks and terrifying teachers. Girls had similar memories, magnified by the particular female pressures of adolescence. The Board of Education probably meant well with its physical education requirement, but the practice was generally a dismal failure, or at best, an interruption in the otherwise boring routine. The very good athletes probably have fonder memories of this gym requirement but the average Bronx elementary or junior high student took physical education as just one of the inexplicable hardships imposed by that near-mythical entity, the Board of Education.

Along the same lines were music classes. It was decided that music made for good citizens, so that Bronx schools rang with the sad efforts of hundreds of kids trying to harmonize on songs like "Silent Night" or "The Anniversary Waltz." The better voices might be inducted into the school chorus, to perform at assemblies and graduations, but the great mass struggled along with ordinary voices and lasting memories of some folk songs. In later years some schools actually taught music and offered instrumental instruction. A few high schools had famous bands and orchestras.

Shop was another enrichment class, a reflection of the "new" educational theories (of the 1900s) that practical skills were important and fulfilling. So, thousands of Bronx boys got to make hideous

wooden tie racks, trays and bookshelves in school shop classes in fulfillment of John Dewey's theories of good citizenship, and in hope that these skills might ultimately produce a paying job. We hefted hammers, ran jig saws, peered down levels and, overall, tried to pretend we were handy, while the frequently enraged shop teacher (a close cousin to the gym teacher) yelled and fretted at the total lack of manual dexterity. There was the occasional student craftsman, who could actually complete a project with something vaguely useful or attractive. For most though, the output was misshapen and clumsy, loved only by the parents who had to store the things for the next twenty years. Some schools had printing shops (We learned to set type in junior high) while a few encouraged crafts like ceramics, electricity or even metalworking. Girls, by contrast, were introduced to "home economics" in those unliberated times and were expected to learn sewing, cooking and home management — preparation, of course, for their careers as housewives and mothers.

Being a highly centralized system, the New York City school curriculum was standard throughout the boroughs. Kids in The Bronx got the same lessons, from the same books, as kids in Brooklyn and Staten Island. The campaign for educational reform was only beginning in the '40s and '50s, with the result that classrooms were rigid little kingdoms, ruled over by teachers with absolute power. Desks were bolted to the floor and

P.S. 6 on East Tremont Avenue

Photo: Spencer Field

still had inkwells from the previous generation. Few remember actually getting ink to use. Some enlightened teachers might venture into a limited freedom, but for most, it was the old regimen of sitting quietly, hands folded, and waiting to be instructed. A "good" student was one who was quiet and neat — especially neat. Notebooks were a sign of a person's mental status, sloppy notebooks equaled sloppy minds and so were much frowned upon by good teachers. There were the standard pictures of Washington and Lincoln at the front of the room, along with an American flag used every morning for the Pledge of Allegiance. Seating was strictly by size, the taller kids sat at the back and the short ones at front, exceptions made only for those who wore glasses. In many classrooms, there was a rigid gender separation. Girls and boys had separate sides of the room, lined up separately in the schoolyard, and generally kept their distance. In junior high school, this kind of discrimination faded away, but the idea of sexual equality was very foreign in The Bronx until the 1960s, and maybe later. In high school the sexes mingled more freely (it would have been impossible to prevent it) but there was still a consciousness of what constituted male and female behavior. Boys, for instance, took shop and played sports. Girls were in the home economics classes, excelled in French and artistic matters, and generally were more sedate than their male classmates. All this was, at least, the theory. The reality could vary considerably depending on the neighborhood and the school culture.

Attendance was a major issue in the schools of The Bronx. There were, in theory, truant officers who tracked down missing students but few ever saw one, and they may have been mythical. Most students never played hookey, or did so only rarely and with great trepidation. The parents and regular teachers were quite sufficient to ensure daily attendance. If one was absent for legitimate reasons, usually sickness, then a note was expected the very next day, written by the parent to the teacher explaining the absence. Such matters were carefully tracked and recorded, most memorably on the Delaney card. Everyone who ever sat in a New York City school was familiar with the Delaney card, a palm-sized cardboard record keeping device which allowed the teacher to record every student's activities. Most crucial was regular attendance, and if there were too many red circles on the Delaney card, some notice would be taken. Delaney

*Photo: Spencer Field*

P.S. 11, located on Ogden Avenue.

cards also had room to show test marks, behavior problems and homework achievements. They were, in short, an unblinking camera upon which the student's life was imprinted.

Delaney cards, report cards and similar official papers were near-religious documents in the average Bronx school. Perhaps most imposing was "the permanent record card" a legendary official document which reportedly followed one throughout his or her lifetime and would (we were assured) affect one's life forever. The teacher, or assistant principal, could always make the ultimate threat to a unruly student: "This is going on your PERMANENT RECORD CARD, YOUNG MAN!"

Threats were always a potent weapon in the discipline wars. Physical force, while not entirely absent, wasn't considered very modern and scientific. New York City schools didn't permit capital punishment and Bronx parents took rather unkindly to any bruises upon their children, at least, to any administered outside the home. A verbal warning was, however, effective and nothing worked better than a threat to involve either parents or principals. There was a hazy upper echelon of school officials who loomed over students in those more innocent days of the '50s. People like the principal, an impossibly remote figure who might be glimpsed at times but who, hopefully, never interacted with the average student. The front line troops, so to speak, were the assistant principals, usually two or three in each school with assorted responsibilities. In elementary school, the APs might be in charge of various grades, or special projects, but the junior high school AP was the true warrior. Most awesome was the AP in charge of discipline, who could sniff out misconduct with supernatural skill and whose office was a waiting room to hell. There must have been kindly APs in some schools, but they were few and one rarely encountered such. There were various Miss

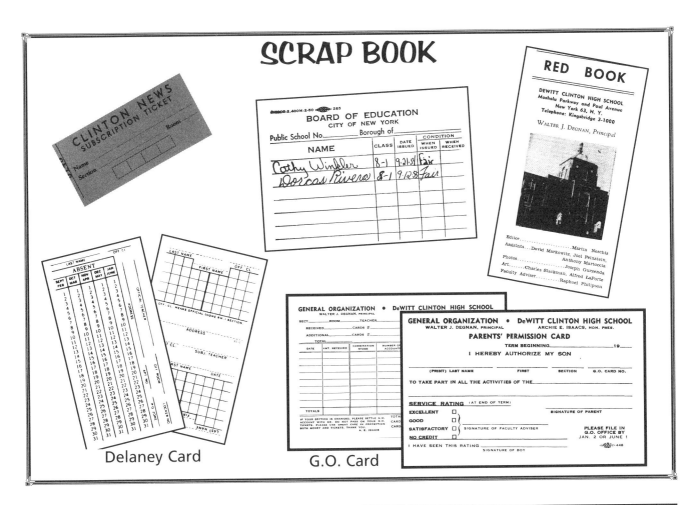

Delaney Card    G.O. Card

somethings in elementary and junior high, who could skin a student with a glance. In high school, there was a real "dean" of students, who handled discipline matters and he was, naturally, a terror. Probably in off-hours, these APs were nice folks with families and friends, but in school, they played their roles to the hilt.

Order was especially demanded in the fire drill, a memorable part of Bronx school life. The Board of Education obviously, and rightfully, demanded periodic fire drills in the schools, and every student was expected to behave to the very highest standards. Based on some erratic schedule, every school in The Bronx held occasional rehearsals for a fire emergency. They involved emptying out the school in perfect military precision, or at least as much military precision as adolescents could manage. Winter or Spring, the classes silently filed out of the building, taking preassigned routes and waiting patiently in the street until the whistle sounded for the return trip. For the kids, it was a generally welcome

break in routine but still a very serious event. Nothing, not anything, could be a worse offense than "talking during a fire drill." This infraction would produce a personal intervention by APs and teachers alike, and maybe a note home to the parent. During the '50s, there were also air raid drills, another reflection of the political state of affairs in those years, that were even more exciting than fire drills. The theory behind air raid drill was that in case of nuclear attack by the Soviets, school children would save themselves by hiding under their desks. There was a prescribed survival technique, which involved turning away from the windows, covering the head with one's hands, and ducking under the wooden desks. All this was incessantly drilled into Bronx students in the '50s, and reinforced with posters and letters home in case one failed to take nuclear disaster seriously enough. Thankfully never needed and almost certain to fail in reality, the air raid drill was, nonetheless, a constant reminder that not all was well with the world outside and that, in fact,

*Photo: Spencer Field*

**Schoolyard, similar to many around The Bronx, was very popular for after-school activities.** Punchball was one game that was well suited to this schoolyard, provided you had a spaldeen and not a pinkie!

*Photo: Spencer Field*

**New York Public Library on Woodycrest Avenue at the corner of West 168th Street.** Further left on **168th Street** was the entrance reserved for children. The main entrance seen here was meant for adult use. Many **Highbridge** youngsters, whether they went to **P.S.11, P.S. 114**, or **Sacred Heart School,** had their first library experience in this tranquil setting.

you might be incinerated at any moment. Sometimes the under-the-desk routine would be varied by a huddle in the hallway, away from windows, of course, to simulate an air raid emergency.

Another well remembered part of the curriculum in Bronx schools was the school trip. Many Bronxites still recall school trips to the *Museum of Natural History*, that enchanting pile of red brick and stuffed animals on Central Park West. The vast riches of the Museum were almost irresistible to generations of teachers in New York City. There the classes could experience nature, biology, anthropology and just plain science in myriad forms and unending variety. So it was

normal that at least once in every school year from the first to the sixth grades the class would pack up their lunches and journey off on the subway to the Museum. As there was an elaborate program of school tours run by the Museum itself, small wonder that teachers were eager to expose their students to this world-class institution. The classes were met at the entry by Museum staff, escorted to the cloakrooms where lunches and coats were stored, and then taken on the day's planned itinerary. Most school age visitors carry with them, even forty years later, the memories of several things: the amazing dinosaur bones, of course, and the towering blue whale hanging from the ceiling. Equally imprinted on the minds of thousands of Bronx school kids was the famous Indian canoe at the basement entrance: a massive wooden boat containing a dozen or so life size carvings of Northwestern American Indians, apparently caught in the moment of high adventure on the sea. The canoe was dramatic and mysterious, but the hall of dioramas was enchanting: a procession of tableaus portraying animals and birds from around the world, frozen in magical lifelike scenes complete with painted backdrops and trees that seemed to tremble in the wind. The dioramas were brightly lit, in contrast to the darkened hall, so that the overall effect was similar to watching a movie or a giant TV screen, and they were, and remain, one of the great marvels of the museum.

For hours, the class would be herded through the displays and educational talks, but, finally, it was lunchtime. And that was the high point for most Bronx school kids on a museum visit. For days before, the teacher would instruct and remind about the upcoming trip, gathering permission slips and sending home mimeographed advisories, and one of the major requirements was to pack a lunch for the child. Taking a lunch to school was not the ordinary behavior of Bronx kids. Most went home at lunchtime and the others ate the dreaded school lunch, but not many were found carrying lunch boxes, except on Museum day, when a picnic was mandatory. Memories of the *Museum of Natural History* has to do with smell. You might recall the lunchroom in the basement pervaded with the odor of apples and scrambled egg sandwiches, generations of lunches stretching back to the nineteenth century for all we know or the endless lines of kids, all carrying their apples and

sandwiches, waiting for the little containers of warm milk, forming an unbroken chain that goes back to the time of our grandparents.

Other kinds of school trips existed, too. There were excursions to the **Statue of Liberty**, or to **City Hall**. In The Bronx, the usual destinations included **Poe Cottage, Van Cortlandt Park** and the **Hall of Fame** at **NYU**. The latter sights were generally pretty boring, especially the **Hall of Fame**. There simply isn't much to excite a kid in a solemn row of bronze busts, although the bus ride to and from NYU was always good for a few laughs.

In The Bronx, schools were commonly numbered, rather than named, at least on the elementary level. What mysterious system was responsible for the number is impossible to say, but to the residents in the district, there was **PS 26**, or **92**, or **l22**. Somebody, we suppose, at ll0 Livingston Street, the school headquarters, had a system and, probably, a committee worked long and hard at the numbers, but to the students they were facts of life. We did have school songs, school colors and school traditions, but the level of excitement about all these things tended to be moderate. Few in The Bronx could identify with the movie or television portrayal of the town high school and the football cheerleader pep rally lifestyle that appeared to be so common in the rest of America. In The Bronx, school was a utilitarian training ground, a place where the student was expected to prepare for a career or a "good job" and where social amenities were just that, amenities. The point of schooling was learning, not social life.

Still, it was the social life that often counted most and that remains so strongly imprinted in

### Clinton Alma Mater
#### Words by Effingham C. Murray

*Clinton, Alma Mater,*
*Thy name we sing;*
*May our endeavor*
*Praise and glory bring*
*To thee throughout the future;*
*Clinton, Alma Mater,*
*Home of our youth,*
*To thee forever*
*Our fondest love*

# *Last Will and Testament*

We, the Graduating Class of 1954, being of sound mind and memory (?) and knowing the uncertainties of this life (now preparing for our Regents) and feeling the necessity for handing down our traditions, heirlooms, possessions and whatnots, do hereby make, publish and declare this to be our last will and testament, hereby renouncing all other wills reputed to have been signed by us heretofore.

To our beloved faculty we give back all the failures they have so graciously bestowed upon us, and make a special request that they be used sparingly on all forthcoming seniors.

To Mr. Feldman, we leave a set of velvet padded chimes so that future Monrovians will not have their morning conversations interrupted.

To Mr. Fineman we bequeth a leather bound copy of "30 Days to Correct Pronunciation and Enunciation."

To the incoming freshmen we leave this observation:
School walls do not a prison make,
Nor high school books a slave.
BUT THEY HELP!

Miss Simon we leave Eco.

Mrs. Witchel we give our sympathy.

Miss Winters and Mr. Adler we leave our silverware )ken" of our appreciation for the famous Monroe

infirmary our undying gratitude for taking care he famous Monroe lunch.

nd Ruth our thanks for helping us get up in the

lich and Co. a poem:
gave

**James Monroe High School: 1940s & 1950s.**

the memory. As every student knew, the really important stuff took place outside the classroom, in the schoolyard, on the street, in the lunchroom. We learned how to interact with our peers, how to talk to girls or boys, how to dress, speak, eat and play softball. All this important education was not on the approved curriculum, but it meant a great deal anyway. Did we really need to know trigonometry, or French verbs, or the mechanics of cell reproduction? In the abstract, the answer is yes, but in the practical world of The Bronx, these items took second place to the really important matters of sports, sex and neighborhood status.

Schools were always social pressure cookers, places that transmitted more than facts and curricula. The schools of The Bronx took a couple of generations of disparate children, from every conceivable ethnic and religious background, and subtly blended them into New Yorkers and Americans. Ask anybody who sat in those classes after World War II, or during the Depression, and the recollections are amazingly similar. Teachers, classmates, the good times in the playground and the bad times in the principal's office, all these are part of the collective memories of Bronxites. Ask yourself, do you still dream about school? Chances are, the answer is yes. And chances are very good, too, that children now in the schools around The Bronx will dream the same dreams years hence.

# SHOPPING IN THE BRONX

**Fordham and the Concourse—The famous Army Recruiting Station occupied the choice sight on the Concourse island directly across from Alexander's.** Dating from World War II, this station regularly topped the list for enlistments throughout the nations. This view shows the busy pedestrian traffic of the neighborhood. At lower left, a teenager in a classic Bronx pose holding up a lamppost.

Like many other activities in The Bronx, shopping had rules. Deciding what was being bought was only the first step in the process. Equally important was the purpose, the season, the age of the consumer and the opinion of the neighbors. Price, naturally, figured high on the list of considerations, but it was not necessarily the decisive factor, even in The Bronx. In the era before malls and nationwide discount stores, the act of shopping brought the shopper into close contact with the neighborhood and its customs. Going out of the immediate

area was allowable, but only as directed by custom. To buy a suit, for instance, for a graduation, wedding, confirmation or bar mitzvah, wasn't a step lightly considered by anyone in The Bronx during the '40s and '50s. Even more, a ladies' dress for a special occasion was an item that demanded all the skills and knowledge handed down from generation to generation. It was never a casual decision.

The Bronx certainly offered a bewildering variety of stores and outlets, with every sex, taste, age and occupation served by one (or many) retail

**Grocery store at 969 Morris Park Avenue, in the mid-30's.** This type of small store was where most Bronxites purchased their groceries before the rise of the large supermarkets.

speculators had understood quite well that apartment buildings wouldn't be easy to rent without close-by shopping, so they frequently added stores to their plans for the still-rural Bronx back in the 1910s and '20s. As the apartments went up, so, too, did the stores and service establishments. Nearly every main street off the **Grand Concourse**, for example, was lined with stores. Along **167th Street,** or **170th**, or **Burnside**, or **Fordham**, any of the wide streets that ran perpendicular to the **Concourse** were the locale for shops and stores.

The assortment of stores was strikingly similar, whether on **Burnside Avenue** or under the El at **231st Street**, on the rough and tumble sidewalks of **Willis Avenue** or even in the planned streets of **Parkchester**. Candy stores probably dominate in memory, but they were, in reality, very small retail establishments. Few candy store owners got rich. Still, every neighborhood and shopping street had a candy store, or luncheonette, or soda fountain, almost by law. More substantial food, in the nature of groceries, was

possibilities. If the item wasn't immediately available in the neighborhood store, then there were options to be found in places like **Alexander's** or **Loehmann's**. Shopping at **Alexander's** was a borough-wide habit. It was almost like going in the neighborhood, no matter what part of The Bronx you lived in. Everybody knew the grand store at the corner of **Fordham Road** and the **Concourse**, and sooner or later, everyone in The Bronx bought something at **Alexander's**. Still, the first stop usually was in the local shopping street. Almost universally, every neighborhood in The Bronx was served by retail establishments of every description. Real estate

**General view of people who lined up, despite a heavy rain, to buy nylon stockings at uptown Alexander's Department store at Grand Concourse and Fordham Road right after World War II.**

*Photo: Max Levine*

**A wide view of West 167th Street looking west at the confluence of several streets including Edward L. Grant Highway, Jerome Avenue, and Cromwell Avenue.** This late 1950s picture shows an interesting mixture of cars, including some from the '30s, '40s, and '50s. Note also that parking was easy in those days, perhaps because of the newly installed parking meters or because cars were not yet commonplace, or both. This is one of the may **Strauss Stores** in the city where car buffs could indulge their hobby. **Hirsch Funeral Home** was also well known in a less pleasant way.

available everywhere when candy and egg creams had paled. There were chain stores, like A&P, or Daitch Dairy and they served well in the era before mega stores. But more congenial were the solid little local grocers and butchers, the stores where personal service was the hallmark. Kosher meats in one neighborhood, Italian sausage in another, and everywhere the need for real bread from bakeries where flour was actually used.

Shopping, though, usually meant clothing. Doing the daily food purchasing was just, well, everyday stuff — to "go shopping" however was a larger endeavor. Shopping was a project for the ladies, in particular, although countless husbands, sons, nephews and boyfriends could be found making the rounds, as well. The same husbands, sons, etc. would soon be found dozing by

> There were chain stores, like A&P, or Daitch Dairy ...But more congenial were the solid little local grocers and butchers, the stores where personal service was the hallmark.

the front door of the dress shop or department store, grumpily waiting for their companions to finish whatever mysterious rites went on in those dressing rooms. **Loehmann's,** on **Jerome Avenue**, had the good sense to provide chairs and magazines for the bored males, and there was inevitably a line up of men, sitting and waiting, upstairs at the bustling **Loehmann's** outlet.

Shoes were another popular item, more a ladies' enjoyment than a male pastime. Along **Fordham Road**, to take only one example, there were probably two dozen shoe stores running from Webster Avenue all the way across to University, with the densest number within a block of the **Concourse**. Day and night the sidewalks of **Fordham Road** were filled with window shoppers, going from shoe store to dress store in search of the perfect fit or the ideal color. Men, too, needed shoes from time to time, and again **Fordham Road** was a rich source. Adlers, Thom McAn and Florsheim were only the best known of the many shoe stores in The Bronx, but there were always others competing for the shopping dollar. The '40s and '50s were a time when children's health was a high visibility subject, perhaps a reaction to the shortages of the Depression and war years. In any case, parents in The Bronx were passionate about their children's well-being. Somehow the idea of proper shoes for children took deep root, and the result was an outbreak of specialty stores catering to youngsters and the special needs of young feet.

310-314 E. Fordham Road in 1951.

The most memorable part of the shoe store, for the kids certainly, was the x-ray machine. In some fever of technology during the late '30s, shoe stores were equipped with machines that x-rayed the feet of young customers. The two appendages were stuffed into a little slot and a kind of eye shade gave access to an x-ray. At least they called it an x-ray, and perhaps it was. One hopes, otherwise given the health risks. But in the mid-'50s, x-rays weren't on the danger list very often and most parents took comfort in the special attention

(and highly modern aura) of these shoe store machines. How much the shoe clerk understood of pediatric bone structure, or could read these supposed x-ray pictures, is debatable, but the point was, after all, to sell shoes, and if the machine made the parents happy, then the machine served its purpose. Every kid who ever stood on the little platform, longing for a glimpse into the mysterious machine and the eerie green lighted picture, would carry that memory into old age. Going for shoes, then, could be quite an adventure in The Bronx, but it paled in comparison to dress buying.

Shopping was, by definition in the '40s and '50s, a woman's vocation and passion. Men tolerated it, but women reveled in it. The pinnacle of shopping skill was reached in places like **Loehmann's** or **Alexander's**, or the sale floors of **Kleins, Hearns** or (for the adventurous) at Macy's, Gimbels, or Bloomingdales in Manhattan. They existed, sure, like Paris or

**West Kingsbridge Road & Grand Avenue.** This neighborhood was a rich educational center. A neighborhood child could have attended **P.S. 86** then **Walton** and continued at **Hunter College**, all within a few blocks. After World War II, history was made here as well, when **Hunter College** was the first home of the United Nations Security Council.

Loehmann's, located on Fordham Road and Jerome Avenue.

*Photo courtesy of Loehmann's*

duced to by their parents and which required skill, strength and total commitment. Consider this: at **Loehmann's** there were no real dressing rooms. Trying on of dresses was done, if at all, on the sales floor or behind a rack of clothes, while a friend or mother held your coat and pocketbook. And at **Loehmann's**, the clothes could vary in price from day to day, according to age and whimsey, all color-coded on little tags that became magnets for the shoppers. If you found a Chanel suit (and it was possible ) the tactic was to clutch it fiercely, try it on, and then hope that nobody snatched it from your hands while you weren't looking. For these reasons, shopping at **Loehmann's** was almost always a team effort. Mothers, sisters, older children and (in the very last resort) a husband, were enlisted to be the aide in the struggle. And it was a struggle. Women returning from a bout at

Timbuktu, but nobody ever really expected to go there.

But **Loehmann's** in The Bronx was another matter altogether. This was a battle ground, a hallowed place, where dresses were remaindered by their original manufacturers at a fraction of the downtown price and where the savvy shopper could make a spectacular buy. But you had to fight for this privilege. Shopping at **Loehmann's** was related to armed conflict or a rite of passage. It was something that Bronx women were intro-

John's Bargain Store at 2375-77 Arthur Avenue in 1963.

Fordham Road & Jerome Ave., facing east in front of Loehmann's.

188th Street facing south shows Messinger's Dress Shop, Dr. Scholl's, and the Irish flavored Peter Reeves Market, one of the many around New York in the early '50s. One could buy an Emerson TV at **Davega's** for around $130, still a hefty price when a week's wages were often less. **Krum's**, although a few blocks away, prominently advertised on the side of this building.

**Loehmann's** had the look of grizzled D-Day veterans. They had the long stare of the combat soldier but the jaunty air, too, of one who had survived the very worst, and if they could carry home a dress or gown from the boiling sales floor, then their victory was complete.

For men, life was easier. Suits were available at **Robert Hall** on **Fordham Road,** or **Alexander's**, or

535 St. Anns Avenue at the southwest corner of East 149th Street in the mid '40s. The policeman seems to have little vehicular traffic to occupy him. Perhaps he is more concerned with pedestrian safety and neighborhood school children. In these years, the concept of the foot patrol was still common. Quality Pet Shop hints at the popularity of pets in The Bronx.

perhaps at one of the discount stores along the **Hub** at **149th Street**. A suit, for most Bronx men, was a special outfit reserved for important events.

Some professional people did, indeed, wear suits to work but they were the exception in a borough where working class usually meant work clothes. School teachers, lawyers, doctors and others of the educated class did dress for their jobs, and in fact in the '40s and '50s, even clerks and manual laborers might leave the house with a shirt and tie. Men's shopping, however, was conducted within narrow margins, unlike the fashion free-for-all of the later '70s and '80s. There were more than enough haberdashery shops in The Bronx, where belts, ties, cuff links and shirts could be acquired but this was a utilitarian kind of shopping. You bought what you needed and went home, as quickly as possible. The idea of a group of men

*Photo: Julian A. Belin*

**The Bronx Terminal Market.** Here wholesalers would sell their goods to local merchants and shopkeepers. It was a busy, noisy and sometimes raucous atmosphere.

**John's Bargain Store on East Tremont Avenue between Clinton and Prospect Avenues.** A retail chain, John's Bargain Stores has replaced several of the smaller shops of an earlier era. The Jewish population of the East Tremont area has been supplanted by an Hispanic and Black population. Still, the needs of working people remained the same and the new stores still supply inexpensive clothing and housewares for the neighborhood.

spending a Saturday going shopping was, on the face of it, absurd — at least in The Bronx.

On a nice June Saturday in 1956, one could take the number forty bus at **University Avenue**, say at the corner of **Burnside Avenue**, and the panorama of Bronx shopping would be displayed out the window. Up **Burnside,** past **Harrison** and **Davidson**, the small neighborhood stores and shops were drawing their usual crowds on a Saturday. Fruit stands displayed their best pro-

**The far west end of Fordham Road at the intersection of Loring Place.** A major Bronx church, **St. Nicholas of Tolentine** rises at left at the intersection of **University Avenue** and **West Fordham Road**. A standard assortment of Bronx stores line the street, including the popular Fordham Hill Delicatessen. This was a neighborhood that was largely German and Irish and this delicatessen catered to their taste. In the early '50s, Fordham Hill Houses were built across the street.

duce, hardware stores and shoe stores had their windows in tip-top order to attract the strollers, and the ladies' stores were showing the newest (to The Bronx) fashions. Nat's Pool Room was discretely hidden down a flight of stairs (under the **Burnside Manor** catering hall) but teenagers from blocks around knew the location well, and the tables and bowling alleys at Nat's would be busy until very late at night. As the bus nears the **Concourse** it passes under the **Jerome Avenue** El, where furniture stores, appliance outlets and some slightly disreputable restaurants do a good business on the shaded street. Those who are well informed can find the **Jerome Bagel** factory, down a flight of iron steps just off **Burnside Avenue**, where teams of bagel bakers are hard at work turning out bushels of the chewy treats. After a late movie at the **Burnside**, or a game of bowling at the **Burnside Lanes** (one flight up), a couple of bagels and the Daily News were a common treat. The banks are closed on Saturday, but during the week the Manufacturers' branch on **Burnside** was a neighborhood landmark, as was the big **Burnside Theatre**, where second run films served the area. There was a **Woolworth** near the **Burnside Theatre**, too, a familiar Bronx variety store and the magnet for every kid with a few hours to kill. Across the **Concourse**, or more accurately under it, the bus continued down **Burnside** until **Webster Avenue** crosses, and there was another level of shopping. **Webster** was a burly and slightly unkempt part of The Bronx, but bargains abounded if you knew your way around. Not far away was **Bathgate Avenue**, home of the bustling street market and the lowest prices in town, and on the corner of **Tremont** was a renowned **Bobkoff's Sporting Goods** store.

As one continued up **Tremont** (which had by now replaced **Burnside** as the cross street) there were little and big shops, running the entire gamut. **Frank's Sporting Goods Store**, a neighborhood fixture since the 30's, served and still serves the area well. **Ungar's Pawn Shop** was a place of mystery and adventure, with its hoard of pawned goods and second-hand binoculars, fishing rods and rings. If one had time and inclination, **Tremont Avenue** continued for miles until it ran almost to the shores of **Pelham Bay** in the far east. But that was a lengthy trip and really not necessary, for the stores repeated themselves every few blocks. The idea of local shopping was strongly embraced in The Bronx of the '40s and '50s, perhaps because automobiles were still a luxury for most. Nobody, at least until the mid-'60s, thought of travelling to malls or even out of the neighborhood for most purchases. So the retail opportunities on **Tremont** were also found on **Pelham Parkway,** or **Jerome Avenue,** or **Morris Avenue** or way off on upper **Broadway.** The names may have been different but the rage to shop was the same.

75 Featherbed Lane in the 1940s.

# GETTING AROUND IN THE BRONX: SUBWAYS, TRAINS, TROLLEYS & BUSES

**This IRT station at 161st Street & River should be familiar to Yankee fans in The Bronx who probably remember peeking out the window for a brief glance at the right field and bullpen area.** Since the IND train also stopped at **161st Street** (below ground), free transfer was given by the transit system which straphangers used to switch from one system to the other. **Nedicks** and the **161st Street Cafeteria** were convenient eating and meeting places before or after **Yankee** home games.

One of the major benefits of life in the Bronx was a remarkably efficient public transportation system. Usually taken for granted, the availability of cheap subways, trolleys and buses throughout the borough made life easy for the great majority of the population for most of the twentieth century. Indeed, the Bronx as we know it wouldn't have been born without access to the subways. It wasn't until the City extended its subway system northwards into the Bronx that the builders and real estate speculators followed. Even earlier, in the late nineteenth century, it was the railroad that brought the first sizable population to the wooded acres of the Bronx. **Mott Haven, West Farms** and **Morrisania** were early communities that owed their existence to the **New York** and **Harlem River Railroad**. It is a simple task to chart the growth of The Bronx population by following the lines of the subway and elevated trains that were constructed during the late teens and '20s. Apartment houses sprang up like mushrooms in the wake of the subway system.

Landlords too, knew quite well that transportation was a powerful selling point to prospective tenants, and so real estate ads always proclaimed "subways close by," or "short walk to IND." This might not always be strictly accurate, of course, and a short walk to a landlord might in reality be ten blocks to the tenant. Somehow, though, it never seemed a difficult hurdle to walk those blocks to the nearest subway entrance, or home again at the end of the day. Perhaps, for the older citizens, it was, but kids accepted a certain amount of trekking as normal, and it could be fun as well. The point remains, however, that Bronxites depended on their public transportation, and for the most part, it was there for them in any weather and at any time.

During the '30s and '40s, cars weren't common family possessions for most Bronxites. A glance at any street scene from those years reveals a surprising abundance of curb space on most streets and suggests that Bronxites relied on public transportation for their travel plans. The oldest system in the borough was the trolley cars, electrically powered conveyances that pre-dated even the oldest subways and retained a valuable rustic charm well into the 1940s. The trolleys ran on steel tracks embedded into the asphalt and paving stones of the major thoroughfares; they click-clacked their way at a modest pace to most parts of the Bronx. Trolleys had an old-world feel to them. They were slow enough not to intimidate the pedestrian and were cleaner (if not quieter) than the buses that replaced them in the late 1940s. Being bound to the tracks, trolleys followed very predictable and invariable routes and they kept to precise schedules. The traffic laws provided for trolley-only lanes, and ensured right-of-way for the trolley cars, so that only rarely did the trolley become stuck in vehicular traffic. Taken as a whole, the trolley network provided excellent urban transit. It was cheap, reliable, faster than walking, and didn't pollute. Naturally, it was replaced with the diesel powered bus at the earliest opportunity.

Trolleys could be particularly fascinating to the kids and teenagers of the Bronx. In the summer, the sides of some cars were removed to allow air circulation, so that the whole vehicle took on the feel of an amusement park ride. There was always the fun of sitting at the rear unused motorman's seat, watching the road recede but still getting the thrill of navigation. Other uses of the trolley system were less approved. Putting pennies on the track to see them flattened was one pastime, but a dangerous one that always

**Here is the interior and exterior of the IND "D" train.** These trains were built between 1930 and 1939 and served passengers for over 40 years! Most straphanger from the 40s, 50s & 60s would recall a 2 hour trip from The Bronx to Coney Island.

**No matter where you went on the IRT chances were good that your car looked like this.** Almost 2,000 of these standard body types were built between 1910 and 1925. This 1916 car had the cane seats that were mostly all replaced with the newer foam rubber and vinyl by the early 1960s.

**This is a 1961 photo of the interior of the old familiar D train as well as other IND line trains.** This picture was taken on the AA train. Still in use, the rattan or cane seats, the bane of women wearing nylon stockings, served on subways and Els for more than 70 years.

concerned parents and motormen. Even worse, the urge to jump on the rear of a passing trolley was something young men could barely control and there was constant shouting from the motorman about such hitchhikers. Naturally, this kind of play was incredibly risky and there was hardly a summer that passed without a story in the Home News about a kid who fell off the back of a trolley and lost either his leg or his life.

The trolley cars in use during the '30s and '40s were powered by overhead electrical wires, connected to the trolley by a long metal pole that occasionally sparked, making for some spectacular fireworks. Trolleys were decorated, if that is the word, with a comfortable yellow paint along with some red trim, and each carried a large letter on the front designating its route. Trolleys were, in fact, a private business, operated by the Third Avenue Railway System and not a municipal service at all. True, they were closely regulated and seemed a permanent part of the city's machinery, but when they were removed in the late '40s, it became clear that political decisions had been made and not business ones. The buses that

replaced them were also privately held, but in later years absorbed (as were all the subways) into the City's structure.

In New York City, the subways ran around the clock, so that late night travellers could always be assured of a ride home. In the Bronx, the major subway lines offered service that extended from **Van Cortlandt Park, Woodlawn, Wakefield** and **Pelham Bay** to the heart of the Bronx at **l49th Street** or **Fordham Road**. Creative travellers could change trains at, say, **l6lst Street** and the **Concourse**, and make their way to the remotest parts of the Bronx, all for one fare. If the subways ended at **Broadway** and **242nd Street**, there were buses waiting to continue the journey so that the intrepid traveller could find a way home, no matter what the hour. They could also extend their travels to every borough in the city (save Staten Island, of course), and many Bronxites could spend whole days at Coney Island or even the Rockaways, thanks to the subway network. Manhattan was, naturally, the biggest attraction to the Bronx wanderer, and it is where many youngsters first explored the possibilities of freedom and non-traditional recreation. A trip via the IRT or the **Concourse** D train to downtown New York was simple enough, and fast. For many years, the fare was five cents, with younger children riding free, so that cost was a minor factor in the subway equation. Nor was safety a widespread concern, as it later was. True or not, the subways in the '40s and '50s were viewed as perfectly safe for travellers of any age at any time of day. There must have been some crime on the subways back then, but it wasn't a burning city-wide issue and rarely disturbed anyone's plans for a late night outing. Bronxites of that era will happily confirm the security issue. "I could come home at two in the morning and never worry," or "My mother told me to take the subway after dark because she thought it was safer than the streets."

The rickety wooden platforms of the elevated lines along **Jerome Avenue** or **Third Avenue** were perhaps more fun than the newer lines under the **Concourse**. Travelling on the El was more than just transport. It was a scenic tour of the Bronx. Underground was, well, underground and it was mostly dark tunnels that occasionally brightened into identical stations. The El, though, had color, charm and sunshine. The most renowned moment of elevated travel was on the **Jerome Avenue IRT**, as the uptown **Woodlawn** train emerged into the sunlight from **149th Street** and approached **Yankee Stadium**. For a moment, if one stood on the proper side of the train, it was possible to peer into **Yankee Stadium** itself and catch a glimpse of the green outfield and the seats. This was a thrill at any time during the season, but when a World Series

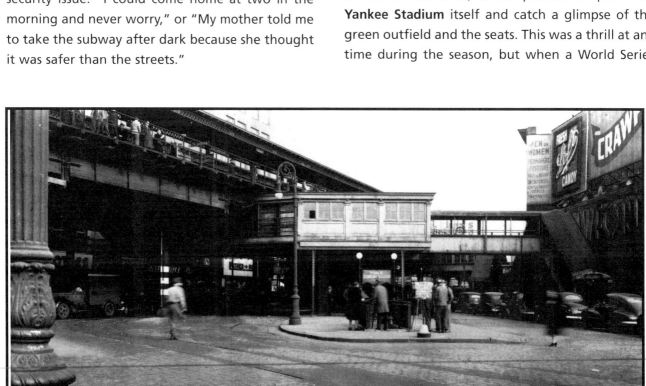

*New York Transit Museum Archives*

**This is the hub on January 13, 1947 looking north from Willis Avenue.** This was one of the early commercial shopping centers in The Bronx. Several subway, trolley and, later, bus lines, converged here making it a thriving area. On the right is **Crawford Clothing Store** and on the next block one of the many **Bickford's Cafeterias.** Nearly every need could be met at the **Hub**, regardless of income. The original **Alexander's** was located on **153rd & Third Avenue**, the grand store on **Fordham Road** followed later.

**This is the 177th Street and Boston Road - West Farms Square Station which is still in service today.**

was in progress (which was almost every year so it seemed) it was a positively exhilarating few seconds. It was, in other words, possible to see Joe DiMaggio himself patrolling the grass of the Stadium, and of course, to recycle this moment to everyone in the neighborhood later that night.

Another widespread enjoyment of the subway, both elevated and below level, was to stand at the very front car and watch the tracks as they rushed past. Nearly every train had a knot of kids bunched up next to the motorman's cab, enthralled by the view as stations and other trains passed by at top speed. And, to be truthful, more than a few adults took part in this sport, too, it was especially colorful below ground when the darkness and the mysterious lights made the first car view even better. On the IND A or D train, there was a famous run in Manhattan from l25th Street to 59th street, when the train went express and the motorman opened up the throttle, giving all the subway fans in the front car a genuine adventure. In the summer, in the days before air conditioning, the motorman would probably have his cab door open so the passenger could get a

look at the driver at work as he manipulated the handles and buttons. All this, remember, for five cents. Not a bad way to spend an hour or so.

For those who preferred to sit during their subway travel, the walls offered much of interest. The advertisements were a constantly changing and intriguing panorama of American commerce. There were the usual cigarette ads, candy or soft drink notices and a bewildering variety of products being pushed on the consumer. But most memorable was the brilliant Miss Subways campaign initiated by the NYC Board of Transportation. Every month the board ran a contest to choose the prettiest of a set of candidates who would reign for those 30 days as Miss Subways. The young ladies were distinguished by being strictly amateur local girls, who would represent the City in its best light and at the same time avoid the taint of professionalism. They tended to look suspiciously alike, being mostly brunettes, with small features and all, naturally, being Caucasian. It is true that, in later years, there were Black and Hispanic contestants in the Miss Subways competition but not during the '40s and '50s. The Miss Subways, therefore, were secretaries, municipal employees, the occasional teacher, entertainer or student, along with some in the "aspiring model" category. Each poster had a short biography of the winner and all seemed jolly, energetic and above reproach. Maybe they were. Some of the Miss Subways winners went on to modeling careers (according to legend) but most returned to their anonymity, although they must have treasured those subway placards for decades afterwards. One notable success story was that of Mona Freeman, who was the first Miss Subways and went on to a Hollywood career. On lower Broadway, just opposite City Hall, is a restaurant owned by a former Miss Subways where contest posters still line the walls and windows.

Subway platforms had their own special pleasures. Gum machines were a standard feature for years in Bronx subway stations, along with candy and telephones. The gum, however, cost only a penny (later a nickel) so it was with-

in the reach of kids and was well used. The same gum might later be found under a seat, and occasionally on a seat, so in its wisdom the Transit Authority finally removed such temptations. Today, eating is strictly forbidden in the subway car. Smoking always was. A few Manhattan stations (such as Times Square) had concessions that offered frankfurters, drinks and other merchandise but this was not the rule in the Bronx. The best The Bronx got were newsstands, and those only in the largest stations. As compensation, the private stores clustered around subway entrances and provided any missing services. You could always count on a newsstand, a candy store, and the assorted food shops to be close to the local subway stop, for obvious reasons. On the trip downtown in the

**NO SMOKING NO SPITTING**

**SANITARY CODE SECT. 216**

SMOKING IN SUBWAY IS PROHIBITED. SMOKING OR CARRYING ANY LIGHTED CIGAR, CIGARETTE OR PIPE IN OR ON ANY STAIRWAY, PLATFORM, STATION OR CAR OF ANY RAILWAY RUNNING UNDERNEATH THE GROUND SURFACE IS HEREBY PROHIBITED.

BOARD OF TRANSPORTATION        BOARD OF HEALTH.
CITY OF NEW YORK

*New York City Transit System, Harold A. Smith*

**This is the 1940s-50s Dyre Avenue "Dinkie" running from Dyre Avenue to East 180th Street at Morris Park Station.** Power was originally from overhead wires.

These three photos were taken at the Trolley Museum. They represent the type of car used on most Bronx routes. The two interior shots are from the 1940s. The trolley below is from the 1930s.

morning, people bought their cigarettes and newspapers. Coming home they picked up bread for dinner, the evening <u>Post</u> or <u>World Telegram</u>, and perhaps the dry cleaning for next day's work. The result was a busy knot of shopkeeping and business within stone's throw of the subway, and it was usually a wise location for the businessman.

The elevated made some of the major streets in The Bronx into shaded and slightly mysterious thoroughfares. **Jerome Avenue, White Plains Road, Westchester Avenue, Third Avenue** and upper **Broadway** (among others) took on a unique atmosphere thanks to the presence of the El; they were shaded, cool and crowded with cars, and there was a special mood of privacy under the great steel girders. Just how powerful was the impact of the El can be measured by its absence. When the **Third Avenue El** was torn town in the l970s, it transformed that street in surprising ways. Sunlight streamed in for

180TH STREET
BRONX

the first time in decades, and the street seemed amazingly spacious, although it hadn't been widened an inch. With the great pillars removed, traffic, both auto and pedestrian, could flow easily, and **Third Avenue** seemed reborn. But something was lost, too, when the El disappeared. It was hotter in the summer and, somehow, the wind blew much harder in the winter, and the sunlight wasn't always flattering to the surrounding stores and apartment houses. The El may have been old and noisy, but it wasn't all bad as many discovered when it wasn't there any longer.

The great changes of the '60s and '70s were felt by the transportation system as well. Trolleys were long gone (sent to Bombay, India, Sao Paulo, Brazil and Vienna, Austria according to one urban legend), and the familiar trolleys were losing favor with the riders. For a time, the bus seemed the answer, being modern, diesel-operated and highly flexible, unlike the track-bound trolleys. Robert

Moses, among other urban experts, vigorously advocated the use of surface buses to bring New York into the twentieth century and modernize the system, and the bus manufacturers were energetically on the same side. As a result, trolleys vanished and New York became a city that ran on internal combustion engines, both private and public.

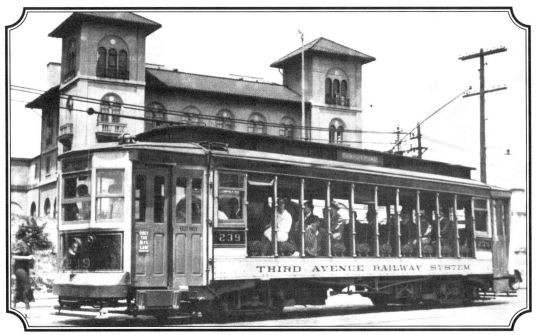

Buses, too, cost a nickel but they were a much slower means of travel and never the choice for really long trips. But when the trolleys were gone, there was little choice. In truth, the bus could be an excellent local conveyance. It went into areas not served by subways, or was the connecting means between the far-flung neighborhoods and the nearest subway station. For school kids, the bus was very important. One of the signs of maturity for Bronx kids was the first bus pass, a bit of colored cardboard distributed by the Board of Education that allowed free (or very cheap) travel between school and home. This was, naturally, for high schoolers who might have to travel outside their neighborhoods, and for the uncommon few junior high or elementary students who, somehow, lived a long way from the school.

Elaborate regulations governed bus passes, regulations which were disregarded on a wholesale basis by every kid in The Bronx who could acquire a pass. Bus passes were controlled by the school authorities. The dean kept a list and handed out the passes to the qualified student, sometimes for the payment of thirty cents or so. The passes were changed monthly, according to some color code, to prevent cheating and fare beating. These rules posed an interesting challenge, therefore, to the clever teenager but hardly an insoluble one. Bus passes could be handed out the rear window at a crowded school stop, for instance (they did not come with ID photos), or simply used for after-school cruising by telling a suitably sad story — "I got sick in school and I had to go to the doctor , and I have no money" when the driver asked why the pass was being used at five thirty in the afternoon at a stop two miles from any school. It worked often enough, and, if not, just wait for the next bus and the next bus driver who might be more pliable.

As the '50s progressed, the fare went up slowly from five cents to ten cents in 1947 to fifteen in 1953, to twenty, and ultimately to thirty cents by the '60s. Tokens came and went, or were redesigned, and the subways became a much

*Across New York*
*By Trolley*
*by Frederick A. Kramer*
**The Third Avenue Railway was developed in the late 1800s and its trolleys were frequently upgraded and modernized over the next several years.** Pictured here is the convertible, a streetcar designed with the side panels removed for open air operation in the summer. The Third Avenue Railway served The Bronx, lower Westchester, and Manhattan.

*Across New York By Trolley by Frederick A. Kramer*

**West Farms Square, Decoration Day 1940.** This major hub in the center of The Bronx where **177th Street, Tremont Avenue,** and **Boston Road** converge, was constantly crowded with trolley cars and, later, buses. This was the terminal point for many lines and helped take families to the **Bronx Zoo** just a few blocks away. The letters on the trolleys indicate their destination. In the background (right) you can see the Coliseum and sports facility. In the early 40s, it was turned into a vehicle storage facility during World War II. After the war, the Surface Transportation took it over and used if for vehicle maintenance.

more questionable means of travel. Stations which once were swept and reasonably maintained declined into shabbiness and worse. The crime issue arose with a vengeance as every subway incident was trumpeted across the newspapers and on television. By the mid-'60s, subways were a danger zone, sometimes in reality and, more often in perception, but in either case, no longer attractive to many Bronxites (or other New Yorkers). The precipitous fall in subway ridership coincided with the public's loss of security and with the other massive population shifts that characterized the '60s. Paradoxically, subway fares increased as ridership dropped, an odd response by the Transit Authority, but somehow deemed reasonable. By

the mid-'70s, fares had risen to nearly one dollar, but by that time, many in The Bronx had transferred their allegiance to the automobile.

Not that cars were rare in The Bronx before. There was more than enough traffic along the **Concourse** in the '40s and '50s, and parking was already difficult on **Fordham Road** or along **149th Street.** But the largest proportion of The Bronx's people did not own autos. They were subway, bus or trolley riders who dreamed of someday owning their own private cars. Well, in the years after World War II, the dreams could come true and private autos became possible for nearly everyone. The glorious economic boom of the '50s brought cheap cars into nearly everyone's price range. The

*New York Transit Museum Archives, Brooklyn*

**This 7th Avenue Southbound train originating at Bronx Park and heading towards the South Ferry was among one of the oldest trains serving The Bronx and more specifically, the East Bronx. This tired family is trying to rest on the familiar wicker seats.**

There were taxicabs in The Bronx but they were reserved for truly special events. Taking a taxi might be a sign of some emergency, somebody was in the hospital or maybe there was a funeral. It might also mark a very important date. Taking a cab to the **Paradise**, in the mid-'50s, was living very large indeed and pretty much guaranteed to impress the girl. It was OK for proms, weddings, graduations or bar mitzvahs, but the idea of hopping into a cab for a normal shopping trip would have been quite unusual; the neighbors would have surely talked. Taxis were, however, interesting. In the post-war decades, cabs were still big comfortable automobiles with specially altered interiors. The most notable feature was the two little jump seats that folded down. These were automatically given to the kids, and always made the cab ride more fun than simply sitting on the regular leather seat. Taxis

Bronx suddenly erupted in automobiles. Where once only a few in the neighborhood owned a car, by the late '50s, nearly everyone who worked could be a driver. Parking spaces suddenly became scarce, stickball games got harder to play thanks to parked cars, and Bronxites found themselves highly mobile in ways they never imagined. Together with television, the auto was probably most responsible for changing the face and nature of the old Bronx. If television kept people inside, the auto took them away. In either case, the old custom of sitting on the stoop, or merely hanging around the neighborhood, faded rapidly with the spread of cars and TVs.

*New York Transit Museum Archives, Brooklyn*

**The oncoming view of Yankee Stadium in the early 40s is a regular sight for south-bounders on the Woodlawn-Jerome IRT**. Macombs ballfield and track is shown below. On game days this stop would become one of the most crowded stations on the system.

were converted Dodges, DeSotos, or were big Checkers; they had massive springs and plump seating, and they seemed to be clean. The junky yellow jobs on the streets today wouldn't have passed muster in the '50s, being far too crowded and too often in terrible condition. Cab drivers, however, were the same. They lived up to their colorful reputation as tough-talking, street-wise, lovable roughnecks who could entertain the rider with New York stories. There was, indeed, the famous cabby hat: a cloth workingman's head covering that often had a union badge to complete the expected picture. What they were, in reality, were the usual low-paid and hardworking immigrant groups: Jews, Italians, Irish and the occasional Black, who struggled through traffic and heat to make a living. Today's East Asian and

**177th Street and Boston Road - West Farms Square Station.** Note the sign that says change from East Side trains here for The Bronx Zoo. This picture had to be taken before August 4th, 1952 because the spur from 177th Street to Bronx Park was abandoned then.

Central European drivers are the latest in an honorable tradition of newcomers to New York who take the toughest jobs, and few are tougher than cab driving.

It is interesting to note that the extraordinary transportation network of The Bronx still exists. The subways are plying their old routes, buses still rumble along **University Avenue** and the **Concourse** as they did in the '50s, and one can still travel from furthest **Riverdale** or **Pelham Parkway** to mid-town Manhattan in an amazingly short time. True, the fare is now $1.50 and the newspaper to read on the trip is fifty cents, but, otherwise, the routine remains the same. People walk to the stations, pay their fares, push into the rocking subway trains and complain about the delays and crowding, and generally repeat the behavior of their predecessors of 40 years ago. Heat is less of a problem since all NYC subways are now air conditioned and the picturesque over-

**This 138th Street IRT subway entrance was below ground, even though the IRT generally ran on elevated tracts above 149th Street.** Subway stations like this and especially the IND stations on the **Concourse** were often used by kids, at the urging of their parents for safe underground passage across the busy **Grand Concourse.**

head fans are gone, but New Yorkers can still make angry noises when the air conditioner breaks down. All in all, the subways are still familiar places. The colors of the faces may have changed a bit but in any given IND car leaving **Tremont Avenue** you might find Soviet Jews, Irish construction workers, Greek waiters and students of every color and language. For most people in today's Bronx, the subways and buses still take them to work and school, to shopping on Saturdays and home in the evenings, and the rumble of those trains still echoes through many bedrooms around the borough.

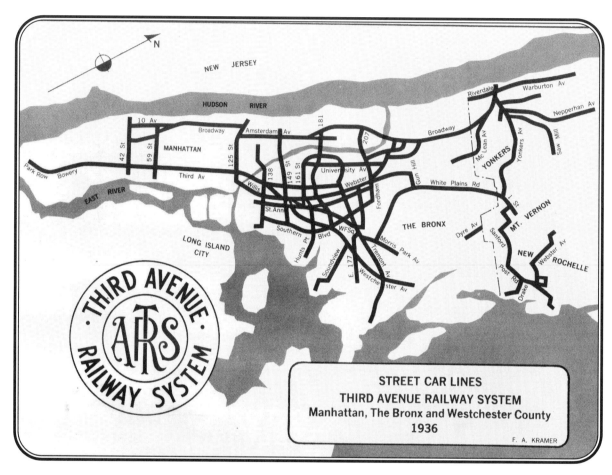

**A map of the street car line Third Avenue Railway System.**

*Across New York by Trolley by Frederick A. Kramer*

| No. | Route | From | To |
|---|---|---|---|
| 1 | Concourse-138th St. | East 38th St.&Grand Concourse | Broadway & 231st St |
| 2 | Concourse Hub | 150th St.& Melrose Ave. | Sedgwick Ave & Fort Independence St. |
| 3 | Prospect Ave | E.138th St. & Jackson Ave. | Third Ave. & Fordham Rd. |
| 4 | Jerome-Bainbridge | Valentine Ave. & Fordham Rd. | 242nd St. & Katonah Ave. |
| 5 | Bruckner Blvd | Westchester & Longwood Aves. | Westchester Ave & Bruckner Blvd. |
| 6 | Throggs Neck | Westchester Square | Ft. Schuyler |
|  | Branch #1 | Miles & Meagher Aves. | Edgewater camp |
|  | Branch #2 | 177th St. & Pennyfield Ave. | Locust Point |
|  | Branch #3 | E. Tremont & Miles Ave. | McDowell Place & Harding Ave. |
| 7 | Boston Rd | Pelham Pkwy So. & White Plains Rd. | Ropes Ave. & Boston Rd. |
| 8 | Williamsbridge Rd. | Benson St.& Westchester Ave. | Burke Ave.& White Plains Rd. |
| 9 | Eastchester Rd | Benson St.& Westchester Ave. | White Plains Rd. & 225th St. |
| 10 | Riverdale Ave | West 207th St. & Bdwy | E. Riverdale Ave. City Line |
|  | Branch #1 | W. 231st St. & Riverdale Ave. | Mosholu Ave. & W. 254th ST. |
|  | Branch #2 | W. 236th St.&Riverdale Ave. | Henry Hudson Pkwy E. |
| 11 | 170th St Crosstown | W. 180th St.& St. Nicholas Ave. | Southern Blvd & Freeman ST. |
| 12 | City Island Fordham | University Ave.& Fordham Rd. | City Island Ave & Rochelle St. |
|  | Branch #1 | Traffic Relief Circle & Orchard Beach Rd. | Orchard Beach |
| 13 | Castle Hill Ave | Pelham Pkwy & White Plains Rd. | Castle Hill Ave. & Zerega Ave. |
| 14 | Edenwald Ave | White Plains Rd. & E. 233rd St. | Boston Rd. & Dyre Ave. |
| 15 | Gun Hill Rd | Jerome Ave. & Mosholu Pkwy | Gun Hill Rd. & Gunther Ave. |
| 16 | Webster Ave | 206th St. & Bainbridge Ave. | Corsa Ave. & Boston Rd. |
| 17 | Allerton Ave | White Plains Rd. & Allerton Ave. | Allerton Ave. & Westervelt Ave. |
| 18 | Macombs Road | Montgomery Ave. & W. Tremont Ave. | E. 170th St. & Teller Ave. |
| 19 | 207th Street Crosstown | 207th St. & Broadway | Souther Blvd. & E. 189th St. |
| 20 | Bronx-Van Cortlandt Park | Broadway at the City Line | E. Tremont Ave. & E. 177th St. |
| 21 | Pelham Bay Park | Westchester Square & Tremont Ave. | Westchester Ave. & Bruckner Blvd. |
| 22 | Burke Ave.-Country Club | Westchester Ave. & Edison Ave. | Campbell Dr. & Country Club Rd. |
| 23 | Crosby Ave. - Layton Ave | Westchester Ave. & Crosby Ave. | Schley Ave. & Ellsworth Ave. |
| 24 | Bailey Ave | Fordham Rd & Sedgwick Ave. | Broadway & W. 231st St. |
| 25 | Morris-Jerome Aves | Lincoln Ave. & 138th St. | Jerome Ave. & Kingsbridge |
| 26 | Boston Rd. & Morris Park Ave. | Third Ave. & 137th St. | Morris Park Ave. & Eastchester Rd. |
| 27 | Clason Point | East River & Sound View Ave. | Westchester Ave. & Simpson St. |
| 28 | Williamsbridge | E. Tremont Ave. & Third Ave. | White Plains Rd. & Gun Hill Rd. |
| 29 | Willis Ave | Fort Lee Ferry | Third Ave. & Fordham Rd. |
| 30 | 149th St. Crosstown | E. 149th St. & Southern Blvd. | 134th St. & Locust Ave. |
| 31 | Southern Blvd | 138th St. & Bruckner Blvd. | Southern Blvd & Fordham Rd. |
| 32 | St. Ann's Ave. | E. 161st St. & St. Ann's Ave. | St. Ann's Ave. & E. 132nd St. |
| 33 | 138th St. Crosstown | St. Nicholas Ave. & W. 135th St. | 134th St & Locust Ave. |
| 34 | 163rd St. Crosstown | Hunts Pt. Ave. & Westchester Ave. | W. 155th St. & Broadway |
| 35 | 167th St. Crosstown | E. 167th St. & Westchester Ave. | W. 181st St. & Broadway |
| 36 | 180th St. Crosstown | Intersection at E. 177th S. & Bruckner Blvd | W. 181st St. & Broadway |
| 37 | Ogden Avenue | 161st St. & River Ave. | W. 181st St. & Broadway |
| 38 | University Ave | W. 181st St. & Broadway | W. 238th St. & Broadway |
| 39 | Sedgwick Ave | E. Burnside Ave., & Morris Ave. | Cedar Ave. & Sedgwick Ave. |
| 40 | Tremont Ave | W. Burnside Ave. & University Ave. | Bruckner Blvd. & E. Tremont Ave. |
| 41 | Webster & White Plains Aves. | Melrose Ave. & E. 149th St. | White Plains & North City Line |
| 42 | Westchester Ave | Third Ave. & 148th St. | Westchester Ave. & Tremont Ave. |
| 43 | Highbridge | 161st St. & River Ave. | W. 168th St. & Nelson Ave. |

This 1946 GMC bus #19 photo taken in 1962 at the corner of W. Fordham Road and University Avenue across from Tolentine Church. This was the 207th Street Crosstown bus originating at 207th Street & Broadway and terminating at **Southern Blvd** and **East 189th St.**

This December 1951 picture shows bus #29 underneath the El at Fordham Road & 190th Street. From here this bus would take you to the Fort Lee Ferry.

This 1951 picture at Westchester Avenue and 233rd Street. The #23 bus would travel the **Crosby Avenue-Layton Avenue** route and would terminate at **Schley Avenue** and **Ellsworth Avenue**. The fare in 1951 was 10¢.

This 1947 GMC bus #11 photo taken in 1962 at 170th Street between Cromwell and Inwood Avenue just below the 170th Street Station on the IRT-Woodlawn-Jerome 170th Street stop.

This 1947 GMC bus #26 photo taken in 1962 on Boston Road at 174th Street. This bus ran from **Third Avenue** and **E.137th Street** to **Morris Park Avenue** and **Eastchester Road.**

This Nov 1951 photo shows the #19 bus in front of the Fordham Road Station of the New York Central Line. This bus would be the 207th Street crosstown route terminating at Broadway & 207th Street.

1947 GMC going eastbound on 170th Street crosstown. This photo was taken in January of 1961 and showed one of several big snowstorms of the year.

**This southbound Woodlawn-Jerome Avenue train has just left the Woodlawn station and is approaching Mosholu Parkway in 1962.** Below you will see the bustling double-parked automobiles between **Mosholu Parkway** and **Gun Hill Road**. If you look closely you could see Schweller's Delicatessen.

**This southbound train at Gun Hill Road & White Plains Road in 1962.** A northbound "Thru Express" used to run express all the way to **Gun Hill Road** in rush hours. A thru express is visible in the distance. This is a double deck structure. The Third Avenue El arrived on the lower level.

**This 3rd Avenue Line northbound train is leaving 183rd Street towards Fordham Road - a mixed train of 1938 World's Fair cars and IRT standard trains.**

**This 1960 train is shown leaving Claremont Parkway toward 149th Street and 3rd Avenue.**

**This is the northbound Jerome Avenue IRT approaching 170th Street station.** A minute earlier and in the summertime, the heat-exhausted straphangers would always envy those bathers cooling off at Cascade Pool less than a quarter mile south under the El on Jerome Avenue.

**This late 1960s shows the Jerome Avenue IRT approaching the 176th Street station with Davidson Avenue in the background.** If you lived west of this station, you would now have to climb those dreaded 150 plus steps leading up toward **Davidson, Harrison, West Tremont** and **University Avenue**.

This 1950s IRT train is departing at the 174th Street north-bound station in the early 1960s. The lead car is a 1957 built R21 type.

This 1962 photo arriving at Intervale Avenue on the Westchester Avenue portion of the White Plains Road Line.

This 1962 photo of a southbound train between Freeman & Simpson Street running Southern Boulevard.

This 1962 track level picture of the IRT Woodlawn-Jerome Avenue train arriving the Mt. Eden Station. Notice the hanging clothes on the clothesline.

This southbound IRT Woodlawn-Jerome Avenue train is approaching the 167th Street Station in 1962. One can see the familiar Santini Bros. warehouse was an area landmark.

Another southbound Jerome Avenue IRT train arriving at the 161st Street and River Avenue station in 1962. The lower portion shows the street alongside Mullaly Park.

# Religion In The Bronx

Photo: Daniel & Beatrice Epstein

**Temple Zion , located at 1925 Grand Concourse. The wedding of Daniel and Beatrice Epstein (1948).**

Brooklyn may have been the "Borough of Churches," but the Bronx had a pretty rich and colorful religious culture. It was a culture that was often unofficial and non-orthodox, but everybody who lived in the Bronx during the 40s and 50s had to confront the question of religious duty. Not so much faith or theology: the Bronx wasn't the place to discuss fine points of belief or practice. But "religion" in a wider sense was made an important part of life for most Bronxites; it made a difference, in other words, where and when you confronted the Deity. For the average kid-on-the

street, religious affiliation could count very much indeed. Neighborhoods, stores, parks, parishes and even buildings were frequently classified by religion: e.g., the Jewish deli and the Irish deli, two very different clienteles and goods. Nothing like official segregation, of course, existed in the Bronx. The civic philosophy was ecumenical and overflowing with brotherhood: every Bronx politician marched in the St. Patrick's Day parade and made sure to wear a yarmulke at a Jewish funeral. Jewish businessmen had Catholic clients, Protestant bankers had no trouble in dealing with

*Photo: Municipal Archives*

**Our Lady of Mercy Church & School** is still located at **2496 Marion Avenue** between **Fordham Road** and **E. 188th Street.** This Church has strong ties to Fordham University because the original Parish Church is now the Fordham Chapel located at the University, and the Parish was originally founded by the Jesuit community at Fordham University. The cornerstone of the Church was laid in 1907 and the school opened in 1915. In the 1940s and '50s the surrounding neighborhood and congregation was comprised of mostly Irish.

Christmas pageants, Channukah displays or other sectarian activities. The Board of Education was, naturally, not inclined to any particular religious practice: it simply upheld Judeo-Christian traditions. This much seemed quite ordinary and was rarely questioned: religion was viewed as a normal element in anyone's upbringing and a vivid part of everyday culture. What would have surprised Bronxites, were schools that avoided religious instruction of any sort.

The influence of the major religions was pervasive in the Bronx, and to a great extent, still is. During the worst days of the Bronx's decline, it was the Catholic Church that fought long and hard for the survival of the neighborhoods. Cardinal Terrance Cook, himself a Bronx native, and dozens of local priests, fed the poor and lobbied the government for help during the crisis of the 70s. The other Christian churches similarly stood

Orthodox Jews and everyone spoke glowingly of the melting pot. There weren't many Muslims, Hindus or Buddhists in the Bronx back then, but they probably would have been embraced by the same public tolerance that kept the other faiths working together.

In the days before school prayer was limited by the courts, and when state/church connections weren't so closely studied, the Bronx witnessed what, in retrospect, seems to have been a remarkable amount of official (i.e. government) religious involvement. Public schools, for instance, had no hesitation about opening each assembly with a reading from the Bible, nor about

for the Bronx in a difficult period, and were often responsible for whatever relief the embattled Bronx did find in those years. The powerful Jewish establishment has less to be proud of, despite the work of the individual rabbi or synagogue in confronting a social crisis. With a large part of the Jewish population on the move out of the Bronx, the 60s and 70s weren't a happy period for the old-line Jewish leaders; their congregations were fleeing and their old political ties had been dissolved by the flood of new immigrants. For many synagogues, these were the years when Jewish life all but disappeared in the Bronx or was at least radically weakened.

**A beautiful July day in 1958 is the setting for a happy event at Our Saviors Church located at E. 183rd Street & Washington Avenue.** The bride is being escorted to her limousine as the wedding party and neighborhood onlookers enjoy the occasion. The Church performed weddings and sponsored other functions for neighborhoods throughout The Bronx.

*Photo: Municipal Archives*

**St. Jerome's Church** is still located at **230 Alexander Avenue at E. 138th Street. St. Jerome's Parish** was established in 1869 and **St. Jerome's Church** was constructed in 1898. A massive reproduction of the Last Supper adorns part of the dome which soars over sixty feet above the sanctuary floor while magnificent stained glass windows enhance the beauty of the Church. The original ethnic composition of the parish was largely Irish, then Germans, then Italians, and later (in the 1950's) Puerto Ricans.

In the years after the War, though, the Jewish impact on Bronx life was very powerful. For most of the 20th century, the Bronx had a predominately Jewish population and that majority made itself felt throughout the borough. Along the **Grand Concourse**, synagogues were imposing structures that anchored neighborhoods and were both religious and political institutions. On the Jewish Holy Days of Yom Kippur or Rosh Hashonah, these grand buildings such as the **Concourse Center of Israel** or the **Mount Eden Synagogue** drew hundreds of worshippers to the services; even on ordinary Friday nights they would be packed with faithful attendees. Bar

*Photo: Municipal Archives*

**St. Paul's Evangelical Lutheran Church of Tremont.** This church is closely connected with the Tremont area. In 1923 the property was purchased and on December 20, 1925, the church was dedicated. The Church is still located at 1986 Crotona Avenue at E. 179th Street.

*Photo: Municipal Archives*
**Young Israel of the Concourse – 1015 Walton Avenue between E. 164th & 165th Streets.** This popular synagogue served the people of the community who lived between E. 161st Street and E. 165th Street.

Mitzvahs and weddings were elaborate affairs in the Bronx Jewish community and further jammed the neighborhood synagogues on a regular basis. There were dozens of smaller Jewish temples in the Bronx too, storefront congregations in the poorer areas of **Mott Haven** or **Hunts Point**, and converted basements in some of the middle-class streets of **University Heights**. The synagogue also doubled as the local Hebrew school, where young boys went to prepare for their Bar Mitzvah, and in many cases as a social center, where basketball and dances were on the program.

Jewish resources often went into hospitals and social service. In The Bronx there was **Montefiore Hospital** on **Gun Hill Road**, named after the famous British Jew who donated funds to the building, and later on, there was **Albert Einstein Hospital** at **Eastchester Road**, named for the most famous living scientist. Jewish charities embraced health, cultural events, social programs and even sports, and the annual Israel Bond Drive was a major day in the Jewish social calendar.

The same role was played, of course, by the Catholic and Protestant churches of the Bronx. In the big churches like **St. Nicholas of Tolentine** on **Fordham Road**, or **St. Raymonds** in the East Bronx, religious life mixed with social and community affairs with great success. The intensely Italian **Belmont** neighborhood was anchored by **Mount Carmel Church**, where all baptisms, weddings and burials took place as a matter of custom...to observe the Sacraments elsewhere wouldn't have seemed right to the people of **Arthur Avenue**. The weekly dances in **St. Raymonds** drew hundreds (maybe thousands) of parochial school

**Tremont Temple Congregation Gates of Mercy, located at 2064 Grand Concourse between Burnside Avenue and E. 180th Street.** This palatial-looking building served the large Jewish community in the decades of the '30s through the '60s. It is now a Baptist Church.

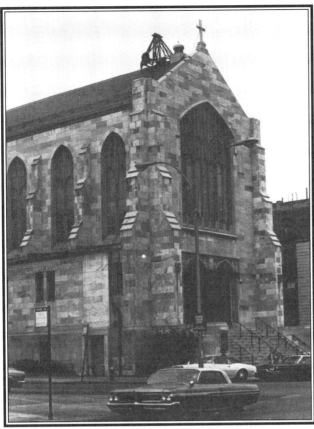

Photo: Spencer Field

**Sacred Heart Church, located on Shakespeare Avenue near West 168th Street.** This church was an anchor for the large Irish community. This church offered a Catholic education for those families who chose not to send their children to public schools.

Photo: Municipal Archives

The **YW-YMHA** was located on the **Grand Concourse and McClellan Street.** In the 1940s, '50s, and '60s the **"Y"** offered some courses in Jewish studies but to most it offered a large variety of youth and teenage activities. Some of the more popular activities included co-ed dances, music lessons, and crafts. Participants were well rewarded by the quality of the instruction as well as the organized social life.

students from around the city, and **St. Anselm's Church** in the tough **Mott Haven** section was renowned for its boxing team. The **Fordham Manor Dutch Reformed Church** on **Kingsbridge Road** or the **Lutheran Church** on **Ogden Avenue** were active players in their neighborhood's social life on all levels, from baptism to basketball. The Catholic Church had a major investment in education throughout the Bronx too: many churches had attached parochial schools that went to the 8th grade, and then there was the possibility of

**St. Nicholas of Tolentine Church, located on University Avenue at the intersection of Fordham Road.**

continuing at such high schools as **Cardinal Hayes** on the **Grand Concourse**. For more ambitious Catholic students (and others as well) there was the world famous **Fordham University** on **Rose Hill** in the **Fordham** section. Run by the Jesuits, **Fordham** boasted a magnificent campus surrounded by trees and ivy-covered buildings, and a first class academic program; it drew students from around the world and still does. Another Catholic center of higher education was **Mount St. Vincent's**, at the northern end of Broadway in Riverdale, where the Sisters of Charity taught generations of young women.

Photo: Spencer Field

**Jewish Community Center of High Bridge located on Nelson Avenue between West 167th and West 168th Street.** Jewish families in **Highbridge** attended services here at this Orthodox Synagogue on the High Holidays and several generations of young men were Bar Mitzvahed here.

All in all, religious activity was highly visible in the Bronx of the 40s and 50s. For most Bronxites however, their religious affiliation was chosen at birth and worn lightly...Bronxites tended not to be the most orthodox in either practice or belief, no matter what their label. By the mid-50s, the old-country orthodoxy, Jewish or Catholic, was fading fast and the younger generation found it hard to follow the traditional rules. Jews rode cars to synagogue and rarely, if at all, obeyed the dietary laws. Catholics bent the rules equally and found their youngest congregants more and more lax in observance of the Church's doctrine. Still, Bronxites felt deeply about the cultural importance of having some religion, even if only a surface obedience to their faith. The family and the neighborhood still expected the young men and women to follow the well beaten path to church or synagogue...and most did.

**Our Lady of Victory, located at Webster Avenue and Claremont Parkway.**

# Bronx Celebrity Interviews

The Bronx has been the birthplace and childhood home of many well-known people, most of whom carry happy memories of their early years. In the following pages we offer some observations and stories from an assortment of people in the entertainment industry, government and business. Remember, when these men and women lived in the Bronx they were, for the most part, just neighborhood kids whose future renown wasn't yet apparent. Colin Powell, for example, unloaded trucks for pocket money and played the familiar games when he lived on Kelly Street... his spectacular career in the military wasn't even imagined in those years. Red Buttons went to PS 44 on Prospect Avenue along with thousands of other Bronx kids, and only dared dream of a show business future.

The famous faces in this section generally agree that the Bronx shaped them in some way, and most give some credit to that early period for their later achievement. But their stories are strikingly familiar to all the other Bronx folks, who went to school and worked at less dazzling jobs but who have equally happy stories to tell about the borough of their birth.

NOTE: Some of these interviews came from the WLIW program <u>The Bronx: The Way It Was</u> broadcast in 1996. Other interviews were conducted especially for this book by the authors.

# Red Buttons

1929 saw the Hoovers move to Washington, the Roosevelts move to Albany, and Chiwatts move to the Bronx. Not just the Bronx. The **Tremont Avenue, Crotona Park North** section of the Bronx. God's little green acres. There was a movie theater on the **Grand Concourse** called **Loew's Paradise**. And that's what The Bronx was when I saw it in 1929. Paradise.

When we got to **176th Street** and **Southern Boulevard**, the van could hardly make it up the hill to number 853, between **Southern Boulevard** and **Marmion**. The second building off **Marmion Avenue** on the right side of the street was the house we moved to. 'Top'a the world ma. Top'a the world.' The hill going up from **Southern Boulevard** to **Marmion Avenue** was awesome. I'm talking about a Mount Everest climb. It was foolhardy to attempt it without a backpack, a supply of oxygen, and a St. Bernard dog with a keg of seltzer. People dropped like flies during the ascent. By the time they made it to the top, you looked like the hunchback of Notre Dame. When

people reached the top of the hill, they planted a flag. Just beyond **Marmion Avenue**, the block between **Marmion Avenue** and **Prospect Avenue, on 176th Street**, in the East Bronx, was as close as I am ever going to get to Shangri La.

It is exactly 61 years ago, in August 1929, that I first set eyes on what, for me, had become, along with show business, a lifelong love affair. Stuck plumb in the middle of a street full of private homes with lawns and a galaxy of flowers, old age rest homes, a school of nuns, the **Sacred Heart Academy**, magnificent oak and maple trees, was the Studio. The Studio. The old silent movie **Biograph Studio**, whose hallowed walls had seen the likes of Mary Pickford and the Gish sisters. The stuff that dreams are made of.... I used Shangri La descriptively, because, like in the movie, when I stepped into that street, I came in from the storm, and into the calm. I felt a spiritual communion between myself and the silence that enveloped me. Ten years after the constant din and cacophony of the Lower East Side had left me shell shocked, I felt like I was back in my mother's arms. My first, and until that moment, last experience with complete tranquility. I had found my lost lullaby. For the next six years, that block was my cradle. And I rocked it. With my dreams.

The Bronx was my Ellis Island. And like Mom and Pop before me, I entered my new world eager to fulfill my destiny. My romance with The Bronx has never ended.

*The Museum of Modern Art Film Stills Archives*
**Biograph Studios, 176th Street and Marmion Avenue.**

My apartment building was four stories. We lived on the first floor, in the front. And that was very important. There was a big difference between the front and the back. You know, it was like the caste system. Really, I'm not kidding you. You know, when you were able to say, *'Oh, we live in the front,'* you know, it was wonderful. Of course, they tell some great stories about that. There're two women talking. *'Did you see, did you see what happened in Russia? Did you see?' 'Oy, I didn't see, I live in the back.'* I mean, that used to be the joke....

When I moved to The Bronx it was, in that neighborhood, about 95% Jewish. Although, we did have a Negro family living on the corner — The Hanes family. We were all friends. Every one of us. We all went to school together, we hung out together. We were in the same little gang together. And thank God, we grew up without the bigotry, without the prejudice. And it was good. It was good.

Most of us who were Jewish came out of orthodox homes. And if you did, I mean, you went to the synagogue, you went to the temple with your father. There was no other way. I mean, the Day of Atonement, there was a Day of Atonement. You know. And I was already singing in choirs. So on the High Holidays, I was singing.

I went to **Public School 44, 176th Street** and **Prospect Avenue.** Our colors were green and white. I wrote the school song. *'To each loyal son and daughter; faithful to the core; let's drink a toast with seltzer water; to P.S.44.'* I was the poet laureate of my block. I loved public school. I clowned my way through public school. I was the class clown. I was the clown on the street corner. I knew, and everybody else knew that went to school with me, that I was going to be in show business someday. There was no doubt about it. I was in the school plays; I sang 24 hours a day.

In 1935, I was going to **Evander Childs High School** in The Bronx. Wonderful school. Bob Hope's Delores went to **Evander Childs.** Whenever we meet we sing the school song. *'Fight for Evander; Evander must win; Fight for Evander; Never give in; We'll do the best, boys; You do the rest, boys; Fight for Evander; Rah, rah, rah.'* And we kiss and hug.

I was on my way home on the Third Avenue El and I was reading the Daily Mirror. At that time, the paper was two cents. And I saw a little ad: *Boy Wanted. Singer. Apply.* And it gave the address and what time. And it was that day. And if I stayed on the **Third Avenue El**, instead of going home, I could make it. So I had a choice. Do I run home and pick up my two little sheets of music, or do I run down and fake it? So I ran downtown, the Strand Theater building, and I met the man who was auditioning the boy singer. His name was Denny Moore. He was the orchestra leader and drummer. I walked in, he took one look at me, and the man went to pieces. I had my little green sweater on; I had my blue eyes, my freckles, my nose which has dropped a little bit since then— my red hair. And he said to me, *'Yeah, yeah. You sing, kid? You sing, kid?'* I said, *'Yeah.'* He says, *'Well, what? what?'* So I named a few things. I said, *'I haven't got my music; I was just comin' home from school.'* He had a piano player there and I sang for him. I think it was *'My mom, I love her. My mom, you'd love her. Who wouldn't love her? My mom.'* I had him crying in the first eight bars. He says, *'Ok, you got the job.'* He sent me down to a costuming house. They put me in a Phillip Morris bell hop's uniform. You remember the little uniform, with the little hat? *'Call for Phillip Morris.'* And I came back with the uniform, and he said, *'Oh, this is perfect. Perfect! What's your name?'* I said, *'Aaron Chiwatt.'* He said *'Oh, my God.'* I said, *'What happened?'* He says, *'This is an Irish place. It's called Ryan's. It's in City Island. They* have an Irish clientele. *You can't be Aaron Chiwatt. You could be Aaron O'Chiwatt,'* he said, *'But I got the name for ya, kid. We're gonna call you Buttons, because of the uniform.'* That's how I got my name. I got the job. They were calling me Buttons. I sang with this band. I was doing little odd jobs around the place. One day, it became, *'Hey, Red; hey, Buttons; hey, Red Buttons.'* So in 1935, Red Buttons was born. That summer was my first year in the Catskills. First year, dollar and a half a week, room and board. I sent my mother a buck a week. With the other fifty cents, I went crazy — wine, women, malteds. It was hilarious. That was the start. Right now we're doing this interview in '98, so this is my 63rd year in show business.

I saw my first game in '29; it was that great Yankees team. It was heaven. **Yankee Stadium.** You'd <u>cry</u> for fifty cents to sit in the bleachers. You'd save up and sit in the bleachers. Then once in a while they'd take kids from the public school or from the Boy's Club. Any kid that lived in The Bronx who was not a Yankee fan, there was a big problem — a mental problem.

We used to get to Yankee games first class: hitch-hiking on trolley cars. On the back of the car. That's what we used to do. We'd go cross town, from the **East Bronx,** down to **Yankee Stadium,** which was right off the **Grand Concourse.** As you know. I used to get a thrill every time I walked into **Yankee Stadium**. I still do. I went to see a ball game there not too long ago. I still do. I walk through and something just happens. It's — I get the same feeling when I land at JFK. I mean, these are my roots, this is home. This is home.

Third Avenue — I grew up with the **Third Avenue El.** I loved the **Third Avenue El.** I used to stand in front, in the front car on the **Third Avenue El.** And like Calvin, of Calvin and Hobbes, I would spin my dreams as we rolled, at the ferocious rate of 35 miles an hour, going from the Lower East Side up to **177th Street** and **Tremont Avenue.** I just absolutely loved it. I mean, it was a nickel high on the **Third Avenue El.** The **Third Avenue El** is one of my fondest remembrances when I was a kid. I didn't like the subway but I loved the **Third Avenue El.**

My fondest memory of The Bronx is the street that I hung out on, in back of the studio, on **176th Street.** That's been with me since 1929. I can shut my eyes and see it vividly. For whatever reason, it's been with me all my life. I just loved that piece of terra firma. I dreamed in back of that studio. I climbed the walls. I used to sneak into the studio. They wired the studio up for sound around 1930, and started shooting again. I was there day and night. Whenever my mother needed me for anything, she knew I was on the wall. Whatever movie they were shooting at the studio, it was always, *'Hey, kid, get off that wall! You're in the shot!'* Ralph Bellamy shot a picture there once. Tossed a quarter at me; said, *'Hey kid, get me a pack'a cigarettes.'* It was a dime at that time. I came back with the cigarettes. He said, *'Keep the change.'* Fifteen cents. That was, believe me, big. Big. You could go to the movies for a dime. Years later, Ralph Bellamy and I became friends. There was a romance about the whole thing. It helped my dreams. It helped my dreams. It was Hollywood. I didn't think of it as **176th Street** in The Bronx. I thought of it as: Hey, I'm in Hollywood right now. I'm at MGM. I'm with Warner Brothers. I'm with Jimmy Cagney. I'm with the boys.

My fondest, most romantic memory of The Bronx was the old **Biograph Studio** on **176th Street** between **Marmion** and **Prospect Avenue.** That's where I spun my dreams. That's where I entertained the guys. That's where I knew, I knew there was no stopping me. I just had to be in show business.

# Judd Hirsch

After we moved away from **176th Street**, I hung out in a neighborhood called **Claremont Parkway** and a couple of blocks from **Bathgate Avenue**. You remember the novel, Billy Bathgate? Dutch Schultz also lived in this neighborhood. I hung out in a building on **Claremont Parkway.** There was a Chinese laundry in the cellar. We all used to hang out in there. That cellar was where Dutch Schultz kept all his ammunition. I remember when we were kids and this big car would roll up. These guys would get out and they'd go down to the cellar. None of us ever knew what it was, until one day my brother told me. He said, *'You know why these guys come around here? They're all Dutch Schultz' guys. All the ammunition's down there in the cellar.'*

I was born in The Bronx and moved several times before settling in what is known as the **West Bronx.** Now, the **Grand Concourse,** to us, was the magic line between one kind of place and another. The magic line was a grand boulevard. To live on the **Concourse** meant you had to have some kind of station, or some kind of money. My aunt lived in a place called **Roosevelt Gardens,** which was a very interior gardened apartment house. So it was kind of a specialty to visit her. We lived on

**171st** and **Walton Avenue** in an apartment house. A red brick apartment house. That's where we finally settled before we moved out of The Bronx. It was a little place with a stoop with concrete planters and railings and two entrances. It was a tenement, a real tenement. But it had a kind of a splendor to it because you felt that you were entering a special kind of a building rather than just off a street. So all of the games that we played had to do with your building. We played stoopball, punchball, slapball, boxball. And they all took place within about four feet of the stoop. In the summer time there wasn't any air conditioning. Air conditioning was a cool night on the street, or up on the roof with a radio. When air conditioning finally came in, we couldn't afford it. So we just tried to get as cool as we could anywhere. Lucky ones got away for the summer. We were stuck.

My father was supposedly the Super but he was actually working on the atomic bomb. He didn't know it. He was away. We were more or less the Super of this apartment house until he came back. He got a good job. He was an electrician and helped in the manufacture of the atomic bomb.

It was an interesting neighborhood. Our house had a schoolyard right across the street. The school was at the end of the street. On the opposite side were individual wooden houses and then a steep drop down to the next street. I believe it was **Webster Avenue.** It had an enormously long flight of stairs that went all the way down. If you were brave, you walked down the entire flight never expecting to come back up again. Well, there is an enormous hill down on the other side of the school. I think it was **P.S. 52.**

I spent my teen years in The Bronx. Those were probably the most formidable years. My teen years started with 1950. The boys had come home from the war. There was an enormous Bronx migration to Long Island. I was trying to make it through high school and keep my friends in the neighborhood. While everybody else was getting interested in all those wonderful things like popular records, girls, and the popular trends of the time, I was one of those people who rejected them all. We were into semi-classical music. We were into reading weird books for our age. You know, philosophy, and those writers who were way ahead of us. We were talking about people who weren't even American. We were reading foreign novels, and going to foreign movies. The English and Swedish movies came to America. Art houses started at the time. The **Loew's Paradise** up by the **Grand Concourse** was the most flamboyant movie house in The Bronx. It had stars in the ceiling that moved. And I believe you could see the heavens. If you didn't particularly care for the love scene, you'd watch the stars. Next to it was the **Ascot.** It was a little art movie house. We went there more often. On **Fordham Road** you could get a thing which my mother called a frappe which was an ice cream soda. The idea was to take a long walk from **171st Street** to **Fordham Road**, and meet the girls. It was a crossroads. And there was **Edgar Allan Poe's House,** just above **Fordham Road,** surrounded by a little park. The idea was to go there for small concerts, where you'd be standing next to people that you didn't know, listening to the music and wondering if you could 'make out.' You know? It was a frightening time for a teenager.

I went to **DeWitt Clinton**, which was an all boys high school. One of the reasons I went there was because a friend told us *'You can make it through.'* He says, *'Nothing to distract you.'* Little did I know that nothing to distract me was because it was all boys.

I believe that when you're born, you're born to a place, a religion, and a baseball team. And the **New**

*Theatre Historical Society of America, Michael R. Miller Collection*

**York Yankees** had the best players. When I was born, they were already great. And their greatness went on through the War. I even kept track of those people who replaced the baseball players during the War. I remember thinking that the great records were made before the war. Now we had a whole bunch of other guys who had no experience. The Yankees were the necessary team to root for. It was like a club. It was like an identification. We didn't wear anything. We never wore Yankee hats or Yankee uniforms. You could wear something that looked like it, but we didn't. If there was somebody in your neighborhood that wasn't a Yankee fan, that person was an outcast, and that was a dangerous individual. That person had to be confronted. I went to Coney Island to live with a close family friend for the summer. My cousin was my best friend. He was a Dodger fan. He would take me to his friends in the schoolyard down the street, and I would be stopped because they'd know me, and they'd say, *'You a Dodger fan?'* And I'd say, *'Yes'*. It was a great cover. I even tried to like the Dodgers so I could feel like I wasn't lying. But as soon as I got back to The Bronx, I was back rooting again for the Yankees. I went to ball games and loved those players.

I remember **Shorehaven** was just developed when I was a teenager. My father got a job there when I was seventeen. He was an electrician. They had a big pool and I believe they had a beach; and they also had entertainment. This was another place to go and try to meet interesting people. We always risked something by going to these places. Believe me, we were such chicken kids. I remember there was a place that you could stand on to overlook **Shorehaven**, some kind of precipice or catwalk. And I'd look down into it with my friends and say, *'How's my hair?'* At the time, we used to have pompadours.

He said *'Looks good.'* I said, *'It's too short, it's too short, I just got a short haircut, I can't go down there. I can't go down there.'* *'Come on, come on, your hair's fine.'* *'No, your hair's fine, mine's not good. It's just not good. I can't go down there today.'* *'When?'* I said, *'Gimme a couple'a weeks.'* He said, *'Your father works here.'* I said, *'Ok, ok, I'll go down, I'll go down with ya.'* *'All right, let's go.'* So we went down there. I remember that Jack Carter, the comedian, was one of the entertainers there.

**Orchard Beach** was a place on the Sound, on Long Island Sound in the Northern Bronx. There weren't any other beaches in The Bronx. You got on this crowded bus. Everybody had a radio. There were as many people as there were radios. You couldn't see the faces because of the radios. They were big, portable radios with tubes and thousands of batteries. This was before the transistor radio. Everybody knew that they were going to get to the beach, plant the radio, which was like the head-stone of your blanket, and try to walk on what they called sand which was really many little pebbles.

My father had a car. My father always had a car. We lived smack in the middle of The Bronx. So of course, part of our life was about parking. The idea was to park your car so that nobody hit the fender.

We always had a used car. Your know, like it was 1950, we had a `36, with a wagging fender. On Sundays we would start to drive upstate. We'd go out about a half an hour before we'd have to come back and have dinner. And at that time, the speed limit was 35 miles an hour.

In The Bronx there was tremendous competition. Stickball was probably the most important sport at that time. There was another hierarchy. There were older guys, who were no longer teenagers, who should be working and for some reason weren't. They hung out. They were called the hang-out artists. They were about twenty years old. They looked like they were forty, but they weren't. They were only a couple of years older than us, but they dressed and they smoked. If they came down to the schoolyard and we had a game going, they simply showed up, looked at us until we stopped and walked off the court. We moved to Queens in 1954. I thought I'd probably never be back in The Bronx again, but something kept drawing me back. So I used to come back all the time. In fact, I would come back weekly so that we could continue playing our games on the court. You couldn't play stickball in somebody else's schoolyard. You had to play where you were trained.

# Mal Z. Lawrence

The Bronx was a very special place, as far as I was concerned. We had about sixty young boys growing up just in my building alone. Every building was almost like a little city unto itself. We had seasons. We had baseball season, football season, hockey season, roller skate season. We had marble season, ticket season. Tickets were legal tender when I was a kid. Mickey Mantle tickets, Willie Mays tickets, Duke Snider tickets. Baseball cards. I had a drawer full of them. I had every ticket. And then my mother threw them out. I cannot believe that she threw out those tickets!

Living in an elevator building, meant your father was making a real good living. My father earned enough to live in an elevator building. I lived in apartment 3E, **200 Marcy Place,** which was right off the **Concourse.** The thing that I always remembered about my apartment building were the smells, the different smells of cooking. We had Italian people, Jewish people, German cooking, and there was Swedish cooking. Few people had telephones. It was a big priority to get a telephone. It was kind of a nice life, a very tight community minded life.

**Posing at Orchard Beach.**

I was a sports nut. I played every sport. Sports in The Bronx consisted of games like *slug* and *saloogie.*

In The Bronx, everybody talked to each other. I went to **William Howard Taft High School.** I was always trying to be the class clown. I would do things in school. I had a dossier with the Principal about 12" thick. I mean, I was a bad boy. I was just trying to be different, trying to cut up. I remember once we were in history class and this teacher had a map that comes down like a window shade. She pulled it and it seemed to rip off and fall to the ground. And I said, *'Well, what do you expect? Look how heavy the world is. How can that little hook hold up'.* Well, needless to say, I was in the Principal's office. We had a teacher who used to lisp, and she used to *th-thay th-thing.* She was a *Th-thpanish* teacher. And whenever *th-the'd— Th-the'd* always do one of those kinda things. And I said, *'Pardon me, could you give out raincoats while you're talking, please?'* She was spraying everybody, and— again, down to the Principal's office.

I wanted to go to **Dewitt Clinton** when I was a kid, because that was a boys school and they had great basketball, baseball teams and a football team, which Taft never had. However, **Taft** had girls. I tried out for every team. I just wanted that jacket. I wanted that team jacket. Oh, with the big T, you know. **"Taft"** written on the back. Even if you were on the track team, or baseball team, you had the same jacket as the basketball team, which was the most popular team in our school. I think it's the most popular in most every school, except the Big 10 schools, which has those big football schools. I wanted that jacket because the girls would look at you if you had that jacket on. You know, you were a big guy in town, in the school. You were athletic, and that always attracted more girls.

When I was a kid, a really young boy in my teens, I lived on **184th** and **Southern Boulevard,** right opposite the **Bronx Zoo,** which of course, is probably one of the greatest zoos. And I never went. Never went to the **Zoo.** My father made a little more money, so we moved to the **Grand Concourse** area, up on **Marcy Place.** And that next weekend after we moved in, my mother said, *'Let's go to the Zoo.'* I said, *'We lived right across the street and you never went to the Zoo. Why would you wanna travel half way across The Bronx now to go to the Zoo?' 'We're going to the Zoo.'* And we went to the **Bronx Zoo.** The first weekend we moved, we went back to the **Bronx Zoo.** Something drew us into it. We had parks everywhere. There was **Claremont Park** and **Joyce Kilmer Park,** and **Franz Siegal Park.** There was always a park. As a Jew in The Bronx, it was very important to have a park. On Yom Kippur and Rosh Hashonah everybody met in the park. I lived in a predominantly Jewish neighborhood. Men would be playing checkers, kids would be running around on the grass, and other kids were playing ball. The parks were really nice. You could walk in the park at all times, and you felt safe, never threatened. We loved the parks. That was the only time we had any kind of contact with nature. Otherwise, it was just cement and asphalt, and curbs, and fire escapes. But that was the best part about The Bronx. We had a lot of parks, a lot of trees, lotta grass. It was really a great place.

Crawford's Department Store at the E. 149th Street hub.

I remember going to the **Paradise** and admiring the blinking stars. It was very romantic, up in the balcony with your date. You always had your arm around her. When the picture was over, two hours later, you'd walk out with your arm permanently frozen in that same position.

And I remember going to a vaudeville show on **Fordham Road,** in a place called the **Windsor Theater.** I saw Cab Calloway there, Lena Horne, Danny Kaye. That's when vaudeville was... Well, that'll give you an idea how old I am.

I used to love to ride my bike in The Bronx. Oh, man! I had a Schwinn, a red Schwinn. And I used to pedal fast down the hill. There was no traffic, so you didn't worry. It had every kind of terrain you ever wanted. And there was always a lot. There was always a lot that had ragweed, and you would sneeze when you'd go by.

There was a place called **Freedomland.** That is where **Co-Op City** is right now in The Bronx. I did a weekend there with Tony Bennett. We had just been touring around 1965. He was appearing two nights at **Freedomland.** The crowds were enormous.

I remember having more baseball suits in my closet than regular suits. I only had one regular suit. It was a blue serge. Every kid had a blue serge suit because it didn't show the dirt, and it would last for a long, long time. It was made like iron. I bought a suit from **Crawford's Department Store.**

It's a beautiful borough and I have very fond memborries of growing up there. "

# DION

I come from a macho Italian neighborhood. I spent the first 19 years of my life standing under a street light on the street corner. You know, a cigarette dangling out of my mouth. My eye was tearin', my lip was burnin', but I was cool. I just stood there and said, *'You talkin` to me?'* You know, you have to, like stand there, like look like you know everything. It was kind of a code in the neighborhood. And it was like a commune, a community, you know; it was just an Italian community. There was one Puerto Rican family in my neighborhood. And they lived about a block and a half from us. Emilio. I mean, cool people. But we used to use them as a point of reference. It was like, *'Hey, Joey could throw a football. Man. Far— he could throw a football from here half way to the Puerto Rican's house.'* You know? It was like a point of reference.

I was living in The Bronx and all you heard when I was growin` up was Jimmy Roselli, Don Cornell, Jerry Vale, you know, Frank Sinatra, those kind of guys. And I caught this station coming out of Newark, New Jersey. Don Larkin. And he would play some country music. You know, and I heard stuff like, *'Well, I left my home down on the rural route;*

*Told my pa I'm goin' steppin' out; Gimme the honky tonk blues; Yeah, the honky tonk blues.'* I said, *'What's that?'* And I started a Hank Williams collection. I owned about 75 records, and I knew every one of his songs by the time I was about 14 years old. Even his Luke the Drifter series. I just got totally taken with that. Then, somewhere along the line, I heard from Willie Green. He'd have his guitar. I'd follow him. And when I was going to **Junior High School 45,P.S. 45,** the teachers thought I didn't know what I wanted to do. But I couldn't wait to get out of school to go sit with Willie Green, because I guess he was into all those John Lee Hooker records and stuff. Sonny Boy Williamson and Lightning Hopkins. But I followed this guy around. Reverend Gary Davis lived in The Bronx. Later on, I went down to see him, because I really got hooked into this kind of music. Growing up in The Bronx had wonderful characters. They're bigger than life, So I started writing about them. Like <u>Runaround Sue</u> and <u>The Wanderer.</u> That was written about a guy named Jackie Burns. He had tatoos all over him. You know, like Flo, Janie, Mary. He had Rosie on his chest. He was like a walking billboard. You know, he was, *'I'm dating Nunzio's...'* you know, he was like that. He was worth a song *'Flo on my left arm; Mary on my right; Janie is the girl I'll be with tonight; Little girl asked me which one I loved the best; I tear open my shirt, show her Rosie on my chest; I'm the wanderer; Hey, I'm the wanderer; I roam around, around.'* It was worth a song. This guy used to swagger down the middle of the street. So The Bronx was full of these interesting people. You could be writing about them all for a lifetime.

Back in The Bronx you had Joe the grocer. It wasn't like today, with the supermarkets and checkout girls. They don't know anybody. Joe the grocer knew the 500 families that he served. You know, he knew who was born, who got married, who died, who went to jail, who's on vacation, who graduated, the whole bit. And he was emotional about everything. I went in one time and I said, *'Joe, give me a mortadella sandwich on white bread with American cheese.'* He said, *'You're gonna ruin my mortadella with American cheese? I'll give you one. Marie!'* He calls his wife. The wife comes out from the back stirring peppers. He says, *'My wife, she makes a good sandwich, and you don't use American bread and you use provolone.'* He makes the sandwich; all the meat is hanging out of the bread. When he slipped it over to me, you know, I— I opened it up and I started folding the mortadella back into the sandwich. He takes the sandwich away from me and unfolds it. He says, *'No the meat's gotta hit your mouth first, then the bread, then the cheese,'* I said, *Why don't you hang the sandwich on the wall?'* It was like a work of art, you know what I mean? It was a very personal thing, you know? My parents used to send me down to Joe the grocer's and say, *'Tell'im charge it.'* And he had the little slip. He would take it out and he would write five fifty; milk, cheese, whatever? And that's the way it was. It was like a community. A commune. You know? A bunch'a crazy Italians. I had about 250 Italian relatives, that all talked at once. Listening was a whole different concept. I learned that when I was in my thirties, to start listening.

**Tally's Pool Room** was a hang out. And I'll never forget, when Willie Moscone came to play Joe Rocko. What a day in The Bronx that was. And Moscone ran 87 balls straight. It was thrilling. And then he showed some trick shots. And all the guys in the neighborhood who were aspiring pool players all wanted to be Willie Moscone five minutes after he left. And we all grabbed our pool sticks and everybody ran off to their different pool rooms and grabbed a table. There were more ripped pool tables after Moscone left, and everybody was tryin` these shots.

My father was kind of like a Johnny Weismuller. And he used to take me to **Botanical Gardens.** Used to call it bare ass beach— BAB. And we used to dive off the mountains. We'd just strip down and dive off the mountains. He'd say, *'Always check the water before you dive.'* He used to tell me the story. When I was a kid, my friend Johnny Scumbazzo' or whatever his name was, *'dove in, and he got his head caught in a milk can, so ya check what's under the water.'*

I went down to the Apollo Theater. And the Apollo Theater had great jazz, rhythm and blues musicians, horn players. They had a big orchestra. And the orchestra would be playing. I didn't have a horn section in The Bronx. So I rounded up a bunch of guys and they were like a poor man's horn section. So I would sing, *'I love a girl and Ruby is her name'.* And they would *'Ruby, Ruby, Ruby, baby. '* They were like my horn section. Ya get it? A lotta that stuff was tryin` to imitate the horn sections down at the Apollo Theater — for me.

I belonged to the **Fordham Baldies** gang. Just a bunch'a guys that hung together and kind of protected the neighborhood. If there was a guy abusing a girl, we'd beat the hell out of him. I mean, we beat guys up that beat up women. That was unacceptable back then. We were rowdy. We used to have these parties, and a lot of the songs that I recorded back then, like The Wanderer, and Lovers Who Wander, and Donna the Prima Donna, all those kinda songs came out of those parties. We would just be bangin` on cardboard boxes. I used to give people parts, and they'd sing for hours, and I'd make up words and stuff like that.Then I'd go down and make the record. When I brought the record back and played it for the **Fordham Baldies**, they'd say, *'You ruined it. It was better at Louie— Louie Spike's party,'* It was a feeling of belonging, for me. It was such a huge family — and at times I felt like I didn't belong. I think being with the guys, with the **Fordham Baldies** was a feeling of belonging at that age. The **Fordham Baldies** wasn't an athletic club. They were just rough guys. There were different gangs for different neighborhoods. There were the *'Young Sinners,'* the *'Scorpions,'* the *'Harlem Redwings',* the *'Golden*

*Guineas,' the 'Imperial Hoods,' the 'Italian Barettas',* They all had different sections mapped out where they came from. The **Fordham Baldies,** we got the name from the— the American Eagle. Nobody wanted to shave their heads back then. It was important to have that loop of hair hangin` right down in front of your face.

I remember riding the subway a lot when I started dating Sue, before I got my first royalty check, and I bought a 1957 silver-grey Thunderbird with black leather bucket seats. I rolled down **Crotona Avenue** like I owned it. *'Ey. Yo. Sue. Take ya to the best places in town.'* **White Castle.** We'd go up there. But before that, when I had to, I'd take the **Third Avenue El,** or the **D train** downtown.

It was like the beat generation. I would like to go down to The Village. I knew a couple of the guys and we started reading some of the philosophers like Plato. We all grew goatees, had bongo drums. Conga. *'Hey, man, you bringin` you conga'* We'd get on the **Fordham Road D Train** and ride down to The Village. We wanted to be beatniks. I was young then, about fifteen. As a kid, growing up on the streets of The Bronx, I remember that the church was like the hub of the community. We had **Mount Carmel.** That was the hub of the Italian community. Then there was **Mount Saint Michael**. That was the Irish community. We had the synagogue over in Pelham Bay and that was for the Jewish community.

I remember when they used to have the feasts. And they were celebrating Saint Gennaro or Saint

St. Anthony's Feast.

Anthony, whatever it might be. They wheeled Saint Anthony, down the streets; he's like 20 feet high. I'm standing there with Ricky, and we're on the street corner. They're carrying him down the street, with the old guys in double breasted suits, playing trumpets and trombones. *Ya-da-da-da-da.* And the feast is going on, and there's, like two hundred elderly women with black dresses and rosary beads and buns, and they're walking with no shoes on, two thousand of them were there. And then the statue, all the merchants and the people, they run out to the statue and they pin twenty dollar bills, ten dollar bills, five dollar bills on the statue. And I turned to Ricky, I said, *'Ricky, this don't make sense.'* He said, *'Dion, who owns the statue? This makes sense. If we could get one of those statues, we could work* **Southern Boulevard.**' So after that, we were looking to rob a statue. Will the real Saint Anthony stand up? Sometimes the religion didn't make sense? I didn't know at the time that a lot of those traditions were visual signs pointing to a higher reality. I only saw what was going on.

All I remember about high school is that I liked to look good during lunch hour, because I knew Susan was going to be sitting at table number five. That was it. I don't remember too much about the other stuff. I was pretty restless, irritable, and discontented at that age. I went to seven high schools. My world was totally taken up with music and Susan. I'm still married to Susan. We're married 32 years, and have three beautiful daughters.

# ROBERT KLEIN

When I was six months old, my parents moved to the North Bronx. **Decatur Avenue,** the last block. It ended there. The beauty of this community, when one thinks of it now, is that 86 families lived in my building. There were, easily, several hundred children in the building, and probably a dozen exactly my age. *'Ma, I'm goin` ta Phil's house.'* All you do is go down the hall. Nobody had to drive you. And I think the women, too, knew how to support each other. There was a very close relationship between women — as was usual then, and probably still exists. In the warm weather, the women and some of the older folks would put out their folding chairs and sit in front of the building on the hill.

I went two years to **Junior High School 80.** I skipped the eighth grade, went 7SP, which was an advanced course, to 9SP; went from top of the class right to mediocre, with geniuses in my classes. And then my father wanted me very much to take the test for **The Bronx High School of Science.** All my friends were going to **DeWitt Clinton,** which was a

**Robert Klein on the Ted Mack Amateur Hour.**

boys school. 4,000 boys, one session. It was traditional in my neighborhood that you went to **Clinton** and the girls went to **Evander Childs,** which was co-ed. My sister went there. So I walked out after half the exam. I have no idea whether I could've made it or not. I'm sorry because I think **The Bronx High School of Science** is probably as good a high school — certainly public high school — as there is in the United States. And **DeWitt Clinton,** at that time, was too easy.

Now, once I went to junior high school, in the warm, fairer outdoor weather, I took to hanging out at **Mosholu Parkway.** On a warm spring night, there may be 150 or 200 teenagers. Mostly good kids. My group and I sang rock and roll on the parkway. Doo wop. We were called the *Teen Tones.* We did make the Ted Mack Amateur Hour in 1957.

The neighborhood was quite remarkable. There was a competition between Brooklyn and The Bronx. My father had a lot of cousins who lived in Brooklyn. Whenever we went there we got lost. Whenever they came to visit us, they got lost. The first half hour of discussion among the men would be traffic. *'What are you talking about? I told ya exit 24, Parkway. Whadda ya—' 'I told ya Ocean Avenue, Ocean Avenue, Avenue Y.'* You know. None of this made sense to anybody.

You would go downstairs to play curbball, you play boxball by putting spins on a ball. Johnnie on the Pony was a very rough game. Five guys lined up, one on another, like horsies. And the other ones would have to leap onto them and try to make them cave, try to all land on one guy making him cave in.

Horn & Hardart.                                    *Photo: Vanishing Americana*

There was also, in this vertical existence, the, *'Ma, I'm goin' down.'* I never said, *'I goin' out,'* until I bought a country house in 1970. I always wanted a backyard and all that.

The other thing was when the ice cream man came in the warm weather. You'd hear, *'Ma,' 'Ma,' 'Ma,' 'Ma,'* and it reminded me of the Galapagos Islands, when you see one of these nature documentaries. Every parent could tell their own child's frequency of their wail. And the parents would throw out a dime or whatever. If they hated their kid, they'd throw it out with five Gs on it, go right through his head. My mother did it lovingly, in a paper bag, so that it aerodynamically floated down. And even two cents more for a toasted almond. Imagine? Twelve cents was the top of the line ice cream pop.

People were always looking out their window. They related very much to the street below. In warm weather, people would sit out and women would put a pillow on the windowsill and sit there for a long time. It was like the equivalent of a terrace if someone was taken away. Everybody looked out for one another.

*'Ma, I'm goin` down.'* And I'd walk the six flights. We, in fact, leapt six flights. Always took the elevator up (except when it was broken) then... jumped down. You sit on the curb, or on the stoop, and you play cards. Sometimes you could get fooled. For instance, an early March day, a late February day, and suddenly a warm day, hinting of spring. We would take out our baseball gloves, which we hadn't used in months, and have a catch — we'd say, *'have a catch.'.* Summer, last day of school — that's a memory in The Bronx. Ooh. Last day of school. Usually around the 30th. They kept you until the end. Our winter in The Bronx wasn't as long as Toronto or Minneapolis. It was long enough.

Food in The Bronx was going to the Chinese restaurant. I tasted the egg roll, chicken chow mein, fried rice combination plate, and I was hooked for the rest of my life. To this day, I try to find chicken chow mein that can match that old Bronx taste. Every morsel was consumed. And the other special treat on that block was the Horn and Hardart retail takeout shop. The ladies with hairnets, dispensing upside down corn muffins. The baked beans, the spinach, the fish cakes were spectacular. And that was a treat for my mother to bring that home from the retail shop.

# SHARI LEWIS

**Parkchester** never felt like part of The Bronx. **Parkchester** felt like **Parkchester.** It was a totally self-enclosed community. Within the community there were four quadrants. It was owned by Metropolitan Life. In fact, A&E did a wonderful biography on it and they called it *The Projects.* They said, *'Shari comes from the projects.'* Which made me titter, because **Parkchester** was so elegant and safe. It was very middle class. But everybody was aspiring to education. The quadrants were divided. The Jewish community lived near **Young Israel.** The Irish community lived near **St. Helena's.** And what were called 'the regular people' lived in the other two projects. It was a fabulous community in which there were lots of park benches — lots of them — surrounding the circle. Everybody sat out there. And you got to know the children playing in the many playgrounds. There were no cars in my part of **Parkchester.** I lived on **Archer Road.** There was an enormous wide hill that circled down. Great for skating and sleighing. I used to ride down on my father's foot. I would sit on Dad. My father skated until he was 78. He may have skat-

ed after that, but I left the City, so I didn't see the evidence of it. But I used to sit on Daddy's foot, and we would come down this enormous hill. Perfectly safe community. My mother was very protective. She let me play outside in the evening. It was a great place to grow up; I really loved it.

I went to **P.S. 102.** My mother was a teacher at **P.S. 106,** which was on the other side of **Parkchester.** It was a place where there was a movie theater under the subway that was eleven cents — and you got a comic book. I loved everything about **Parkchester,** except the travel to the places where I knew I had to go. I started going downtown for my dancing and other lessons when I was eight. And the subways were a bummer. A bummer. Oh, it was the elevated, of course. It was terrible. It took too long to get anywhere. I went to **Music** and **Art High School.**

Well, I learned everything in The Bronx. I learned to horseback ride in **Pelham Bay Park.** I learned to bicycle — bicycling from **Parkchester** to **Honeywell Avenue,** where Grandma lived. Grandma had moved to **Honeywell Avenue,** which is right near the zoo. So my Papa and I, every Friday night, would bicycle first to the zoo, and then to the grocery store to buy food for Grandma. And then we'd bring the food to **Honeywell Avenue,** where all of the many cousins would descend for Friday night dinner. It was terrific.

I went to **Herman Ridder Junior High School, P.S. 102** was nice. And there were some wonderful

> **Note: Shari died on August 3, 1998, before this book was published. Her credits include: a dozen Emmys, a Peabody award, the John F. Kennedy Center Award for Excellence and Creativity, seven Parents' Choice Awards, the Action for Children's Television Award, and in 1995 the new ROM-MIE award for her CD-ROM "Lamb Chop Loves Music."**

teachers there, Mrs. Kirschner, particularly, who started putting me in all the plays. It was a time of good teaching. At **Herman Ridder Junior High**, I was in 'The Rapids'. And so we were— we considered ourselves pretty spiffy. And there was a lot of unconscious competition. The teachers were wonderful. Unconscious competition? I don't know. A lot of competition.

It was an era of good teaching. Teachers didn't have to be policemen, which, of course, makes all the difference in the world. And Mrs. Rothstein at **Herman Ridder** used to pull me out of the classroom constantly to read the Bible in the auditoriums. And to this day, I know the Psalms and Genesis — I mean, I'm really well versed, thank you to Mrs. Rothstein. Sid Oaken, who ran an award winning newspaper — he won the Columbia Journal Review, or whatever that is called,

HERMAN RIDDER J.H.S.

each year, he threw me off the paper in my second year of the school, and said, *'You're gonna be an entertainer. The fact that you write is irrelevant. Concentrate on what you're doing.'* You know, they were focussed teachers. *'You belong in* **Music** *and* **Art High School.'** *'Your musicality is swell; but you play badly. Bring a bag lunch, I will give*

**Parkchester.**

*you a piano lesson all year at lunch time.'* And he did so. And I got into **Music** and **Art**, thanks to him.

My first job was all around **Parkchester,** in schools, because many of the principals were friends of my parents. Sid Siegelschiffer and other people from The Bronx had big schools, and I did shows in the auditoriums, shows at the churches and synagogues all 'round The Bronx.

My parents were members of the Orthodox community. But we weren't terribly observant. We were culturally, historically, and socially very much committed to the Jewish way of life, but not committed to the traditions in the home. That was true in most of the homes around me.

The movie theaters were great. It was the **Loew's American,** up near **Tremont Avenue.** The only problem was getting from my house, at the bottom of **Archer Road,** up to **Tremont Avenue** where you went through a veritable Arctic air tunnel — wind tunnel. It was freezing. And the wind whipped down. And you know, in those days, girls weren't allowed to were slacks. You wore those miserable stockings. Not even black tights, you know? And you were cold. I mean, I remember freezing walking up to the movie theater, **Loew's American.** And then the other theater was the one down under the subway. **Parkchester** was very patriotically involved in the war, as I think every community was. And we had uncles in the war. One uncle was taught Arabic languages because he spoke Hebrew. And he was a spy when Rommel was being chased in Africa. And he fell in love with an Arab girl, which caused some consternation in our family. But we had a lot of members of the family in the war, and we did a lot of bond rallies.

The Bronx was a place where people were aspiring, through education, to get someplace else. It was a place where people were working to educate their children, so they could live in Great Neck. I mean, it was that kind of thing. And I think Brooklyn had more frivolous attitude toward that sort of thing.

# GERALDINE FERRARO

I was eight when my father died. We were living in Newburgh, New York. My mother, because she had to go out to work and didn't have anybody who could take care of me and my brother, sold our house up in Newburg and we moved down to **1148 Longfellow Avenue,** which is in the South Bronx, right off of **Whitlock Avenue.** She moved to that block directly across the street from my aunt, who was also widowed. Her older sister lived there with three of her children, one of whom was also married. So we had a real extended family for me and her and my brother to reach out to and enjoy.

I lived in a three story building. When we first came down from Newburg, I remember walking into the apartment. Our house in Newburg was very big. I walked into the apartment and I was absolutely stunned by how small all the rooms were. I had just lost my father and now I had lost my home. However, it was very nice. It was three bedrooms. A railroad type of apartment with a very small dining room and living room. I had a piano. My mother brought it down from Newburg and put it in the living room. It took up almost the whole living room.

It was an interesting neighborhood. Italian and Irish. There were some Jews on the block. One black family moved in and they actually bought the building I lived in. They lived upstairs. It was a nice neighborhood where everybody was very, very comfortable. The kids all played out in the street. We played stickball in the summer. Actually, boys played more stickball than the girls. We played stoopball and handball and all kinds of boxball. It's amazing what one can do with a spaldeen when you have nothing else to play with. The Bungalow Bar used to come everyday and we'd all hang out and get our ice cream. Duggins used to sell cakes. If there was money for a cake that day — that week — my mother would buy some of those Duggins fresh baked goods. People used to come around with horses for nickel rides. It was a very interesting neighborhood. Kids really did play outside and had a lot of fun.

1102 Longfellow Avenue & Westchester Avenue

I liked to play jacks. In fact, I still like to play. I'll try and teach my grandson how to play it, but I don't think little boys have the dexterity like little girls have.

As a child, I can remember coming home from school. I'd go to my aunt's house, which was right across the street, and wait there until my mother came home from work. As I got older and started travelling on the subway, I went to Marymount College. I had received a scholarship and I remember coming home on the subway, the **Pelham Bay line,** at nine o'clock at night. I'd get on the subway at nine, get to **Whitlock Avenue** at about nine-thirty or so. I'd get off the subway and walk up to **Longfellow Avenue,** which was a big, long block. I would turn on **Longfellow Avenue** at about nine-thirty or a quarter to ten at night. I never worried about my safety. It was funny, my mother would be on the windowsill, which is something that parents used to do back then. They would put a pillow on the windowsill and lean on the window and watch all the activity of kids playing outside and making sure everything was all right.They were like a bunch of guards at all the windows, watching the kids playing games. And my mother would be at that window when I'd come up that street at nine-thirty, twenty of ten at night. She'd be leaning on the pillow, looking out the window, watching for me to make that turn, and she'd say, *'Ger—'* And I'd hear her all the way down the block. Of course, that was a warning to anybody who ever would think of harming me, that my mother was watching. But here she was, less than five feet, a very tiny woman with this authority: *'Ger—'* to let everybody know she was watching. I don't want to give the impression that it was all wonderful.There were unhappy times, too. But it was a safer time for kids. Much safer.

We used to go up to **Southern Boulevard** to the movies. We'd go on Saturday matinees at eleven o'clock in the morning and see some great movies. I can't remember how much it cost, but I don't think it was more than fifty cents, if it was that much. It was probably closer to thirty-five cents. After the movies, we'd all stop at a wonderful bak-ery on the way home. Other kids would stop for candy, but we'd stop for what they called a Charlotte Russe  It was a cupcake loaded with fresh whipped cream that went to a spiral. And it had a cherry on top. Delicious. None of this canned whipped cream stuff. It was real whipped cream. I think it cost about a dime.

**Orchard Beach** was a large beach with lots of people around. We'd bring blankets and  just bake. As you got to be an older teenager, you'd flirt with other teenagers who were around. I'm a good swimmer, and always have been. I used to go to swim. We'd get there at ten, ten thirty, eleven o'clock in the morning and leave at four, four thirty and that was it. My mother expected me home. I didn't go out afterwards. When we went to the beach, we went to the beach. I didn't say to my mother, *'I'm going to the beach,'* and go someplace else. My mother was very strict and I was not allowed to date. **Orchard Beach** was very crowded then and very safe.

The focus of attention when I lived in The Bronx, was the church. You were identified by your parish. *'What parish do you belong to?'* if you saw another Catholic. And it was, *'I belong to St. John up in...'* I don't remember exactly where it is, but I think it's **Westchester Avenue.** It was five or six blocks from where I lived. I told you I didn't date. What I did do was, because my cousins and everybody were in the Second World War and because they joined the Catholic War Veterans, I joined the woman's auxiliary. I would get to meet other people who were slightly older than I. I would get to meet some of the young guys who had just come back from service. Things were focused around the Catholic War Veterans. Dinners that they did, dances they held. Even as a child, I went to **St. Johns** for a very short period of time, I remember learning to do the Irish jig because I was a good dancer, so they taught me the Irish jig for St. Patrick's Day. But it focused around the church and the parish. It's funny. If you're talking to someone now who's my same age category, invariably, they'll say, *'What Parish did you belong to when you lived in The Bronx?'*

The street that was the focus of attention in The Bronx was always the **Grand Concourse.** The Catholic War Veterans Memorial Day parade was always down the **Grand Concourse**. It ended at the **Concourse Plaza** where they would have some sort of an event afterwards.

**Orchard Beach** was a summer getaway. I mean, when you lived in the South Bronx, what do you think, we went away on a cruise? I went to camp. And it worked well. But a summer getaway was **Orchard Beach**. My poor mother never even got to go to **Orchard Beach.** She couldn't afford it. She had to work all summer.

There was a time, right before Christmas when we used to get our Christmas tree the night before Christmas, because they were cheaper then. A Christmas tree was maybe about two or three dollars by Christmas Eve. My mother finally had the money to purchase one. I remember going out one Christmas Eve. She came home from work and she said, *'We're gonna go right out.'* And we went out to **Southern Boulevard**, and we went into a five and ten because she hadn't eaten dinner. She had a piece of cake and a cup of coffee, which was going to be her dinner. Afterwards we would get the Christmas tree and a few last minute items. After finishing she got up to pay, and her purse was gone. I'll never forget the desperation, and how we went into the **Simpson Street Police Station**. And they said, *'Lady, what do you want us to do? It's Christmas Eve.'* And she was desperate. We went home and she then went to her sister who had very little money herself, who was a widow for God knows how many years, with six or seven kids. She managed to give my mother the money she needed. We had a Christmas tree. And I will never forget that Christmas. I will never forget it as long as I live. As much as there are wonderful memories of us together and reaching out, there are a lot of unhappy memories of not having money to pay for different things, and watching the struggle. When I went back to the South Bronx, I saw Mrs. Barker, my landlady, who was 91 at the time. She died about three months later. I was devastated but pleased to know that I had gotten this chance to see her. My reaction as I was standing at the foot of those steps looking up at those kids was: I got out. I got out through a very good education; I got out because my mother worked hard trying to give me a better life than she had; I got out because there were people willing to help me get the education and the scholarships, and to push me ahead. Those people are still there. It wasn't a bad life; it was a good life; because I had a wonderful family. I'm a very lucky person.

# ED KRANEPOOL

I was born on **Castle Hill Avenue,** and I lived there for 17 years. I finally moved out of The Bronx right after signing a baseball contract with the New York Mets in 1962. We lived right off the main road. There were a lot of two-family, three-family homes, tenement houses. It was a lot of fun back in those days. We also had a little playground, which gave you the opportunity to participate in lots of sports. I lived in a three family house above the shoemaker. He had a relative right across the street that owned the barber shop. I could get my shoes fixed pretty quickly, and if I wanted to get my hair cut, his relative, Joe the Barber, did it. I spent a lot of time there. These people really took care of me. Like surrogate fathers, they really watched after me. My life was spent in the playground. The neighborhood was a very close neighborhood. People really looked after one another.

There were plenty of parks. If you went down on the east side there, you had **St. Mary's Park.** Then **A.J.**

**Foy Park,** named after A.J. Foy, who had a great career with Boston and Kansas City. Then if you went into the center of the borough, you had **Crotona Park.** I think it was famous over the years for guys like Rocky Colavito who played in that area. My school had a great field, and of course, we had a great ballplayer coming out of **Monroe High School** prior to myself, whose name was Hank Greenberg. I had the pleasure of meeting Hank before I signed a contract. He was working with the White Sox, and I almost made it to the White Sox but I chose the Mets at that time. We also had **Macombs Dam Park,** which is right along side of **Yankee Stadium.** We played the championship in that park and had a lot of fun. It is unfortunate that they're not parks today. I was really very fortunate back in the fifties and the early sixties to grow up in The Bronx. There was a lot of organized activities. Little League was formed in my area when I was as young as ten years of age. I played Little League baseball. And then, of course, I went on to sandlot baseball in The Bronx. And we had every kind of league imaginable. The New York Federation, The Bronx Umpire's Association, which was called the BUA. After playing three years there, I played in sandlot ball. And we had a number of leagues that played during the week at night and then on the weekends. So I used to play five, six ballgames a week. Back in those days, we had a lot of newspapers. One happened to be the Daily Mirror. We had much fun playing softball for the Daily Mirror Championship. My club in The Bronx won the championship back in the late fifties and the early sixties.

The Bronx was a great place to play. Many fields around the area, and many sponsors. You had YMCAs, leagues where you could play basketball. The police leagues, the PALs. There was always opportunities to play sports which never gave you time to get into mischief.

There were many, many developments in The Bronx. Later on we called them projects. However, the largest development prior to that was **Parkchester**. The trains and the busses both went through the development. I had a lot of relatives that lived in that area. It was kind of upscale. Upscale-medium income. There were high rise buildings, maybe fourteen, fifteen stories up, and many families. And it was a great community. They had a tremendous shopping area. It was like the mini malls they have today, but they had developments around there, a lot of housing. But that was not my area. I was closer to The Bronx **Whitestone Bridge.** It wasn't as developed. I really liked it there. I would pass **Parkchester** all the time on my way to **Monroe High School.** When I think about The Bronx I think about the local delis that we used to visit around school. Whether it would be the candy store, where we would have an egg cream, a chocolate egg cream. I spent many an afternoon in the local candy store, right down from **Monroe High School**. I'd go down every afternoon and get a malted milk shake or an egg cream and a donut. After signing a contract, they all wanted you to come back to the area. I was a big ice cream eater back in those days. Unfortunately, today, being a diabetic, I don't have that luxury anymore. I remember going to **Jahn's** on **Fordham Road** and eating the 'kitchen sink' with three or four of my friends. The 'kitchen sink' was a tremendous bowl of ice cream and you would get an the opportunity to get a second one for free if you finished the first one. Well, obviously, most people couldn't eat the first one. But I think we used to take them at their word, and we'd eat the first one and we'd eat part of the second one. I think we got our money's worth.

I would have a black and white sundae, vanilla ice cream in a tall dish, with chocolate syrup on it. I would have one of those every night. And I'll tell you what, I loved it; I looked forward to it. When we were working out, we always had ice cream, and when I think about working out, I think about **Monroe High School,** and walking down to the El. You had the delicatessen on the corner. Every afternoon, after basketball practice in high school, I had a knish and a cream soda or something like that. By the time I got home, I wasn't very hungry. We had

a routine back in The Bronx. You know, you walked the same walk everyday. People knew who I was, especially when I went to high school, because I had some kind of a recognition factor back in those days. People would wave and wish you good luck because they knew the ball clubs were interested in signing me.

You had the opportunity to go to the movies, which I think was twenty five cents. I had a choice. I could either pay for the movie or ride the bus. I didn't have enough money back in those days to do both. So I'd go to the movie theaters. They were very inexpensive. Saturdays was an all day affair. You got cartoons, the newsreels, and two movies. I remember going there for two movies. You would spend the whole day in the theater. Later on, as you got a little bit older and you started to date, you went to the **Loew's Paradise.**

Most of the dates in The Bronx , on a Saturday night, fancy night, involved going to the movies, and afterwards getting a slice of pizza or something like that. I only went out one night a week. If I did go out in high school it was going to the movies. And if it was really a top date, you might go for pizza afterwards. When I was growing up things were tight. I think most of us in that area really didn't have much money.

My mother ran a strict house. She wanted me home at a decent hour, so most of the girls that I dated lived near the high school, and I lived about twenty- twenty five minutes away so I had to watch my time pretty good. Some nights I would run home, and some nights I was lucky enough to catch the bus and save my energy.

Growing up was fun. I didn't move out until 1962 when I signed a contract with the New York Mets, and I obviously was a **Yankee** fan. I loved the **Yankees** and I loved Mickey Mantle and Yogi and Hank Bauer and Bill Skowran. Back in those days, you were either a Yankee fan or you were the enemy. I never went to Ebbetts Field. I went to the Polo Grounds on a number of occasions and saw some of the great rivalries between the Giants and Dodgers. I played one ball game there later on in my career in high school. I remember fondly going to **Yankee Stadium** many times as a guest of the Journal American newspaper, and getting seats, in the bleachers or in the upper deck, and working my way around to the lower level. And if I were to buy a ticket In The Bronx, the place I wanted to sit was in right field, because you had, in the pre-game practice, a lot of guys hitting home runs over there. The Yankees had some great left handed hitters like Yogi, Mickey, and then later on, Roger Maris. I followed the Yankees. I was hurt that I didn't sign with them, but I was looking for an opportunity to play in the major leagues in a hurry and I signed with the New York Mets. But deep down, I wanted to be a Yankee in pinstripes. I would've liked to have finished my career in **Yankee Stadium.** The Yankees really meant a lot to The Bronx. They were a prestigious organization. What they meant to the fans was a winning attitude, a great tradition. I think if you look back at the Brooklyn Dodgers, the Brooklyn Bums, they were the working team. I think the Giants were the middle of the road guys. But I think Yankee fans were an elite group. You knew they were going to finish on top. They had class. When you looked at that organization and that uniform, you respected it. And I think that's really what it meant. The Yankee fans really hated the Giants and Dodger fans. In my neighborhood if you weren't with the Yankees in The Bronx you really were the enemy. What makes The Bronx different from the other boroughs? I think it is the people. The borough is unique in itself. It had everything, I guess like recreational facilities, good schools back in those days, the **Zoo**, and a lot of things to do. But the people were different. They minded their own business. We didn't have many street fairs back in those days.

We might've been at the bottom of the totem pole economically, but people kept nice homes, they got involved in the community activities, and it was a great place to live. I looked forward to it and I enjoyed my seventeen years in The Bronx. And I still miss it when I ride through it. I have fond memories of **Castle Hill** pool because my sister used to go there. I only had the opportunity to swim there on a couple of occasions. I wasn't much of a swimmer back in those days. I was a baseball player. But my sister was there. I used to sneak over the back fence. I remember that fondly. You'd sneak into the pool. Only one of us in our family could really afford the price of getting in. But later on, after signing a contract, I was an invited guest many, many times. **Shorehaven** had two pools and really had a great environment for the people. They had the beach areas and cabanas. It was a way of life for a lot of people. They enjoyed themselves and it was always a great summer.

# REGIS PHILBIN

I delivered **The Bronx Home News** to all those apartments and I can remember the sights, the smells, the sounds, everything. The one thing that I remember best of all was walking down these different hallways and hearing laughter coming out of each apartment. It was something.

Stickball! Everyday there was stickball. The thrill of connecting with a spaldeen with a good solid broomstick and driving it who knows how far. When I came back here from Los Angeles the first thing I wanted to do was go back on my street and the first thing I wanted was to see if I could still hit that stickball. So I got the camera crew from ABC and I went back to **Crueger Avenue** and I stood right at the same sewer

that I stood at when I was a kid and I had the guy go out and pitch the ball to me from where they used to pitch it and I couldn't hit a damn thing. Twenty-one times I swung and missed. It was so frustrating. The eye was gone. I used to be great. I used to be a contender!

Doo Wop music was very, very important. It was uplifting and it was fun. An awful lot of guys became part of that music, sang that music even though they didn't pursue music careers.

I would take Inez Brown to the **Park Theatre** and when I think about it, the torture, the pangs of guilt, and everything else! The fact is Inez Brown asked me out for the first date if you want to know the truth. She came to my house and asked me in front of my mother if I could go to her junior prom. How do you like that?

**Orchard Beach** was our escape from the stifling, sultry humid heat. We would get on the bus at **Pelham Parkway** and go out there. As you got closer and closer to the beach you could feel that breath of air.

I think sometimes...was it that good or does everything mellow in retrospect. When you are looking back and everything becomes nostalgic and warm and fuzzy, my though is that...Yeah!...It really was that great!

# LLOYD ULTAN

24% of The Bronx is park land. And they range from parks that go miles and miles and miles to areas, you know, that are just little triangles in the street. There's hardly a neighborhood in The Bronx that doesn't have a neighborhood park. And people in the thirties, forties, and even the fifties, used to go to the parks to sit on the benches and enjoy themselves, especially on a hot day before the advent of air conditioning. They would sit under the trees in the shade and they would converse. And this is how people would get to know their neighbors, reconnect with their family and their friends. It would also be an area for kids to play. Robert Moses had a great effect on The Bronx. He was best known to the people of the area as the New York City Parks Commissioner. As the Parks Commissioner, he had a very strict regime. All of the 'parkies,' as people called them — were the park attendants and had to wear uniforms. They enforced very strict rules. Nobody was supposed to walk on the grass. Nobody was supposed to lie on

the grass. The place to stay was on the park benches. But of course, all the kids tried to evade those rules. There was always one kid, whenever a game was played on the grass, who always had an eye out for the parkie. As soon as he would say, 'The parkie is coming,' everybody would run.

Robert Moses was the guy in charge of slum clearance and building highways. After World War II, there was a great sentiment for the generation that lived through the Depression and World War II, to do something to provide housing for poor people. Robert Moses was put in charge of that. A number of public housing projects were built. Since Robert Moses was also in charge of parks, great open spaces with playgrounds and grassy areas with trees and benches were built. He was also in charge of building highways. He built the major highways in The Bronx , the **Major Deegan Expressway,** the **Cross Bronx Expressway,** the **Bruckner Expressway** that led to and from areas and out of The Bronx. In doing so, he caused a lot of upheaval for many people who were in the paths of his proposed highways. One person, who later became a Bronx borough president, lived above his father's candy store, where the **Major Deegan Expressway** was planned to go. He and his family had to move so that the **Major Deegan Expressway** could be built. Certainly, one of the areas that was hardest hit was in the central part of The Bronx, which was very densely populated and had loads of apartments houses. The **Cross Bronx Expressway** went right through that area. All of these things certainly had an effect upon The Bronx.

As the Parks Commissioner, if there was a park in the way, he would give permission for the highway to go through a park; and that's why highways go through **Van Cortlandt Park** and **Pelham Bay Park.** As the City Planning Commissioner, he would approve the overall plan. Robert Moses had a great reputation for getting things done because he had complete autonomy. **Orchard Beach** was originally a bungalow colony made up of people who rented their little bungalows from the City of New York in **Pelham Bay Park.** Many of them were Irish, but not all of them. Many of them were civil servants, but not all of them. Some were politically connected. It originally started out as a place to pitch tents, and later became more and more permanent. When Robert Moses became the overall City Parks Commissioner in the middle of the 1930's, he did not want anyone living in the parks, so he expelled the entire bungalow colony. However, what he did do was create a brand new **Orchard Beach. Pelham Bay Park** took its name from a bay called **Pelham Bay.** He imported sand and filled up what was the original Pelham Bay in a crescent shaped sandy strip which he named **Orchard Beach,** taking the name from the original bungalow colony. And he provided dressing rooms and locker rooms and places like that, a beautiful terrace to overlook the lapping waters of Long Island Sound, which came over his brand new beach. And almost immediately, The Bronx Chamber of Commerce started calling **Orchard Beach** 'the Riviera of The Bronx.' And of course, it attracted many people, and still does today.

I grew up on **165th Street** and **Walton Avenue** which was one block west of the **Grand Concourse.** The area is very, very hilly. It is filled with five and six story apartment buildings. The apartment house that I lived in was highly unusual. It was a five story walk-up apartment. In every apartment there was somebody from a different ethnic group. We had people who were Hungarian, German, Russian, Filipino, and Chinese. Everybody got along. During ethnic festivals everybody exchanged foods. Everybody knew each other and was friendly.

There was always more than one candy store in a neighborhood. But wherever the candy store was, that's where people gathered — especially kids. That's where all the goodies were. That's where you could get egg creams, sodas, candy, chewing gum. You would pick up the latest version of comic books at the candy store. And of course, the adults would

go there to buy the newspapers. If my pen was broken, I could go there and buy a pen. All of those things were available in the candy store. It was the place where teenagers would gather at night. The bright lights from inside the candy store would remain on the sidewalk outside and people would congregate and tell jokes and laugh. The streets were used in those days for more than just walking and getting from one place to the other.

The apartment that I lived in was a three room apartment. That was the normal size apartment. There was a kitchen, a living room, and a bedroom. As families grew, the living room would be a part-time bedroom for the kids. There was an old fashioned gas stove in the kitchen. There was a place to bake, which was on the side of the range in the stove. You could actually stand up, open it and put it in. In the 1950s these old stoves were taken out and the new type of range was put in. You had to bend in order to open up the oven. There was a bathroom, a single bathroom. Only one bathroom per apartment. Nobody considered it unusual to have only one bathroom for a family. There was a dumbwaiter, where the superintendent would have a box that was pulled up by ropes and winches which would go up to a particular floor. He would ring a bell, you would open up a door, and there would be the box. You would place your garbage on the dumbwaiter, and he would take it and lower it down. At one point, the dumbwaiter became inoperable. From that point onward, we had to deposit the garbage in the backyard in a garbage can. The garbage cans were made out of metal, not out of rubber or plastic. The boiler that created the heat for the hot water and the steam heating system was fired by coal, not by oil. Periodically, the coal truck had to come over. The back of the coal truck would be lifted with a hydraulic lift and the coal would come down out of the back, down a sluice, through a door at the bottom of the apartment house near the sidewalk. It was piled up in the basement near the boiler. The coal-fired boiler had created ashes after it was burned. The ashes were not like ashes you would get from a cigarette. These were lumps, tan and brown lumps. The superintendent had to take those ashes and shovel them into the metal ash cans, or garbage cans, if you will. On collection day, he had to haul them out to the sidewalk, which wasn't easy. Superintendents had to be very powerfully built people in those days to do that sort of thing. The superintendents also had to clean the hallways. And they did, starting from the top floor, going down the steps with buckets of water. They also cleaned the sidewalks. Up until sometime in the mid-1940s, when we had one of our droughts, the superintendent would take a hose and hose down the sidewalk to clean it off. When we had the drought, the City discouraged that sort of thing; so the only thing that the superintendents could do was take a

*The Bronx County Historical Society*

**Molly Goldberg**

broom and sweep it out. In the winter time, when the snow covered the sidewalk, it was the job of the superintendent to clear the snow off the sidewalk. In our case, the relationship between the superintendent was always good. The superintendent was basically considered one of us. The superintendent had an apartment — albeit it in the basement — but it was an apartment. He had to come up to the main floor in order to collect his mail from the mail boxes that were there. I always liked to say that people who moved out of The Bronx into the suburbs and got their own homes actually went down a peg because by living in an apartment house, you had a servant who took care of everything — clean off the snow, the sidewalk, make sure that the boiler was working correctly — I never had to do that because I had a superintendent to do it for me. The interesting thing is that we never referred to it as apartment houses and never referred to the places where we lived as apart-

ments. We would refer to them as houses. You know, *'Where's your house?'* Almost as if we had the proprietor's interest in the thing. But it was, *'Where's your house?'* or *'My house is over here.'* *'That's my house.'* The word apartment was never used except, *'Come over to my house, it's apartment 4A.'.* That's the only time you would use the word apartment.

The Goldbergs were an institution. They lived in The Bronx — supposedly in an apartment house on **Tremont Avenue,** which never really existed. The real mover and shaker in the family was the mother of them all, Molly Goldberg. She always fractured the English language with her Yiddishisms and other ways of speaking English. She had a big heart and an amazing intellect. Whenever a problem arose, she was able to solve it by the end of the episode. Certainly, she was not the public conception of a Jewish mother. She was very considerate and kind . In many ways, it reflected life in The Bronx in a humorous vein. Whenever you saw The Goldbergs, there was always a warm feeling that came out of it. You'd say, *'Yes, that's the way it is.'* And the fact that Molly Goldberg lived in The Bronx and this was a nationwide show, always made us proud and now the nation would know what living in The Bronx is like.

There were street singers in The Bronx. They were much more common in the thirties, forties and into the early fifties. Without any prior notice, and without any warning, somebody would come down the street singing a popular song at the top of his or her lungs. People would come and open up their windows so they could hear the music — unaccompanied by any musical instrument. Usually a dime or a nickel would be thrown down and the street singer, after finishing the song, would shout, 'Thank you,' and pick up all of the coins. Depending on the configuration of the apartment, the street singer would go into the back alleys of the apartments and sing there. The very last time this ever happened was also most unusual. This was in the the mid-1950s, when of all things, a Mexican mariachi band came down **Walton Avenue.** They were dressed with their mariachi outfits and sombreros, strumming their guitars and singing. They were treated the same way. They got all the coins and everybody said, 'Well, gee, isn't that unusual?' They brought their own instruments and they sang but that wasn't the usual street singer. That was the very last time I remember that happening. Street singers declined about that time, because people had television sets. They didn't have to go to their windows to see it. It was all there.

There were people who actually serviced the people in the apartments with all sorts of services — some you might think was highly unusual. One man would come along with a portable grinder on his back that was on a collapsible tripod. He would shout out in the street, 'Knives. sharpen knives.' And people would come to him with their dull knives, kitchen knives. And he would sit down with a collapsible chair, in front of the grindstone, and the grindstone would move and he would sharpen the knives. Then there would be a man who would come around and shout, 'Clothes. Buy old clothes.' And anyone who had old clothes would send it down to him and he would give a little pittance to buy it. Eventually, he would freshen up the clothes and resell them as used clothing. There would also be icemen, who would come around in ice trucks. This was an especially valuable if there was an interruption in electric service and you needed to do something to preserve the food that was in your refrigerator. You could always look for the iceman. He would have huge cakes of ice, a hammer and something that looked like an awl, and he would cut up the ice. He would have a piece of cloth that he placed over his shoulder and with tongs, he would take that cake of ice and put it over that cloth and climb up the stairs to the apartment that wanted it. He would sell the ice to the person who had shouted down to him, 'Ya got a cake of ice?' There would be people who sold vegetables. Most of these people were Italian in origin. A horse-drawn wagon would carry the vegetables. On a particular day, and at a particular time of day, he would be at a particular curb where he would have a slate surface on the wagon with various wooden boxes filled with potatoes, tomatoes, carrots, lettuce, and other things. In back of every box there would be a wooden stick. Over the wooden stick would be a brown paper bag that was folded. On the surface of the paper bag would be the name of the produce and the price in big, thick crayoned letters. Women would come down, and look over produce. They would say, 'Well, give me five pounds of potatoes.' He would immediately take out a bag and put in five pounds of potatoes. You could do your produce shopping that way. It was always cheaper than the neighborhood vegetable and fruit store because he didn't have to worry about paying rent. I remember one time on a very hot day, his horse dropped dead right there in the street. He was very upset, but he also had to make arrangements for the horse to be carted away.

Later on, in the 1950s, the horse-drawn wagon was replaced by a flat wagon that was propelled by motor. So it became more of a truck rather than a horse drawn wagon.

# COLIN POWELL

Growing up on **Kelly Street**, there was quite an ethnic mix. A large percentage of Jewish families, Eastern European strains; Hungarians, quite a few blacks, colored or Negroes as we were known in those days, a new infusion of Puerto Ricans and many other eastern European strains. It was quite a melting pot in the old traditional New York sense of melting pot because each one of us was a minority.

In those days, you could take a swipe at somebody's ethnic or religious background without it resulting in a war or without being accused of being politically incorrect. It wasn't always nice and happy. I have to remind myself that we had gang fights in those days, the Puerto Ricans and the blacks sometimes didn't get along. It was one of those places where you established a family, you earned a living, and you lived for the day when you could move out and up.

We played all the traditional New York City games: 'sluggo', 'kick the can'. I explained to my children the other day the process by which you took a bottle cap and filled it with melted wax in order to give it weight and they just stared at me vaguely wondering why anyone would want a bottle cap filled with wax.

Or how you would pitch marbles against a cigar box that had three little holes in it of increasing size. Whichever hole you were able to get your marble through had a different value, depending on the difficulty. Those were wonderful games, all of which you could play for less than a dime, all of which involved just junk that was lying around your house. I don't recall ever having expensive toys of any kind. We didn't need toys. We had the streets, the hydrants,the back yards, and broomsticks to play stickball.The only toy expense I really remember was that everybody had to have a bike and a spaldeen. It cost ten cents at every candy store in The Bronx.

It was a great neighborhood. It was a playground. We invented games to amuse ourselves. We flew kites off the roof. We made glass cord, an old New York thing where you would take regular kite cord and glue powdered glass on it so that you could cut down somebody else's kite as you flew your various kites from roof to roof and street to street. Of course, there was always the joy of just taking a nickel and getting on a trolley car and going all over the city. We all were able to do that by age nine or ten.

It was a very patriotic time for me during World War II. I was five through nine during the period of the War. All of us had a cousin or an uncle who had gone away to the War. Bad news tended to be suppressed. The government had a very effective propaganda machine at work in those days to stir up patriotism, and it was terribly effective. It was a noble war, in a noble cause, and we were enormously successful in that war. I remember the block parties in 1945. In my memoirs, I included a picture of Kelly Street being prepared for a block party, with banners being stretched across the street, and food starting to come out on the street, and all the cars cleared. Very patriotic time. We all had relatives who brought something home for us. In my case, I got a German leather belt from one cousin, and a German Africa Corps helmet from my uncle. The Africa Corps helmet I kept for many years, and then it disappeared on one of my moves back from Germany. I have a hunch the German movers decided to reclaim the Africa Corps helmet.

We had block wardens, parents who would go up on he roofs and look for bombers. And this was serious stuff. It was only many years later that it occurred to me that no bomber from either Japan or Germany could ever reach the South Bronx. Nevertheless, we were on those roofs looking for them, with little helmets on. We blacked out our apartment every evening with shades that came down. We took all that stuff very, very seriously.

My extended family lived in the **Kelly Street** neighborhood. I had an aunt on every block. I just remember a warm nurturing environment provided by my family and the public school system of the City of New York. They gave the sort of services that made us all feel like we were in a city that cared about us and and gave us the opportunity to move up.

Church was a very important part of my life. I'm still in touch with my church, **St. Margaret's Episcopal Church.** It was a central feature of my family life. There were many other churches and synagogues in the neighborhood.

I worked at a toy store known as Jay Sickser on **Westchester Avenue** and I started working there when I was 15 and the first job that Mr. Sickser gave me was, *'young boy, come here in the back and unload this truck and I'll give you a few bucks.'* And I learned how to unload a truck and move all of that merchandise into a warehouse. He gave me a few bucks and he asked me to come back the next day because I had done a good job. Work hard, earn a few bucks and there's a new opportunity the next day. I learned a lot from Jay Sickser over the next six or seven years. I'm still in touch with his family.

You got your baseball affiliation genetically from your father. My father was Giant fan so I was a Giant fan and you never question anything like that, just like you don't question why you are an Episcopalian. It comes to you from your lineage. In those years, Willie Mays came along, and that really made something of it all. We hated everybody else. We hated the Dodgers and the Yankees. That was the order of the world. This is what brought stability to our lives, knowing which team you supported and which ones you hated. Brooklyn really had the Dodgers. It was a paranoia in Brooklyn that you had to be a Dodger fan. In my section of The Bronx, it was acceptable to be a Giant fan, because it was just a little bit across the river.

Those were the days of wonderful ballads, the World War II ballads. Frank Sinatra, Bing Crosby, and the great crooners came along. In my ethnic neighborhood there was also a mix of jazz and blues. Rhythm and blues hadn't quite been categorized as such yet. There were the ethnic mixes, such as from my family. The Calypso was a major musical influence in my early years and still is today. Everybody was learning to cha-cha and to mambo. I was better at the cha-cha because the cha-cha is almost like marching because I can count the steps and figure out where I'm supposed to be and what I'm supposed to be doing. The mambo required a certain degree of sophistication, which I did not have.

I think people who move to The Bronx have the same dream that my parents had when they moved to The Bronx so may years ago. They want to provide a good home and a good life for their children and for their family. And then move up sooner or later. Move on up sooner or later. That was The Bronx dream. *'Love livin' in The Bronx, but, man, if I could only get to Westchester County or Long Island'*. That's what it was all about and I will never forget The Bronx. It was a pleasurable part of my life.

*Photo copyright by Fight Back!*

# DAVID HOROWITZ

" I lived at **108 Marcy Place** on the corner between **Walton Avenue** and the **Concourse**. It was the first brownstone apartment building on the block. There were also two white buildings, 120 and **130 Marcy Place** which were called the new buildings because they were the only buildings in the neighborhood that had elevators and were six stories high. And of course the new buildings were the upper class buildings.

We shopped on **170th St**. **170th St** was enormous. There was a little candy store that sold newspapers and egg creams, jelly apples and charlotte russes. There was a fish store, a Chinese restaurant called **Jade Gardens** and a fruit and produce store, and smaller shops, a barbershop and another Chinese restaurant.

The interesting thing about **170th St** was that there was a tunnel that ran under the **Grand Concourse**. There was a luncheonette which was a real hangout and on the other side were two competing candy stores. There was **Pop's Candy** store. Pop was a crotchety curmudgeon who would sell anything. He would sell you a two cents plain for three cents. If you wanted a little syrup in the water he would charge you two cents extra, a scoop of ice cream and he'd charge you

a nickel, and so for a grand total of a dime you would have an ice cream soda. These people were so cautious. They never let you stay in the store without following you a r o u n d . Across the street was **Resnick's**. It was originally a candy store that turned into a luncheonette. There was **Olinsky's**. **Olinsky** had the best appetizers, the best lox, and the best pickled herring. The best place for baked goods was the two bakeries on **170th St**. There was the **Garden Bake Shop**. They had the best black and white cookies. I only ate the vanilla and my sister ate the chocolate. Next to Woolworth's was another bakery called **Friedhoffers Bakery**. You would buy your rolls at **Friedhoffers**. They had the best rolls.

I used to deliver newspapers right opposite **Taft HS** on **Sherman Ave**. My route was between **Mt. Eden Ave** up to **170th St**. They were mostly walkups, maybe a few elevator buildings and a couple of private houses as you went back towards **Lebanon Hospital**. I delivered the **Bronx Home News**. I remember that you really schlepped in those days. You had to cross over the roofs and you had to go up and down stairs and customers used to beat me out of my money. When you rang the bell they either didn't answer or, if they opened the door they would say that 'you know, I didn't get my paper three days this week.' So they would deduct two or three cents for each newspaper and we were responsible for the shortfall. Our little newspaper store was on **169th St** off **Morris Ave** where the **Bronx Home News** carriers went. On Sunday we would have to stuff our newspapers with the funny sections and other sections of the newspaper. "

# JERRY VALE

My parents were both born in Mt. Vernon. My grandmother had a grocery store in Mt. Vernon on 7th Avenue and used to make and sell her own booze to the people who lived in the area. This goes back a long time ago. Actually the grocery store was like a front. She may have sold a loaf of bread once a month and the rest of the time people used to come in and they would call her 'Mom' and they would say 'Mom, let me have a 25 cents plain' which meant that they wanted a shot of booze.

My mother was 15 and my father was 18 when they got married. They eloped and moved away and came back after they were married and lived in a house that my grandmother owned in the Bronx that was right on the borderline of Mt. Vernon. One street was **Mundy Lane** and the other street was Sanford Blvd. I was in the Bronx. I lived on **Seaton Ave**. I'll never forget the address, **4255 Seaton Ave**. My house had very little heat and in the winter on a real cold night my mother would throw all the coats over the kids. My sister and I and my brother and other sister all slept in the same room with two beds side by side. I slept with

my brother and my two sisters slept on the other side and I remember always being cold. The first thing my father would do on real cold mornings was to turn the oven on in the kitchen so we could all huddle near it. I was always cold and I thought that everyone lived like this until I was a little older when I realized that I was living a very sheltered life. You see, we lived in one of those apartment houses where they shoveled coal into the furnace basements and the heat depended on getting coal into the furnace to keep the apartments warm. To this day, in our house my wife and I are constantly arguing about the heat. I say it's too cold and she says its too warm. That's because she always had heat in her house in Brooklyn when she was a youngster and I lived in an apartment building that never had heat.

As I mentioned before, there was a time when my father was sick and didn't work and my grandmother would send us loaves of bread and lentils. My grandmother would take two or three day old bread and put it in a plate, boil water with lentils in and pour it over the bread and that was a delicacy for us. It was lentil soup with Italian bread soaked with the juice and we thought that was a great meal.

I used to shine shoes in a barbershop and used to sing for the customers while I was shining shoes. The owner recognizing my talent sent me to a woman in the Bronx. She wasn't a vocal coach but she played the piano and I used to sing in her school plays. At this time I realized that I wanted to be in show business. Where can you go and do what you love and get paid for it and not work too hard. That's the reason I decided that I was going to be professional singer.

Even today I go back to the **Belmont** section when they have their Feast. I am happy and proud that I grew up in the Bronx.

# JAN MURRAY

My parents came from the Polish-Russian border. Twenty minutes it was Poland, twenty minutes it was Russia. When they couldn't stand the Russian winters they called it Poland. My parents came to the United States when they were very young, maybe nine or ten. When they first came here, like everyone else, they lived on the east side. They all ran to the east side. They had a different kind of work ethic, a different kind of dreams than we have today. They worked day and night and their main thing was to educate the children. I am talking specifically of Jewish people because that's what I am and this is what I knew. I'm sure that the Irish, Italians and all were much the same. They all did pushcarts, any type of manual labor, anything that they could get their hands on to make money, to make a living, to exist, but the main thing was to educate the children.

No matter how hard they worked they thought about the next generation.

Those that started to do fairly well started to move uptown. At that time, peculiar enough, places like Harlem were where the elite lived. But when the Jews and other immigrants started to encroach and they started to do well, they got out of the ghetto of the east side because they wanted a little apartment where they had their own bathroom instead of sharing it with ten other tenants. The elite turned their nose up and they ran. They ran out to Long Island, to

Westchester, whatever, and those immigrants, Jewish, Italian, Irish and so forth settled in Harlem and in later years when they started to do good they moved to the Bronx.

I was born on **East Tremont Ave** and **180th St** near **Longfellow Ave.** I went to **PS 75** on **Faile St** and **Bryant Ave.** It was almost like living in the country. There were little four family houses that were built and in front of each house was one small tree. It was such a nice thing. We had a park that we used to call Kitsel Park because the boys and girls used to neck. 'Kitsel' in Jewish translation means to tickle. So I spent my growing up years on **Longfellow Ave** during the Depression. Thank G-d we had a good landlord. His name was Mr. Gotlieb and he lived upstairs and we lived downstairs. We had the flat in the front. Our big fear when I was growing up in the Bronx in those years was simply food and shelter. Those years the landlord would have the people out on the sidewalk if they didn't pay their rent. We were lucky in our little apartment. My father was doing fairly well when we took this $40 a month apartment. My father was in the pleating and stitching business. He had a lot of employees. His big thrill was that he had a Packard car.

In those years you worked six days a week and all day Saturday, but when Sunday came we all had to go for a ride in the car. He pulled out his 3 cent cigar and we loved it except in the winter because the car wasn't heated and we'd freeze to death but we had to take that ride. He would drive us up to **Mosholu Parkway** and into Westchester or Yonkers and we thought we were in the middle of the country some-place-we thought we were in Utah! When the Depression came everyone lost their job including my father who went under.  I remember that my uncle (my mother's brother) was a cab driver and he loaned my father $300 which I'll never forget because it seemed like it was all the money that there was in the world and my father had to use it to convert this Packard into a cab. He was lousy at it and had to stay out 20 hours because he didn't know how to hustle. After all he was a businessman and not suited for this type of work.

But we always remembered Mr. Gotlieb, the land-lord, because he was so nice to us. This was one of the good things about living in a four family house where the landlord was one of the families and you could become friendly. It wasn't like a big apart-ment building where the landlord had no feeling towards you  and if you didn't pay the rent your fur-niture was on the street. He carried us a great many times. In fact about 13 years ago when I periodical-ly played the condominium circuit down in Florida and I love it-I relive my life there. Periodically peo-ple come backstage after the show and there is always a half dozen people who knew me from The Bronx. We would talk about **PS 75** and **Longfellow Ave** and so many people would come backstage who knew me, my kid brother and our family. One day a balding guy came backstage and says his name is Bernie Gotlieb and I say 'You aren't that landlord's kid' and he says 'I certainly am'. Your memory goes back to the last time you've seen him (more than 50 years ago). So I asked about his father and mother and he says his father passed away a few years ago but his mother is still alive. I said, 'Why didn't you bring her?' He said he didn't this time and made some excuse. I said the next time you come be sure to bring your mother. A few years later I got a notice backstage that Bernie Gotlieb was there. I asked that they bring him in, and would you believe it, he came with his mother who was in a wheelchair. She gave me a gift, a bottle of some

cologne or after shave lotion. And I said to her 'Did your son tell you my act stunk?'

My mother passed away in 1942 in the Bronx when she was only 43 or 44 years old and that's when the family dispersed. I was married and I already had a little room in Manhattan because I was traveling to nightclubs all over the country. In 1939 I moved out of the Bronx. I went to **DeWitt Clinton** but only attended one year. Years and years have passed and now I'm a TV star and personality and have my own show. This was in 1961 or '62. I had the #1 daytime show in America called 'Treasure Hunt.' It was my show, I created it. Whenever I had a contestant that was a teacher or a pretty girl I would say 'When I went to **DeWitt Clinton HS** I never had teachers like you-my teacher was so old she didn't teach history she remembered it. She was so fat that every time she turned around she erased the blackboard.' One day my personal secretary came in with the mail and a telegram. She says you are going to find this telegram very inter-esting It said 'Dear Mr. Murray you have the faculty, the student body and everyone crazy. Every so often when you have a teacher on your TV show you often talked of your days at **DeWitt Clinton**. We furiously looked through our records and we can't find that you attended. Why would you be talking about **DeWitt Clinton**? Can you enlighten us?  We take such great pride that one of our alumni became something so important.' It was signed by the principal, Walter Degnan. In those years I could-n't walk on the street without somebody recogniz-ing me. So I sent a telegram to the principal and I said to look under the name 'Murray Janofsky'. I get a letter back and it says we see that you only went a year and we are grateful that you did attend and so on and so forth. I wrote back to say that because of family circumstances I was unable to attend for more than one year but is was always my regret that I didn't get a better education. At that point I thought everything was answered appropriately. I received a letter from **DeWitt Clinton**  and it said that they spoke to the Board and because of my good deeds and because of my charitable contribu-tions that they read about   and the benefits I attended and the good causes I supported, and this and that, that they would like to give me an Honorary Diploma. I accepted it. I think the year was '62. That was the year. It was January 1962. I went up on the stage with the dignitaries and I was the valedictorian. On stage with all the dignitaries was my son who was a freshman at NYU and I'm now graduating high school. I pointed that out to the audience and said that I can't help it that my son is smarter than me.

So I took my diploma under the name Jan Murray, (it was legally changed by then) and I jumped into my limo and ran back because I had to be on the air. We had a three story house in Rye with two major playrooms. All over the walls were pictures of my life-me with presidents, with stars, starring at the Paramount and at the Copacabana and other things and in the middle of all these pictures is my framed school diploma. It was 1964 or '65 when someone looks around and says, 'So how old are you?' Whenever someone asks my age, I say 'How old can I be, I graduated high school in 1962!'

Back in those early years in the Bronx, young teenage boys didn't have money to take a girl to a movie or have lunch or have dinner so there sprung up social clubs all over The Bronx. They were called cellar clubs. Twenty or thirty boys would belong to the club and would pay 25 cent dues per week to the landlord upstairs for rent. They put in a few couches and a radio and a few chairs and that's where they went Friday and Saturdays. They would dance and maybe neck a little, nothing really raw went on but it was a place for boys and girls to congregate. I would perform shows with a few of my friends at these clubs where they would charge 25 cent hat check fees. These shows were so popular and this went on for a year or two. When I was 16 I performed at a bar mitzvah that my girlfriend took me to. Someone there saw my act and asked me to play this act up in the mountains in Ellenville. That was my real start in show business. I will always remember the Bronx and the opportunities that it gave me.

# MARVIN SCOTT

I grew up in the area known as the West Bronx, just down the hill from **Lebanon Hospital** on **Mt. Eden Avenue**. It was a middle class Jewish neighborhood, where the men, mostly blue collar workers, went to work and the women stayed home to take care of the kids. My formidable years were spent in a fourth floor apartment at **1585 Townsend Avenue**. The six story tenement with about fifty families was like a kibbutz, a commune. There was a special sense of togetherness. Our neighbors were not neighbors. They were more like family. As a kid, I truly believed Aunt Selma in apartment 5B and Aunt Etta in 3C and Uncle Jack were blood relatives. We were always in one anothers apartments, sharing food and clothing and special occasions. At times, I felt more comfortable talking with my neighbors about problems than I did with my own parents. Why is it that to a kid anyone but your own parents seem so much wiser? The bond between neighbors, particularly during Jewish holidays, left me with warm feelings and impacted my future sentiments about the importance of family cohesiveness. My mother Frieda had a great influence on my brother Jerry and me, if for no other reason than that she was there more than our

father George. He was a hardworking man who owned a window cleaning business. He always saw to it that his family was provided for. We were treated to such luxuries as a new car every few years and a two week vacation each summer in the Catskills. My Dad's religion was his family.

A visit to **1585 Townsend Avenue** was unforgettable, if for no other reason than the scent that permeated the halls. Odor is more like it. The smell of cats camping out in the basement, combined with the pastrami and corned beef aroma from **Mos Kov's** delicatessen and the sour pickles from **Jack's** appetizing store on the ground floor, set our building apart from any other on the block. What we lacked in a favorable aroma, we certainly had in our view. Located on the corner of **Mt. Eden Avenue**, our windows afforded us an excellent perch from which to observe our limited world. We could watch the comings and goings of everyone in the neighborhood. Many had to pass our building as they came up the block from the IRT station on **Jerome Avenue**. Instead of sunrises or sunsets, the view from my bedroom window changed only with the seasons. That's when the scaffolds would go up for painters to change the Seagrams liquor sign that graced all six floors of the tenement across the street. In those days we had no need to call movie phone. A peek from the window enabled us to see what was playing at the **Surrey Theatre** across the street. If we strained our necks from another window, we could check out the bill at the **Mt. Eden Theatre**, usually a double feature with lots of cartoons, all for 25 or 50 cents a kid, and that was with the candy.

In those days before cell phones, we had a much simpler way of communicating with one another. My mother and Etta would talk for hours as their heads hung out their kitchen windows one floor apart. And we had no need for pagers to summon us back then. A deafening screech MARRRVINNN by my mother from the fourth floor window would send chills up my spine, and me running home. My brother Jerry, the little brat who was four years younger than me—-all younger brothers are brats, aren't they—had a unique way of communicating with his friend Don two floors below. They would get each other's attention with three taps on the radiator with a spoon. And they would exchange toys and other things with a string between the two apartments.

There were other sounds indigenous to **Townsend Avenue**, like *High Cash Clothes,* the weekly refrain from the visiting used clothing buyer or *Seltzer Man,* the cry of the man who would deliver his weekly supply of gaseous water and, of course, another bottle of chocolate syrup.

I was kind of shy when I was a kid. I liked girls a lot, but didn't know how to approach them. I remember having a crush on a girl named Vivian. She was so pretty. She reminded me of Lucille Ball. I wanted to date her, but lacked the courage to ask. Sitting around one Saturday afternoon with my friend Steve, we decided to set up a double date with Vivian, and her friend Isabel. I was too bashful to get on the phone. So Steve did, and instead of asking Isabel for a date he had the opportunity and asked Vivian instead. I was crushed, but somehow survived the following day when we all got together to go to the **Bronx Zoo**. Isabel lived just across the street from me. Her father owned the Jewelry store on **Mt. Eden Avenue**. So I was going out with wealth, right? It was a moment to behold. I wore a new pair of pants and sweater, and all the neighbors were either hanging out windows or spying from behind venetian blinds at **1585 Townsend Avenue**. They qvelled (that's a Yiddish word for pride or joy) as Isabel and I walked up **Mt. Eden Avenue**. This was my first date. Sure, I was nervous for a kid of 13 with raging hormones. We had a fun day at the zoo and while I enjoyed being

Taft High School gymnasium.

with Isabel, I kept looking at Vivian, regretting that I hadn't asked her out. When I returned home that evening, the critics were waiting, Mom loaded with questions and admonitions, like *"You know Marvin, when you go out with a girl, you should walk on the outside."* Selma chimed in, *"She's so pretty."* Then someone observed, *"She was wearing a crinoline skirt...wasn't that too dressy for the zoo?"* Not only were my neighbors critics, but matchmakers as well. Everyone, it seemed, had a girl for me to meet.

The place to take a date on a Saturday night was the **Loew's Paradise** on the **Grand Concourse,** near **Fordham Road**. It was a majestic and cavernous movie palace that accommodated more than 4,000 people. Usually, there was a double feature. I remember the atmosphere of the place more than the movies, particularly the glittering little stars in the sky blue ceiling. It was there, in the balcony, where I got my basic training in necking.

No Saturday night date was complete without a stop across the street to **Krum's**, the ice cream and sweet tooth emporium that made the best frappe in the world. So what's a frappe? A giant glass filled with your favorite ice cream, bathed in chocolate syrup, a mountain of whipped cream, and topped with nuts and a cherry. If you didn't care for a frappe, there was always a delectable **Krum's** eggcream. Never understood why they called it an eggcream. There was no egg in it, just lots of chocolate syrup, milk or cream and seltzer. It was heavenly. The check at **Krum's** never came to more than two or three dollars, and that was with the tip. We didn't count calories back then. Afterall, we were all svelte and beautiful, and oh so young.

I went to **Taft High School**, which could very well have been the model for Grease. Although I was a student leader involved in many activities, I somehow managed to find time to attend classes, at least most of the time. I was a judge of the student court, editor of the yearbook and the newspaper, The Taft Review. I was very popular because I was also the unofficial school photographer, along with my best friend Danny Mayer. My Rolleiflex camera became a part of my appendage. We had a run of the school and access everywhere, including the girl's gym. Afterall, we needed pictures for the yearbook. We even started a small business, Dan-Mar Photographers. We cleaned up, selling pictures of school functions to the students.

We were so brazen that we entitled ourselves to certain privileges, like riding the school elevator. Well, we tried and Danny succeeded. Unbeknownst to me, he signed my name to an elevator pass which the operator accepted as valid. Danny would ride the elevator at will, while I schlepped up and down the stairs. I didn't learn of his scam until after he and his family moved to Florida for the winter. If it worked for him, I figured it could work for me as well. I got my hands on a blank authorization form, filled it out and signed Danny's name to the document. My first elevator trip was short—from the basement to the first floor— to the office of the Dean of Boys, Simon Jason. The crime: forgery and unauthorized use of the elevator. The elevator operator recognized the

pass was bogus. My luck. I was admonished and threatened with suspension, but was spared because of my outstanding school record. There were so many activities, that I often cut my gym class. It caught up with me in my senior year. Instead of going home in the last period with the rest of my class, I had to make up the missed gym classes, under the threat of not graduating. What a drag it was being out in the running field in my gold gym shirt and blue shorts, getting teased by my fellow seniors on the other side of the schoolyard fence.

Danny and I are immortalized in the 1954 and 1955 yearbooks. Not only did we take pictures of our class-mates, but we took plenty of ourselves. As matter of fact we are so visible in our class yearbook that one classmate inscribed in mine: *May you have as much success in life as the number of times your picture appears in this book.*

My journalistic career literally started from the ground up, as in walking up. I delivered the **Bronx Home News** to tenements along **Morris Avenue** and the **Grand Concourse**. I schlepped this little red wagon with creaky wheels from **Townsend Avenue** to **167th Street**, where I picked up the papers. At the age of 11 or 12, the walk was exhilarating. The air was fresh. The Bronx was safe and clean. I remember the beauty of the tree-lined **Grand Concourse** and the sun glistening off the facades of the graffiti-free buildings. My routine was simple. I carried a batch of papers up five flights of one building, then hit the roof and crossed over to the next building, and walked down five flights. Up and down, down and up through rain and hail and snow. For my efforts, I earned about $10 a week. That was a pretty good supplement to my dollar a week allowance. After a year, I got tired of getting up early and retired from my newspaper route. Photography became my passion. Once I took a picture of a fire and offered it to the **Daily**

**News**. It never got published——the negatives were fogged——but the newspaper sent me seven dollars as an incentive to try again. It worked. I kept chasing fire engines and police cars until I caught a dramatic photo of a fire on **Mt. Eden Avenue**. A catering hall was ablaze and I was the first on the scene with a camera. The Daily News paid me $25 for the picture, gave me a credit line and wrote a story under the headline: *Student Finds Pix Pays.* That was my baptism in the news business. Usually when I would return from an accident or fire, the neighbors would gather around to ask me what happened. Guess I was destined to be a reporter.

For a while I worked at **Pordes Pharmacy** on the corner of **Walton** and **Mt. Eden Avenues**. I cleaned bottles, filled in stock and delivered prescriptions. The job didn't last too long. I was fired because one day as I was enroute to deliver a prescription, a fire engine raced by. With camera in hand, I took chase. Sure, I got a good picture, but forgot about the delivery.

After all these years, it is time to confess that I left the Bronx with a criminal record of sorts….illegal use of fireworks. Yup, half a dozen friends and I were setting off firecrackers in the vacant lot through which the **Cross Bronx Expressway** now passes on **174th Street.** A police car pulled up, my friends ran faster than me, and I was left holding the bag, or more correctly, several bags of firecrackers. Here I was, a juvenile delinquent at the age of 14. A few days later, my parents and I were summoned to the local precinct where I was read the riot act and told about the hazards of playing with fireworks. The cops tried to get the names of the other kids, but I never ratted on my friends. Needless to say, I've gone straight ever since. It seemed ironic that years later I returned to this same street to report about crimes of a far more serious nature, including a triple murder.

Among the many memories of the Bronx are the nights spent in my apartment, watching television with our neighbors. We were one of the first families to own a television set. It was a Dumont with a six inch screen. We'd put a magnifying glass in front of it to enlarge the picture. On Friday night, the men would cram into our living room to watch the wrestling matches. On Monday or Tuesday, the women would show up to watch Molly Goldberg, the most popular soap opera of the day. She was no Susan Lucci, but Molly certainly had a way of making the Jewish ladies laugh or cry. Watching television in our apartment was an event, and always there was plenty of coffee and cake. As others in the building bought their own tv sets, the crowd in our living room diminished. It just wasn't the same, watching television alone.

Over the years, I have received calls and mail from a number of viewers inquiring whether I am the same person with whom they grew up on **Townsend Avenue**. After watching me anchor a newscast, my former high school English teacher sent a letter in which she observed, *"You look just like one of my former students, but his name was Marvin Oppenberg. Are you related to him?"* she inquired. Helen Griffin was delighted to hear from me and learn that Marvin Oppenberg and Marvin Scott are indeed the same person. We became pen pals and stayed in touch for several years until she passed away. She often told me how proud she was to see how successful one of her students had become.

Looking back on it all, a myriad of kaleidoscopic images fill my memory bank. The days growing up in the Bronx were so innocent and so impressionable. Our surroundings were filled with love and hope for the future, sentiments that influenced our lives and helped motivate us to achieve our goals. The fifties, they were wonderful years. "

# THE BRONX CANDY STORE

**This classic scene was repeated thousands of times all over The Bronx on a daily basis.** This candy store, **Zimmerman's,** was located on Allerton Avenue near Bronx Park East.

Every few blocks in the Bronx, on the main avenues and often on the side streets, there was a fiercely independent enterprise that offered much more than candy, although all knew the place as the "candy store." These crowded little shops were the cement that held the neighborhood together, giving it an identity for better or worse. One could be associated with the candy store, as in "he hangs around *Skippy's*" or "she's one of the girls from *Red's.*" The candy store had sharply defined characters, inherited always from the characters who ran them. And they could be outrageous characters:

tough as concrete if necessary but soft as oatmeal to a local kid who needed five cents to make the price of an egg cream. The man or woman behind the seltzer spigot had to be a cook, cashier, manager and janitor, and they required finesse in public relations, child psychology, labor law and occasionally self defense. Candy store owners usually came from other professions, scraping together their money over years in the dream of owning their own business, and willing to make great efforts to keep their little stores profitable. There never was such a thing as a candy store chain, the concept of a 7-ll being

Photo: Scott Mlyn

**The Daily News truck didn't stop for deliveries.** Owners had to be alert as bundles bounced in the general vicinity of their store.

evening deliveries: the next day's edition of the News and Mirror. Waiting for the News and Mirror was a Bronx habit that became elevated to near ritual; it was a ceremony engaged in by thousands every night, rain or snow, winter and summer, but most avidly during the baseball season. Around 7:30 or so, the knot of men would assemble outside the candy store, combining perhaps the dog walking, ice cream purchase or odd errand with the imminent newspaper delivery. It was the occasion for neighborhood small talk and kibitzing, meeting and greeting, getting some air and generally hanging out with a purpose rather than aimless loafing.

Around 8 a.m., whatever the weather, the paper trucks could soon be heard rumbling down the

unknown and unimaginable in The Bronx of the 40s or 50s. Yet, the need for an all purpose convenience outlet, open far into the night, was unmistakable. The niche for aggressive business persons was there, and the ambitious rushed to fill the need. But only the hardest working and strongest skinned need apply for the position of candy store owner— it was no picnic.

Candy stores opened with the dawn to catch the early commuters on their way to the subways who needed newspapers to read on the train, and gum to chew, and cigarettes to smoke in those innocent years. So one of the first sounds on many Bronx streets, as the sun rose over the fire escapes, was of the local candy store owner, and often of his wife, tearing open the packs of newspapers. Like abandoned orphans, forlorn bundles of newspapers dotted the sidewalks all over The Bronx, waiting for the storekeeper to arrive and free them. The News was there of course, and the Mirror, Herald-Tribune and the Times — these were the morning deliveries. Later, as the day progressed, the Telegraph, Journal American, and Post would arrive for the afternoon crowd. The real excitement, though, were the

Photo: Scott Mlyn

**The Daily News published a one star edition that appeared at 9:00 pm.** For many Bronxites it was eagerly anticipated. Getting the evening paper was a social ritual and a chance to meet your neighbors.

*Photo: Scott Mlyn*

**A Bronxite's dilemma at Zimmerman's candy store: Too many choices and too little money.**

his front window. Many candy store owners employed (in the loosest sense of that word) kids to pick up the papers, meaning that one of the local teenagers might be persuaded to carry in the bundles from the street in return for a soda or a candy bar. On Sundays, this became a bit more complicated, or rather on Saturday night when the Sunday papers were delivered. The problem was they were delivered in pieces, and the pieces needed assembling. The News, Mirror, Journal-American had famous comic sections, and somehow the machinery at the printing plant was unable to produce a complete product. For the beleaguered candy store owner, Sunday papers were an ordeal. He had to store the various sections, find a place to display them, and more important, get somebody to put them together in proper order, or any order, in a rush.

Once assembled, the Sunday editions, with the comics always facing outward, were handed out to eager buyers. The remainder went on the traditional newsstand, a usually wooden shelf that sat outside the candy store and displayed the var-

street. Both the News and the Mirror, the city's popular morning papers, were delivered by a species of rough, tough men driving even rougher, tougher trucks. Paper trucks were somehow muscular, they looked as if they could carry lumber or steel, not a few dozen bundles of newspapers. And they were driven by men who matched the trucks — hard-eyed, hairy-armed, strictly union drivers who had zero tolerance for traffic, fools or slow talkers. The drill was that the truck slowed, not stopped, at the corner and hurled out a bundle of papers. If the candy store owner was alert, he would be waiting for the delivery. If not, too bad. The paper landed on the corner, or maybe in the gutter, and from then on it was his worry. The papers had been delivered. Foolish the store keeper who complained to the driver about any of this, or even worse, complained to the newspaper company. The next delivery might accidentally land on his head, or through

**Leftoff's Candy Store on Bathgate Avenue in the '30s.**

The "boys" in front of Maxie's Candy Store in 1951.

ious editions. Naturally, the newsstand was an ideal seat for the corner crowd, and the age-old counterpoint went on all day long. "Hey, get offa' the papers, will ya'?" answered by "Yeh, yeh, okay. I'm goin'."

A paper unique to The Bronx in those years after World War II was the home edition of the New York Post, known to all as **The Home News**. The Bronx had delivery boys back in the '50s, although none ever used bicycles and there was little Norman Rockwell color to the job. Getting a Home News route was a familiar first job for many pre-teens. One had to buy the first bundle of papers, and then collect the money every Friday from the households on the route. On Sundays, early, The Home News delivery boys would assemble at the local depot (usually an empty store) and put together their papers; the Post, too, had comics on Sunday. Usually employing a shopping cart, or sometimes an old baby carriage, the deliverers would fan out to their routes, trudging up and down stairs and occasionally luxuriating in an elevator building. The Home News would be dropped outside the apartment door, or under the threshold, or, if nothing else worked, in the general area of the residence. Deliveries were, of course, after school and so the hallways were always thick with cooking smells making the poor Home News boy very hungry. There were dangers in the job: stolen or vandalized papers, run-ins with gangs or marauding tough guys, and even worse, customers who never paid. Accounts were kept on a cardboard ledger, more or less neatly, and it was strictly up to the delivery boy to collect the fees, about 35 cents per week. There were many customers who carefully avoided the collection day, or yelled (through the closed door), "next week."

For the candy stores, of course, papers were a cash and carry business. In those low wage days, papers cost literally pennies. The most expensive was the Times at five cents, and that was a kind of showy purchase. More familiar was the News or Mirror at three cents (yes, three pennies!) or maybe

Candy Store at Corner of Jerome Avenues and Marcy Place in the 1950s.

the Telegraph or Tribune. Newspapers were, however, only a portion of the candy store's wares. Inside there was a complex assortment of items, goods, services and amusements that filled a hundred different needs for The Bronx inhabitant.

Some of the goods stocked by the average Bronx candy store were comic books, ice cream, pencils, notebooks, spaldeens, combs, soda, cigarettes and cigars, Bromo Seltzer, toys, baseball cards, yo-yos, magazines and of course, candy from the one cent pieces to fancy Valentine boxes that might cost as much as three dollars. The services were even more varied: telephones, juke boxes, a soda fountain where an egg cream was always available. Depending on the size of the store and the humor of the owner, the candy store could also serve as a teenage club or retiree's hang out. One thing it was not, definitely, was a library, as in, "Hey, this ain't no library. Put back the comic book unless your gonna buy it, will ya'?" It was, however, a source of much information.

The most discussed subject was sports, and mostly baseball at that. When the season was in full swing, the local candy store was a seething arena of baseball debate, with Yankee fans strutting their usual winning news, and the Giants' boosters occasionally celebrating some good results. Even in The Bronx there were Dodger fans, odd misplaced Brooklyn devotees who delighted in their eccentricity. These Dodger supporters were allowed their delusions with good natured tolerance, but real fandom, as any Bronx kid knew, focused on the Yankees, or, at the very minimum, the Giants. End of the summer brought pennant fever, and in the days when New York teams almost always figured in the race, the temperature in the average candy store went up by a considerable factor as desperate fans pored over their newspapers and argued the latest strategy. Would the Yanks beat the Red Sox in the crucial series? How were DiMaggio's (or Mantle's) legs holding out? Is Maglie pitching tomorrow? Did Durocher really say that on the field yesterday? "Yeah, I'm tellin ya, you could read his lips on television."

In the off season (i.e. when baseball wasn't being played) the talk in the candy store turned towards local gossip, politics and sex. The last was modestly

Dorothy Seibel Schancupp, a friend, and Joseph Seibel at Morris Seibel's Candy Store, located at 549 East 168th Street.

discussed among the guys, never in mixed groups, but more than a few Bronx males learned the facts of life around a candy store table, or leaning against a newsstand outside. As for politics, somehow the candy store was apolitical; the inherent good sense of most Bronxites dictated that politics was a verboten topic, unless, of course, you were looking for a fight. In the Cold War atmosphere of the '50s, with McCarthy a fresh memory for many, political opinions tended to be tempered by caution. A good safe topic in the candy store was anybody who wasn't there at the moment.

If conversation grew stale, the traditional Bronx treats were always available at the soda counter. Egg creams, malteds, two-cents plain and handpacked ice cream were the standards, but the owner could (usually) be convinced to make an ice cream soda or even a concoction like a banana split. Exotic cocktails like lime-rickeys or cherry cokes were usually on the menu too, and a freezer full of bottled sodas as well. Pretzel sticks were a good side dish with any soda or malted, and they were considered normal counter-top offerings — two for a nickel. The basic pick-me-up after stickball or school was a simple soda — syrup and seltzer water. The affluent might go for an egg cream, or malted, and/or one of the bottled choices — Coke, Pepsi and a number of local brands like Hoffman, Hires or the popular Yoo-Hoo. The truly impoverished had to order a "two cents plain" which was merely seltzer in a cup, or else hang around hoping for charity from a pal.

These are typical 1930s & 1940s candystores. Murphy's, located at 729 East 165th Street also had a shoeshine stand.

**Foster's Candy Store – 933 East 165th Street.**

*Photo: Frank Arce*

**Murphy's Candy Store – 729 East 165th Street.**

*Photo: Frank Arce*

**Richard's Candy Store – 1084 Forest Avenue.**                                    *Photo: Frank Arce*

**Richard's Candy Store – 1084 Forest Avenue.**                                    *Photo: Frank Arce*

The candy store might often serve as communications center. In the days before telephones were standard home appliances, the candy store acted as telephone central for the neighbors. Messages were relayed or summons yelled up a stairway, "Moskowitz, you gotta' phone." It was good form to tip the kid who carried such messages, and somehow the candy store owner tolerated this arrangement. In some neighborhoods, the candy store was also the betting parlor. It was, in plain language, a bookie joint. Not that the store owner was a criminal, but taking bets or allowing the premises to be used for such was a community service. I doubt that anyone involved in friendly gambling would imagine themselves as lawbreakers, and, pretty obviously, the police didn't. It was more or less an open secret that certain stores would handle the action on the Series, or a horse, or on CCNY basketball. Most neighborhood candy stores came complete with a cast of characters, local guys who

Photo: Spencer Field
**Nadelberg's Candy Store on West 169th Street in Highbridge between Plimpton and Nelson Avenues.** Pictured here is Mrs. Nadelberg. Everyone knew and loved her and she made great egg creams. It would open at 4:45 a.m. and closed around 1:30 a.m.

added color to the pedestrian business. There was frequently a swinging bachelor, a couple of shady guys of uncertain occupation, and a changing crowd of neighborhood kids who started out in the candy store with lollipops and hung out long enough to smoke Camels as teenagers. Housewives, truck drivers, local businessmen and school kids came and went according to the clock and the season. In the summer, the kids were pretty much a permanent fixture in or around a corner candy store.

One of the special events that involved candy stores was the yo-yo contest. For reasons probably unknown, The Bronx was a hotbed of yo-yo activity and Duncan Yo-Yo was smart enough to run local contests to promote their product. The natural locale was, of course, the candy store and so periodically a yo-yo master would

**Measer's at 1661 University Avenue and Tenny Place in the 1950s.** This was a big time hangout for **Andrews Avenue** kids. They made great egg creams although Mr. Measer wasn't particularly likeable and the kids loved to drive him crazy. (Jeff Weinstein)

arrive, put up signs and the games were on. The kids would have to demonstrate their skills at walking the dog, sleeping, round-the-world and cats-cradle, and, after an elimination tournament, awards were given. The big prize was a "diamond" studded yo-yo, and runners-up got patches for their jackets.

Even more popular than yo-yos were baseball cards. Anybody could buy and flip cards; the skill level was minimal so even the worst athlete on the block was a potential terror at card flipping. Naturally, the cards were bought in the candy store, traded and discussed at the counter, and competitions took place on the sidewalk outside, until chased by the owner. In the proper season, marbles would be on sale at the candy store too, and kites, skate keys, crayons and rubber balls. Nobody from The Bronx, of course, ever asked for a "rubber ball." It was generically a "Spaldeen", although a real spaldeen, made by the Spalding company, cost a quarter or even forty cents, while other lesser breeds could be had for a nickel or a dime. Genuine Spaldeens did really

The location is at the corner of Allerton Avenue and Barker Avenue. This candy store has had many names: 1930s-Bergman's, 1942-43-Mintz's (pictured above in the inset), 1944 - Lum & Eddie's, 1945 - Raine's, 1946-9 - Rogofsky's, 1952 - Harry & Murray's, 1952 - Murray's.

bounce higher and last longer; there was a certain quality feel to a Spaldeen that imitators could never match. They were especially prized for stickball and off-the-stoop games, and the wise owner inked his name on the ball to avoid disputes.

The candy store did, in fact, sell candy, and lots of it. Somewhere in the crowded premises could always be found a candy counter or showcase, jammed

**not one will make an egg cream like Rubin's on 174th Street.**

with delicious temptations and tooth corroding wonders. A dime could fill a small bag full of penny treats, including the famous buttons on a long strip of paper, and unspeakably sweet little tins filled with flavored sugar and eaten with a tiny tin spoon. There were lollipops, gums, cheap chocolates, sour balls, gum balls, marshmallow creations, fake bananas and licorice. All this was usually the kids' domain; the grown-ups were tempted with higher quality sweets. The cash register in a candy store might often be surrounded with boxes of Joyva halvah, or marshmallow twists, or

*Photo: Spencer Field*
**West 169th Street looking towards Ogden and Plimpton Avenues adjacent to P.S. 11 schoolyard.** The candy store was called the **Cozy Corners**, Sid and Thelma operated it from early morning to late evening. It attracted scores of school children from **P.S. 11** and **Sacred Heart School.**

chewy caramels. Some favored the chocolate covered jelly circles while others picked toasted coconut marshmallow squares. The famous gum brands would certainly be on display, too, as well as all the nationally advertised candy bars, such as Hersheys, Milky Ways, Baby Ruths and Tootsie Rolls. Somewhere near the soda fountain would sit the tall container of pretzels, three for a nickel and a very nice accompaniment to an egg cream or a cherry coke.

Just how and where they learned is a mystery, but all candy store owners were soda alchemists; they knew how to whip up superior egg creams, creamy malted and even the more elaborate ice cream creations for those special customers. Even the smallest candy store was well equipped with a soda fountain and all the syrups, nuts, creams and tools to make memorable sodas and sundaes, including deep freezers for the gallons of ice cream. Malteds were the result of the powerful mixers, and a dollop of special malt powder that only candy stores seemed to have. The owner was also the ice cream dispenser, mostly in cones and cups, but with variations. Ice cream could also be ordered by the pint or quart, and for that the owner could reach down into the recesses of the freezer with his scoop, and hand pack the cardboard container. If he was generous, the ice cream mounded over the top so that the container was still open as it was transported home. This being long before the days of thirty flavors, or even fifteen, the standard choice was vanilla, chocolate or strawberry, or some combination of these. Prepackaged ice cream might be a bit more elaborate, but not very much. There were Eskimo Pops, Dixie Cups and the legendary Mello-Roll, the last being a wafer cone holding a cylinder of ice cream horizontally. Getting the Mello-Roll into the cone was a small trick which involved holding the ice cream with one hand while

unrolling the wrapper with the other; often the result was ice cream on the sidewalk. Children were generally the only customers for Popsicles since they (the Popsicles) were cheap and, under the right conditions, could last a long time. They were also garishly colored, imparting a bizarre purple or red tint to the child's tongue, lips, cheeks and, maybe, clothing, depending upon neatness. Popsicles and their ilk were the bane of parent's lives, but the kids cherished them, at least partly because parents were so opposed to them.

Still, most parents were tolerant of the candy store culture. It was so obviously a neighborhood utility that the occasional irritation could be well overlooked. For every sickening candy or forbidden cigarette that originated at the local candy store, there was always the benefit of its role as community center and general store. How, after all, could fathers condemn the candy store for its "loafers" when he spent as much time there as the kid, talking baseball, getting newspapers and passing through its doors a dozen times a week on various errands.

On a summer night, the age spectrum at any Bronx candy store could run from babies in their mothers'

**Drinking a 2 cents Plain, a true Bronx tradition at Zimmerman's Candy Store.**

A family getting ready to enjoy Mae & Al's at 827 Melrose **in the 1940s.**

80-96 Featherbed lane at Jessup Avenue in the 1950s.

arms to grandfathers (and mothers) buzzing around outside. Whole families strolled to and from the candy store. It was, if nothing else, a destination on a quiet night where for a few cents there could be conversation, color, excitement and a cold soda. Not a bad invention in the days before television, and even later, when there was ample competition for time and resources, the candy store held a special place in the hearts of Bronxites. The neighborhood candy store did finally pass away, done in by changing behavior, television, automobiles, chain stores and just different times. One of the last of true Bronx candy stores was **Hafts** on **White Plains Road**, which closed its doors in 1996 after a run of sixty or so years. A few lonely survivors of the breed may still exist, carrying on a tradition that goes back to the days of Calvin Coolidge. The familiar bodega carries on some of the function of the candy store, and perhaps the local McDonald's or Korean grocery can recall a bit of the old candy store atmosphere. With any luck, these hold-overs and questionable substitutes are still making memories for the neighborhood kids and providing an anchor for the whole block. But they won't have the character of *Abe and Molly's* on **Creston Avenue**, or wonderful juke box from *Ike's* on **Willis Avenue**, and not one will make an egg cream like *Rubin's* on **174th Street.**

*Photo: Scott Mlyn*

Zimmerman's located at corners of Allerton and Ollinville Avenues was also known as "Zimmies" by the neighborhood crowd. Close by was P.S. 96, where it seemed everyone stopped there for a little something or just to hang out.

# Candy Stores in The Bronx

These above photos represent the collection of **Anthony Santarelli's** ice cream parlor memorabilia. With amazing detail he has replicated The Bronx Candy Store appearance with all its charm in his basement.

● ● ● ● ● ● ● ● ● ● ● ● ● ● ● ● ● ● ● ● ● ● ● ● ● ● ● ● ●

## Aaron's

Neried Avenue & E. 238th St.
1951-1957
Owner: Aaron Abrams
*My dad's candy store in the North Bronx was located in the flight path between several church-es and Mt. St. Michael's High School. It was the magnet for people going to and from those places. My dad was famous for his Sealtest hand-packed ice cream, fabulous malteds and egg creams, ice box full of Mission, Coke, Pepsi and Hires bottled sodas and real, highly comp-ressed whipped cream.— Harvey M. Abrams*

Aaron Abrams

## Abe's

West Tremont & Harrison Avenue
1940-50's
*We always brought our empty bottles back to the candy store where you would receive two cents (5¢ for family size). At Abe's you could exchange your pennies for a 5¢ chocolate candy bars (Mounds and Almond Joy were 10¢) and these were big. Not like the "sons of" chocolate bars at inflated prices passing as treats for today's unknowing kids. I usually bought "Goobers" or "Raisinettes" (or both) and spilled the boxes' contents into my pockets, picking them out (with lint) one-by-one and plopping them carefully in my mouth while walking back to JHS 82 after my eat-at-home lunch. Abe was middle-aged, stout, balding (reddish hair and moustache). His relationship with the kids was strictly business. Patronizing Abe's Candy Store helped make me what I am today—FAT! — Jerry H. Wartell*

## Abe & Helen Candy Store

White Plains Rd & 223rd St
1960's
*My folks owned the candy store, which was located 1/2 block from the elevated train. —Bernie Liebman*

## Abe & Molly's

E. 184th Street and Creston Ave.
1951-1970

*Abe & Molly were my great grandparents. My grandma is Abe's & Mollie's daughter. Both of my grandparents worked in Abe & Mollie's Luncheonette through the 50's & 60's. Abe & Mollie fed most of the students from the Bronx H.S. of Science. The hand-packed chocolate fudge was the most popular ice cream. Mollie's famous homemade meatloaf, pot roast, tuna fish sandwiches, and egg creams were loved by all. Abe faithfully opened the luncheonette at 5:30 every morning.*

*Abe & Mollie's first luncheonette was on 140th & St. Ann's Ave., from 1945-1950. Then from 1951-1970 they were on 184th & Creston Ave. —Harriet Muskatt Irwin*

## Abe's & Molly's

Off of East 172nd Street

*Right next to the P.S. 77 schoolyard – on a side street , across from Monroe was a little hole-in-the-wall candy store run by Mr. Abes who was the father of my friends Jerry and Judy Abes. It was there that I got the most refreshing drink I've ever tasted-a very large glass of ice water spiked with lime syrup. An absolute necessity after a vigorous game of softball or touch football —Marty Herlands*

## Abe & Sylvia

Hoe Ave & E 173 St
1934-1937

*My parents, Abe & Sylvia Muskatt owned a broken down candy store, and we lived above the store at 932 E 173 St. Candy and cigarettes were one cent. There was an empty lot across the street where we went sleigh riding.*
*—Harriet Muskatt Irwin*

## Abram's

Holland Ave, Antin Place & Bronxdale Ave
1940's-1950's

*This wasn't a busy shopping area, so this store was busiest when the Delicia Candy Factory and the Electronics Factory, that occupied the old Bronxdale Pool (both factories were just across Antin Place), took their lunch break. Neighborhood people went in for a black & white malted (25 cents), or a Three Musketeers (5 cents), or a creamsicle. The Abrams, who ran this store, were the parents of former Bronx Borough President Robert Abrams. —Victor Rosenblum*

## Abramson's Candy Store

1632 Washington Ave (between E. 172 & E. 173rd St)
1940's

*I remember this store being right across from the original Bronx House. I lived at 1636 Washington Ave. and remember my mother being called down to their telephone because we didn't have one at home — Joan Alpern Gross*

## Adelson's

Watson Avenue near the corner of Ward Avenue
1948-1955

*This tiny little store had just about any toy or game ever made somewhere in stock. Only Sid could find them. "Big Sid" also sold us loose cigarettes for 2¢ each.*

## Al & Alice's

Davidson & W. Tremont Avenue (just west of Davidson)
1950-1965

*One guy had "credit" there (his parents would pay) so he'd get a spaldeen and candy and we would get nothing and share his candy. — Clifford Horowitz*

## Al & Murray's a/k/a United Cigar Store

W. 231st Street

*Al and Murray always serviced customers from in front of their soda fountain, and were always very business-like preferring adults as customers. However, they had a nickel embedded on the lowest shelf of their candy bar display which many a kid tried unsuccessfully to pry off when Al's and Murray's backs were turned — Jerry Sullivan*

## Aldus St. Luncheonette

Corner of Longfellow Ave & Aldus St

1934-1945

*This store was long and narrow with a newsstand outside. There was an open counter window, on Aldus Street, where you could see the display case showing the d e l i c i o u s Charlotte Russes.*

*We loved the mello-rolls. —Bernard and Shirley (Blitz) Mandel*

## Alice's

Corner of Hone Ave & Morris Park Rd

1938-1950

*Alice's was run by Alice and her mentally-handicapped sister. Alice chain smoked Camels. She sold "looseys" for a penny, made a 3-cent chocolate soda, (or it costs you 5 cents if you didn't also buy cigarettes). She kept us away from the magazines and candy, or anything we could (and did) steal. Two doors up Hone Ave was "Patsy's" Barber Shop, another institution. —Professor Raymond O'Keefe*

## Angelo's Candy Store

E. 189th Street & Cambreleng Avenue

1935-1960

*This is the place where all the boys met before basketball at PS74 on our way to Orchard Beach years before WWII. This oblong store had 3 fountains and three stools, a juke box and pinball machine. Around 1950 Angelo passed away and his brother Jitney (nickname) ran it until around 1960. — Sal Spadafora*

## Applebaums'

Lowell Street on Longfellow Avenue

1960's

Owner: Henry Applebaum

*I liked Henry because every time I went in there with my mother, Henry would always give me a vanilla cream sandwich cookie. He knew my mother since she grew up on the same street. Henry was (from what I remember) a fairly tall man, balding on top but dark hair on the sides. He was slender in build but always wore a white shirt and a white grocer's coat. He made great malteds. Plus his candy selection was pretty good, too. His wife would always joke with us as well. Applebaum's was the place to buy the Spaldeens, the paddle & ball, the wooden tops, etc. — Dan the NYC Deli Guy*

## Archie's Candy Store

Corner of Mt Eden Ave & Walton Ave

1947-1973

*Archie's was across from the Surrey Theatre. The owners were Archie Finkel/Max Serlin. I worked there as a soda jerk from 1957-1963. —Bill Sperling*

## Atlas Candy Store

SW corner of Bainbridge Avenue & W. 204th Street

Owners: Mr. & Mrs. Atlas

1930's

*— Robert B. O'Connell*

## Babe's

Between Castle Hill Ave & Watson Ave

1945-1980

*Babe's was the "hang-out" hub of the Unionport section of the Bronx. It was where everyone gathered prior to a sojourn or shortly thereafter. Babe was a good-natured proprietor who gave you what you wanted, even if you had no money. He would always say "pay me later". He was noted for his egg creams, cherry cokes, and his frappés. Mixed sodas were 10 cents, sundaes were 20 cents, and a banana split was 25 cents. He would have to clear the store, of non-paying customers, so that paying customers could get in. He always did this very reluctantly and only when it got unmanageable. He was a great person who loved people. Babe and his two brothers went to Italy, married three sisters, and lived happily ever after. —Joseph Leahy*

## Baratz

University Avenue & W. 176th Street
1940's
*Sam and Henrietta Baratz were very friendly, and wonderful around people. Mrs. Baratz made over-sized ice cream concoctions as well as sandwiches. — Vivian Malkoff Kornet*

## Bard's

Prospect & corner of Boston Road
1940's
*Mr. Bard was not too friendly, however, the sodas came with real fruit.*

## Bar's

Monroe & Weeks Ave
1950's
*I lived at 235 east 173 St. Bar's was our favorite candy store. I can remember drinking the best egg creams while eating a jelly bar after playing a nine inning softball game at P S 70 along with friends.— Victor Tadelis*

## Barney's

La Fontaine Ave between 178 St & Tremont Ave
1940's
*Barney kept a running charge, for me and my sister, that my mother paid off at the end of the week. In the 1940's, before we had a phone, we got calls on his pay phone. Someone would yell up to us "phone call". —Luciano Siracusano*

## Baum's Candy Store

West Farms Rd & Hoe Ave
1939-1962

*Upon entering the front left was the counter where we had our chocolate malts, egg creams, etc. To the immediate right was the comic book rack, where my brother and I purchased everyone in creation. It was a quaint cheerful place with great owners. In the 1940's Mr. Baum owned it, he was a kind gentleman. From about 1949-1953, Edwin and Miriam Gitow owned it, they were a loving husband and wife; and from 1953 on, Max Weinstein owned it. He easily made the biggest and best maltoss, unbelievable, and all for 25 cents. —Rev. Jerry Caterino*

## Bea's

E 182 St & Mapes Ave
1955-1968
*Typical Bronx candy store with 5 red metal stools on the left side as you entered. On the counter were spaldeens, tops, national pretzels, assorted gums and candy (1-cent Bazooka gum and bullet and string licorice stick candies). Three fountains for malteds, egg creams, cherry cokes, lime rickeys, 3-cent and 5-cent seltzers. Seeburg juke box in rear, on the right, next to the refrigerated sodas (10 cents, or 3 for a quarter). —Michael Siano*

## Beck's

235th Street & Johnson Avenue
1960's
*You refer to it as Costa's Luncheonette, a name entirely unfamiliar to me. The name I remember, and this very clear is Beck's, short for Beckerman's, the owner's name. One of my favorite drinks was a cherry lime rickey. Snapple makes a pale substitute. — Jim Graham*

## Beckenstein's
## (later Goldberg's, then Ellis')

1940's-50's
*In the 40s and early 50s it was owned by the Beckenstein family. After school hours the fountain was manned by the Beckenstein sons, Jerry and Hy. By the time I was old enough to "hang out" at a candy store it was owned by the Goldberg family, and after school, sons Mel and Jerry ran the store. It was later owned by the Ellis family, and the after-school workers were sons Bob, Don and Bill, with an occasional assist from cousin Ron.*

*Through all the ownership changes this place stayed as a traditional candy store; a newspaper stand out front, a fountain with six or eight stools, a magazine rack, a candy case, and a couple of tables in the back. To this day, I haven't found anything to match a chocolate malt made by Mel Goldberg. — Lester Stoller*

## Beller's

Corner of Teller Avenue & 165th Street
1930-1949

*If you wanted to know what was happening to the local young men in the service, you would stop by Beller's. You did not have to buy anything; you could sit on the stool and listen. If a relative had to contact you with good or bad news (99% was bad news, a death), they would phone you at Beller's. They would leave the message with Mr. Beller, his wife, daughter, or son. Or, if it were very urgent, they would come to your home. I remember him selling 2 cigarettes for 2¢ You could buy a chocolate marshmallow strip, licorice, and buttons on the strip of paper for a penny. Most of all, I remember the contact with the people of the neighborhood. — Jeanette Venderosa*

## Ben & Sid's

E. 174st off of Vyse Avenue
1940's

*Inside was a great place to meet during the cold weather. A very busy hangout during the summer. Here you could quench a thirst with a 5¢ coke or a mouth-watering egg cream for 6¢. Better yet, indulge yourself with a deliciously rich malted (two full glasses for just 12¢). Don't forget the penny pretzel. There were also many characters in the rest of the group that never failed to make life interesting. The fact is we never knew the real names of many of them. We knew them as Filthy Milty, Crazy Kalen, Zilch, Wheel, Gooch, Eagle, Gash, Shuckleup— to name just a few. We all have our nostalgic moments, — but in my case, I have to believe that some of my favorite and most memorable occurred at Ben & Sid's almost 50 years ago.*

## Ben's Luncheonette

200 Holland Avenue
Owners: Ben & Dotty Abrams
1950's

*Ben and Dotty Abrams, parents of the former Bronx Borough President Robert Abrams, fashioned an egg cream in May 1951. This was one home of the authentic Bronx Egg Cream.*

## Benny's

Center of Silver Beach in Throgs Neck, near the mansion
Owner: Benny Bredon  Specialties: "Broadway Flips"
1940's-1960's

*Every Fall, word would spread throughout St Frances de Chautal School: "Benny's is closing for the winter!" Kids would come from as far away as Bruckner Boulevard to enjoy 4 or 5 days of free ice cream & candy as Benny cleared out his stock before going to Florida with his wife for the winter — Kathleen McGrory*

## Benny's

East Mohegan Ave & 180th St
1940's-1950's

*It was called Sally's from the late 1930's to early 1940's. I worked for Ben as a soda jerk from 1947 till 1951. —Robert Kaminsky*

## Bernie & Jimmy's

Corner of University Avenue & W. 175th Street
1940's

*It was a home away from home and a gathering place for the "Blackhawks". Eventually, it became employment after school and during the summer for several of us. We became, and probably are still, adept at making egg creams (both vanilla & chocolate), packaging bulk ice cream, handling merchandise and cash, and relating to people on a one-to-one basis. We still recall those times as a great learning experience and a fond part of our teenage years. — Gary Linderman*

*Bronx County Historical Society*
Ben & Dottie Abrams owned Ben's Luncheonette.

## Bernstein's

Whitlock Ave. and Tiffany Street
Owner: Mr. Bernstein
1935-1958
*A very friendly store. Mr. Bernstein was very tolerant of kids. It had a few pinball machines. A nice family candy store — Margaret Lorenz*

1949
*Entering its (Bernstein's) doors brought the sweet aroma of a penny Hershey bars, and the sound of the seltzer fizzing into an egg cream. — Leatrice Isler Bell*

## Bib and Sam's Luncheonette

Barnes Avenue off Lydig Ave.
1950's
*I worked at this establishment and was known as a "Sweet Water Chemist" (not a soda jerk!) —Ray Unger*

## Binnie's Candy Store

Morris Ave between E 164th St & E 165 St
1930's to late 1950's
*The address was 1009 Morris Ave. Mr. & Mrs. Bill Binnie were the owners. Bill was a World War I veteran "gassed" by Germans in France. The store was located across the street from the Fleetwood theatre. I lived in the building (1009 Morris Ave) at the far right of the picture. I remember the malteds and egg creams that were made by Bill. I also remember the single cigarettes (loosie), sold for 1cent. The Daily News and Mirror sold for 2 cents, and I bought my first Superman and Batman (Action Comics) books for 10 cents. I wish I still had them! —John K. Reid*

*The candy store was known as "Bill Binnies" and was the local hangout. To the immediate left was the garage where those who were lucky enough to own a car could park it there. —Joseph Hayes*

## Birnbaum's Candy Store

SW corner of Davidson Avenue & Fordham Road
1940-1960
*This narrow rectangular store had one fountain and two stools with a big soda cooler in the back. It had a front window where you could purchase newspapers.*
*—William Fulham*

## Blackman's Candy Store

Creston Ave & Kingsbridge Rd
1940's to early 1950's

*Mr. Blackman owned the candy store. He was Michael Marks' grandfather. Michael went to PS 86 with me. At various times through our years we had crushes on each other. Mr. Blackman was always screaming at the kids who stole comic books and chewing gum. We sat on red leather bar stools and slurped up every drop of egg creams. — Roberta Nussbaum Graff*

## Blum's

Home St between West Farms Rd & Westchester Ave
1920's to 1950's
*Mr. Blum owned this small intimate store. Sold penny candy, egg creams for a nickel, and pretzels for 1 penny.*

*During WWII he had a phone. When I called my parents from California, he would ring my mother's bell, she would go to the window and he would tell her that I was on the phone. Mr. Blum had bought the store from Mr.Landau, and later sold the store to Mr. Mazin.*
*—Leslie Schneider*

## Blumenthal's

Hunts Point and Garrison Avenues
Owner: Samuel Blumenthal's Father
1940's
*Next to the store was Rosenberg's Bakery and a large lot where the neighborhood boys played sandlot baseball.*
*— Norman Blumenthal, grandson*

## Bond's

208 Street near Jerome Avenue at 210 St.
Owners: Mr. & Mrs. Bond
1940's-50's
*The Bonds knew everyone and everything that went on in the neighborhood. A small Coke cost 5¢, a large was 10¢. Ice cream cones were 12¢. Bubblegum was 1¢. —Bruce Havsy*

## Bootsy's Luncheonette

Jerome Avenue & Minerva Place
1950's-60's

## Brandt's

E 138th St & Brook Ave
1930's to 1940's
*It was the best ice cream parlour in the neighborhood. All three parishes met there; St Jerome's, St Luke's, and St Pius. It was a wonderful place to meet, before and after dances, to see the old crowd. Everyone knew one another. Terry our waitress was a doll, and Pete was Pete. In 1947 Wally became the second owner, and named it Wally's.*
*—Pat Flanagan Mc Glinchey*

## Broder's

Sherman Avenue & McClellan St.
1950-65
Owners: Harry & Eva Broder.
*It was a hobby shop and candy store in one. A pleasant place where everybody stood tall. It was a hangout and it drew people from everywhere. — Len Rinaldi Sr*

## Brown's

East 170th Street and Bristow Ave.
1940's

## Bunny's

Starling Ave
1950's
*This was a classic candy store with a soda fountain.*
*—Hank de Cillia*

## Cantor's

Clay Avenue and E. 173rd Street
Late 1940's & 50's
*A large meeting place for egg creams. Sold loose cigarettes.*

## Cappy's

Gun Hill &White Plains Roads
1960
*Though I never lived in the Bronx my dad, "Cappy", owned and operated 2 candy stores (luncheonettes) in the Bronx in the early 60's. His store at Gun Hill Road and White Plains Road was also known as the Evander Sweet Shop. This store was the home of the Cappy's hamburger, french fries, small coke for 55¢! His second store was located at Boston Post Road and Gun Hill Road. Here again the fame of Cappy's lived. I worked behind the counter in each of these locations and can still make a great egg cream as well as the almost extinct lime-rickey. — Bart D. Kaplan*

## Captains

Bryant Ave & E 173 St
1938-1954
*It was to the right of Levine's Drug Store (pictured). Good egg creams, malteds w/pretzels, large soda cooler, on right side mid store, where we ran to after playing ball in the PS 50 schoolyard, down the street. I can still taste the chocolate mello-rolls ice cream with sprinkles, which sold for 6 cents. The front right side was the comic book wall. Rear left side was the candy counter. —Marvin Olarsh*

## Carrie & Larry's

Briggs Ave near 196 St opposite Our Lady of Refuge Church
1952-1966

*There was a wooden newspaper shelf chained to the front, but it was only used for papers on Sundays. The rest of the week, we used to sit on it and drum with our heels. When business was slow, Larry would come out and chase us, otherwise we were ignored. There was also a gum ball and pistachio nut machine outside. A green canvas awning hung above the front window, which Larry operated with an iron hand crank.*

*There was very little floor space inside. The interior was like a corridor with a glass candy display case, cash counter, and fountain counter with 5 stools, all lined up on the right side. On the left was a wall with mirrors. The stools were chrome with red plastic seats. The counter was pale green formica with "free-form" thin line designs (pink, white, and purple), similar to the Newport cigarette logo. Behind the counter were tall graceful chrome fountains-one for seltzer and one for water. There were syrup pumps with white porcelain labels: "coke, cherry, chocolate, vanilla, coffee, lime"; and there were three Hamilton Beach mixers for malteds. All the way in the back was a cooler with bottled drinks, one wall phone, and shelves for school supplies. They made good egg creams, malteds, cherry cokes, and excellent chocolate sodas with just Fox's U-bet & Seltzer. They also sold all the penny candies. We had yo-yo season, water-gun season, and pea-shooter season; all equipment were sold there*

*Carry had the first Poodle hairdo I ever saw. She wore cat eye eyeglass frames. I once saw Larry smile and it made me realize that I'd never seen him smile before. I never did see him smile again. —Joel Isaacson*

## Charlie & Maureen

Cypress Ave & E 141st St
1940-1965

*A small store with very friendly owners (Maureen and Charlie O Brien). Laughter and happy talking could be heard when you opened the door. Always many people sitting at the long counter, drinking malteds, eating strawberry sundaes (my favorite!), or reading the News or Mirror while smoking. Lots of kids looking through the comics. Sometimes customers would sing along with the radio. —Ellen McGahey*

## Char-Rock Luncheonette

East Burnside Avenue between Ryer & Valentine Avenues
1957

Owners: Grace & Murray Small

*This store was located opposite Echo Park. Formerly Ed-Mar Candy Store, which started in business approximately*

Char-Rock Luncheonette, E. Burnside Avenue between Ryer and Valentine Avenues.

*12 years earlier. The Char-Rock, where you could enjoy Grace's double scoop ice cream cones for 10¢, a one-of-a-kind egg cream also just 10¢, or a thick malted for a quarter. It also had a barbecue grill in the front window facing the park, a full soda fountain service and a long counter with 15 stools. The rear of the store accommodated teens from all neighborhoods. They could sit and listen or dance to their favorite Rock & Roll hits from the juke box, complete with psychedelic fluorescent lighting. It was a taste of disco before its time. — Eddie Small*

## Chubby's

E 155 St & Tinton Ave
1935-1944

*It was a large candy store. All the boys and girls hung out there. It was across the street from St Anselem's schoolyard. —Marie Ryan O Connor*

## Cohen's Luncheonette

Clay Avenue and
E. 170th Street
Owners: Fay & Irving Cohen
1950-60's

*My parents owned this store for 15 years. We also lived in the building right next door-so the customers were also our neighbors. It was a hangout for boys who played ball across the street in the park. Although the family hated having to work in the store to help out, I did meet my husband Ron Cohen while working at the store. We are married 41 years so you can see why this candy store/luncheonette has real special memories. — Harriet Cohen*

### Cohen & Rosenzweig

Hoe Ave & E 174th St
1930's 1960's
*The candy store is the one with the overhead white sign. Cohen sold to Rosenzweig in the mid-thirties. They sold candy, sodas, ice cream, toys, newspapers & magazines. Made the best malteds. —George Lewin (Lifschitz)*

### College Avenue Luncheonette

E. 166th Street and College Avenue
Owners: Mr. Sevens, Mr. Dill and others
1930's-50's
*The candy store was a meeting place and many who met there were in the garment trade and came out at night for their plate of ice cream and the penny machines outside. They also cracked pumpkin seeds and indian nuts between their teeth, leaving a mess on the sidewalk to be discovered in the morning! — William DeSimone*

### Coopermans Candy Store

Sheridan & E. 166th Street
1940's
*The store was operated by old man Cooperman and his two daughters, Betty & Zelda. This was also the hangout for the 'Darts' team.*

*Cooperman's was bought just after WW II by a fellow named Izzy and was known by that name until he sold it, around 1950, to two men named Al & Nate, and the candy store was known by that name until we moved away. — Aaron Elkind*

### Cooper's

Spofford Avenue and Coster Street
Owners: Mr. and Mrs. Cooper
1940-50s
*The NY Post was delivered there for us paperboys to pick up and deliver. As we were loading our shoulder bags we played the juke box (5 for 25¢). Charlie Brown, The Chipmunk Song, Stagger Lee and Tom Dooley.
—Thomas Cronin*

### Cooper's

Corner of Bailey Ave & Summit Place
1932- late 1950's
*Mr. & Mrs. Cooper ran the candy store. Mr. Cooper ran the soda fountain, and Mrs. Cooper sat halfway down the store, near the 5-cent bars of candy. There were a few booths in the rear. Although Mr. & Mrs. Cooper were not particularly kid-friendly, they knew most of the kids on Bailey Ave. by their first name. They made great egg creams, milk shakes, & sundaes, (made with Breyers Ice Cream). On Saturdays, our dad would bring up a pint of hand-packed Breyers chocolate ice cream for the family. —Eileen Shanley Draper & Theresa Shanley Massimi*

### Corner Candy Store

E. 141st and Alexander Avenue
Owners: Miss Lynn until 1942
1930-1942
*I passed this store when going to PS9 (1929-35) and when going to Clark Jr. High. Miss Lynn would fill my fountain pen with ink and sharpen my pencils and told me not to be late for school. — Charles Bruno*

### Corner Candy Store (Newman's)

376 Gun Hill Road
1938-1950
*The store was owned by my grandparents. I worked there as a young boy. I remember that there was a tin can for the newspaper, and customers would drop money in that tin can, and even pick up change when it was due them. When sales started to slack, my grandfather, Harry Newman, initiated the sale of greeting cards. – Mike Newman*

*Bronx Historical Society*

Costa's Luncheonette.

## Costa's Luncheonette
W. 235th Street and Johnson Avenue
1950's

## Cozy Corners
205 West 169th Street
Owners: Sid & Thelma
*Sid & Thelma operated it from early morning to late evening. It attracted scores of school children from P.S. 11 and Sacred Heart School.*

*Photo: Spencer Field*
Cozy Corners.

## Cruger Candy Store
Allerton Ave between Cruger Ave & Holland Ave

1940-1950's
*We used to stop there every morning on our way to Columbus HS in order to buy five cigarettes, each for 1 cent. We would also stop there after leaving the Allerton Theatre.*
*It was also frequented by members of a club called Aloha, which was formed by me and my neighborhood buddies, after WW II. —Irving M. Hyman*

## Cunningham's
E 138 St between Willis Ave & Alexander Ave
1930's to 1940's
*Mrs. Cunningham owned the store next to my house at 351 E 138 St. She was kind to children; for 5 cents you could get a surprise little brown bag full of candy, and for 1 cent you could pick out a chocolate with white or pink filling, and win a prize if you got pink.*
*Joe Stark owned the deli on the other side of the building.*
*—Marie Ryan O Connor*

## Cy's Candy Store
Creston Ave & E 181st St
1955-1959
*It was owned by two brothers, and was across the street from PS 79. Ice cream was 20 cents, a hamburger with fries and soda was 50 cents, and candy was 1 cent, 3 cents & 5 cents.*
*—Jerry D Leibowitz*

## Dall's
Mid block, W. 239th/240th Streets, East side of Katonah Ave
Owner: Mrs. Dall and her son, Bobby.
*Prime attraction: only candy store where a behind-the-counter worker, i.e., Bobby, was an on-the-street associate of neighborhood kids, i.e., us. However, no special treatment when Bobby was wielding taps and scooper. — Jim Ryan*

## Danny's
E Tremont Ave & Harrington Ave
1955-1980
*It was very "bare bones". It had 2 candy counters, (no fountain), just canned soda. I used to get my father's cigarettes there. The neighborhood kids went there all the time. When you walked in you could look in the back and see his apartment; his wife was usually at the kitchen table, eating! (I think he used to take numbers there). I don't know how he could survive on the candy business! —Robert Guarascio*

### Dave's

2020 Washington Avenue
1940's-60's

*Professional prize fighters and friends of Jake LaMotta hung out there. They wore wide-brimmed fedoras, usually grey with a black band and camel hair coats with a tie around belt. Some also wore zoot suits. You chose a "pick" of candy from a large box. If you got the pink cream center candy you got a large bar of candy free!*
*—Patricia Harrison*

### De Angelis Ice Cream Parlor

4222 White Plains Road
1960's

*De Angelis Ice Cream Parlor sponsored the Bronxwood Little League team called the Ravens. The team went on to winning the championship 5 years later and the team was known as the "Celtics", the team I managed.*
*— Andrew J. Powers*

### DeLuca's

Jennings Street and
Longfellow Ave
Owner: J. DeLuca
1956-59

*We were a nice bunch of girls and boys who hung out together and watched over everyone.*
*—Barbara Eisenberg*

### Divack's

Bainbridge Avenue &
Reservoir Oval West,
1940-50's
*— Neil Harrow*

In front of DeLuca's (left to right) Back: Frankie, Angelo Joe S., Howie, Richie. Middle: Harry, Jimmy, Jackie, Al M. Front: Rosanne, Elaine, Bobby, Terry and Barbara Eisenberg

### Dutch Mart

White Plains Rd. between Lydig Ave & Pelham Parkway
1940-50's

*This was an old fashioned candy shop that also sold toys.*

### Eckhoff's Ice Cream Parlor

North side of 204th Street just west of Mosholu Theatre between Perry Avenue & Bainbridge Avenue & 205th St.
1940-60's

*Eckhoff's, one of the last of the classically decorated ice cream parlors of the Bronx, with its tiled floors, marble soda fountain, walnut and mirrored back-bar, locked candy cases, darkwood mirrored and paneled walls, and bentwood chairs with marble topped tables in the rear where lunches were served, and at one time featured in The New York Times.*
*— Robert O Connell*

*Eckhoff's Ice Cream Parlor stood on the north side of 204th Street directly across from the Mosholu Theater between Perry Avenue and the intersection of Bainbridge Avenue and 205th Street. Eckhoff's was one of the last of the classically decorated ice cream parlors in The Bronx. It had tiled floors, marble soda fountain, walnut and mirrored back-bar, locked candy cases, darkwood mirrored and paneled walls and bentwood chairs with marble-topped tables in the rear at which lunches were served. Eckhoff's was, at one time, featured in the* New York Times. *—Neil Harrow*

### Eddie's

E. 176th Street between Walton and Townsend Avenues
1940-50's

### Ekman's

Lydig Ave & Wallace Ave
1939-1956

*Mr. Ekman was a curmudgeon of the old school, who, though dependent on us kids for a lot of his business, never really wanted us to hang around, unless we were actually spending money. Reading comic books in the store was considered a cardinal sin, and raised Mr. Ekman's blood pressure to undoubtedly dangerous levels. The dairy store, visible next door, was eventually subsumed into Daitch supermarket in the 1950's. —Sy Kotler*

### Eli's

Macombs Road between 175th &176th Streets

*Eli suffered from a pronounced stutter which, at times, made it most difficult to understand him. He attempted to compensate for this by raising his voice an octave or two which didn't help his condition, but tended to make him sound rather unpleasant. At such times, I wondered why we didn't give the guy across the street the benefit of our patronage.*
*— Walter S. Freedman*

## Eli & Meyers

Macombs Road
1940's-50's
*I lived at 1665 Macombs Road from 1942-1957 and went to PS 82 and Taft HS.*

*Eli & Meyer were brothers and fairly friendly with the kids who hung out there. We used to take the long pretzel-sand twirl them in our malted milk and suck the foam off of them. On certain occasions I'd get a vanilla egg cream and two other favorites, a Charlotte Russe and walkaway Sundaes, which consisted of a pointy paper cup filled with ice cream, syrup, nuts and whipped cream and a wooden spoon. In the 1940's you could buy a single scoop, waffle ice cream cone with sprinkles for 9-10 cents.* — *Joan Shaw*

## Ellis'

Northeast corner Burke Avenue & Holland Avenue
(see also Beckenstein's)

## Ellman's Candy Store

Fox St between Longwood Ave & 156th St
1940's-1950's
*The store was long and narrow. It had a soda fountain and stools on the left as you entered, comic book racks on the right, penny candy, etc. Further down on the left were phone booths in the rear and large red Coca Cola soda bin in the back, filled with ice and various brand drinks. I purchased penny candy & comic books, (some purchased, some borrowed!)* —*Bill Goldberg*

## Elsie Hells

Fordham Road between Grand Avenue and Davidson Ave
1940-1970
*We always called it "Elsie Hells", but the owner's name might have been Elsie Hellman, or a similar German name. During the daytime mothers would leave their babies in carriages outside while they had their refreshments. Glass front windows, on either side of middle doors, displayed candy boxes and small gift items. The floors had standard white/black tiles.*

*The rear was center partitioned by a glass divider. The marble top tables were rectangular and seated four. My food memories included grilled cheese with pickle served on beige plastic plates. Of course vanilla cokes with fries and malteds were standard orders. It wasn't fancy, but it was our "hangout".* —*Denise Carusos Bendo*

## Engelstein's

Corsa Avenue and Boston Post Road
(adjacent to Hillside Homes)
Owners: Mr. Engelstein & his 2 sons, Jerry & "Red"
1940-68
*Candy and newspapers were in the front on the right side of the doorway. Inside, there was a long counter and about 10 stools. Toys and games were along the left and to the back of the store. I often called my grandmother from the pay phones located at the rear of the store.* — *Joyce Epstein*

## Ernie's

Off the corner of Jerome Ave & E Mosholu Pkwy
1950's
*Ernie was the owner. He took in a partner, Hal; and when Ernie left and Hal owned it, it remained Ernie's. It was next to a large corner drug store that had a great lunch counter. On the other corner was the Mosholu Cafeteria, also with good food. The El station was across the street, as was the park and the path to DeWitt Clinton.*

*All during the 50's, every afternoon, we would head to Ernie's, get an egg cream for 8 cents and a pretzel for 2 cents. Big spenders! The counter had the usual red plastic stools and a juke box, where I would play Johnny Ray's "Still", over and over again. If you remember that song you can understand why Ernie hated it and finally pulled it out. We hung out in the back, which had 2 red booths, right next to the pay phones. When they rang, one of us would answer "Breyers calling" until the day someone said, "no this is Sealtest". Sometimes we bought a Spaldeen, or some penny candy, or a gill of ice cream.*

*Neither Ernie nor Hal was "Mr. Nice", but when I think back, they must have been pretty okay guys to put up with us. That candy store holds warm and fuzzy memories.* —*Louise Dichter Wilson*

*Ernie was a bowling nut and loved telling his bowling stories. His specialty was "Suicide Egg Creams" which cost 25¢ and were terrific!* —*Martin Buchholtz*

## Esther's Candy Store

E 156 St & Elton Ave
1950's
—*Albert Dinsmore*

## Evander Sweet Shop

Corner Gun Hill & White Plains Roads
Owners: Mr. & Mrs. Friedman
1940-1965
*This great place was run for more than 25 years by Mr. & Mrs Charles Friedman, their son Norman, and brother-in-law Sol. They were all wonderful people and watched us grow up and have kids of our own* — *Frank Porricelli, Sr.*

## Falkowitz'

Avenue St. John & Fox Street
1930-1941

*This was a large candy store where they delivered papers at night. As a nine year old I would pick up the papers when the truck stopped at E. 149th Street and Southern Boulevard. The store had a large soda fountain with 6 stools and served Breyers Ice Cream. There were different age groups that hung out there. — Larry Pfeffer*

## Fanny & Sol's Candy Store

Nelson Ave & W 168 St
1950's-1960's

*They had the typical candy store at the time, a window onto the street, and inside there were counter stools and booths in the back, near the telephone.*

*Fanny and Sol watched out for you. You could count on them to keep your mother informed of your activities. Fanny knew all the local kids. She would scoop out ice cream cones from cardboard tubs, (single or double scoops), onto plain or waffle cones. She made terrific egg creams in the familiar metal cone containers with the paper cone cup insert, malteds, 2 cents plain, cherry cokes, and seltzer that tickled your nose.*

*The store had the usual comic books, Spalding balls, yo-yos, bubble gum, stick pretzels, chalk, and the large chalk to mark the sidewalks for "potsie."*

*Sol could always be seen sitting towards the back discussing the daily races with his customers. Around 10 PM nightly, the Daily News delivery truck would drop the bundled papers onto the sidewalk, and everyone would hurry to get their copy. Fanny's sisters, Yetta and Clara, would stop by, and sometimes you would see Fanny & Sol's daughter, Jean, work behind the counter. —Eileen Hawe*

## Farbers

W. 162nd Street & Ogden Avenue
Owners: Max Farber & Family
1940-1950

*Last candy store with a double fountain located at the foot of Highbridge hill. Also serving Mission soda from a real icebox. —Eric R. Gustavson*

## Feldman's

E 156th Street & Grand Concourse
1940-1965

*Run by Abe and Miriam Feldman. Technically, Feldman's was a pharmacy but it also had a soda/sandwich counter and large candy store. Mr. Feldman was old when I was born and older still when I came home from college. He never really communicated with youngsters and would always check our money close to his eyes (cataracts), but in his own way helped raise dozens of children over the years. Mr Feldman once smiled (in 1956, I think) and knew every family and their children. Everyone met at the store, waited for the bus and shared ice cream and candy there. — Dr. Eugene Alexander*

*Mr & Mrs Feldman gave me my first charge account. They were always very friendly. Mr Feldman made the best chocolate malted and I had two at a time; and don't forget those salted stick pretzels! When I bought candy & malteds too frequently my grandfather ended my charge account at Feldman's. —Debra R Blackman*

## Feldman & Tannenbaum

170 St & Jerome Ave
1941-1948

*My parents operated the store with the help of their children and two partners. It was a store with a soda fountain but with no seats. They had a big newspaper stand at the foot of the 170th St station (Woodlawn-Jerome) as well as a very active cigarette and cigar counter. It was a very small store.*

*They also owned a luncheonette on the other side of Jerome Ave in the Short Line Bus Terminal on the southwest side of 170th St & Jerome Ave. —Selma Zwecker*

## Fialkoff's (formerly Wendy's)

Owners: Mr. and Mrs. Wendy Morris
*Also run by Frances and sons Seymour, Calvin and Howie. Made great egg creams, lime rickeys in the summertime, and sandwiches, ice cream sundaes, sodas and malteds. What I would give to be back there! — Norman Erlichman*

## Fisher's

Castle Hill Ave between Blackrock Ave & Chatterton Ave
1936-1944

*Fisher's reminded me of 2 purchases: egg creams & chocolate candies-that if you got a pink inside, you got an extra 5 cents worth of candy. —Ed O'Connor*

## Five Corner Candy Store

Unionport Road near Van Nest Avenue
Owners: Bill & May Higgins and Al (Chill) DiZenzo
1950-60's

*This was a hangout for over 90 (Boys & Girls), from St Dominic's, Our Lady of Solace, and PS 34. This candy store hosted Damon Runyon characters such as: Pete the Hag, Harry the Horse, Babalu, Mona, Moose, Saba Juan, Zeff, A-2, Miggs, Bird, Swede, Sal the Barber, Spud, Chill, Buzzy, Dell and Zeke. Most have moved to different states or out of the area and some are no longer with us. But we had our time and will never forget "The Five Corner"*
*— John (Bird) Martignetti*

## Fly's Candy Store

Corner of Sherman & E. 166th Street
Early 1940-50's

*Fly's always had a great supply of Mission sodas-all flavors. This was the hangout for the "Lions" team.*
*— Aaron Elkind*

## Frank's

Southeast corner of Katonah Avenue and E. 237th Street
Owner: Frank, wife, son, daughter
*The first option for soda after PS 19 schoolyard basketball, stickball, any-kind-of-ball. —Jim Ryan*

## Frankie's

West Tremont Avenue & Harrison Avenue
Owners: Frank & Rosalie Moraldo
Early 1960's
*This six stool and fountain sold your usual fare, but Frankie began selling 25¢ sandwiches in the early 60's to the consternation of Al's Kosher Delicatessen located next door. —Marty Pollinger*

## Fred's

St Ann's Ave between E 146 & E 147 St
1951-1958
*The candy store was directly across from St Mary's Park playground. PS 27 was one block north. Fred's candy store was a small walk-up shop with an outside counter service. A small ice cream cone was a nickel, the large was a dime. The egg creams were great. Inside there were 4 swivel stools at a counter. The floor was black and white with one-inch square tiles, in a diamond pattern. To the left of the counter was a candy display case, and on the rear wall was a jukebox, which received all our loose change, nickels at a time. By the time we stopped going to Fred's, the jukebox cost a dime. When Fred couldn't stand our 'singing' any longer, he would call for a break and asked us to come back later. —Sigmund (Siggy) Latarski*

## Frieda's

University Ave & W 179th St
1940's-1950's
*The store was owned by Frieda and her mother. One of my memories of Frieda was that she never allowed us to look at any of the comics for more than a minute or two before she insisted that we put it back or buy it! Frieda was one of the first neighborhood candy stores to have bubble gum for sale, after WW II. When the first "Double Bubble" packages became available, they were 8 cents each. —Jim Kravit*

## G&Z Sweet Shoppe

1003 Freeman Avenue and West Farms Road
Owners: Max Ziegelman and Max Gruber
1948-60
*My father and his partner were both named Max. To distinguish the two owners my father was called "Little Max" or "Skinny Max" and his partner, my cousins' father, was "Big Max" or "Fat Max". Looking back, I can see how they might have appeared to be the Laurel and Hardy of candy store owners. — Danielle Harris*

## Gable's

East 172nd Street between Rosedale & Commonwealth Aves
Owners: Jake Gable, his wife, and daughter Dorothy
*Each day I would pick up the Jewish Daily Forward which was reserved for my grandmother. Most memorable was the large soda chest filled with icy water, where I had to fish around to find my favorite flavor of "Mission" soda. The bottle caps were great for all kinds of street games, especially Skully with caps filled with melted candle wax. Also my brother and I would go there for a hand-packed pint of cherry vanilla and vanilla fudge ice cream, or at other times, a Mello-Roll, pretzels and, as necessary, a spaldeen. — Marty Herlands*

## Garber's

Middleton Road and Hobart Avenue.
Owners: 2 brothers and one woman
1950's-early 1960's

*One of my fondest memories was going with my friend to Garber's. It was located down the block from PS 71. The man behind the counter was named Artie. He always wore an apron, and had a coin changer tied around his waist. We secretly called him four-finger Artie, because he was missing a thumb. He made the most delicious egg creams & malted. The most popular item sold was a confection called a "Walkaway" —a tube- shaped ice cream which had to be unraveled from a paper wrapper, and placed in a cone shaped cup. Chocolate syrup was poured over it and topped off with whipped cream and a cherry on top. Artie would hand the finished product to you as you paid and then walked away. Hence, the name! In the back of the store on the left was a big glass-enclosed counter with wooden shelves inside. On these shelves sat rows and rows of the most delectable sweets you ever tasted: money candies, shoestring licorice, jawbreakers, toasted coconut squares, malt balls, candy buttons, mallow cups, all kinds of bubble gum, O'Henrys, Hersheys, Sugar Daddys, Sugar Mamas, Sugar Babies, Chocolate Babies, Goobers, Red Hots, Juju Bees, Dots, Pez, Tattoo Gum, Bonomo Turkish Taffy, and candy cigarettes. At Halloween time you could buy candy corn, wax harmonicas, wax lips complete with vampire teeth, costumes, and chalk. My friends and I would put chalk in a sock and smash it against the street to turn it to powder and commence to hit each other with it.
—Guy Chiapparino*

*Garber's had walk-away sundaes, mello-rolls, great malteds, a lot of comic books, 2¢ pretzels, little things that were made of wax where you could suck some weird sweet liquid out of little round candies on a long strip of paper, spaldeens, pez dispensers, egg creams, and a lot of toys in the window that you didn't even think about because they cost more than a dollar. Garber's was where you went to relax over an ice cream soda. Even later on when we played basketball on Wed. nights in the gym at PS 71, we would stop at Garber's for a malted & pretzels. No matter what we did, it was the natural conclusion to the evening.
— Frank Schmidt*

*It was a pretty decent size candy store with a soda fountain and red round swivel seats. It also had a glass enclosed candy display. When you first walked in, the comic books and the register were across from them. They also had cigarettes behind the register, and toys. The owners were 2 brothers, who were very friendly. They made the best egg creams and cherry cokes. They also had tons of penny candy, which is the one thing half the neighborhood went there for. —Flo Giannola*

## Garber's

E 181 St & Ryer Ave
1940-1950

*This store was located opposite the 46 precinct, and was owned by Dotty and Hymie Garber who had two lovely daughters, Carol and Tina. Many years after leaving the neighborhood, we heard that one of the girls became a doctor and the other an accomplished musician.*

*In addition to great sandwiches, egg creams, cokes, etc., Garber's featured a great juke box full of records of Glenn Miller, the Dorseys, Artie Shaw and other big bands. Although a sign indicated 'no dancing allowed', we would sneak a fast 'Lindy' now and then. Garber's was a great gathering place, where old friendships strengthened and new ones were formed. Some people may say that the reason for the store's harmonious atmosphere was because of the proximity of the police station, but we think it was the way Dottie set the tone. —Rita & Tom Tiernan*

## Gert & Hy's

Near Vyse Avenue
1940's

*My Aunt and Uncle owned this candy store. I loved going there on Saturdays to help Aunt Gert behind the counter. She taught me to make delicious egg creams and, of course, we only used U-Bet chocolate syrup!— Harriet Jacobs*

## Gilberts

Third Ave & E 138 St
1930's-1940's
—Marie Ryan O Connor

## Glass' Candy Store

Cypress Ave & 141st St
Late 1930's-early 1940's

*My parents, Jennie and Barney Glass, owned this candy store in 1939, and maybe one or two years before and/or after. Catty-corner was PS 65. There was a window out front where he kept charlotte russes, and sold chocolates. It had a long counter, cash register, 2 tables & chairs, cigarettes behind the counter, (rolled-up cigarettes). It had an older crowd, (teenagers to 20's).* —Phyllis Glass Fielding

## Gluth's

1248 Castle Hill Ave
1930's-1960's

*It had homemade ice cream, homemade chocolate sandwiches. During the cold weather, they served hot chocolate and cookies. Customers were the neighborhood teenagers and adults. It was the busiest ice cream store in Unionport (Castle Hill Ave), Westchester to Long Island Sound.* — Louis Timothy Golly

## Goldberg's

Northeast corner Burke Avenue & Holland Avenue
(see also Beckenstein's)

## Golden Rule Luncheonette

SE corner of Burnside Ave & Anthony Ave
1940's-1960's

*I have wonderful memories of it. It served cherry cokes, BLTs, hot fudge sundaes, pretzel sticks. Henry was the charming Englishman at the fountain. My very first job at age 10 was to assemble the Sunday New York Times on Saturday night. I was paid $0.50.*

*I went back two years ago to visit. The store is now a bodega; but I was still able to buy a Three Musketeers bar from the same candy rack.* —Barbara Schenker Sontz

## Goldfarb's

Burnside & Grand Avenue
1950's

*Goldfarb's was located next to the Granada Restaurant and across the street from Nat's pool hall. I was the soda jerk who worked there after school for 3 or 4 years during the mid 50's. They made malteds with 6 ot 7 scoops instead of the usual 2 scoops, all for 25 cents. It was so thick that you needed a spoon to drink it, also I used to put the Sunday papers together, Saturday nights, so fast that people used to come in just to watch.* — Ralph Micklowitz

## Goldman's

Corner of 181st & Daly Avenue
1950-65

*This was a small store that you had to step down to get in. Mr. & Mrs Goldman (we never knew their first names) were strict and proper. We bought our pretzel rods, candy and egg creams, and we hung out until we were asked to leave. They knew all our families and always asked how they were doing. It was a real community on 181st St!*
— Marcia Cooperman Jamison

## Goldstein's

863 Southern Blvd.
1950's

*My mother, Rose Goldstein, owned the candy store. The store was located between Tiffany & Intervale Ave. It was located around the corner from St Anthonatious Catholic Church. Cardinal Cook was a priest and a customer. He was most friendly and always nice to my mother. I can remember the cost of Camel cigarettes was 14 cents, a mello-roll was 5 cents, cigarettes could be bought for 1 cent each. There was a kitchen in the back, and my mother prepared all the meals. My father died when I was seven, and my mother supported me and my two sisters from the income derived. The store had a pinball machine and served as a meeting room and center of discussion.* — Nat Goldstein

## Goldstein's

Bruckner Blvd & Castle Hill Ave
1930's-1940's

*I remember purchasing cigarettes for my dad, and toys for Christmas.* —Ed O'Connor

## Goodman's Candy Store

Cauldwell Avenue and E. 149th Street
1940-1944

*This picture was taken at Goodman's Candy Store where we spent many happy hours inside and outside. The 4 fellows belonged to the "Comet A.C." namely Frank Goltz, Bill Balfour, Ernie Morris and Phil Marciano. The little boy on the left sticking out his tongue was just passing by and thought he'd be a smart guy. In the background is a hill called Cara's Mountain. That's where I lived. We had to walk up approximately 40 steps then a passage way through*

*the six houses facing E. 149th St and across a road and another 20 steps to our home. — Rosemarie Reiff Winkler*

## Green Dot (The "Dot")

Ogden Avenue and 168th Street
Owners: Mike Klein and his son Al
1950's

*Our lives revolved around the "Dot". We met there before and after school and after dinner, Friday nights before dances and on weekends.You could get 5¢ Cokes, pretzel sticks, juke box (6 songs for 25¢), greasy but delicious cheeseburgers, comic books and everything else. This place had it all! —Ray Axberg*

## Greenberger's Candy Store

1406 Townsend Avenue, next to the P.S. 64 schoolyard
1935-1942

*This candy store meant a lot to me. It was owned by Abe Greenberger who had two daughters, Lenore and Dorothy. Dorothy was my best friend and her parents were very generous to me. I would be the recipient of many Breyers chocolate and vanilla dixie cups, the lids of which had pictures of all our favorite movie stars.*
*— Sondra (Sandy) Marilin*

## Gun Hill Luncheonette

Corner Gun Hill Road & Bainbridge Avenue
(across from St. Ann's Church)
1955-65

*For my brother Phil and I, growing up in a place where we didn't have to wait for our parents to come home from their day's labors was very special: the whole neighborhood was family! We'll cherish those memories always. —Ed Zemmel*

## Gus's

Boynton & Westchester Ave
1940-1966

*Gus always had his top teeth out. He was a tall thin man who seemed to always have a dirty left hand, but he served the best egg creams and malteds in the Bronx. Fresh seltzer cost 2 cents, an egg cream 8 cents, and a malted 20 cents.
—Lorraine Capaldo Filosa*

*Opposite corner from Sam's was our stopover before we went to Monroe HS in the morning. We also hung out there after school before we split and went in different directions.*

## Halpern's Candy Store

140th St & Cypress Ave
Late 1930's to early 1950's

*It was a long rectangular store with about 6 stools and a counter. I'm sure that most of the candy store made delicious egg creams, but the "schmoozing" that accompanied those egg creams made them exceptionally delicious. The store had everything from 10 cents comic books to school supplies, yo-yos, tops, "immies", magazines, newspapers, candy, jelly apples, and charlotte russes. The light emanating from the store at night provided a haven for the "older guys" to talk about any topic from yesterday's stickball game to last night's "conquest". —Alvin Eli Stameisen*

## Harms

Jesup Ave & Featherbed Lane
1940's & 1950's

*Harms was an ice cream parlor where you could get sodas, malteds, and sundaes (we called them "frappes"). They also served sandwiches and had booths in the rear, as well as counter service. —Harold (Hal) Podgur*

## Harry's

Lydig Avenue between Bx Park East & White Plains Road
1940-50's

*Owned by Harry and Henny, husband and wife. I would buy one and two cent candies, egg creams and candy dots on paper.*

## Harry's

Anthony Ave & E 176th St
1950-1970's

*A small candy store, with a soda fountain on the corner. We all called it "Sam's" but the owner's name was Harry, and over time, it came to be known as Harry's. This is where we bought Spaldeens, comic books & egg creams. Harry had some sort of accent, and was loud and scary- especially to those under 10 years old. We were thrown out many times, usually for no reason. We always insisted that the cokes be filled right to the top. It made Harry crazy. His wife worked there. She was nice. —Harold Schwartz*

## Harry Gordon's

*—Submitted by Daniela Nugent*

## Harry and Phil's

W. 170th Street and E.L. Grant Highway
1950-1960

*Owned by two brothers-in-law with very different dispositions but great egg creams and malted and Breyers/Reid's ice cream. Best soda jerk - ME! — Stan Agines*

## Helen's

Cypress Avenue & E. 141st Street
1940's

*Helen's on Cypress Ave and E 141 St had the best egg creams. Sunday afternoon saw many families heading to a large ice cream parlor on St Ann's Ave between E 141 & E 142 St. – Ellen Keating Horan*

## Herman's

Bainbridge Ave & E 194 St
1940's and 1960's

*In the 40's Herman's had a soda box which dispensed the usual coke, seltzer, egg creams and ice cream from the large packed containers. He sold newspapers, loose candy, cards and small toys. He had a few tables where you could sit for a short time and enjoy your soda. In the 50's the soda box was removed so room could be made for a refrigerator and display cases. —Pat Quinlan*

## Hermax

3891 Sedgwick Ave
1960's-1972

*It used to be called M's, when it was owned by 2 men named Murray and Max, then it became Hermax when Murray sold it to Herman. For description of store look up M's. —Mindi Marra*

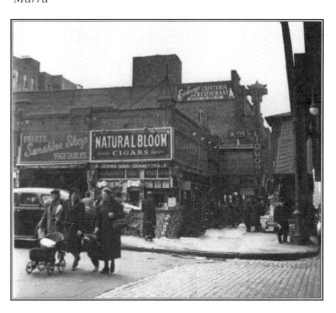

## Herskowitz

E 170 St & Jerome Ave
1950's

*As you descended the IRT #4 train at the 170 St station you hit upon this corner candy store. It was located alongside Mel's Key Shop, and next to the famous pickle-man. Yes, a nickel a pickle! The candy store was a convenient place to stop for a cool drink, especially an egg cream served in a cone-shaped paper cup with a 2 cents pretzel rod. Other items sold were candy, gum and cigarettes. —Marvin Soffer*

## Hilda & Moe's

W. 231 Street near Broadway
1950's-60's

*Hilda and Moe Waldman and their three children: Harvey, Joel and Judy worked in this oblong shaped store. It had a six stool counter and they sold Rockin' Root Beer dispensed from a fountain and served in a frosted mug. They had terrific soft pretzels and only used Breyer's ice cream in their malteds. They offered credit to their patrons. — H. Brian Samtur*

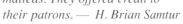

Moe at work in the late'50's

## Hink's

Located across from the Loew's Fairmont on Tremont Ave. *"Ice Cream Parlor" is a term that isn't used much anymore. Hink's was a typical mid-20's emporium that served frappes, which we now call "sundaes" and "banana splits" for those who were in the upper brackets because it cost 20¢. They also sold ice cream sodas and variations of the same such as a "Broadway" which was Coke, vanilla ice cream, and a dash of chocolate syrup. Hink's was a narrow fronted store with white tile flooring and a dark mahogany counter, which ran halfway down the length of the store. — Norman Raines*

## Hochstein's

Corner of Wilkins Avenue & Crotona Pk East
1940-50's
*This store was owned by my parents and grandparents. The store was opened 23 hours a day (closed to clean and mop floors for one hour). We used to decorate the store windows with displays of area kids in military service. Store was owned by partners Mike and Lou through the 1960's.*

## Hoft's

3200 White Plains Road
1947-1998
*Hoft's was a remarkable candy store/luncheonette. The store was located on White Plains Road at the corner of Burke*

Hoft's

*Avenue. John Hoft and his wife Betty, along with their son, Al, operated the candy store for over 50 years. As you entered this tile-floored store you would find a long counter with about 10 stools on the left side. There was a mahogany and glass display of Mr. Hoft's wonderful homemade chocolates on the right side. He would make very large chocolate displays for Easter and other occasions. Mr. Hoft made his chocolate and home-made ice cream right*

*from their store cellar. What was particularly interesting was that the store actually had its own elevator or lift that was used to bring the ice cream up, which was then placed in the silver bucket dispensers. Since the store was located near the Telephone Company, many employees (and bus drivers) would stop there for lunch. Mrs. Hoft (Betty) was the cook. She made*

Mrs. Hoft

*all of her meals from a low 2´x 2´ grill. As she got older, her posture seemed to get worse and worse, and many of us think it was related to her many years of stooping to make lunches. This candy store was a fixture for two generations, and in the 1990's the* New York Times *did a story about the owners and the store. – Thomas & Eileen Socci, and Michael Porcaro*

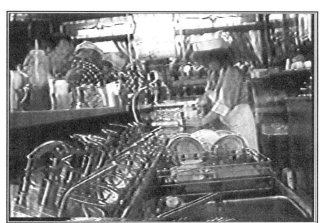
Hoft's soda counter.

Hoft's counter

Mr. Hoft

## Hopengarten's Candy Store

665 Burke Avenue - corner Olinville & Burke Avenues
Owners: Louie and his wife
*The owners, Louie and his wife and two daughters were all vertically challenged and I have wonderful memories of this store. —Joan Levine-Krinsky Soslowitz*

## Horowitz

Longfellow Ave & E 172 St
1930's to 1940's
*Mr. & Mrs. Horowitz lived in my building at 1564 Longfellow Ave. I played with their son, Paul. They always had a big jar of chiclets on the outside counter. It was on the honor system. You took two chiclets, and left a penny on the counter. –Sheila Eller Berman*

## Horowitz's

131 East Gun Hill Rd & Rochambeau Ave
1928-1930
*My father's candy store was a gold mine. Montefiore Hospital did not have a coffee shop, so we did big business, selling cartons of cigarettes and boxes of candy. A small egg cream was 3 cents, and a regular size was 5 cents. Customers had a way of getting their money's worth. They would either say it's too sweet or not sweet enough, so we would have to add more seltzer. It was a very busy store, and my mother, Dad, a clerk and myself had to man it. My mother would pray for a rainy day so she could rest her feet. —Mildred Newman*

## Howie's

White Plains Rd &
 Archer Ave
1958-1970
*I lived at 1514 White Plains Rd and worked at this candy store from 1961 until I went to college in 1963. It was owned by two brothers, Charlie & Howie Schneider. They were*

*both WW II vets, and married two sisters. Saturdays were a long day for me working from 9:00 AM to 9:00 PM. The store became very crowded around eight in the evening And people waited for the early edition of Sunday's Daily News. Usually the paper arrived late, and my day was extended to 11:00 PM. However, the free egg creams made up for the extra time. —Thomas McCarron*

## Huggins Candy Store

Burke & Westchester Avenues (next to Pilgrim Theatre)
1950-1965
*The owner had a large supply of magazines and papers, candies etc., like a small five and dime, great egg creams. It was a huge hangout. — Fran Lombardi Traietta*

## Humphrey's Candy Store

Morris Ave/163rd St opposite St. Angela Merici Church
*Mr. and Mrs. Humphrey owned the store but he passed on; and for several years she ran the store with the help of her teenage son. She was a lovely woman. —Jeanette Verderosa*

## Hy & Romeo's Luncheonette

Jerome Avenue & 190th Street
1955-1965
*This luncheonette/candy store was long and narrow and had two telephone booths in the back. It also had two tables and ten fountain stools. The store sold newspapers, spaldeens, comic books and candy. In the 50's, parents would call Hy (the owner) if they wanted their kids home for dinner. They made the best black & white ice cream sodas in the Bronx! Hy watched out for all the kids, and on the weekend many of them would come in for hot lunches. — Allan Glynn*

## Hy Chaiken

White Plains Road & Pelham Parkway Station
1940-60s.
*I bought Ricchardi's Bulk Ice Cream in all flavors that was served by Pearl and Hy Chaiken.*

## Hymee's

Brady Ave & White Plains Rd.
1938-1949
*My father Hymee had the best little candy store in Pelham Parkway. It was a classic with a soda fountain, a comic book wall, cigar humidifier and an outside newsstand. We all worked, Mom and pop, Jeanne, Marty (Mendy) and Leo. —Martin Kornfeld*

## Hymie's (Cohen's Sweet Shoppe)

Allerton and Holland Avenues
1940-50's

*Sacks of nuts stacked on the floor. Delicious candy showcase. Sold bags of 5¢ polly seeds, malted, cherry lime rickeys (made from real squeezed limes!), and loose cigarettes.*
*—Dee Verdecanna Fabian*

## Hymie's Candy Store-

Between Allerton Ave & Cruger Ave
1934-1950's

*Had 2-cent seltzer, 5-cent egg creams, 10-cent malteds, 5-cent candy bars. When I was discharged from the army in 1946, the first place I stopped in, after getting off the subway on Allerton Ave., was Hymie's, and the first person I saw was Hymie in his store. —Bernard Fogel*

*Hymie ran the candy store with his brother for many years, and even after his brother's death from cancer. Some of the kids referred to the brothers as "Happy" and "Grumpy". Hymie was the "Happy" one. —Sam Goldman*

## Ice Cream Parlour

Castle Hill Ave & Bruckner Blvd
1940's

*It had booths to eat ice cream, and a long polished ice cream bar to sit at. It was great for egg creams, or one cent plain. The ice cream sodas were terrific. I think we paid 25 cents for a super duper sundae! The owners were pleasant. It was located just down from Joe & Joe's Bar & Grill.*
*—Father Fred Hill*

## Ifshin's

500 Southern Boulevard at E. 149th Street
1930-40s

*Owned and operated by Morris Ifshin. After delivering the Home News in the summer, I would stop here to get a 5¢ soda to quench my thirst. The phone booths in the back were used to make dates and usually would bring into the booth 10 or 15 nickels. Ifshin's always had a big selection of Classic Comics that I bought for 15¢ and used to make my book reports instead of reading the book.— Daniel Blau*

## Ike's

E. 143rd Street and Willis Avenue
Across from Gramercy Boy's Club
1950-60's

*Ike was the quintessential matchmaker. The store had a great 50's juke box which played records for only 5¢. Sold loose cigarettes, loose penny candy and wonderful chocolate egg creams. — MaryAnn Barbish*

## Irene's

1940-60's

*They sold sandwiches and sodas and malted milks. Frosted glasses were used for cold drinks.*

## Irving's Candy Store

One block north of Gun Hill & White Plains Roads
on White Plains Road
Owners: Irv & Helen Gelber, daughter Helen
*This was a real old fashioned candy store with a four-seat soda fountain and great egg creams. At ten PM each night we would wait for the next day's Daily News and Mirror.*
*— Frank Porricelli, Sr.*

## Izzy's

Nelson and W. 169th Street
1950-56
*— Submitted by Pat Cosby*

## Izzy Balsam's

Sheridan Ave & Mc Clellan Ave
1950-1975

*Known as Izzy's or Balsam's, it was owned by Izzy Balsam and his wife Sarah. Their red headed son, Butch, also worked in the store. It was opposite PS 90, and you could always find a group of kids hanging out in front of the store, by the red alarm box. There were several booths in the rear of the store behind the soda fountain, two phone booths, and displays for candy, comics, magazines, and cigarettes. Browsing through the magazines & comics was discouraged; and if you tried you were sure to hear Izzy's refrain of "You want to buy a book, ha, ha, ha- 25 cents, ha, ha, ha".* —Stephen Bernstein

## Jack's

Corner of Gun Hill Road and DeKalb Avenue
Owners: Slatky family
1940's — Steve Slatky

## Jack's

W 231st Street
Owners: Ben and Sadie Brazinsky
1940's-50's
*– Jerry Sullivan*

## Jack's

Corner of Oneida Avenue and E. 233rd Street
Owners: Jack and Rose Krasnof
*Great view of tombstones and mausoleums of Woodlawn Cemetery. Specialties: Egg creams (of course) and dust-covered boxes of balsa wood model planes.* —Jim Ryan

## Jack's

W. 162nd Street and Ogden Avenue
Owner: Jack and Molly
1950-1960
*Formerly Farber's (1940-1950). It was the last candy store going down Highbridge hill, which also served Mission soda from a real icebox.*

## Jack's

Corner of Bryant & Seneca Aves.
1950-1956

*Jack's was located at the base of a residential 6-story building. The entrance was on the left. It had a large window, framed with a Coca-Cola decal, and a gum and pistachio nut machine in front of it. On the right, there was a wood newsstand with rectangular iron paperweights, that also served as coin collectors. When there were no papers on the newsstand, teenagers would sit, talk and hangout. The locals were schoolmates and many visiting friends from other neighborhoods. Jack's was a mecca, attracting as many as 50 or more teenagers during certain summer nights. Rough and ready guys would also socialize, harmonize and romanticize.*

*Going in, you had to pull the brass door handle open, and once inside, there was a stainless steel soda fountain on the left, with black vertical tap handles that would dispense seltzer at 2 speeds, a low and high pressure that created one of Jack's special egg creams. Just in front of the fountain was a large candy display that held every sweet treat you can imagine. It rested on a long marble counter with a cylindrical pretzel stick tin in front, just handy, to go with your soda. Cigarettes were against the wall. Going along the counter were ruby-red, padded, vinyl covered stool seats, with chrome base, and a step up from the floor, that ran the length of the counter, to rest your feet. In the rear of the store was a wood telephone booth that had a circular ceiling lamp. A lot of Jack's customers, that did not have privacy at home, came to the store to make their calls to arrange for dates.*

*Along the entire right side of the store were padded vinyl booths. In the front, right wall, was the comic book section and a revolving wire paperback stand. The floor was checkered black and white tiles. Above, at each end, were 2 ceiling fans, which hung fly paper, in the summer. Jack's always had a warm and friendly atmosphere, like Jack Saperstein, himself. He was a man trying to make a living, maintain a marriage, and raise two daughters, who worked there part time. In spite of all the responsibilities and the pressures of running a business, handling teen wise guys and shoplifters, Jack always had time to listen and give good advice to teenagers, like me.* —Stan Fine

*It had about 10 stools and 4 or 5 booths. It was a long store and was a big hangout for all ages of kids. Jack and his wife worked the store and they were known to have the best egg creams.* — Sandy Weiss Cohen

## Jack's Candy Store

Northeast corner of Bainbridge Avenue & E. 194th Street
1930-40's

*All through the 30's it was a great hangout for the guys from Marion Ave. There was a 12 ounce bottle of Mission Orange, self-served from a cooler just outside the front door and filled with chopped ice, all for 5 cents.*

*However, Jack's unique claim to fame came about from events totally beyond his control. For most of the decade the #4 Bainbridge Ave/City Line bus ran from Fordham Rd north on Valentine Ave to E 194 St, then a right turn down the steep 194 St hill to Bainbridge. Then it made a 90 degree left turn to go north on Bainbridge. One particular cold winter day, a bus came down 194 St and skidded on the ice and snow right into the side window of Jack's.*

*Then the unthinkable happened! Within weeks of the first incident, another bus came down the steep hill a little too fast and you guessed it, right into Jack's. However, within three months, the #4 bus was changed.*

*Coincidence? The paper sign posted on the inside window of the bus said "for the convenience of our readers on the inside window of the bus said, 'the bus still went by Jack's but at a different angle. The folks inside Jack's relaxed.* — *Raymond Bogert*

## Jack's Candy Store

White Plains Road and Archer Street
1942-1946
Owners: Jack & Mal Cohen

*This was a large square style store with 12-15 stools, 2-3 booths and two soda fountains. During the war years Jack's was the gathering point for information. Telephones were scarce so any calls from families were directed to Jack's for forwarding to those who had no phone service. Unfortunately, during those years (1942-1945) many sad tidings would arrive. The front window had a patriotic board with the names of the servicemen who went to war from the neighborhood, and there were a few gold stars placed next to the "kids" on the block. We had a small luncheonette. Sandwiches, some hot food, and Breyers Ice Cream. We were known for the best egg creams, ice cream sundaes and malts. PS 102 was "up the hill" so we carried school supplies and penny candy.* — *Martin Cohen*

## Jack's Candy Store

2153 Starling Avenue - corner of Purdy Street
1947-1977
Owners: Jack & Mal Cohen

*The store was rectangular, long and narrow, somewhat small in size, perhaps 20 feet wide by 50 feet long with a back room for storage. As you walked into the store you would find a huge penny candy case (glass enclosed) on the right side containing the best selection available, dots on a paper, syrup drinks in wax containers, nonpareils, etc. The left side had two soda fountains with ten stools and two booths. On the left*

*side, after the fountain, was a large enclosed cigar counter containing the finest cigars. During these years, cigars were almost as large a seller as cigarettes.*

*We carried an extensive line of Breyers Ice Cream, both packed and loose. My father was the "heavy hand" and never closed the top of the container when he packed a "half-pint" of ice cream. My mother always said "Jack, you are giving a half pint, not a pint." My mom was so conservative and gave everything they paid for, but was not a "heavy hand". But everyone came to Jack's for ice cream sodas, malted milks, etc. We had a large selection of bottled sodas, including Hoffman's, and we also had a freezer full of Milky Ways, chocolate jellies and fudgecicles.*

*The building where the store was located, (Starling Gardens), was a four-building complex of over 240 families. Many tenants brought their chairs down to get away from the heat (before air conditioning), and they sat in front of Jack's, waiting for the Daily Mirror and News to arrive. The store opened at 5:30am and closed at midnight during the week, but Friday and Saturdays we were open until 2:00 am. The store didn't serve any sandwiches or hot foods.* — *Martin Cohen*

## Jack & Edie's

Davidson & W Tremont Avenues (just east of Davidson)
1948-1965

*It was a long narrow store with some stools run by husband and wife. We'd have 10 guys go in thirsty after a stickball game-one to buy soda and nine asking for water.* — *Clifford Horowitz*

## Jack and Milt's

Allerton and Wallace Avenues
1960's — *Submitted by Joe Florio*

## Jack Bernstein's

E. 168th and College Avenue

*A family run candy store that was a lunchtime spot for the students of P.S. 53. School supplies and small toys were also a favorite here.* — *Susan Honickman Samtur*

## Jaffe's Luncheonette

E. 170th Street and Grand Concourse (next to Luxor)
Owner: Mr. Jaffe

*We never knew Mr. Jaffe's first name, but we did know that he never smiled and was usually grumpy, but he made the best toasted bialys and egg creams.* — *Ron White*

## Jake's Candy Store

E 141 St between St Ann's Ave & Cypress Ave
1930's

*Jake Levine was my grandfather, and he owned and ran the store with my grandmother Minnie. We would visit every other weekend. Since I was the first grandchild I never paid for anything, and therefore cannot quote prices. The pay telephone in the store was the central phone for most of the people living in the surrounding buildings. I would run upstairs to tell somebody when they got a call.*

*Jake's was known for its malteds. My grandfather would freeze the milk so that when it was placed in the malted machine it would whip up to an extra thick and large malted. Also, you received the remainder left, which provided about 2-1/2 glasses. Kids came from all over the South Bronx for Jake's malteds. Lastly, the salesman, who sold the ice cream to my grandfather, eventually purchased the small Bronx ice cream company called Smith Brothers, and proceeded to change his name to Haagen Daz. —Morton S. Levin*

## Jake's Place

Castle Hill Ave near Westchester Ave
1930 to 1950's

*Jake's was a combination a "self-service" newsstand on the outside, and a wonderful glass-enclosed display of candies on the inside. During the depression, at age 9 in 1931, I was fascinated by the people who left their pennies on the papers, as commuters selected late editions, as they streamed off to the IRT elevated trains. To be helpful, I thought I'd bring the coins inside to Jake. Grabbing a fistful in my right hand, and two pennies in my left, I had visions of buying 1-cent Hooten candy bar. When I handed Jake the huge batch of coins, he stared down at me raising his eyebrow and growled, "Is that all"? My left hand shot out and I dumped the 2 pennies into his outstretched hand and he said "Thank You!" I quickly left without the candy bar, but relieved that I never fell into a life of crime!*

*Soon after, I took a paper route delivering to the Unionport area, earning enough to buy all the Hooten bars I wanted, and plenty left over to get to the local Loew's Paradise Theater, and I thought of Jake often...for he practically save my life. "Thanks Jake!—Jules W. Gordon*

## Jake/Gussie's

Minerva Place and Jerome Avenue.
1940's-early 60's

*None of us ever knew the real name of this store, run by Jake and Gussie and their son and daughter. We all got our daily ice cream cones there, and sometimes even a Mello-Roll. If the ice cream fell out of the cone, and you were really polite, they would replace it free of charge. They sold the daily papers, and had the latest comic books. We were always chased out for trying to read the comics without buying them. Great old time soda fountain and booths with stuffed red leather benches. Of course, we all learned what egg creams were and the combination of egg creams and 2¢ pretzels were what nourished our Bronx souls! — Tina B. (Kasloff) Carver*

## Jarma's

Tiffany and 167th Streets
1943-44

*My most vivid recollection was during the Second World War during a time when sugar and bubblegum was scarce. Well, the word got out that Jarmas got a shipment of bubblegum and as you can guess, the kids came out of the woodwork to line up outside Jarmas. Unfortunately, there was not enough to go around - But what is rare is wonderful! — Jerry Toplitsky*

## Jarmin's

Tiffany and East 167th Streets
1950-1960

*Pop and his son Louie worked in the store. After playing ball across the street (Tiffany schoolyard) we stopped in for soda. — Norman Kaufheil*

## Jaycee Coffee Shop

Pelham Parkway N. & White Plains Road
Owners: Jacob & Tillie Cohen, Charles & Sylvia Group
*The Pelham Parkway hangout from 5:00 in the morning 'til 9:00 at night. Known for those famous lime rickeys, egg creams (with a dash of cherry syrup for that special taste,) hand-packed Breyer's Ice Cream, Roses's delicious hot lunches, malteds with real malt.*
*Marc, Esther, Bruce and Howard have the best memories ever from growing up in the candy store era.*
*— Esther Group Klein*

## Jerry's

E. 183rd Street and Cambreling
*—Submitted By Dorothy Budica*

In front of Jerry's Candy Store at 183rd Street) (l-r) Norma, Isabel, Terry & Dotty

### Jerry's
West Mosholu Parkway between Knox Place and Jerome Avenue
Owners: Jerry and his wife
1940-50's
*This store was located next to PeeWee's Grocery-a fruit store and cafeteria. Jerry's made the best egg creams and malteds. What I remember most is that before we had a phone, if someone called the store for me they would send a kid to ring the bell in my apartment house. I would then run down the 5 flights and the one block to get my phone call. — Harriette Kaminsky Jordan*

### Jesse's
2130 Lydig Avenue and White Plains Road
1948-55
*It was located on the same side of the street as the RKO Pelham. Before the movies, kids would come in to buy their Raisinettes, Goobers, Dots or JuJubes. They did this because they got more for their money! —Erwin Schussel*

### Jessie's Luncheonette
Creston Ave & E 181st ST
1948-1949

*My father, Hyman Kornfeld, and brother-in-law, Herman Soifer, bought Jessie's Luncheonette in 1948. I helped out at night, for about a year or so. — Leo Kornfeld*

### Jessie & Louis
271 E 156 St
1939-1942
*This candy store/luncheonette belonged to my parents, and we lived in the back of the store. It had 8-10 stools, and 4 moveable tables. For a nickel you got a bag full of penny candy. You could also get an egg cream, a charlotte russe, coffee, pie, soft drinks, cigarette, cigars, and newspapers. There was a jukebox, and all the boys would stand around it. My parents are still friends, after more than 55 years, with their patrons. —Yvonne Mazzella Fusco*

### Jim & Joe's
Corner of Burke Ave & Wallace Ave
1944-1952
*I lived in the apartment house above Jim & Joe's. One day I suggested to Jim to make up a "Joe Di Maggio" egg cream He put it on his counter sign that day: "Joe Di Maggio Egg Cream-Extra Large 13 cents". It became a big seller, especially for all of us Yankee fans. —Robert Sturner*

### Jimmy DeRosa's
2359 Beaumont Avenue & E. 187th Street
1950-60's
Owner: Jimmy DeRosa.
*Malted 25¢, egg creams 10¢, snowballs 5¢, candy 1¢ & 2¢.*

### Jimmy's
East 172nd Street and Commonwealth Avenue
1950's — *Myrna Shinbaum*

### Jimmy's Candy Store
Corner Prospect Ave & E 187 St
1940's-1950's
*In the early to mid-fifties, when my sister Donna and I were kids, our mother used to hide an egg in her pocketbook when she took us to Jimmy's for a "real" malted. (We refused to drink her homemade egg-malteds because they tasted "funny"). Jimmy's son Nicky would surreptitiously take an egg from my mother and blend it into one of his sweetest-tasting malteds in the neighborhood. We never guessed! Leave it to my mother to figure out a way to make sure we had a "nourishing" breakfast.*
*P.S. After, Jimmy sold it to my uncle Tony Mastroianni. — Paula De Marta Mastroianni*

### Jippy's
Corner of Sedgwick Ave & Fordham Rd
1960's-1970's
*It was across the park and the #12 bus stop. I sat at the soda fountain, ordering many egg creams and cokes, and bought candy bars for 5 cents. —Elizabeth Baga Bryden*

### Joe's Candy Store
Continental and Westchester Avenues
— *Lou Nigro*

## Joe's Candy Store

Intersection on the Northeast corner of Watson Ave & Olmstead Ave
1940's-1950's

*Joe's was a small rectangular room with red linoleum floors, beige painted walls and a gray ceiling. It always seemed dark from tobacco smoke. As you entered, immediately to the left, was the candy counter, a glass enclosed case that displayed various candy in large jars and colorful boxes. Immediately to the right, as you entered, was a free standing soda cooler, with "Hires" imprinted on the side. The soda was cooled with chopped ice, delivered daily by the ice man. There were also cold cut display coolers.*

*The owner/operator was the Farfarina family. They owned the building and lived on the second floor. The family consisted of father Joe, mother (name unknown), and the daughter Mary. They were Italian immigrants, and the mother and father spoke little English. Mary spoke perfectly and would translate for her parents what the customers needed. Mary was crippled from birth with polio, and used a wheel chair, or sometimes she used crutches, since the store was so small. Joe smoked a little cigar called cheroots. He had it in his mouth all day long. When he needed to cut off the chewed portion of his cigar, he would use the same butcher knife that he used to cut cheese or bread to make us guys a hero sandwich. Some of the guys joked that the cigar could only improve the sandwich. This store was very important to us. It was where we met, hung out, and where our parents could find us. We played king, queen and box ball against the side wall, and stick ball in the street in front of the store. —Richard J. Melville*

*The daughter, Mary, sat behind the counter, always with a smile. The store always had the sweet smell of candy. They sold charlotte russe for 5 cents, milk, eggs, cheese and Italian specialties. Mary and her parents were one of the nicest people you could meet. —Father Fred Hill*

## Joe's Candy Store

NW corner of E 184 St & Webster Ave
1940's-1960's

*The owner, Joe, was a Russian Jewish immigrant. The most memorable item was the great chocolate malts (16 cents). One day he had his fountain changed over (new syrup containers, etc.), and as they were taking out the old container, we saw the inside of them. They were filthy because he had never changed them. It never seemed to affect the taste, and we never got sick from the filth. —Frank Roberts*

*It was owned and run by Joe & Fanny Ashman, and later by their son Irving. —Regina May Imperato*

## Joe's College Luncheonette

Jerome Avenue & East 198th Street
1950's-60's
*— Stuart Silverman*

## Joe's Luncheonette

Corner of Hunts Point & Seneca Avenues
Owners: Joe and sons Harold, Jerry and Martin Schein
*I am the daughter of Joe, sister of Harold, Jerry & Martin. Dad's store was THE meeting place. He had the first TV set in the neighborhood. Everyone met there on Tues. nights to watch the Milton Berle Show. — Florence Prentiss*

## Joey B's Quick Lunch

1101 Castle Hill Avenue
1961-1967

*Across the street from PS 36 and Holy Family Church and School. Known for its fine soft and creamy ices that was homemade, delicious egg creams and malteds. Ice cream, syrups, and chocolate Easter rabbits were homemade on the premises. Sunday mornings were heavy in newspapers, coffee and roll sales. Many parents would bring their children in for lunch on Monday through Friday. It also had a juke box and played rock & roll music of the 50s & 60s. — Joe Burgi*

## John's

653 E. 182nd Street, between Hughes and Belmont Avenues
*This small rectangular candy store had 4 stools, one fountain and one telephone booth. It served soda, ice cream and school supplies. —M.A. DeBellis*

### John's Candy Store

Cortland Avenue between E. 149th & E. 150th Street
1931-1936

*John Dello Iacono posing behind the counter was the owner, while his young son Michael stands in front of the*

*counter. This store sold many things including candy, ice cream, sodas, and even wine, but was particularly noted for its fine cigars. As a sideline, John would repair customers' smoking pipes. — Frank & Dorothy Dello Iacono*

### John O'Neill's Candy Store

E 153 St between Elton Ave & Melrose
1920's-1930's

*I am almost 83 years old and I fondly recall John O'Neill's Candy Store. My house is also in the photograph. I lived there, right up until I had my children and moved to the Northeast Bronx. John O'Neill also lived just two doors down from us. He was a very*

*kind and caring person. His store had the only telephone in the neighborhood, and he was always running to deliver messages I graduated from PS 3 on E 157 St in 1931, and my favorite purchase, there, was my school notebooks that cost a dime. I always bought two.*

*After I moved, it was my custom to call my grandmother at John O'Neill's, each week. I remember the Wednesday I forgot! She waited for hours, all the while John telling her to go home, but she kept waiting. I've never forgotten how disappointed she was that I let my new life distract me from calling her. But I was glad she was in John O'Neill's, a safe neighborhood spot, run by a caring neighbor. —Concetta DiStefano Schembre*

### Julie's Candy Store

Corner of Kingsbridge & W. 238th Street
1950's

*Yes, I was one of the kids who got up early every Sunday in the freezing snow to assemble the New York Daily News and New York Times for the boss lady. — Peter Oreckinto*

### Kaplan's

Corner of E 167th St & Teller Ave
1940's-1955

*My parents' candy store had a stand in front, and it sold newspapers, comic books, magazines, ice cream, sodas-(especially egg creams), toys, etc. In 1948 my father installed a TV set (like in bars), to be viewed by customers. Tuesday nights were wild with The Milton Berle Show. The candy store was packed on those nights.*

*My father died in 1955, and my mother and grandfather, "Pops", could not handle the 6 AM-to-midnight/7-days-a-week schedule, necessary to running a candy store. In 1955 we left The Bronx. Growing up owning a candy store was unique. —Martin Kaplan*

### Kaplan's

Townsend Avenue between W 170th & 171st Streets
1948-1963

*The store was adjacent to the south side of P.S. 64 school-yard. Kaplan's had a truly extensive collection of penny and 2¢ candy. Please note that "Eddie's" on W 176th St between Walton & Townsend was not "Eddie's." It was either Eddie's Nut House," or Eddie's Crazy House," or something like that. Here's an interesting story about Eddie. In the old Bronx candy stores the place was run by the entire family. Eddie, himself, almost never worked the store. He set himself up with a bridge table in the back room, with a single light bulb hanging above him. Since most of the purchases came from Wade JHS kids just up the block, most purchases came to under one dollar. Eddie, in the back room, with his light bulb and magnifying glass spent most of his time examining pennies, nickels, dimes, etc. looking for those 'valuable' ones that he would keep. Since I was also a coin collector we became buddies. He said he made more money from the rare coins he found than the candy store business. Smart guy, no? — Mark Axelrod*

*Nat Kaplan ran this store with assistance from his son Lenny. Store was immediately next door to PS 64 school-yard, and it was a common occurrence for us to go in for a "Meyer's Orange" and a pretzel after several hours of 3 on 3 basketball. I think we paid 12 cents for both.*
*—Mort Glick*

It was adjacent to PS 64's schoolyard. During lunch hour, we would line up to get into the store and stand in front of a glass showcase, in order to buy our "penny candies". When we became too noisy and were too much to handle, Mr. Kaplan would lock us out and tell us to come back tomorrow. —Marvin S. Soffer

A classic candy store, about fifty feet long and ten feet wide, where children from PS 64 and the immediate neighborhood frequented. It had a soda fountain on your left, and a magazine rack on the right wall. In the back you had the glass display candy counter on the left, the soda coolers on the right, and a phone booth in the rear of the store. My most vivid memories were buying candy for a well-balanced lunch. I particularly loved the little pies in tins, with serrated edges and little metal spoons, so sharp that you could lacerate your lip. But the delicious hardened custard inside (if that's what it was), was 90% or more sugar, and they came in yellow, pink, and brown colors (flavors?). They were a penny each. I recall the so-called "nickel nips", wax bottles filled with a liquid version of a super-sweet mixture costing two cents. Mushy bananas were a penny each.
—Martin Adelman

## Kaplan's
Corner of Gun Hill Road and Decatur Avenue on the southwest corner.
1940's-50's
Owners: Sam and Sarah Kaplan
My grandparents owned and operated this candy store with the help of their daughter Esther (my mother) and their two sons, Jack and David. Sam continued to operate it until Sarah's death in 1957. I remember my mother telling the story of how the salesmen from Fox's U-Bet Syrup would come around and teach the candy store owners how to make the latest concoction: The "egg cream".
—Mark Stilz

## Kappy's
E. 176th and Walton opposite Wade Jr. High
1950's-60's
One of the most popular and well known candy stores for the time. — Estelle Bart

## Kappy's
Corner of E Gun Hill Rd & Hull Ave
1959-1980's
It was first called Sam's from 1940's-1959, and was run by Sam & Irv. Then it was sold to Murray & Terri Kaplan, becoming "Kappy's" from 1959-80's. It sold newspapers, baseball cards, malteds, toys, pretzels, and of course, spaldeens. It was the neighborhood hub. —Rick Herman

## Kasten's Candy Store
1809 Crotona Avenue
1940-50's
My grandfather, Nathan Kasten, ran this candy store with my grandmother, Sarah until 1950 when they bought another candy store in Parkchester. Their store had three or four round tables with wire-backed chairs. They sold newspapers, candy, fountain drinks and ice cream. It was open 6 days a

week and closed on Mondays. They lived in the apartment building over the store and took turns watching the store during the day. My father also helped out part time before he was drafted. One customer, the delivery boy for the grocery store next door, was a frequent kibbitzer and became my father's lifelong friend. My cousin and I would always play with the vending machines. The store remained open and was run by someone else until the building was demolished for a housing project around the same time that the Cross Bronx Expressway was built. — Ellie Schweber

## Katie's

E 153 between Elton & Melrose
1950-1963

*This store was originally owned by Katie Meyers. When she died in late 50's, John Crudo purchased it ("Nino's"). It had six stools and a counter where you could get an egg cream for 15 cents, and a stick pretzel for a nickel. The wood floor was traffic worn to the point of having ruts, yet it was the neighborhood kids' home-away-from-home! —James Sweeney*

## Katz's Candy Store

Longfellow Ave between Freeman St & 174th St
1935-1942

*It was owned by Mr. Schwartz, and had 1 counter with seats, and a showcase with various sorts of candies. The store was approximately 200 feet long. Mr. Schwartz was stingy with water, and would try to sell you seltzer if you requested "a drink of water". He paid me 5 cents to pick up the Sunday Daily News at the newsstand on Freeman St & Southern Blvd, under the #2 subway. —Frank M. Finck, MD*

## Kaufman's

E. 183rd Street & Walton Avenue
1950-60's
Owner: Ann & Ziggy Kaufman

*I bought my spaldeens and egg creams there. I used to hang out there all summer because it was air conditioned.*
*— Ronald W Bolte*

## Kent Luncheonette

E. 167th Street just off the concourse
1951-1969

*The owners were Al Promisel and Nat Datlow. Many of the doctors and dentists, in the building where the store was located, frequented the store as well as their patients. It was a popular lunch spot for school children whose parents sent them there knowing the store got a fresh meat delivery every day from the butcher shop. The owners opened the luncheonette in 1951, after being discharged from the service, and were there for 18 years. It became a gathering place for neighbors and families. Al was his own best customer. After he would close the store and clean up, he would sit down with a soup bowl full of different ice cream flavors and indulge himself. — Penny Promisel Contente*

## Kitty's Corner Luncheonette

E. 183rd Street and Beaumont Avenue
1950's-1960's

*This store was across the street from PS 32. It was run by Kitty, Blackie and their daughter. They served lunch and the best tuna sandwiches I've ever had. The luncheon area was in the back with tables and chairs and a view of the kitchen. Sometimes my mom helped Kitty with the cooking. They also had a long counter, school supplies and tons of Beatle stuff at the height of BEATLEMANIA! —Christina A. Packer*

## Kleinman's Candy Store

SW corner of Nelson Ave & Featherbed Lane
*Mr. Kleinman was often assisted by his son, Sid.*
*—Judith P. Sussholtz*

## Kornberg's Candy Store

E. 184th Street & Tiebout Avenue
1945-1960

*Every morning before getting on the bus on my way to DeWitt Clinton I would stop at Kornberg's Candy Store and order a tuna sandwich and soda for lunch. The sandwich was $.85 and the soda was a quarter. My father would pay Mr. & Mrs. Kornberg every Friday for the lunches that I had ordered.— Shepard Horowitz*

## KornBlooms

1696 Washington Ave, between 173 & 174 St.
1934-1940's

*Sold egg creams for 5 cents, candy for 1 cent, cigarettes for 10 cents a pack. —Herman Rosen*

## Kornfeld's

Corner of Brady Ave & White Plains Rd
1940-1949

*I was 8-13 in 1940-1945 when my parents, Hyman and Helen Kornfeld, owned the candy store at 2070 White Plains Rd. I remember the secret of making great malteds: use frozen milk shavings and not a lot of ice cream. Our store had a plaque with white stars on a blue background with the names of neighborhood boys in the service during WWII, including a gold star for a soldier named Harvey, who did not come home. I also remember that long block and a half walk I would take every night to pick up the next day's early edition of the News and Mirror, particularly heavy on Saturday night. A dozen neighborhood candy stores would pick up their bulk deliveries in front of the RKO Pelham. —Leo Kornfeld*

## Kramer's

163 West Tremont at University Avenues
1950-55

*Mr. & Mrs. Kramer ran the store. Mr. Kramer looked just like Hopalong Cassidy, and his wife reminded me of Harriet Nelson. Sold school supplies, egg creams, baseball cards, rubber balls and an assortment of bottled sodas. Various ice cream, including mello-rolls, were affectionately dispensed by Mrs. Kramer. — Steve Samtur*

## Kramer's

W 231st Street

*Owned by a hard working couple with Nazi Concentration Camp number tattooed on their arms. — Jerry Sullivan*

## Kranz's Candy Store

NW corner of 163rd St & Jackson Ave
1929-1944

*It was run by my parents Rubin & Clara Kranz, and the whole family. I remember that we were the telephone number for families-all around, like a radius of a block. We brought men and women to the phones for dates. We called people who had applied for work- with our number as their contact. In the winter, with few customers, my father and his friends played poker, only to be interrupted by a stray customer. — Rabbi Abraham Krantz*

## Krause's

Beekman Ave & Beech Ter
1950's
—*Joyce McGrail*

## Kresse's

Southwest corner of Morris Avenue and E. 174th Street
Owner: Mr. Goodman
1930s-46

*It was the big hangout in the thirties. Technically it might be called a luncheonette but it sold candy, too. — Marvin Nick Resnick*

## L&L Confectionery

1891 Gleason Ave
1940's-1950's

*The store was purchased, from the original owner, by 2 veterans, under the GI Bill, around 1945. It was named L&L after its owners: Lou Weinstein and Lou (?). They were known as "Fat Louie" and "Skinny Louie". Neither took offense in those years. They expanded the original store by breaking down a wall to the next storefront in 1946 or 47. The expanded counter space never caught on, and was used to store toys and other miscellaneous junk.*

*The store was the local gathering spot in the days before air conditioning; and like Cheers, everybody knew your name. I was the soda jerk for L&L, from 1949-1955, which was a high status job for a teenager, that paid 60 cents an hour-(minimum wage). —James I Levine*

## Landsman

E. 164th Street off Morris Avenue
Owners: Mr. and Mrs Landsman, son & daughter
1935-1960

*We would pass this store on the way to school - P.S. 35 on 163rd Street. Mr. Landsman was not too patient with all the kids that would come into the store at lunch break. It was not a place to socialize but it was the one store on the way to school to get penny candies. — Jeanette Verderosa*

## Lapin's

East 234 Street & East Gun Hill Road
1940-50's
*They had everything and anything every other store had. They were there so long that people thought they bought Gun Hill Rd. from the Indians. Ask anyone who grew up in the 40's and 50's about Lapins' and you'll get an earful.*

## Larry's

Gun Hill Rd & Tryon Ave North
1960's
*Larry's was a direct competitor to Milty's, being that they were catty-corner of each other. Larry specialized in pretzels and comic books, and would get pissed if you came in with goods from Milty's. He was a good guy though. —Arty Conliffe*

## Larry's Luncheonette

1534 Westchester Avenue
1955-1965
*My father owned this little luncheonette. It was located underneath the #6 IRT elevator train at the Elder Avenue station. In 1989, I had a book published about my father's shop called "My Father's Luncheonette" by Dutton Children's Books. Larry is still alive and kicking living on Hilton Head Island SC. He would love to hear from those who remember his place.— Melanie Hope Greenberg*

## Lavin's

*—Submitted by Daniela Nugent*

## Lee's

Corner of Fish and Boston Post Road
1940-78
*Lee was a friendly man with a generous heart. If you didn't have enough money he'd complain but let us have it anyway. He also took the time to know all the kids by name, and he always had a smile for us. It was a safe and friendly place. — Carol Friedman Lefkowitz*

## Leedman's

Leland & Westchester Avenues
Owners: Abe Leedman
1945-60
*Loose penny candy in glass jars, Hootens-plain and peanut, mello rolls, ice cream pops (3¢ and 5¢), plain seltzer, fountain made sodas, NY Daily News and Mirror (2¢ ea.) loose cigarettes, 2 phone booths in the rear of the store. It was a daily meeting location for everyone. —John Bredehoft*

## Leff's

Near Dover Theatre
1950's — *May Siegel Wilde*

## Leftoff's Cut Rate Candy Store

Jennings Street Market - Witkins Avenue, Charlotte Street, Minford Place and Southern Boulevard, also near the Freeman Street Train Station.
1930's
*The store might have been a hole in the wall. It was between Mittleman's Pickle and Herring stand and Rosenblatt's Dry Goods, but this little hole in the wall stood out like a shining light blinking.*

*In the early 1930s the store was bought by my mother, Becky Leftoff, as a family enterprise. For that period of time she was so business-wise, like she was born before her time. Eventually, the business was operated completely by my brother Dave. Everyone knew and loved him. If anyone needed a favor or help, he would be the first one there.*

*We sold candy, nuts and dried fruit by the pound, and occasionally by the piece. The aroma from the fresh hot roasted peanuts in the big burlap sacks got to you. They stood next to the Indian nuts, pumpkin seeds, sunflower seeds, walnuts, etc. Dave was one of the last retailers that Hershey Chocolates and Nestles sold to.*

*We didn't live in luxury in those days, but we all have such wonderful happy memories when we lived at 1412 Charlotte Street near the store, meeting and sitting on the closed stands and laughing and playing games, having fun with a feeling of safety. Are any of these friends around who recalls my memories? — Shirley Kirschbaum*

Leftoff's Cut Rate Candy Store in 1938. Dave (second from left), Bella (far right, Becky (third from far right), and Shirley (fourth from far right).

## Lefty Moe's
E. 183rd St. and Beaumont Avenue
Owners: Moe and Minnie
1947
*This place was great. There was always at least 200 kids hanging around Lefty's. I remember "The Big Guys," (guys who were 8 to 10 years older than us- who had just come back from WWII), playing records on the juke box until they wore out. There was a newspaper stand outside where they sold The Daily News, Daily Mirror, Times, Journal American and the Herald Tribune. — Russell Marrapodi*

## Leiblein Candy Store
Fox St between Westchester Ave & 163rd St
1940's
*Isidore Leiblein owned it, and his wife worked with him. His trigger finger was missing from his right hand. The candy store had an outside stand with newspapers, and inside, it had a counter and showcases.*
*—Phyllis Glass Fielding*

## Leightner's
Kingsbridge Avenue and W 231st Street
1950's
*Harry Leightner was the major domo with a frog-like voice and sourpuss wife. — Jerry Kopf*

## Lemme (Tony & Anne) Candy Store
Corner of Bronxwood Avenue & E. 213 Street
1950's
*This candy store had all the normal fountain drinks, bottles of Martin sodas (made in the Bronx), loose Cavalier cigarettes (3 for 5 cents), a terrific jukebox with all the early rock and roll records. My hangout (1952-1957) had Tony & Anne and her three daughters working the store. They treated all of us teenagers as family. It was a small store, one telephone booth, and maybe 6 stools. Tony always had a cigar in his mouth.— Joseph Schiavone*

## Leo's
Williamsbridge Rd between Mace & Waring Aves
Late 1950's-early 1960's
*A large store with full fountain & lunch service. It had large displays with all the popular 1-cent, 5-cents candies, soft pretzels, baseball cards, gum machines (1 cent), papers, magazines, comic books, Spaulding stick ball bats, tops, yo-yos, and hula hoops —Jack Albert*

## Leo's
East Tremont & Vyse Avenue
1938-1942
*Located across the street from PS 6. Leo's was like most candy stores in that it sold egg creams, two cents plain, malts and shakes. When we could afford them, Spaldeens cost 15 cents. However, in those days (1938-1942), we used a white ball called a "leader" which cost only a nickel. If there was a stickball game each team was required to buy a "leader". A new one would last about half a game, so two were needed. They did not bounce as high as a spaldeen but the bounce was truer!*

*Leo's had a fountain going from front to back and covered about half the length of the store. In the rear were two tables near a telephone booth. I was playing sandlot football (Firemens Field) when I badly sprained my ankle, and had to use crutches for two weeks. My mother didn't approve of me playing football and was sort of happy that my injury prevented me from playing. I managed to keep my equipment in his storeroom and several Saturdays in a row, I would "crutch' my way to the candy store and replace my crutches for football gear and reverse the procedure after the game, and Mom never found out! Hey, we "vyse guys" were a pretty tight group back then!*
*— Phil (Pat) Farrell*

## Leo's Candy Store
Northwest Corner of Field Place and the Concourse
*— Hoffer Kaback*

## Leverah's
Corner of W. 165th Street & Woodycrest Avenue
1940-50's
## became Sam's Candy Store
1950-60's
*A big hangout for kids from PS 73 and Anderson and Woodycrest Avenues.— Bobby Johnson*

## Libbys
321 East 166th St
1928-1948
*This store was located next to "Faders" Fruit & Vegetable Market and a Barber Shop and Grocery Store all on the ground floor at the corner of E 166th St & Findlay Ave, which was a 20 apartment building.*

## Lieflander's Candy Store

Honeywell Ave between E178 St and 179 St
1950's-1960's

*This store was located opposite PS 67, where every afternoon I would take 10 cents and buy my father's Jewish paper and an ice cream, often a "mello-roll", which was an ice cream cylinder wrapped in paper that could be placed, vertically or horizontally, in a wafer cone. One of the Lieflanders was deaf, and the tough guys would always harass them. —Ruth Albert Spencer*

## Lifer's

Creston Avenue & E 198th Street
1950s-60s

*Here I bought baseball cards with that lousy gum for five cents and my emerald green Duncan Yo-Yo for $1.00*

## Lou's

3rd Ave & E Tremont Ave
1947-1965

*My Aunt Lil & Uncle Lou owned this store. It was long and narrow. There was a counter with stools from the middle of the store to the back. In front was a window open to the street, where candy and gum were displayed. They made the best egg creams and malteds. All the bus drivers would stop in on their breaks. I used to love going behind the counter to help customers. —Sandra Krentcil*

## Lou's

Gun Hill Road and Tryon Avenue
Owners: Lou Guyer (daughter Ellen)
1950-60

*Lou's was a long oblong shaped store with the front door at the lower left corner. On the rack behind the front door were the comic books- 10¢ for the regular size and 25¢ for the giant Christmas annual. Along the opposite side of the store ran the counter, split into 2 parts: the short left side with rows of candy, gum and trading cards, and the longer right side with stools in front and soda machines and a griddle in back. Lou was cook, sandwich maker, cashier and keeper of order and, if I close my eyes really tightly, I can still smell and hear the sound of the burgers frying, and Lou telling us not to read the comics unless we were buying them. — Alan S. Gordon*

## Louie and Ann's

Grand Avenue between Buchanan Place and E. 182nd Street.
1933-1955

*I have the fondest memories of growing up in a store that was the center of that neighborhood. Anyone who went to PS 91 would remember it fondly. — Ed Zemmel*

## Louie's

Lydig Ave and Wallace Ave
1940's-1950's

*I worked there after school in 1957. The place was owned by Mr. Lombardi. I earned $1 an hour and worked there from 4 PM to 9 PM on Mondays, Wednesdays, and Fridays. I filled the syrup reservoir in the fountain and stocked the cigarette shelves. Mr. Lombardi actually gave me lessons in the preparation of cherry-cokes, lime rickeys, and vanilla sodas. I was given very special lessons in the creation of both chocolate and vanilla egg creams and malteds. There was a fierce competition in the neighborhood as to who made the best egg cream. People would actually go out of their way to find their favorite.*

*My Mom and Pop would stop by the store from time to time and would always comment "your boss looks like Chester Morris", (a movie star in the 30's and 40's). I don't know if that was true, but I do know that Mr. Lombardi took great pride in his candy store; and if he is still alive, I'll bet that he is still trying to make the best egg cream in the neighborhood. —Richard Meduri*

## Louie's Candy Store
Leland & Archer
1946-1949

*My father purchased the store in 1946, and operated it with the help of my mother Fritzie and me. Our biggest business was fountain service and cigarette sales. We even sold cigarettes as singles, for those who couldn't afford the 20 cents pack. I learned to make a variety of sundaes and ice cream sodas, shakes, etc., and treated myself to one, practically everyday. The kids, who played stickball just down the block on Leland, always stopped in for sodas after the games. —Marty Silverberg*

## Louie's Candy Store
E. 181st Street and Crotona Avenue
Owner: Louie
1940-1960

*The store was long and narrow with a counter on one side and comic books and magazines on the other. Great place to buy an egg cream and pretzel and read all the comic books. We had dozens of guys form various age groups hanging out who would not co-mingle with other age groups until their age group was depleted and the remainder of the group had to drop down and consolidate with the next age group. Louie was a confirmed bachelor, short and bald, and worked the store alone. I would guess a million Spaldeens were sold from his store as the P.S. 57 schoolyard and Crotona Avenue playground were on the same street. — Carmine Fiore*

## Luboff's
Quimby and Houghton Avenue
1930's

*If the funds permitted, I bought Mello-Rolls, Hootens, and the Daily News. Luboff's was next door to Pep Cerbone's fathers' deli. — Patricia Donohue*

## Lujack's Candy Store
Andrews Avenue & West Fordham Road
1955-1965

*This rather large candy store could hold up to 60 kids. It had a candy counter on one side and two telephone booths on the other side along with three fountains and ten stools. This was a big lunchtime hangout for Tolentine High School male smokers. —William Fulham*

## Luxor Sweet Shop
210 E. 170th Street
Owner: Harold Bernholz
1947-63

*Soda fountain and eight stools. You could get egg creams and other sodas from the "outside" window. Milkbox outside held newspapers. Inside you could buy cigars from a humidor. Local kids would purchase their candy there to save a few pennies instead of buying at the Luxor movie theater next door. — Harold Bernholz*

## M's
Sedgwick Ave Near Van Cortlandt Ave
1950-60's

*This was a large hangout that had fountain service as well as a short order cook. School supplies were a big sell as P.S. 95 was a block away and Clinton was about 4 blocks away. —Scott Willmarth*

## M's Candy Store
3891 Sedgwick Ave
1956-1960's

*M's was owned by 2 men named Max and Murray, thus called M's. When you walked in, the cash register was on the left, along with a counter, with approximately 20 stools. We would buy egg creams, cherry lime rickeys, burgers and fries. They always had a big jar of pretzel rods on the counter. On the right side were newspapers, comics, magazines, plus a rack with 5 cent bags of potato chips and pretzels. There were approximately 6 tables and some booths. Back in the late 60's, I remember so many "Hippies" hanging out in front of the store. They were always high and stoned. The owners of M's would throw them out, all the time, because people were afraid to go into the store. Thankfully, by the time I started hanging out there, it was pretty cleaned up, as most of them were either shipped off to jail or Vietnam.*

*Murray sold his share to a man named Herman, and it ran under the name of Hermax, but we still referred to it as M's. About 1971 or 72, Charlie Licata bought the store and we called it Charlie's. Then Charlie put in a pizza oven in the back and made the store larger. Later on about 1975, it became Pizza Italia. —Mindi Marra*

Mae above outside the store. Sign still reads O'Leary. Al below inside the store

## Mae's Candy Store
E 182 St & Crotona Park
1940's-1950's
—Michael Martorana

## Mannie's
Grand Concourse between 150th & 151st Streets
1940-50's
*This candy store was located one block from Cardinal Hayes HS and Mannie became an adopted son of Hayes. Moving from his former shop to a larger and more modern place, he was able to accommodate more Hayesmen; although with the crowd he had every day after dismissal, one wondered what place would be large enough to accommodate them. When I moved to Eagle Ave in 1939, our candy store located on 563 Eagle Ave was owned by Mr.*

One of the highlights of the year was the opening of a new store by Mannie who was an adopted son of Hayes H.S. Moving from his former shop to a larger and more modern place, he was able to accommodate more Hayes men; although with the crowd he had every day after dismissal, one wondered what place would be large enough to accommodate them.

## Mae & Al's
827 Melrose Ave.
Owners: May & Al Hedrich
1940-45
*This 6 seat fountain service sold greeting cards, comics, papers and had 2 tables on one side for luncheonette service. It had a cigar and candy case and sold individual pieces of candy. Mae & Al made great egg creams, sundaes and banana splits. Sold Reisman's Pretzel Rods: 3 for 5¢. Formerly O'Leary's — Peg Rivera*

*Goodman. In 1940 he sold out to Mr. Anshel, and opened another candy store a block away on the corner of Caldwell Ave and 149th St. His business flourished and within a year moved right next door to my apartment building at 569 Eagle Ave. Every candy store had its share of unusual people. One that comes to mind was a young man with a physical affliction. His eyes were turned, he was knocked-kneed and walked with a limp. He probably had cerebral palsy but no one knew about that in the early forties. Because of his appearance, he was called Gizmo. Gizmo achieved fame when on a summer day he asked Mr. Anshel for something unusual. He wanted a 'Mello-Roll' in a small coke glass, (the kind he used for a two-cents plain), with a spritz of chocolate syrup. The Mello-Roll' fit into the bottom of the glass like they were made for one another. Mr. Anshel charged him a dime for the concoction. Another kid saw this and asked for "one of those things you just made for Gizmo." With that the 'Gizmo Special' was born circa 1942.*

## Manny's
E. 178th Street and Bryant Avenue
1940-45
*Next to Frank's Barber Shop. Big hangout for teenagers. Penny candy, mello-rolls and cream sodas.*
—Ethel Weissman

## Manny's Candy Store
SW corner of Beach Ave & Randall Ave
1955-1964
*It was a small candy that sold a coke for 5 cents, and an egg cream was 6 cents or 10 cents. There was a large comic book rack in the front, and a small toy section in the rear of the store. —Bob Spinicchia*

## Marshack's
On W. 169th Street & Plimpton Avenue
1930-40's
*This candy store was sold in the early forties to the Nadelbergs (Harry). The Nadelbergs must have been saints to put up with us, like stealing his wooden paperstand and leaving it in front of his apartment door. G-d forgive us. — Arthur Trump*

## Marty's
Tremont Ave & Anthony Ave
1950's-1960's
*Marty's was approximately 1-2 stores W of Anthony, on the North side of Tremont. It was owned by Marty. His wife worked the card shop on Tremont (same block). —Linda Messite Bell*

## Max's (later G & Z Sweet Shoppe)

1003 Freeman Street
1945-1951

*They made the best malted, egg creams and lime rickeys in the summer. Every day after school, 1945-51 my mother would order a vanilla malted & a long pretzel. As we got older I remember that Fat Max could not tolerate us very long if we didn't buy anything, and eventually lost his patience and would ask us to move on. However, he did not wish to alienate us completely – he didn't want to lose our 'spaldeen' trade. His brother, Skinny Max, had a more tolerant personality. —Richard L. Warshaw*

## Max's Candy Store

E. 182nd Street and
Prospect Avenue
1938-1942

*This was my folk's candy store. I was quite young and, therefore can't remember any details except for egg creams, 2 cent pretzel rods and Nestle coffee in beige cups and saucers.
— B. Plisco*

## Maxies

Corner of Gun Hill Road & Putnam Place
1939-1955

*Owned by Max Lipschitz and his wife and their son, Leo who played sax in the Evander HS band. Had the best egg creams. Mrs. Lipschitz would often congratulate a young bride when she ordered a malted because the common wisdom at the time said that a malted (or the malt in the malted) was healthy for pregnant women. — Miriam Gerchman Albert*

"The Boys" in front of Maxie's Candy Store, 1951.

## Maxies

On Melrose Avenue & E. 151st Street
1940's-1970's

*Maxie's Candy Store was across the street from Immaculate Conception School on 151st Street. As you entered from Melrose Avenue, there were 10 stools at the soda fountain counter on the right. Two booths for group seating were on the left side of the store towards the back. A window counter for payment without entering store was available on Melrose Ave. I remember getting a soda and standing next door at the TV store watching the 1956 World Series. Next to the store was Tiny Tim Clothing Store. Maxie was competing with Mike's Candy Store, located between E. 151 and E. 152nd St.
— Albert D'Amato*

*The jukebox was in the rear along with some booth. That is where the boys and girls would meet after school. Immaculate Conception Catholic school segregated the genders in the sixth, seventh, & eighth grades, due to puberty.
—James Sweeney*

## Mayer's (then Guenthers)

E. 219th Street & White Plains Road
1960-1966

*This was a large store with marble tile. It had more than a dozen stools and nine booths in the back of the store. It had a very nice candy showcase and served breakfast and lunch. It was a big hangout for White Plain Rd. kids in the 60's and it had a jukebox. — Carlo Gambino*

## McMahon's

Cypress Avenue between E. 138th & E. 139th Street

*This was a favorite stop on the way to St. Luke's Grammar School, St. Helena's on Cypress Avenue and E. 141st Street. It had great egg creams. — M.A. DeBellis*

## Measer's

1661 University
Ave. & Tenny Place
1950-55

*This was a big time hangout for Andrews Ave. kids living between W. 175th & W. 176th Street. Sold all newspapers including the Forwards. Owner worked with his wife and made great egg creams. Mr. Measer was not particularly likable and the neighborhood kids would love to drive him crazy. —Jeff Weinstein*

## Mendel's

Allerton Avenue and White Plains Road.
Owners: Mr. Mendel
1940-55

*Mendel was Hymie's brother who owned Hymie's Candy Store. You could place an order or make a request at their shop window that opened to the street. Kids from the Coop and PS96 found the store convenient.*
*—Dee Verdecanna Fabian*

## Menschel's

West Burnside Avenue & Hennessey Place
1933-43

*I lived in the building of Menschels. How do I know? It was my candy store for those years. Every morning on my way to school (PS 26), I would bring the change left for the newspapers on the newsstand into the store and give it to Mr. Menschel. Along about 1937 I had been yearning for a particular airplane model kit. I had saved 14 cents and needed 25 cents to buy it. One cold snowy morning I passed the newsstand and there was 11 cents I needed. I took the 11 cents and days later bought the model for 25 cents from Mr. Menschel.*

*In 1945 I returned from the University of Wisconsin, during vacation, to visit a friend in the old neighborhood (my family moved to Washington Hts). I went into the store to return the 11 cents with interest, but the Menschels were gone. Apparently, the store was sold in the early 40's and the store was called Pops. — Sanford Buchsbaum*

## Meyer's

121 Mt. Eden Avenue

## Mike's Candy Store

On Melrose between E. 151st & E. 152nd Streets
1950-1970

*Sodas were 5 cents and the newspaper was 3-5 cents. Long rod pretzels were 2 cents each and the egg cream was 6 cents in a paper cup. Seltzer was 2 cents a glass or cup. This store competed with Maxie's just a block away, also located on Melrose Avenue. – Albert D'Amato*

## Miller's

Corner of E. 152nd Street and Jackson Avenue
Owners: Mr. and Mrs. Miller
1943

*There were several previous owners before Mr. and Mrs. Miller took the store over and gave it a warmth and charm of its own. They had the familiar newsstand out front, a window that slid open to cater to the hurrying customers for a pack of butts, an egg cream, or some other libation. It kept a Coca Cola ice box out front which housed Cokes, Pepsis, and Mission Orange. At the counter were the usual revolving stools and just within reach beyond the counter was an impressive array of candies. The glass enclosed cases in the rear housed many school supplies and some token toys just to cover all the bases. My favorite pastime on a Saturday morning was a visit to Miller's for a chocolate malt and a pretzel stick while I perused the sample issue of Life magazine. —Chet Wargocki*

## Miller's

E Tremont Ave. between Southern Blvd. & Marmion Ave;
1920-1930's

*This ice cream parlor was my family's favorite because of the terrific Tutti Fruitti ice cream. They made their own ice cream. —Robert J. Henessy*

## Mintz's

Corner of Allerton &
Barker Avenues
mid 1930's
— *Harry Kulkowitz*

## Miss Lynn's Candy Store

SW 141st & Alexander Ave
1925-1960's

*It was a small store with a soda fountain and candy counter. Inside entrance was on the left side, with a glass case for cigarettes. Miss Lynn used to sharpen my pencil and fill my fountain pen, when I stopped on my way to PS 9. There was a newsstand out front. Miss Lynn sold the store to Sonny Conklin during WWII, but she stayed in the neighborhood until the late 50s. A couple bought the store from Sonny in the late 50's, and in the 60's it closed. —Charles J Bruno*

## Mr Dee's Store/aka Mr. DiBenedetto

Corner of E 173 St & Boynton Ave
1953-1979

*Our neighborhood candy store was perpendicular to Bronx River Ave and was the last vestige of a real 'candy store'. The candy store functioned as a 'gathering point', wherein we met before school, then after school, after supper, and before we went on dates with our girlfriends. The candy store served also as a 'warm place' in the winter before we rented a neighbor's basement for a clubroom. Popular items at the time were mission soda in the water, Mary Janes before you could smoke them, Bonomo's Turkish Taffy. The Bazooka bubble gum sold for a penny and the triangular pretzel seven cents. All of the candy store owners lived in the neighborhood: Mr. Dee, Frank Pisello Sr, in partnership with Pauline and her husband Casper, Louie and Sylvia Manniacci, and Fabio and Margie Delonoy, respected and guided us kids while our parents respected and trusted them with us. —Edward Jackson*

## Mr. Di

Bronx River & Boynton Avenues
1950-1970

*At age 13 I was a soda jerk at Mr. Di's. I remember a black and white tile floor, and mopping it at night. Everyone who walked into the store would spin the stools, and many left chewing gum underneath the counter. The thing I remember most was making Ed Kranepool and his high school coach egg creams when they came in. You were able to get an ice*

*cream cone for ten cents, with a penny extra for sprinkles and a malted cost 35 cents. You would get your soda from a soda bin that was kept cool in summer with ice water. On hot summer days, Mr Di left the candy store window open for lime rickeys (10 cents), soda water (3 cents) and loose penny candy. —Richard Grunner*

## Mr Gordon's

St Anne's Ave & E138th St
1950-1964

*Mr Gordon's was a small candy store, on the first level of a five-story walk-up, on the SE corner of the intersection. It had a marble counter that was typical at that time. It wasn't very long, but was easy to clean. He sold egg creams for 7 cents, and later raised it to 10 cents. He sold Pepsi, Coke, and Mission sodas. I remember that the Mission sodas were a penny more than Pepsi or Coke because the deposit on them was 3 cents, instead of 2 cents. Long pretzels were 2 cents each, or 3 for a nickel. In addition to the typical newspapers, candy and school supplies, he also sold loose cigarettes--2 for a nickel-(naturally they were called "two cents loose"). In the back, there was a shooting gallery machine with one rifle, which after a while we could play blindfolded. Our big thrill was when Mr Gordo would "trust" one of us to tend his store while he ran errands. —Steve Solcz*

## Mr Lester

Corner of Ogden Ave & Merriam Ave
1940's

*Mr. Lester introduced me to my first chocolate egg cream, mallomar and charlotte-russe. My dad would send me for a pack of Lucky Strikes. They cost $0.20, but had two pennies enclosed, which I got to keep.*

*When I opened The Jumbo Luncheonette in Somers, NY, I served Mr Lester's egg creams. It was amazing and exciting when customers recognized where I was from.
—Barbara Boreman*

## Mr. Yellen's Candy Store

E 187th Street & Park Avenue
1945-1962

*A little candy store that sold everything, including syrup of Coca-Cola that doctors recommended back then for an upset stomach. The store was opened 7 days a week, and Mr. Yellen worked with his wife. The store had four stools, and Mr. Yellin was very good to the kids. He had a dog who had puppies, and I adopted one of them. —Ottilie Giampa*

## Moishes (Pyramid Confectionary)

Jennings Street & Longfellow Avenue
1938-53

*Owned by Moishe & Laibel Ginsburg. Located across the street from PS 66 where we purchased the "Clincher" for $1 for our weekend softball schoolyard games. It had a news- stand which had all the NY papers for $1. I would often make the trip up to E. 138th St & Prospect to purchase the pink edition of the Daily News. There were racks for comic books and magazines. They had the best egg creams (U-bet Syrup) and 1¢ cigarettes. When it became too crowded, Moishe would yell "TIME" and we all left only to return 5 minutes later. — Larry (Sonny) Hoffman*

## Moishe's

Fox Street between Prospect and Avenue St. John
1941-1945

*This was a long rectangular store with 3 stools and one fountain which served ice cream, malted and ice cream sodas. — M.A. DeBellis*

## Molly and Izzy's

W. 231st Street
1930's-1970's

*Molly and Izzy ran their store for 20 plus years before retir- ing and selling it to Moe in the late 50's. Moe ran it for about 15 years. As youngsters, we bought cherry and vanilla cokes, egg creams, sundaes, malteds, 2-cent candies and hand packed ice cream. Molly was a friendly, motherly redhead. Moe was friendly too, but had many customers accuse him of shortchanging them. — Jerry Sullivan*

## Moskoff's (was Spector's previously)

E. 170 Street & Stebbins Avenue
1930's

*Located between Stebbins & 170 St . I lived on the 3rd floor of that building. The store in your listing identified as Stephens, B at 1204 Union Ave in the 60's was known as Kiel's in the 30's & 40's. My wife, (then Miriam Richman) lived in that building. Her family owned the grocery store next door. Our happy marriage still continues.—Victor Feigelman*

## Mt. Eden

Corner of Mt. Eden Avenue between Townsend & Jerome
1940-45

*This was a very narrow and long store with black and white floor tile. They sold penny candy, egg creams, wax lips, and pink liquid in wax bottles. The newspapers were sold on the outside for the convenience of those taking the Woodlawn- Jerome IRT. I remember being in the candy store the day WWII ended, and a lady upon hearing the news gave me candy. I was thrilled because I had mistakenly thought that from that day forward all candy would be free! —Marvin Scott*

## Mukin's

E. 175th Street and Clinton Avenue
*Two men, Hy and Norman, ran it. They had wonderful frappes and egg creams (of course).— Susan Krochmal*

## Mumm's

Layton Avenue & Northern corner of Eastern Boulevard
Late 1930's

*The Bronx Historical Society*

Mr. Mumm, the proprietor, stands on the left, while Mr. Schmidt is on the right.

## Murray's
Gun Hill Road & Hull Ave
1950-1980

*The nighttime corner-spot for the teenage Gun Hill crowd who hung out in The Oval. Murray was a patient man who tolerated the lunatics of this group for many years – especially '70-75. His specialty was all sorts of egg creams and breakfast fare. —Arty Conliffe*

Photo: Mike Newman
Murray's Candy Store at Gun Hill Rd & Hull Aveue.

## My Brothers Luncheonette
749 Astor Ave
1981-1985
*Down the block from Columbus HS and JHS 135.
—Sid & Bob Roffman*

## Nadelberg's Candy Store
W. 169th Street between Nelson Ave. & Plimpton
1960's
*— Spencer Field*

## Nat's Candy Store
Northeast Corner of Seneca and Bryant Avenues
1950's
*It was a long store with about eight stools. Towards the back of the store Nat would sell penny candies. His ice cream was hand-packed and he made delicious sundaes. Nat wouldn't let the kids hang out there too long. —Sandy Weiss Cohen*

Photo: Spencer Field
Nadelberg's Candy Store.

## Nemeroff's Candy Store
1565 Wilkins Avenue
1940's
*Ralph Petracca home on furlough (Air Force) with Joe Nemeroff.
— Celia Keats*

## Ness's Candy Store
Marmion Ave. near E. Tremont Ave. & Southern Blvd.
1945
*When my father died in 1925, my mother bought a candy store. It was a dry store at the time so we installed a soda fountain facing the side wall where we dispensed egg cream and malted milk. In 1925, the Biograph Studios were on E. 176th Street and Marmion Avenue and Ralph Bellamy, Milton Sills, and Mary Pickford frequently dropped in for refreshments. My neighbor and schoolmate was Dr. Jonas Salk who discovered the polio vaccine and who also helped out in the candy store. — Hy Ness*

## Newman's Candy Store
911 Southern Blvd.
(early 1920's)
*The photo is taken at 911 Southern Boulevard in the early 1920's. In front of the store stands Harry Newman (owner). His wife Becky is sitting with their three children: Sol is the youngest at age 3; behind him is Sylvia, age 5 and Hal, age 7. – Mike Newman (grandson)*

Photo: Mike Newman

## Nick's

E. 174th Street between Noble and Rosedale
1959-67

*The counter had about 6 stools. Nick's thumb was messed up. It was injured and had a big, heavy nail which somehow always managed to get into your egg cream! Big hangout for Rosedale Ave. guys from PS 106. — Paul Narson*

## Nicky's Candy Store

896 Melrose Avenue
1950's-1960's

*Owned and operated by Nick & Helen DePerto. Helen's mother, Nancy, also worked, and threw kids out regularly. Helen's brother-in-law, Emil also worked there and made the biggest ice cream cones. Everyone wanted to be there when Emil was on duty. Nick had a newsstand on the outside and a jukebox in the rear of the store. Plays were 6 for 25 cents. There was always music playing when the gang was in the store. Nicky made the best egg creams this side of heaven, and everyone used a 2 cent stick pretzel as a stirrer. — Maureen Corallo*

## Normandy Candy Store

corner of E. 170th
Street and Walton
Avenue
1950-60's

*It was a great luncheonette/candy store combination that was lined with a counter on one side and booths on the other. Large picture windows along Walton Avenue and E. 170 Street gave us a great view of local passers-by. — Michelle Newmark Cahill*

## Nuts & Butts

Between Morris & Creston Avenues on E. 184th Street
1939-48

*Located directly across from Bronx Science, where most of the students would go after school. One nearby candy store, back then, had some type of advanced technology where they were able to produce a frozen malted. —Myron B. Kurtzman*

## Olshen's

E. 154th Street and Melrose Avenue
Owner: Mr. J. Olshen
1932-42

*Olshen's served the usual egg creams and fountain drinks, plus you could strike up great conversations with the other patrons. —James Montesarchio*

## Paley's

Hunt's Point Ave & Faile St
1940's-1950's
—Stan Fine

## Patsy's Candy Store

203rd Street off Mosholu Parkway
(down the street from PS 8)
Approximate date: 1935-1950

*Patsy was a man of endless patience, gentle humor and constant friendliness. He made the greatest sundaes in the world, after explaining in his thick accent that he couldn't because it was Monday or Tuesday or Friday!!! They were architectural wonders. I spent whatever money I earned delivering prescriptions for Lefkiewitz Drug Store at Patsy's and have never forgotten the pleasure they brought. — Jack Getman*

## Pensky's

1208 Stratford Avenue
1935-45

*Mr. Pensky always wore a white smock behind a very high counter. He was more businesslike than friendly. Papers were always available on the stand outside the store. — Joe Behar*

## Peppermint Bar

Commonwealth & Beach Avenues
Owner: Mr. & Mrs. Cummings
1949-57

*It was a second home to many of us growing up in the area. The Academy Gardens was located across the street, a private apartment complex. When most of the boys went off to the Korean and Vietnam wars, the owners displayed all their photos. — Mario DeSantis*

*1953-1956 Egg cream, 12 cents. The owners (when I remember them) never smiled. — Kathleen Dunn Washington*

## Pete's Candy Store

E 167 St between Hoe Ave & West Farms Rd
1940's to mid 1950's

*Pete was a great Latin gentleman that owned this store. —Rev. Jerry Caterino*

## Pete's Candy Store

Williamsbridge Rd between Mace Ave & Waring Ave
1940's-1950's

*Pete was a friend, priest, rabbi, and confidant to all the kids in the neighborhood. He made the best egg creams in town. In the summer he created drinks. His most famous drink was called 'beat the heat'. I remember cigarettes were 24 cents per pack, and if you were short of cash, Pete would extend credit. God bless him. —Nicholas Zeoli*

## Phil's Candy Store

Creston Ave & East Kingsbridge Rd
1940's-1950's

*Phil's was a meeting place that sold egg creams, ice cream, ice cream sodas, newspapers, cigars, and cigarettes. My best memories were at the counter drinking egg creams or ice cream sodas. —Myrna Leavitt Goldberg*

## Pinchick's

Boston Road near Prospect Avenue
1930's

*Mr. Pinchick sold candy and school supplies. I remember him being small and unfriendly.*

## Pippy's Luncheonette

Courtlandt Ave between E 155 St & E 156 St
1950-1952

*This store was the third candy store my parents owned before they moved to New Jersey. Pippy was my father's partner. My parents names were Nick and Nettie Massella. Both my sisters (Bernice and Milli) helped in the store. We had a soda fountain, and made lots of ice cream sodas, egg creams, sundaes, etc. We also did some short order cooking.
—Joan Massella Dahmer*

## PMP Luncheonette

Kingsbridge Road and Creston Avenue
Owners: Paul (ex-fighter), Phil (horseplayer) and Abe (poet)
1940-60's

*The best egg creams, great "sendviches". Employed successive generations of neighborhood boys. Their basement was always available for a card game for a small "cut".
—R. Randy Lee*

## Pop's

Corner of West Burnside Avenue & Hennessy Place
1940-50's

*This store (under 2 names) was such an important part of our lives as kids growing up in the Bronx. Originally called Pop's. Pop Wagner was the owner. Later owned by Willie & Nat. It had everything and was a Dolly Madison Ice Cream Shop.*

## Pop's

2001 Clinton Avenue corner 179th Street
Owner: Abe Goldstein
1950's

*Across the street from PS 92 —Hector Luis Colon*

## Pop's Candy Store

E. 189th Street and
Beaumont Avenue
*I believe the owners' names were Sam & Rose. We just called him Pop.
—Joseph Brutto*

## Pop Sivics'

162 St near
Woodycrest Ave
1940s-1950s

*My father would send me down, with 2 cents for the N.Y. News, and if they were all sold out Pop would say "No more Nooses." He also packed Breyers loose ice-cream by hand which, I'm sure, was as good as Haagen-Daz anyday.
—Harriet Paget Ritzer*

## Portnoy's

N.E. corner of St. John Avenue and Southern Boulevard.
*Mr. Portnoy didn't like people, especially the dozen or so teenagers who hung out in front of his store. Probably because we hardly ever purchased anything, maybe a pretzel stick or an occasional malted. Our attraction to Portnoy's was its vantage point to the candy store across the street where the older guys hung out. —Anna Belle Meisler*

## Raider's Candy Store

Sheridan Avenue & McClellan Street
1940's-1950's
*Raiders Candy Store had the largest selection of comic books and was the hangout for the Spartans team. — Aaron Elkind*

## Ralph DiBenedetto

Bronx River Avenue - corner of Boynton Avenue
1943-62
*Ralph made the absolutely best Cherry Lime Rickey! It was served in a tall frosted glass with a cherry. You could get Mello-Rolls, Nedick's Orange Drink in a bottle from an iced case; spaldeens, and on the counter next to the chocolate covered jelly candy were two rectangular shaped cookies with jelly inside edged with chocolate sprinkles!!*
*—Rosalyn Steinberg Pulfer*

## Ramm's Ice Cream Parlor

3805 White Plains Rd and E. 219th St
1900-1950
*My grandparents owned Ramm's. They made their own ice cream and candy. People came for miles for their home-made confections. My sister Millie and I used to love to go to the store to get our treats and have the opportunity to walk behind the counters and look at all the candy and once in awhile "help" a customer.—Florence Ramm Lagergren*

## Rand's

1566 Watson Avenue between Ward & Manor Avenues
*—Submitted by Honey Rand*

## R&B Luncheonette

650 East 233rd Street
Owner: Ralph Martinez, his wife and two sons Ralph and Bob.
*—Ralph Martinez*

Ralph of R & B

## Rappaports

College Avenue and
E. 170th Street
*We walked two steps up into a candy store that was wedged between the Young Israel of College Avenue and the neighboring building. The small interior supplied us with all our sweet needs. —Susan Honickman Samtur*

## Rauch's

St. John between Fox & Beck
1944-1950
*I spent these years working as a "soda jerk," among other chores after school. It was a hangout for lots of kids, but my mother, Beckie, didn't mind because she loved people of all ages. —Selma "Rauch" Brawzinsky*

## Rauch's

973 Avenue St. Johns
*It was an ordinary store-no stands-a stand up counter. It did have 3 tables and chairs, a greeting card display, a magazine and comic book rack and 2 coin telephone booths. They served egg creams, of course, ice cream sodas, frappes and sundaes, ice cream cones, malteds, hot chocolates, cigars, cigarettes, toys, balloons, and the usual candy store items of the era. Oh yes, bottled and fountain sodas. —Florence Jurgrau (nee Rauchweyer)*

Rauch's on Avenue St. Johns

## Reiser's

170th St & Findlay Ave
1937-1957
*Small homey store owned by Mr. Reiser, who knew all the local kids. He made great egg creams for 5 cents. I always got my grandmother her "forvetz" (Forwards) there.*
*—Judith Busman*

## Rendezvous

Northeast corner of E. 182nd and Grand Concourse
1950-1973

*For many years, Joe, Charlie and Paul owned this place. How they all derived an income from this place could not have been from what they sold. The wagering that took place there must have been the forerunner of OTB. Charlie worked in the Post Office full time, Joe came in to collect his money, and Paul must have been independently wealthy. For many years, a lovely but miserable heavy-set bachelor named Mitch was the soda fountain guy. They never had any supplies, decent magazines or stock to sell, but, boy, could Mitch make the best egg cream and vanilla cokes. To date, I still drink vanilla cokes. We often hung out there after basketball or a date, but you weren't permitted to stay too long, because the excitement wasn't good for Joe's heart.*
— Warren Tockerman

## Rendezvous

Corner of Ward Avenue & Westchester
1946-1955

*This was a great place for teens to meet and have a social and enjoy egg creams, ice cream sodas and malteds. It also had a juke box and some of us danced to the latest popular music and swing bands. – Al Alster*

## Richman

E. 176th Street & Anthony Avenue
1938-1947

*This was a corner store with an enormous tree in front. In addition to the regular New York newspapers, Mr. Richman would also sell ethnic newspapers like* The Forwards, Il Progresso, the Staat Zeitung, The Irish Echo *as well as a Civil Service newspaper called* The Chief. *It had a little fountain and sold the usual egg creams, ice cream sodas, etc. At the front of the store (along the glass) were several phone booths. They were very popular until 1948 when families were able to afford their own phone. Echo Park, across the way was renamed Richman Park because of Mr. Richman's family who were active in civil affairs.*
— Gary Grahl

## Ritzers

Decatur Ave & Bedford Pk Blvd
1950's

*This neighborhood-gathering place, run by Mr. and Mrs. Harry Ritzer and their two sons, featured a sweeping soda fountain, and a number of phone booths. We would call our girlfriends from there, for 5 cents, and Harry would sometimes have to pry us out for another paying customer, who*

*needed to make a call. The 10-cent egg creams were good, but not the pretzels. So many of us loudly gathered outside, and the lady living just above the store would occasionally throw a pail of water on us. —Ed Costello*

## Rockwood Place Candy Store

Between Walton Ave & Grand Concourse
1948-1958

*Small store, with lending library, owned by a young couple, Shirley & Al Bush. Shirley's brother, Willie, worked in the store every night. I married him in 1957. From 1951, when I started to go out with him, he brought ice cream to my father every night. When he made an egg cream, (7 cents), he put the syrup in last, and called it a "straight up". —Judy Schall Rubin*

## Rogoff's

Corner Lydig Ave & Holland Ave
1952-1956

*This candy store was owned by Max Rogoff. I went to high school with his son Jay, and we both worked there, as soda jerks and short order cooks, after school. The training got me a job, in Loch Sheldrake in the Castskills, as a short order cook, the summer before I started college. —Sy Kotler*

## Romeo's Candy Store
Hoffman St between E 187 & E 188 St
1940-1948

*My Dad owned this candy store and coffee shop. We used to roast Italian and American coffee. I felt lucky to be able to eat all the candy and ice cream I wanted. Cigarettes sold for 14 to 18 cents a pack. Loose cigarettes cost a penny, and you got a wooden match with your purchase. Black market cigarettes sold for 25 cents a pack (1941-1945), if you could get it. Candy, ice cream bars, and sodas were 5 cents.*

*It was a hangout for many of the Italian immigrants in the area. They left their families back in Italy during the 30's and 40's, in the hope of making their fortune in America. After the war, they were able to bring their families to the Bronx, for a better life. —Anthony Chirico*

## Ronnie's Sweet Shoppe
755 Allerton Avenue
1955-65

## Rose's
1793 Montgomery Avenue
Owned by 2 Brothers
1940's

*The brothers were drafted and then another man owned the store. Then the store was taken over by a woman named Rose and her husband together with their son who worked for the American Chiclet Company. Rose's was the most convenient candy store/luncheonette to P.S. 109 located on Popham Avenue. Rose always looked out for the kids and you could telephone them at lunchtime. Those were the days of 2-cent pretzels, egg creams, vanilla sodas and penny candies. —Phyllis (Goldberg) Lerner*

## Rosie's
1717 Hoe Avenue - corner of E 174th Street
1930's-50's

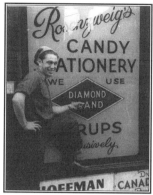

*Mr. Rosensweig, my father, owned the store from the mid 30's until the mid 50's. Open 7 days a week from 5.30am to 1a.m. except on Saturday, when it was opened all night. There were 5 sons. They all started when they were 8 or 9 years old. The store was the local meeting place. The only person not allowed in was the numbers person. During the summertime he would 'rent' out a table for the use of the 'hackies' for limo service up to the Catskills. He also had a contract with the Mountain Transit Bus Co. who provided daily service to the Catskills. —Alex Rosensweig*

## Roy's
E. 174th Street and Selwyn Avenue
1950-55

*It was long and narrow. Counter had ten stools. Magazines were on the right when you entered. Sold malteds and terrific hamburgers. –Stephen Schwartz*

## Rubin's
Corner of Charlotte St & Boston Rd
1940s-1950s

*It was owned by Mr & Mrs Rubin, right across from PS 61. As you walked in, on the right side of the store, was a stand where you could buy greeting cards for birthdays, etc. Beyond that, to the right, was a glass enclosed case with sliding glass doors where you could choose 1 cent candies – like fudge in a small container with a small metal spoon, edible finger nails, bazooka gum and more. The counter had stools, where you could have a malted and pretzel for 25 cents, or you could have loose ice cream by the pint, or a 2 cents plain seltzer. This store was the corner hangout, and it sold seasonal items such as tops, spaldeens, and more...—Gloria Scheinfeld Stockhammer*

## Rubin's

E. 172nd Street between Fteley and Croes
1940-51

*Mom was always concerned with how thin I was, so we had a popular "date" at Rubin's for a malted. I would order an egg cream and drink half and say, "feh, too sweet, needs more seltzer."—Roy Schlachter*

## Ruby's

Corner of Anthony Ave & Burnside Ave (SE)
1940s-1960s

*This was not a hang out store. We bought comics, pop song books, movie magazines, malteds, mello-rolls, egg creams-11 cents, spaldeens-11 cents. It had shelves & tables of light wood, a long counter, cards in drawers, candy bars-(5 cents), Reids ice cream, dixie cups with celebrity photo inside covers. Great BLT sandwiches. —Sara Hirsch Berlan*

## Rudy's

Northeast corner of Katonah Avenue & E. 235th Street
Owner: Rudy
1940's-50s

*Prime attractions: Hirsute, perspiring Rudy and his enormous forearms. Hand packed Breyer's ice cream always had a saline tang from Rudy's exertions and related facial drippings. —Jim Ryan*

## Ruth and Moe's Luncheonette

Gun Hill Road & Putnam Place
1960s-early 1970s

*It had all sorts of egg creams, models, stick ball equipment, and candy for the kids at PS 94. —Arty Conliffe*

## S & W

1717 University Ave - near W. 176th Street
1940-1955

*In The 1940s we even danced to the music playing on the juke box at the rear of this ice cream parlor. It was the biggest 'hang-out' for all the teenagers. Good clean fun! MOM and POP Plotkin took care of us all and Nat Plotkin was the best. We all received important messages on their public phone-i.e. my "boyfriend" had called my home to say he was returning from the Air Force after 4 years. My Dad called S & W to make sure that I received that message and I went home to wait for Muzzy. Remember Murray Sohmer-better known as Muzzy? Yes, we did get married and I have been Roslin Weiss Sohmer for over 54 years! — Roz Sohmer*

## Sabatelli

396 E. 154th Street
1940-46

*During war time kids would congregate here to buy postcards to send to servicemen. Newspapers, metal and rubber drives were collected from here for war use. The store was also used for incoming telephone calls.
—Rita Perota Sabatelli*

## Saddie's

Corner of Watson & Elder Avenues
1948-55

*The best ice cream sandwich made with Breyers Ice Cream on wine crackers. New York Daily News & Daily Mirror were only 3¢.*

## Sal & Dave's

West 168th and Nelson Avenue

*I worked there from 1948 to 1951 as a soda jerk and short order cook after school and on weekends. Sal (who had been there forever) taught me how to make the best egg cream in The Bronx, (consequently, the best in the world). The prices at that time were: 2¢ plain (seltzer), glass of soda 5¢, egg cream 7¢, ice cream soda 15¢, milk shake or malted 20¢, chocolate covered cherries 2¢, egg sandwich 20¢, ham and egg sandwich 30¢, pack of gum 5¢, big pretzel 3¢, banana split 25¢ to 30¢, and the fastest selling item, Charlotte Russe 5¢. Whenever we got a shipment in, it was gone in a few hours. Somewhere in the 1948-51 time frame, a new comic book, "Mad", was introduced, and all the kids were crazy about it. I met a lot of great guys and girls while working there, but sadly never kept in touch. — Ralph "Buddy" Geraldo*

## Sal's

Corner of Creston and E 181 St
1940's-1950's

*At the time that this picture was taken it was called Sal's. Then a friend of my parents, Jeff Lance, bought it. My house (in the picture) was located at 2150 Creston Ave. I used to buy all sorts of penny candy, dots, pez, bubble gum, chocolate ice malts. I loved their Breyer's vanilla fudge ice cream. —Sharon Gelbaum Dolinsky*

## Sam and Anna's Candy Store

Coster St and Spofford Ave
1938-1943

*My parents, Sam and Anna Swerdling, owned this candy store. It was located diagonally opposite PS 48. WW II affected the business adversely, since most of the young men who patronized it went off to the war.*

*Cigarettes sold for 15 cents per pack, a small fountain soda was 3 cents, an ice cream cone was 5 cents, a model airplane kit cost 10 cents. My parents welcomed customers to the store as friends and neighbors, often selling to them "on the cuff", waiting till they were able to pay for their purchases. Nearby was a city playground, and opposite our store was a church. —Irwin Swerdling*

## Sam and Anne (later Phil and Ruth)

Teller Avenue & E. 162nd Street
1930-1947, 1947-1961

*This store was only two blocks from where I lived. —Jeanette Verderosa*

## Sam & Henry's

176th Street & Jerome Avenue
1940-60's

*Sam & Henry's was around the corner from "the steps" which led from Davidson Ave down to Jerome. There were two other candy stores in the little "alley" at the bottom of the steps, but Sam & Henry got the most business because it was closest to the 176th St stop on the Woodlawn IRT. There was a father, son, daughter and son-in-law behind the counter. Magazines and comics to the right, 6 stools to the left. A black & white ice cream soda with whipped cream and a cherry was 25¢. The best thing was that it was adjacent to an appetizing store and a bakery. On Sunday mornings when my mother sent me down "the steps" I came back with lox, egg bagels and from Sam and Henry's, a Daily News. Very convenient!—Susan Schlachter Thaler*

## Sam & Lou's

Woodycrest Avenue about 1/4 block south of 167th Street
*That's where I bought my candy and comic books.*
*— F.S. Hedl*

## Sam & Rose's

Corner Boynton & Westchester Avenue
1950's

*This was our teenage hangout. Sam would ask us not to take up 3 or 4 tables for just sitting but we would always drop10¢ into the juke box and say, "just let us listen to this song." Since it was located near our club room, all the guys from "Club 36" would meet in Sam's after our date and discuss our success or failures.*

## Sam and Sol's

Corner of Davidson and W. 184th Street
Owners: Sam and Ester Turkowitz
*I always started my work day with a well-balanced breakfast- one of Ester or Sam's egg creams! Their store was a great place to stay if you were feeling down or lonely. —Eisenberg*

## Sam Chatinsky's Candy Store

Davidson Avenue near W. 181st Street.
1940's

*During the week I picked up the Daily News and Mirror from the news trucks on Jerome & Burnside Avenues and delivered them to the candy store for which I earned the grand sum of 5 cents! Saturday night the guys met outside the store, where for a penny we could get a handful of Indian nuts. We would then hang out discussing our dates and exaggerating our conquests. — Norman Horowitz*

## Sam's

E. 176th Street & Anthony Avenue
1948-1960

*Sam, the owner, was short, wore glasses, had bushy hair and was sharp tongued. He would wipe the floor with any kid who dallied too long reading comic books. No one misbehaved in his store or in front of his store because he took no nonsense from any of the kids. I worked around the corner at Simon Reinisch's Cleaners and Tailor. Mr. Reinisch came from Austria and I was one of the few kids who could understand German.— Gary Grahl*

## Sam's

1685 University Avenue
1950's-60's

*This rectangular store was owned by Mr. & Mrs. Sacks. Entering the store one would find large magazine racks on the right, and on the left was a counter with 5 stools. This store was a convenient loca-tion for those living on*

*Andrews, Montgomery and Popham Aves. School supplies were sold here along with the standard egg creams, rod pretzels and candy. It was the only candy store in the neigh-borhood that delivered the One-Star Daily News at 9:00 p.m. —Arnold Taubman*

Photo: Bruce Sacks

*Sam was grouchy and always wore the same gray pullover sweater. His son Bruce was always nice to me. One time I went in to purchase my very own brand new Hoola Hoop. I asked Sam how much they were? He asked me how much I had. I told him $4.00, and that's how much he said they were. Glad I didn't have $10.00 on me. I liked the "walk-away sundaes" for 11 cents. —Betsy Russell Pellitteri*

## Sam's

Southwest corner of Katonah Avenue and W. 239th Street
Owner: Sam, his wife and a daughter
1940's- 50's

*Prime attraction: Aside form the diminutive size of the own-ers, none. —Jim Ryan*

## Sam's

Corner of McGraw Avenue and Unionport Road

*Sam's was located between St. Helena's Grammar School and Parkchester, and the number one hangout. It was the one place where you could not only buy candy and an after school Cherry Coke, but was convenient enough to get that last minute school supply needed for the day. It was owned by two brothers that were survivors of the Holocaust, and the numbers tattooed on their arms were visible during the summer and the topic of questions from the kids in the lower grades. Sunday was a particularly busy day, with the after-Church crowd, and the corner in front of the store was the place to be on Friday and Saturday nights before and after the St. Helena's dances. —Jim Fay*

## Sam's

E. 173rd Street and Boston Post Road
1950-59

*There was a window in front (Boston Rd.) that opened to the street. Four chrome stools with red seats. Opposite an old time soda fountain facing the counter was a mirrored wall and glass shelves holding Coke glasses. Ice cream cones were 10¢, 2¢ for sprinkles and could be charged to your parents' tab. Newspapers were outside on a wooden bench. —Barbara Levy Wunsh*

## Sam's

Webster Ave and 205th St
1940's-1970's

*In the early 1940's it was called Max's, and sometimes in the 1950's it was called Sam's. Sam Mandell and his wife Vickie ran the store. I can remember his terrific selections of penny candy---marshmallow bananas, and a chocolate rectangle that I called four centers. My father and I visited Sam's frequently after dinner to get a pint of fresh packed ice cream. He never sealed the top so the ice cream pint would overflow. Sam was lucky; he got all the traffic from the Yonkers commuters who rode the Webster Ave bus to the beginning of the IND subway line at 204th St I believe that the candy store was at an ideal spot for their newspaper, cigarettes, gum and candy. —Susan Perez Aldrich*

*Sam's was a long and narrow store with 4-6 stools. It was owned by Sam Mandel, and his father and wife helped him. A big part of his business was selling newspapers to commuters. It was a great place to get ice cream sodas, egg creams, mello-rolls, and Smith's Natural ice cream. Sam was a big N.Y. Giant fan, and had to endure the 1951 loss to the NY Yankees, in 5 games, in a neighborhood of largely Yankees fans. —Louis Mirando*

## Sam's Candy Store

Astor Ave and Holland Ave
1950's
*I used to be the head soda jerk there. —Dr. Neil Stern*

## Sam's Candy Store

E 169th St between Clinton Ave and Franklin Ave
1933-1942

*Sam and his wife worked in the store seven days a week, from early morning until late at night. They were nice to the kids who hung around waiting for the phone to ring so that we could go fetch those who were being called, hoping for a 5-cent tip. I remember the way Sam carefully placed the 5-cent mello-rolls onto the cone. Here we purchased the Daily News and Mirror, the cost placed on my father's tab until it was paid. It was a glorious shop where I spent many happy hours. I lived at 1309 Clinton Ave, just down the block. —Emmanuel Bierman*

## Sam's Candy Store

Boston Rd & 173rd St
1950's-1970's

*Sam's was special to my friends, since it had a jukebox. We played the top 40 over and over. Sam would get so tired of hearing the music that he would unplug it and tell us it was out of order. Soon we learned to plug it in ourselves so we could continue to sing along with our Rock & Roll idols. We drank our lime rickeys and cherry cokes, which we bought for a dime, and stayed in the store for hours at a time. — Joan Migden Brock*

## Sam & Sadie's Luncheonette

Elder & Watson Aves
1945-1965

*Sam & Sadie's Luncheonette had a counter the entire length of the store, as well as several booths for those eating full meals. In addition there was a bank of telephone booths in the very back. I remember, every Wednesday, we all ate "Chow Mein" for 50 cents, and a soda for 7 cents, egg creams and ice cream cones went for 8 cents and 10 cents. Up front there was a large counter for candy & gum, and all the eight NY daily newspapers available at the time. It was a meeting place for all of us. —Gerald Wintner*

## Sarah and George

East 193rd Street two blocks east of Grand Concourse
Owners: Sarah and George Aitman
—*Norman Kaufheil*

## Sarah & Izzy's

197 McClellan Street corner of Sheridan Avenue
Owners: Sarah & Izzy Balsam
1957-1980

*My parents bought the store from the Schreiber family and inherited all the guys who would line up outside the phone booth on Monday night to make their dates for Saturday night. Many met and married girls from the "luncheonette." Daily News and Mirror were 3 cents. Cigars, the rage of today, sold for 25¢ (Berings) Havatampas (10¢). "Gills" of ice cream were 38¢ and a cone with sprinkles was 12¢. Most kids who attended P.S. 90 ate the lunch special at Sarah & Izzy's and their parents maintained "charge accounts" for them-no mileage! —Geri Jacobs*

## Sarah & Mike's

Beach & East Tremont Avenues
1944-1966

*My parents, Mike and Sarah Hendelman owned this candy store and luncheonette for 22 years. It had eight stools and a juke box. My parents were oftentimes invited to weddings of their patrons. —Joan Hendelman Efrom*

## Sarin's Candy Store

Ogden Ave between W 170 St and W 171 St
1947-1966

*When I greeted Mr. Sarin, the owner, he would reply "I feel so dandy, I'm opening a box of candy". His radio was always tuned to WQXR, and he was always in a good mood. What I most enjoyed there were the egg creams, Halvah, and the 2 or 3 cents Nestle bars. —Irving Edelstein*

*As you entered Sarin's there was a counter with stools on the left, penny candy, cookie cans and 2-cent pretzels cans on the right. The back right side had a few small tables; I cannot recall anyone ever sitting there. Because I was so skinny my mom took me, after school 3 times a week, for a vanilla malted (25 cents). I would watch Mr. Sarin hand pack Breyers ice cream so full that you couldn't close the carton. He was, (in my mind as an 8-13 year old), short, old, balding, grouchy, (a typical candy store owner). Newspapers were outside on a stand, protected by the awning with wood and metal weights to keep them from blowing away. Customers always laid the right change on top of the papers. In those days you were on the Honor System. —Karen Liss May*

*Jacob Sarin and his wife owned the store. They had two children (a son Harold and a daughter). My uncle owned the hardware store about three stores North. —Norman Schaumberger*

## Schiff's Candy Store

Astor Place and Holland Ave
1930's-1940's

*Mr. & Mrs. Schiff owned this store. They were both about five feet tall and five feet wide, and were wonderful people. When a call came in, they were kind enough to inform my mother that her brother, (my uncle), called. It was the only candy store between the Pelham Parkway station and Christopher Columbus HS, so teachers, as well as students, would stop there. This was a big hangout for kids, and the Schiffs treated us well. —Sam Sulsky*

## Schuman's

533 E. 171st Street Between 3rd Ave. and Fulton Avenue
1940's

*Made the best egg creams. Owner would ring a bell if a phone call came in. —Elaine Palmgren Demaria*

## Schwab's

Corner of Woodycrest Avenue and 167th Street one block west of Anderson Avenue

*I went there more for "tops" and "yo-yos" than for candy or egg creams. —F.S. Hedl*

*Schwab's had a fountain and sandwich counter and sold just about everything...plastic models, toys, candy, newspapers, magazines and, of course, Spaldings...in a space, which by today's standards, was tiny. Their egg creams, malted and cherry-lime rickeys were great, but economics forced most of us kids to stick to a 6¢ or 12¢ Coke or to a 2¢ plain. On the rare occasions that my Dad would send us for a quart of ice cream I can remember how they would heap it far over the top of the cardboard container.*

*I can recall Mr. and Mrs. Schwab perfectly. Mr. Schwab was a thin fellow with a curmudgeonly approach to children who always seemed to have a cigarette hanging out of his mouth. Mrs. Schwab was heavyset, short and more pleasant to us kids. Every now and then their grown son Oscar (who they, and all the neighborhood kids, referred to as "Okkie") would come to work in the store.*

*What a pleasure to go into that air conditioned space on a broiling hot summer day and have a cold drink served in one of those conical paper cups!!! It irks me to see the famous high bouncing rubber ball referred to as "Spaldeen". The real article said "Spalding" right on it. I recall that a "real" Spalding cost the princely sum of 25¢, but that a lower-priced version, called a "second", could be had for 15¢. The "seconds" looked the same but were unmarked. A boy's ritual was to go through the entire box of Spaldings and drop each one from a fixed height to see how well it bounced...both the height of the bounce and the degree of deviation from vertical were important. This would drive Mr. Schwab crazy!!! —Jay M. Prager*

## Schwartz

Mohegan Ave. & E. 180 Street
1930's

*It was an old-fashioned neighborhood candy store, located just South of 180 St., one block from PS 6. Benny's Pool Room was next door, one flight up.*

*I enjoyed the egg creams mostly. Mrs. Schwartz was always the good guy. Her son Willy wore thick glasses, and knew every baseball player and statistics there was to know. — Stanley Dichter*

## Schwartzberg's

181st St & Creston Ave
1950-1959

*It was an expensive store. It had a counter/service place for seating. It sold egg creams, malteds, sodas such as Dr. Brown, and chocolate covered bonbons. It also had comic books, yo-yos, Spalding balls, and other small items. — Irwin H. Forman*

## Seibel's

Mace Avenue and White Plains Road
1932-1940

*Owned by Joseph and Dorothy Seibel and worked with their entire family. Sold all types of candy and fountain items. Sold cigars and cigarettes and chewing tobacco. Poker and craps took place downstairs in the back of the store.*
*— Ronnie Seibel Liebowitz*

This was the old location for Seibel's located at Mace Avenue and White Plains Road. This store had it all, candy, fountain, cigarettes, stationery, and even poker and craps in the basement.

## Seibel's Stationery Store

549 E 168th Street
1933-1942
*Owner Morris Seibel worked this candy and stationery store with his daughter, Dorothy Seibel Schancupp.*
— *Ronnie Seibel Liebowitz*

Joe & Jack Seibel - 1937

## Seidler's

709 East Tremont Avenue & East Crotona Avenue

Seidler's on E. Tremont Avenue.

## Seidlitz

White Plains Road & Gleason Avenue
1934-46
*The entire Seidlitz family worked the candy store. Music was played on the juke box so loud that the neighborhood kids would Lindy outside the store.* —*Joe Behar*

## Semel's

E. 196th St and Briggs Ave
Owner: "Pop" Semel
1920-35
*It was a small penny candy store selling MaryJanes, Dots and Tootsie Rolls all for 1¢ each. Also sold Charlotte Russes for 5¢. He also invented the ice cream pop, which was a ball of ice cream on a stick dipped in milk chocolate for 5¢.* — *Marvin Bueton*

## Shakespeare's

One block east of the SW corner of Shakespeare Ave & Featherbed Lane
1950's
—*Judith P. Sussholtz*

## Sheps Candy Store

180 Street between Mohegan & Honeywell Avenues
1940's-1950's
*Here are some pictures of my parents, George and Sally Sheps. In 1954 they closed it to build a new lunchonette called the Stanbar for Stanford and Barry. It had 4 booths and 12 stools. I worked in the store after coming home from high school. It was the neighborhood hangout with jukebox and all. If I remember, the price of an egg cream was 10 cents, tuna*

*fish sandwich-35 cents, and a hamburger deluxe was 50 cents. It was a great life.* — *Barry Sheps*

## Sheridan's

Willis Ave between E 144th St and E 145th St
1946-1956
*The owners were an Irish couple, Mr. & Mrs. Tom Sheridan. Right around the corner on E 144 St was St. Pius Catholic School, and as a result, this store also sold school supplies. Besides selling malteds and egg creams, they were the main outlet for various Irish newspapers. To the left of the picture was Henry Scholte's optometrist shop, and to the right, on the corner, was a German bakery that was packed every Sunday after mass.*

## Shore's
Belmont Ave & E Tremont Ave
1940s-1960s
*Two brothers named Hy & Willie opened the candy store in the late 1940s. The crowd from Belmont Ave and Hughes made it their home. Above the stores, on the Hughes side, the building housed some offices, and the top floor was a loft that the Painters Union occupied. When they left in the mid 50s, the crowd from the candy store, (15 guys), rented the loft and made a club from 1958-1965. My wife and I had our engagement party there in 1958. —Larry Epstein*

## Sids Candy Store
956 R. 174th Street,
between Vyse & Hoe
Avenues
*—Dorothy Greifer Braunstein*

## Silver Rods
Corner of Simpson Street
& E 165th Street
1940's-1960's
*This was a rectangular store with about 6 fountain stools and 3 booths. This store was a luncheonette and sold egg creams and ice cream sodas. — Sam Abramson*

## Simon's
West Tremont & Cedar Ave
Late 1920's-early 50's
*Mr. Simon and his family lived in the back of the store originally. They later moved to an apartment. During WWII, cigarettes were sold by Simon's one at a time, (no whole pack). His son, Stanley Simon, went on to become the Bronx Borough President. —Mary Kruger Piper Placko*

## Sinnigen's
Bedford Park Boulevard and Decatur Avenue
1950's

## Skippy's
West Burnside Avenue and the corner of Andrews Avenue
1950-55
*This was a popular hangout located opposite P.S. 26 and across from Fried's Delicatessen. You could get everything there including the familiar egg cream, sodas, pens, papers and notebooks for school. They held Yo-Yo contests and had Yo-Yo masters there sponsored by Duncan.—Marty Jackson*

## Sloppy Sam's
Woodycrest Ave & W 165 St
1940's-1950's
*This store was located at the top of the hill of W 165 St and Woodycrest Ave. During the memorable winter of 1947, the candy store was the starting point of a sleigh ride down the steep hill to Anderson Ave.*

*This swell store, (never a hangout like Schwab's on W 167 St and Woodycrest Ave), had just 3 or 4 red and chrome stools, greeting cards- 25 cents, comics- 10 cents, and a large penny candy case in the back, where the nervous owner stood guard. Dads would pick up a late Post, a pack of Chesterfields, or some hand-packed ice cream, coming off the bus from IRT and IND lines by Yankee Stadium. On Friday nights, after Boy Scout at PS 73, my buddy Stanley and I, and about a dozen husky sized scouts, would invade, and overwhelm the nervous owner and his frantic wife, and order a 25-cents sundae, frappe or soda. Later on we discovered girls, and abandoned the store for parties.*
*—Jan Polatschek*

## Slotnicks Candy Store
Teller Avenue between E. 161 Street & E. 162nd Street
1940's
*Sam's was a fairly large and wide candy store. Fountains on the left, small tables and a hangout for the Gales, Brewers and local sport groups. Sam was small and quiet and sold everything. — John Hanrahan*

## Smitties
Lydig Ave between White Plains Road & Cruger Ave.
1930-65
*Jerry & Hy Smith sold sandwiches& malts.*
*— Susan Hope Godell*

## Snookies

W. 238th Street and Bailey Avenue
Owner: Josie
1960-early 70's
*Hamburger was 35¢, cheeseburger 40¢. Large hangout for kids. School supplies were purchased here due to its close proximity to the #38 bus which stopped across the streets.*
— *Scott Willmarth*

## Sol's

E 169th St & Sheridan Ave
1948-1958
*The store was small and narrow, and had a newsstand in the front. Sol, the owner, was bald with an ample belly. There was a 4-stool soda fountain counter, which was always cluttered. They had a 2 cent pretzel, along with Knickerbocker chocolate covered jelly. Magazines and joke books were on the left wall. —Marvin Trief*

## Sol's Candy Store

174th Street between Noble Avenue and Rosedale Avenue
Owners: Sol and Rae Green
1949-1953
*My parents were the owners. My dad was a clever businessman. Every couple of weeks, he'd order a new toy and send my sister around to Rosedale, and me around to Noble, to play with them. In no time kids were flocking in to buy the toy. There was a candy store crowd that hung around, and while dad welcomed them, they knew they had to behave appropriately around the store. — Adrienne Green Levinthal*

## Sol & Dave's Candy Store

W. 168th Street & Nelson Avenue
1940s-50s
*I worked there from 1948-1951 as a soda jerk and short order cook after school and on weekends. Sol (who had been there forever) taught me how to make the best egg cream. The prices at the time was 2 cents seltzer, glass of soda was 5 cents, egg creams-7 cents, ice cream soda-15 cents, milk shake or malted-20 cents, chocolate covered cherries-2 cents, egg sandwich-20 cents, ham and egg sandwich-30 cents. Somewhere around this time a new comic book called "MAD" was introduced and all the kids went crazy about it. — Ralph "Buddy' Gelardo*

## Sol & Moe's

Corner of Kingsbridge Road & Morris Avenue
Owners: Moe Goldstein and Sol Shapiro
1940s-50s
*A Nestle "Square" cost 2¢; an egg cream was 5¢. I could afford neither but it felt good to be in that store.*
— *Marilyn Prager Klein*

*Sol and Moe's candy store was my absolute favorite because my father, Moe Goldstein, was the owner. I could have all the comic books, "Spaldeens" and Fleer's Double Bubble I want-*ed. *Sometimes after school, he would make me an egg cream that I would have with a long pretzel. I thought my father made the best egg creams in the Bronx and I was the luckiest kid in the world.* — *Helane Goldstein Zeiger*

## Sophie & Sam's

E. 178th Street between Vyse & Daly Avenues
1955
*Sophie & Sam were wonderful Russian immigrants who were very trusting people and extended credit to everyone (including kids!). Their store was so small and cramped that the door could not be opened completely and you had to walk in somewhat sideways! — George Giorno*

## Spa Luncheonette

1500 Olmstead Avenue
(around the corener from PS 106 and PS 127)
Owner: David and Nathan Kasten
1950-1978
*The store was the local lunch spot for teachers and students at the two schools. The store was open seven days a week. My father, mother, grandfather and grandmother all worked there at some time during the day. Parents would set up an account for their children's lunches. The allowance usually included some candy for dessert. The house specialty was hot brisket on a roll. After the lunch trade the coffee klatches from Parkchester would arrive and sit for hours over coffee and danish. Cherry cokes, egg creams, malted milk, ice cream sodas, sundaes and lime rickeys were big sellers. Parents with fussy eaters would ask for malteds with extra malt to add nutrition, and I learned that malteds were better with frozen milk. In addition to food, they also sold newspapers, cigarettes, spaldeens, candy pretzels and some school supplies.*

*When I was 10, I learned to put the NY Times together at 4 in the morning. I helped serve the rush from St. Helena's at the end of each mass. Years later my 5 year old daughter would stand on the pretzel can to "help" her grandma take cash.*

*Outside of NY, in places such as Ann Arbor, Michigan, Princeton NJ, Los Angeles, CA, I continue to meet people, who remember hanging out at the store at lunchtime or after school. — Ellie Schweber*

## Spa

St. Raymond & Castle Hill
1950's
*We went to it, most afternoons, with the teachers from PS 106, (my mother and Shari Lewis' mother were one of them). The teachers would sit in the booths, and we, the kids, would get pretzels and candy, and stay around the store or go outside. There was a long row of booths to the left, and a counter opposite that. The candy was in the front of the store. —Rosanne Feld Greenstein*

## Spector's

E. 170th Street and Stebbins Avenue

## St. Murray's Candy Store

On the corner of 161st Street
1964
*— Submitted by Bonnie Maser Fraser*

## Stan & Hy's

Corner Walton & E. 183rd Street
1940-50's
*Stan & Hy were an an odd couple long before Oscar and Felix came on the scene. Stan was a young man probably in his 30's, a rather distinguished looking gent, with a fine head of wavy black hair and a manner which exuded a carefully nurtured dignity which remained intact even as he bent over a carton of cherry vanilla or drew a lime rickey. He was clearly a man who read well and widely and who wished it to be known that he was out of place behind a candy counter. The racks of paperback books opposite the fountain always contained volumes of Dostoyevsky and Aldous Huxley, along with such candy store staples as The Amboy Dukes and Mickey Spillane novels. Hy, perhaps 20 years older, was more the stereotype: "Hey, Hy, how about an egg cream?" Then, several sips later, "It's not sweet enough, Hy it needs more syrup." A few more sips and, "Now it's too sweet, Hy how about another spritz of seltzer?" Finally, Hy would catch on. "Drink it the way it is and get outta here, wiseguy," brandishing the dish towel he invariably carried on his shoulder.*

## Stellings

4301 Katonah Avenue
Owners: Henry and Betty
*A true ice cream parlor, complete with two aisles of booths in the back, and a centrally located juke box. Enter to the marble-topped soda fountain with backless, spinning stools embedded in a black and white mosaic tiled floor. Two sets of fountains, silver sleeves (with handles) for the tall, tall glasses of ice cream sodas served with long, long spoons. Opposite side, a glass-case of chocolates, nougats, jelly bars dusted with powdered sugar and more, much more. — Jim Ryan*

## Stevie's

Mace Ave between Paulding Ave and Colden Ave
1940's-1950's
*Stevie's was located right across the street from PS 89. I was in the store twice a day on every school day. My folks would give me 10 cents to spend every day, and I would spend it all on candy. My favorite was the candy buttons.*

*Stevie and his wife ran the store. They had to put up with hundreds of kids every day. While Stevie would always yell at us, his wife never said a word, (because she was checking to make sure nothing was stolen). Stevie's claim to fame was that once a year, right in front of the store, a major happening would occur. The Yo-Yo Men would come and put on an incredible show for all the neighborhood kids. First the Cheerio Man , then a few days later, the Duncan Man, and then every kid would try out his or her skills. —Richard Meduri*

## Stube's

E. Tremont and Mapes Avenues
1935-1942
*This shop was still in existence in 1942 because I took a picture of my future wife in the back of the store seated at a fountain with a gnome water spray in the background. Here they made their own ice cream. — Robert J. Hennessy*

## Stuhls Candy Store

Plimpton & W. 172nd Street
1940's-50's

*I'm writing on behalf of my father, James Gips. He purchased penny candies and "extra thick", "world's finest" comic books for 15 cents. — James Gips*

## Surenko's

Brady Ave and Bronx Park East
1940's-1950's

*This was a small candy store with fountain service and four stools. —Robert Black*

## Sweet Shoppe

Northwest corner of Bainbridge Ave and W 198 St
1940's-1960's

*The interior of the store was bigger than most local candy stores, and it had booths just like the Fonz. The façade has changed quite a bit since this picture, but the two private houses are still there. —James E Hurley*

## Sweisky's

Corner of Vyse Avenue and E. 172nd Street
Owner: Mr. Sweisky
1934-1950

*I never heard Mr. Sweisky's first name. His wife worked there with his two grown up daughters. Sometimes his daughter Edith, who was my friend, helped out. The store was quite large as candy stores go. — Thelma Rosen Kimble*

## Syd's Spa

Holland Ave and Lydig Ave
1952-1962

*I know the store very well because my father owned it. My mom, sister and I worked there. —Arnold Greenspan*

## Taft Sugar Bowl

E 170th & Morris Ave
1940's-1960's

*Known all over the Bronx for its famous egg creams and great tasting lime rickeys. It was the hangout for all the neighborhood kids and a special place for all the older crowd to socialize. – Esther Group Klein*

*The store was run by Jake and his wife. It served malts, cherry lime rickeys and egg creams. It was a corner hangout for local bookies: Moishe "The Senator", Morris "Taxi", "Cigarette Sam", "Irv The Tooth", and his wife "Mrs Tooth". —Raymond Marcus*

## Tares

Corner of 181st St & Morris Ave
1950-1959

*It was across from J.H.S. 79, and was a hangout for students at lunch break and after school. Items were inexpensive — Irwin H. Forman*

## Tasbirn's

Colgate and Westchester Avenues

## Tempsky Candy Store

Beekman Ave & Oak Ter
1950's
—Joyce McGrail

## Tess and Tony's Candy Store

E. 183rd Street between Hughes Avenue & Adams Place
1964-1988

*Looking back at yesterday, when everything seemed simpler, I think of my mom and dad's candy store. It was on E 183 St between Hughes Ave and Adams Pl off the corner of Arthur Ave from 1964 to 1988 and everyone knew it as Tess and Tony's. In the beginning it was just a candy store. It had egg creams, malts, penny candies, stationery, and who could forget the Manhattan Special.*

*The jukebox would blare out those fabulous doo-opps for the girls from Aquinas high school who would pack in wall-to-wall, while the boys from the football team they sponsored, would meet and talk about their games. I remember when they won the championship and we had a dinner and dance. The trophy stood behind the counter for years.*

*As the years went by, the sounds from the jukebox faded and were replaced by conversations of the men having their expressos and Sambuco. They would wait for the number runner; it was fun to watch them play the first, second, and third number. it's a time of my life that I will never forget.*

*I would like to say for my parents, who are no longer with us, to the girls at Aquinas High school, the boys of the football team and all those who came in and out, it's a time of my life that I'll never forget. — Jolaine Cambria*

## Three Corners Candy Store

Home St, Longfellow St and West Farms Rd
1930's-1964

*My father owned this store that was located at 1045 Home St. It was named Three Corners because it was located on the corner where three streets came together. The photo is probably from the 40's, when the Mazin family owned it. When Mr. Mazin died in 1954, his son Walter put the store up for sale. The year before, my father had suffered a heart attack and was unable to go back to being a nailer in the fur trade. He looked for something easier. For the princely sum of $300, he became a proprietor.*

*Sealtest came in and put in an ice cream freezer and a new counter. The store was small and narrow, and the back wall had a very large water-cooled soda box. Images of Mission Pineapple soda and Doc's Root Beer come to mind. On the window counter was a dual Hamilton Malted machine. When malteds cost 15 cents for a large one I used to make one for myself that at retail would be worth a dollar! My egg creams were the best. They had a pure white head. The secret was to hold the spoon in the left hand, and let the seltzer run off it to the sides of the glass. Many of my school buddies remember me letting them make their own ice cream cones. We had the store from 1954 to 1964.—Stanley Starr*

## Tompkins

Gun Hill Road between Jerome & Knox Place

*Tomkins had several special things going for it. It was the outlet in the neighborhood for Dolly Madison ice cream, and they seemed to have started charge accounts by which families could buy newspapers and other items. A friend, Steve Tennebaum used to pick up the newspapers on Saturday morning for his father. — Eliot Tiegel*

## Tony's

Corner of 178th St & Washington Ave
1940's

*He sold 3 cigarettes for a nickel. He also kept a running charge account for me. He made a great egg cream. —Luciano Siracusano*

## Tony's Candy Store

E. 182nd Street and Hughes
1960-1964

*A long store with front counter having 3 soda fountains and about 6 stools, a juke box and a small candy counter. They made terrific frozen malteds using frozen milk and Sealtest ice cream. Kids from Roosevelt would come in after school. Joe and Cosmo and sister Rachel would help serve behind the counter. — Cosmo DeRosa*

*This store was operated by Tony DeRosa, his wife Louise, daughter Rachelle, son Butch, and his sister-in-law Carmella. Tony was a rough, tough guy with a soft heart. He served excellent egg creams and lime rickeys. Tony had tatoos on his big arms, and wore a famous white tee shirt. —Louis Mazza*

## Two Little Streets

Castle Hill Ave & Starling
1940's-1970's

*I owned this candy store from the middle of 1958 to beginning of 1961. I married Frances Perillo in April 1959, and*

*my father bought this store as a wedding present for us. He owned the fruit and vegetable market next door at 1506 Castle Hill Ave., from 1943 until his death in December 1960. It was called Two Little Streets because we lived in Lyon Ave in the 40's & 50's, and you had to cross two little streets (Lyon & Starling) to get to the candy store. —Anthony J. Pepe II*

## Umlands Ice Cream Parlor

E. 149th Street between Brook & Bergen Avenue (next to South Bronx Opera House)
1940's — *Edward Boyle*

## Veeter's

Hoffman St between E 187 St and E 188 St
1950's-1960's

*This is the candy store that the Jewish girls went to hang out with the Italian guys. — Ruth Albert Spencer*

## Village Green Candy Store and Luncheonette

Concourse Ave and E 181 St
1950's-1975

*This store served great lunches for JHS 79 students. Your mom or dad could run up a tab and pay weekly so the student could eat a wholesome lunch as opposed to a leaky tuna fish oil sandwich that many of us had to endure. —Robert Baram*

## Wailus Ice Cream Store

Corner of Clinton Avenue & Boston Road (McKinley Square)
Owner: Wailus Parker
Early 1930's

Andy Benedict and Andy Powers in front of Wailus Ice Cream Parlor - 1934.

*His son Walter and I tried out for amateur hour. He played piano and I sang. Hangout for the crowd. Andy Benedict, his brother William, Ed Sullivan, Catherine O'Connor to name a few. Piano in the rear of the store. — Andy Powers*

## Wally & Joe's

Ogden Avenue and W. 165th Street
1946-62

*The owners were Herb Wallis (Wally) and Jack Silberman (Joe) and their wives, twins Mollie and Bobbie. Danny (my husband) and Matty Wallis worked in the store from the time they were tall enough to reach the counter. They also sold toys and was a luncheonette.*

## Weinberg's

181st St & Corner of Daly
1941-1960's

*This was a hangout store, especially on weekends (Friday nights). It was a small candy store with a few steps going down. They had a soda fountain, made egg creams, and sold a variety of candy and gum. —Lillian Luftig Abeles*

## Weiner's

E. 172st between Fteley and Croes Avenue
Approximate date: 1950-53

*My dad and mom, Mr. & Mrs. Irving Weiner had a candy store at 53 E. 172 St when I was about fifteen. They bought it from Mr. Rubin. My fondest memory of this store is that I was proposed to in the telephone booth by Irving Abel. — Arlene (Bubbles) Abel*

## Weiner's

Tiffany between East 167th Street and East 169th Street
Owner: Jake and Beatrice
— *Norman Kaufheil*

### Weinstein's

137 West Tremont Avenue
Owner: Mr. Weinstein
1954-1965
*Mr. Weinstein was generally in a good mood as far as kids were concerned. They sold the usual newspapers, candy, stationery, soda fountain, and ice cream, and was sort of a bookie place for the older crowd.*
*— Russell S. Teasdale*

### Weiss' Candy Store

Bryant Ave & Lafayette
1940's-1950's
*—Stan Fine*

### Yellin's

Brady Ave and White Plains Rd
1940's-1960's
*The store was owned by Mr.Yellin. We called him a mean man because he always charged us 2 cents for cups of water. The mothers stood on Brady Ave, basking in the Winter sun and rocking our younger siblings in their baby carriages, while we kids played street games, ran around, threw snow balls and got thirsty. Our moms knew the deal and gave us 2 cents to go in and get water from Mr. Yellin's. As we got older we bought small cokes for 5 cents, and egg creams for 8 cents. There were two small tables and a five-stool counter. He sold among other things, newspapers, comic books and magazines. —Alice Brown*

### Zacks

Faile St and Lafayette Ave
1940's-1950's
*—Stan Fine*

### Zahler's

W. Burnside Ave between Phelan Pl. & Sedgwick Avenue
1940-50's
*Originally, a Mom & Pop candy store. Joe Zahler was hard of hearing and we had to yell our orders at him. Later it was owned by Abe Fox and his wife. His son Lester worked the counter when he wasn't in school. They were wonderful shopkeepers that had the patience to put up with all of our "schticks". In my younger days I went to Zahler's and Fox's and later, before I moved from the West Bronx, we hung out at Willie's and Nat's. — Richard Copans*

### Zelkins

205th Street near the Concourse
1940's-50's
*I remember the egg creams that I got at Zelkins when I visited my grandfather's house. —Gerald Basciano*

### Ziede's

*As each grandchild hit their teens, we were obligated to stay alone and tend the store while "Pop" went to synagogue on Saturday morning. On Sunday there was an enormous sale of newspapers to worshippers at Our Lady of Refuge across the street. On Sundays our father helped out. The store closed in 1945 with Pop's passing. — Rima Chenetz*

### Zimmerman's

Corner of Allerton & Ollinville Avenues
Owners: Abie and Morris Zimmerman
1960-80's
*In the direct path of PS 96 and a necessary stop en route, I would buy 1 or 2 chocolate covered cherry sticks for 2¢*

*each. Years later we would all go to Zimmies to buy egg creams and look through the magazines. Abie and his wife, Helen, hated when people looked through the magazines. I remember my father saying that Zimmies was a goldmine. Both financially and as a gold mine of memories for many.*
*—Danny Kaplan*

*Photos: Scott Mlyn*
Mr. & Mrs. Zimmerman working in their store.

### Zimmerman's

Hoe Ave & E 173rd St.
1940-1953

*The store was about 10 feet wide and 25 feet long. In the back was the comic book rack; and there was a long counter, with the different candy on top, where you could be served a great chocolate egg cream.* —Allen Gross

### Zimmy's

Corner of Watson & Boynton Avenues
1948-1955

*Best place to have lunch when mom wasn't home during school lunch hour at PS 93. Frieda was a wonderful lady that knew everything about everyone.*— Walter Salidor

### Zombie's

Faile Street between Hunts Point and Spofford Avenue
Owners: Eli & Tillie Cohen
1950's

*We gave him the nickname 'Zombie'. The store featured many different candies, ice cream, egg creams, pretzels,caramels, Charlotte Russe, etc. One of the big features was the pinball machines which were always in constant use. Spofford playground was directly across from the candy store. It was the hangout of the Spofford Maple Leafs, a well known basketball team who later became the "Collegian All Star."*

# THE CONFECTION CONNECTION

This alphabetical listing of around 900 candy stores should help you find your local candy store.
Owner's last name will identify many candy sotres. Dates are approximate.

| | | |
|---|---|---|
| A & L Confectionery | 5572 Broadway | 1960's |
| Aaron's | Neried Ave & E. 238th St | 1951-57 |
| Abe's | W Tremont & Harrison Ave | 1940-50 |
| Abe & Helen Candy Store | White Plains Road & 223rd Street | 1960's |
| Abe & Molly's | E. 184th St & Creston Ave | 1951-70 |
| Abe's & Molly's | E 172nd St | |
| Abe & Sylvia | Hoe Ave & E 173 St | 1934-37 |
| Abram's | Holland Ave, Antin Place | |
| | & Bronxdale Ave | 1940's-50's |
| Abramson's Candy Store | 1632 Washington Ave. | 1940's |
| Adams & Co | 840 Westchester Ave | 1940's |
| Adelson's | Watson Ave | 1948-55 |
| Al & Alice's | Davidson & W Tremont Ave | 1950-65 |
| Al & Murrays | W 231st St | |
| Albed R I & Son | 1752 Morris Ave | 1960's |
| Aldus St. Luncheonette | Longfellow Ave & Aldus St | 1934-45 |
| Alf, E | 335 St Anns Ave | 1940-50's |
| Alfaro, A | 869 Longwood Ave | 1940's |
| Alfred's Sweet Shop | 2934 Bruckner Blvd | 1950-60's |
| Alice's | Hone Ave & Morris Park Rd | 1938-50 |
| Allied Candy/Tobacco Co | 2125 Boston Rd | 1950's |
| Americican Candy Dist. | 26 E 175th St | 1950-60's |
| Anagnosti | 3416 Jerome Ave | 1940's |
| Anderson Prince | 1035 Caldwell Ave | 1960's |
| Angelo's Candy Store | E 189th St & Cambreleng | 1935-60's |
| Anne's Luncheonette | 1136 E. 165th St | 1950's |
| Applebaum A | 572 Westchester Ave | 1940-50's |
| Applebaum's | Lowell St | 1960's |
| Archer Sweet Shop | 1886 Archer | 1940's |
| Archie's Candy Store | Mt Eden Ave & Walton Ave | 1947-73 |
| Arhontaky, N | 1284 Southern Blvd | 1940-60's |
| Arsenlau, N | 864 Westchester Ave | 1940's |
| Adie's Candy Store | 811 East 161 St | 1960"s |
| Ascone, Jason | 561 Morris Ave | 1960's |
| Aswal Chocolates | 3416 Jerome Ave | 1960's |
| Atlas Candy Store | Bainbridge Ave & 204th St | 1930's |
| Attis, R E | 996 Ogden Ave | 1950-60's |
| Avenue Sweet Shop | 1147 Tinton Ave | 1960's |
| B & S Candy Shoppe | 1154 Woodycrest Ave | 1950-60's |
| Babe's | Castle Hill Ave & Watson Ave | 1945-80 |
| Bailey's Candy Store | 1246 Stebbins Ave | 1960's |
| Bainbridge Sweet Shop | 287 E 198 St | 1950-60's |
| Baker, Jason | 83 Hewitt Pl | 1960's |
| Baleny, L | 694 Melrose Ave | 1950's |
| Balzo, J | 1960 Bathgate Ave | 1960's |
| Banguera, P | 869 Longwood Ave | 1960's |
| Bar's | Monroe & Weeks Ave. | 1950's |
| Baratz | University Ave & W. 176th St | 1940's |
| Bard's | Prospect & Boston Rd | 1940's |
| Bar's | Monroe & Weeks Ave | 1950's |
| Barner's Confectionery | 2383 Westchester Ave | 1960's |
| Barney's | La Fontaine Ave between | |
| | 178 St & Tremont Ave | 1940's |
| Baron, M | 3942 White Plains Rd | 1940's |
| Barriccini Candy Shop | 262 E Fordham Rd | 1950-60's |
| Barriccini Candy Shop | 2190A White Plains Rd | 1950-60's |
| Barricini Candy Shop | 90 E 170th St | 1950-60's |
| Bartel's & Hansen | 5572 Broadway | 1940's |
| Bartel's Confectionery | 1554 Westchester Ave | 1940's |
| Barton's Bonbonniere | 72 E Burnside Ave | 1950-60's |
| Barton's Bonbonniere | 2443 Grand Concourse | 1950-60's |
| Barton's Bonbonniere | 3404 Jerome Ave | 1950-60's |
| Barton's Bonbonniere | 7 E Kingsbridge Rd | 1950-60's |
| Barton's Bonbonniere | 2161 White Plains Rd | 1950-60's |
| Barton's Bonbonniere | 64 E 161 St | 1950-60's |
| Barton's Bonbonniere | 70 E 167th St | 1950-60's |
| Barton's Bonbonniere | 28 E 170 St | 1950-60's |
| Baskin's Luncheonette | 749 Lydig Ave | 1950's |
| Baum's Candy Store | West Farms Rd & Hoe Ave | 1939-62 |
| Bea's | E 182 St & Mapes Ave | 1955-68 |
| Becker's Sweet Shoppe | 885 E Tremont Ave | 1950-60's |
| Beck's | 235th St & Johnson Ave | 1960's |
| Beckenstein's | | 1940-50's |
| Bell Soda/Lunch | 1101 Westchester Ave | 1940's |
| Beller's | Teller & E. 165th St | 1930-49 |
| Belmont Candy Shop | 2371 Belmont Ave | 1950's |
| Ben & Sids | E 174th & Vyse Avenue | 1940's |
| Benen Sweet Shop | 1132 Gerard Ave | 1950's |
| Benitez, F | 840 Jackson Ave | 1950-60's |
| Bennewitz, W | 3468 E Tremont Ave | 1940's |
| Ben's Luncheonette | 200 Holland Ave | 1950's |
| Benny's | Silver Beach | 1940-60s |
| Benny's | East Mohegan Ave & 180th St | 1940's-50's |
| Berchin & Cohen | 1053 Southern Blvd | 1940's |
| Bergman's | Allerton Ave & Barker | 1930's |
| Bernie & Jimmy's | University & W 175th St | 1940s |
| Bernstein's | Whitlock & Tiffany St | 1930's |
| Bernstein's | E. 165th St & Longfellow Ave | 1935-1958 |
| Berrios, V | 1569 Hoe Ave | 1960's |
| Besen, David | 785 E Tremont Ave | 1940-60's |
| Beyerman & Kohler | 5572 Broadway | 1950's |
| Bib & Sam's Luncheonette | Barnes Ave & Lydig | 1950's |
| Binnie's Candy Store | Morris Ave between | 1930's-50's |
| | E 164th St & E 165 St | |
| Birnbaum's Candy Store | Davidson Ave & Fordham Rd | 1940-60 |
| Blackman's Candy Store | Creston Ave & Kingsbridge Rd | 1940's-50's |
| Blum's | Home St between West Farms Rd | 1920's-50's |
| | & Westchester Ave | |
| Blumenthal's | Hunts Point & Garrison Ave | 1940's |
| Bob's Ice Cream Parlor | 362 E Tremont Ave | 1950's |
| Bon Bon Sweet Shop | 2411 Grand Concourse | 1950-60's |
| Bond's | 208th St near Jerome Ave | 1940-50's |
| Bootsy's Luncheonette | Jerome Ave & Minerva Pl | 1950-60s |
| Brand, H | 335 St Anns Ave | 1940's |
| Brand, P | 510 E 138 St | 1940-50's |
| Brandt's | E 138th St & Brook Ave | 1930's-40's |
| Brandt's Confectionery | 706 E Tremont Ave | 1940's |
| Breden, B | SilverBeach | 1940-50's |
| Briggs Ave Candy Store | 2619 Briggs Ave | 1940's |
| Broder's | Sherman Ave & McClellan St | 1950-65 |
| Broger & Luessen | 2362 University Ave | 1940's |
| Brooks Candy Company | 1835 Washington Ave | 1960's |
| Brooks, L | 1835 Washington Ave | 1940-50's |
| Brown, Sylvia | 364 Bruckner Blvd | 1960's |
| Brown's | East 170th St & Bristow | 1940's |
| Brunning, G | 5989 Broadway | 1940's |
| Bruno, E | 874 Morris Pk Ave | 1950-60's |
| Bruns, Henry | 664 Jackson Ave | 1940-60's |

# THE CONFECTION CONNECTION

| | | |
|---|---|---|
| Bunny's | Starling Ave | 1950's |
| Burgazoli, T | 4227a White Plains Rd | 1940's |
| Butecke & Liesegang | 291 E 204 St | 1950's |
| Candy Bar | 121 Mt Eden Ave | 1940-50's |
| Candy Box | 733 Lydig Ave | 1940-60's |
| Candy Pantry | 503 E Tremont Ave | 1940-60's |
| Cantor's | Clay Ave & 173rd St | 1940-50's |
| Cappy's | Gun Hill & White Plains Rd | 1960 |
| Captains | Bryant Ave & E 173 St | 1938-54 |
| Carousel Sweet Shoppe | 1007 Allerton Ave | 1960's |
| Carrie & Larry's | Briggs Ave near 196 St | 1952-66 |
| Carvel Dad-Freeze Stand | 911 Morris Park Ave | 1950-60's |
| Cavalier Chocolates | 2893 3rd Ave | 1950's |
| Champ Freeze | 1011 Ftely Ave | 1950's |
| Charles Bake Shop | 2347 Arthur Ave | 1950-60's |
| Charlie & Maureen | Cypress Ave & E 141st St | 1940-65 |
| Charlie's Candy Store | 1497 Southern Blvd | 1950's |
| Charos, S | 1429 Ogden Ave | 1940's |
| Char-Rock Luncheonette | E Burnside Ave | 1957 |
| Chris' Candy Store | 759 Melrose Ave | 1950-60's |
| Chris's Candy Store | 137th St & Willis Ave | 1930's |
| Chubby's | E 155 St & Tinton Ave | 1935-44 |
| Cirillo, A | 919 Allerton Ave | 1940-50's |
| Cisca, D | 938 Allerton Ave | 1940's |
| Claire's Sweet Shop | 103 W Kingsbridge Rd | 1950's |
| Cohen, E | 918 Hunts Point Ave | 1950's |
| Cohen's Luncheonette | Clay Ave & E. 170th St | 1950-60s |
| Cohen & Rosenzweig | Hoe Ave & E 174th St | 1930's-60's |
| Colangelo, F | 320 E 148th St | 1950's |
| College Ave Luncheonette | E. 166th St & College Ave | 1930-50's |
| Colon, P | 1023 Kelly Ave | 1960's |
| Cooper, T G | 867 Home | 1950's |
| Coopermans Candy Store | Sheridan & E. 166th St. | 1940's |
| Cooper's | Spofford Ave & Cooper St | 1940-50's |
| Cooper's | Bailey Ave & Summit Place | 1932-50's |
| Cornelius, L & W | 811 East 165th St | 1960's |
| Corner Candy Store | E. 141 St & Alexander Ave | 1930-40's |
| Corner Candy Store (Newman's) | 376 Gun Hill Road | 1938-1950 |
| Costa's Luncheonette | W. 235 St & Johnson Ave | 1950's |
| Counes, A J | 6 E Fordham Rd | 1950-60's |
| Cozy Corners | 205 W 169th St | |
| Crawford, Ernest | 1326 Barker Ave | 1950's |
| Crillon Chocolates | 1380 Jerome Ave | 1940's |
| Cruger Candy Store | Allerton Ave between Cruger Ave & Holland Ave | 1940-50's |
| Crystal Creme | 3400 Boston Rd | 1960's |
| Cunningham's | E 138 St between Willis Ave & Alexander Ave | 1930's-40's |
| Curry, R | 1081 Boston Rd | 1950-60's |
| Cy's Candy Store | Creston Ave & E 181st St | 1955-59 |
| Dall's | W. 239th/240th Sts | |
| Dal Pra | 5605 Broadway | 1940-50's |
| Dammann | 2645 Jerome Ave | 1940's |
| Danny's | E Tremont Ave & Harrington Ave | 1955-80 |
| Dave's Candy Store | Bainbridge & E. 206th St | 1950-60's |
| Dave's | 2020 Washington Ave | 1940's-60's |
| Davis, J | 1403 Prospect Ave | 1940-60's |
| De Angelis Ice Cream Parlor | 4222 White Plains Rd | 1960's |
| De Ronner, H | 1275 Webster Ave | 1940's |
| De Jesus, O | 921 Longwood Ave | 1960's |
| Delgado, A | 920 Prospect Ave | 1950's |

| | | |
|---|---|---|
| Delgado's Candy | 920 Prospect Ave | 1960's |
| DeLuca's | Jenning St / Longfellow Ave | 1950's |
| DeSpirt, A I | 5605 Broadway | 1950's |
| Diner, Benjamin | 1062 Westchester Ave | 1940's |
| Dino, Josephine | 11 E 200 St | 1940-60's |
| Divack's | Bainbridge Ave & Reservoir | 1940-50's |
| Du Berry, John | 886 Morris Pk Ave | 1950's |
| Duke's Candy Store | 1000 Hoe Ave | 1960's |
| Duncker, H | 2921 3rd Ave | 1940's |
| Durey Product Company | 1691 Anthony Ave | 1950's |
| Dutch Candy Mart | 2150 White Plains Rd | 1940-50's |
| Dutch Mart | White Plains Rd | 1940-50s |
| Eckhoff's Ice Cream Parlor | 204 St. bet. Perry & Bainbridge | 1940's-60's |
| Eagle Candy Store | 649 Eagle Ave | 1950's |
| Eddie's | E. 176th & Walton/Townsend | 1940-50's |
| Eddie's Candy Store | Westchester Ave & Parker St | 1950's |
| Edgewater Confectionery | 10 Edgewater Center | 1950-60's |
| Egiziano, C B | 1779 Westchester Ave | 1950's |
| Ekman's | Lydig Ave & Wallace Ave | 1939-56 |
| Eli's | Macombs Rd, W. 175th & 176th St | |
| Eli & Meyers | Macombs Road | 1940-50's |
| Ellis' | Burke Ave & Holland | |
| Ellman's Candy Store | Fox St bet. Longwood & 156th St | 1940's-50's |
| Elsie Hells | Fordham Road between Grand Avenue and Davidson Ave | 1940-70 |
| Emanuel, A | 2139 Boston Rd | 1940-60's |
| Emmer, R | 318 Cypress Ave | 1950's |
| Engelstein's | Corsa Ave & Boston Post Rd | 1940-60's |
| Erba Food Products | 910 River Ave | 1960's |
| Ernie's | Jerome & Mosholu Pkwy | 1950's |
| Esther's Candy Store | E 156 St & Elton Ave | 1950's |
| Eugene's Candy Store | 953 Prospect Ave | 1940's |
| Evander Sweet Shop | Gun Hill & White Plains Rd | 1940-65 |
| Falkowitz' | Ave St. John & Fox St | 1930-41 |
| Fanny & Sol's Candy Store | Nelson Ave & W 168 St | 1950's-60's |
| Fanny Farmer Candy Shop | 3825 Corleer Ave | 1950-60's |
| Farbers | W. 162nd St & Ogden Ave | 1940-50's |
| Farm Luncheonette | 1004 E 167th St | 1950's |
| Feldhusen, Frank | 476 Willis Ave | 1940-60's |
| Feldman's | E. 156th St & Grand Concourse | 1940-65 |
| Feldman & Tannenbaum | 170 St & Jerome Ave | 1941-48 |
| Feldman's Candy Store | 155th St & Grand Concourse | 1955-68 |
| Fenster, R | 550 E 171st St | 1950-60's |
| Fialkoff's | | |
| Fiech J Company | 1578 Bathgate Ave | 1940's |
| Fisher's | Castle Hill Ave between Blackrock Ave & Chatterton Ave | 1936-44 |
| Five Corner Candy Store | Unionport Rd | 1950-60's |
| Fly's Candy Store | Corner of Sherman & E. 166 St. | 1940-50's |
| Forbes Confectioners | 368 E Fordham Rd | 1950-60's |
| Forest Ave Candy Shop | 867 Forest Ave | 1950's |
| Fossa Stationery | 3221 Westchester Ave | 1950's |
| Foster's Candy Store | 933 E. 165th Street | 1930's-40's |
| Foster's Confectionery | 2411 Grand Concourse | 1940's |
| Fountain of Youth | 2151 Grand Concourse | 1940's |
| Frances Bonbonniere | 61 E Gun Hill Rd | 1950's |
| Frank's | Katonah Ave & E. 237th St | |
| Frank's Candy Store | 597 Creston Ave | 1950's |
| Frank's Candy Store | W. Tremont & Harrison Ave | |
| Frank's Ice Cream Parlor | 975 Morris Pk Ave | 1950-60's |
| Frankie's | W Tremont Ave & Harrison Ave | 1960's |

| | | |
|---|---|---|
| Frawley, J | 3009 Heath Ave | 1960's |
| Fred's | St Ann's Ave bet. E 146 & E 147 St | 1951-58 |
| Frieda's | University Ave & W 179th St | 1940's-50's |
| Fulton Sweets | 50 E 167th St | 1940-50's |
| G & Z Sweet Shoppe | 1003 Freeman St | 1948-60 |
| Gable's | E 172nd St | |
| Garbers | Middleton Rd & Hobart Ave | 1950s-60's |
| Garber's | E 181 St & Ryer Ave | 1940-50 |
| Garcia, Bruno | 567 Southern Blvd | 1950's |
| Geller Brothers | 1589 Bathgate Ave | 1950's |
| Geller, E | 1639 Monroe Ave | 1950's |
| Georgie's Candy Store | 811 E 165 St | 1940's |
| Gert & Hy's | Near Vyse Ave | 1940's |
| Gieseler's Confectionery | 4222 White Plains Rd | 1940's |
| Gilberts | Third Ave & E 138 St | 1930's-40's |
| Glasberg's Luncheonette | 83 E 184 St | 1950's |
| Glass' Candy Store | Cypress Ave & 141st St | 1930's-40's |
| Gluth, J | 1248 Castle Hill Ave | 1930-60's |
| Gnewikow, Karl | 1294 Washington Ave | 1940's |
| Goldberg's | Burke Ave & Holland | |
| Golden Rule Luncheonette | Burnside Ave & Anthony Ave | 1940's-60's |
| Goldfarb's | Burnside & Grand Ave. | 1950's |
| Goldman's | 181st & Daly Ave | 1950-65 |
| Goldstein's | 863 Southern Blvd. | 1929-1948 |
| Goldstein's | Bruckner Blvd & Castle Hill Ave | 1930's-40's |
| Gonzalez, J | 998 E 163 St | 1950's |
| Good, H | 317 E 169th St | 1940's |
| Goodman's Candy Store | Cauldwell Ave E 149th St | 1940-44 |
| Goodwill Sweet Shop | 144 E 170 St | 1940-50's |
| Greco's Pastry Shop | 653 Morris Ave | 1960's |
| Green, A | 3766 White Plains Rd | 1950-60's |
| Green Dot | Ogden Ave & W. 168th St | 1950's |
| Greenberger's Candy Store | 1406 Townsend Ave | 1935-42 |
| Greenfield, M | 3420 Boston Rd | 1940's |
| Greenspan, P & M | 1053 Southern Blvd | 1950-60's |
| Greenstein, Louis | 650 Southern Blvd | 1940's |
| Gruber, W E | 398 E 195 St | 1950's |
| Gun Hill Luncheonette | Gun Hill Rd & Bainbridge | 1955-65 |
| Gun Hill Tobacco/Candy | 3564 White Plains Rd | 1940's |
| Gus's | Boynton & Westchester Ave | 1950-60's |
| Gutierrez, M | 920 Prospect Ave | 1940's |
| H & M Sweets | 3140 Bainbridge Ave | 1940-50's |
| Halpern's Candy Store | 140th St & Cypress Ave | 1930's-50's |
| Halter, C | 870 Freeman St | 1940's |
| Hargood Candy Company | 961 Teller Ave | 1940's |
| Harlem Tobacco/Candy | 678 E 187 St | 1940's |
| Harm, C | 80 Featherbed Lane | 1940's |
| Harms | Jesup Ave & Featherbed Lane | 1940's-50's |
| Harriet Nut Shop | 1733 University Ave | 1950-60's |
| Harry's | Lydig Ave & White Plains Rd | 1940-50s |
| Harry's | Anthony Ave & E. 176 St | 1950-70's |
| Harry & Murray | Allenon Ave & Barker | 1950's |
| Harry Gordon's | | |
| Harry and Phil's | 170th St & E.L. Grant Hghwy | 1950-60 |
| Harry's | Lydig Ave | 1940-50's |
| Harry's | Anthony Ave & E 176th St | 1950-70's |
| Hartleb & Haack | 387 E Fordham Rd | 1940-60's |
| Harvey's Sweet Shop | 2000 Holland Ave | 1940's |
| Hastedt, H | 3200 White Plains Rd | 1940's |
| Hastedt, J | 975 Morris Park Ave | 1940's |
| Hatties, Ann | 1779 Westchester Ave | 1940's |

| | | |
|---|---|---|
| Hecht, A | 1380 E Gun Hill Rd | 1950's |
| Hegamin, E | 585 E 167th St | 1950's |
| Heilpern, J | 667 E Fordham Rd | 1940's |
| Heipel, G | 1013 Castle Hill Ave | 1940-50's |
| Heise, H | 2717 3rd Ave | 1940's |
| Heitmann, J | 209 St Anns Ave | 1940-50's |
| Helen's | Cypress Ave. & E. 141 St. | 1940's |
| Helene's Confectionery | 989 Morris Ave | 1950's |
| Helfrich's Confectionery | 3204 3rd Ave | 1940's |
| Helmedach, John | 45 W Fordham Rd | 1940-60's |
| Herman's | Bainbridge Ave & E 194 St | 1940's-60's |
| Hermax | 3891 Sedgwick Ave | 1960's-72 |
| Herskowitz | E 170 St & Jerome Ave | 1950's |
| Higgins, R | 2927 Westchester Ave | 1940's |
| Hilda & Moe's | W. 231 St. near Broadway | 1950-60's |
| Hill's Candy Store | 1426 Crotona Ave | 1960's |
| Hinck, H | 4301 Katonah Ave | 1950-60's |
| Hindenberger, J | Silver Beach | 1950's |
| Hink's | Tremont Ave | |
| Hochstein's | Wilkins Ave & Crotona Pk E | 1940-50's |
| Hochhauser, Arnold | 972 East 165th St | 1950's |
| Hodon, Arthur | 541 East 166th St | 1950's |
| Hoft's Candy Store | 3200 White Plains Road | 1947-98 |
| Hoeft & Marcodes | 291 E 204th St | 1940-60's |
| Hoffman Conf/Tobacco Co | 1159 Intervale Ave | 1950's |
| Holsten, M | 1191 Castle Hill Ave | 1940's |
| Hopengarten's Candy Store | 665 Burke Ave | |
| Horowitz | Longfellow Ave & E 172 St | 1930's-40's |
| Horowitz's | 131 East Gun Hill Rd & Rochambeau Ave | 1928-30 |
| House of Kramer | 730 Hunts Point Ave | 1940's |
| Howie's | White Plains Rd & Archer Ave | 1958-70 |
| Huggins Candy Store | Burke & Westchester Aves | 1950-65 |
| Humphrey's Candy Store | Morris Ave & E. 163rd St | |
| Hurwitz, Samuel | 1322 Metropolitan Ave | 1940's |
| Hy & Romeo's Luncheonette | Jerome Ave & 190th St | 1955-65 |
| Hy Chaiken | White Plains Pelham Pkwy Station | 1940-60's |
| Hyde Pk Candies | 1324 Metropolitan Ave | 1940-60's |
| Hymee's | Brady Ave & White Plains Rd. | 1938-49 |
| Hymie's (Cohen Sweet Shoppe) | Allerton & Holland Aves | 1940-50's |
| Hymie's Candy Store | Allerton Ave & Cruger Ave | 1934-50's |
| Ice Cream Parlour | Castle Hill Ave & Bruckner Blvd | 1940's |
| Ifshin's | 500 Southern Blvd at E. 149th St | 1930-40's |
| Ike's | E. 143rd St & Willis Ave | 1950-60's |
| Irene's | | 1940-60's |
| Irving's Candy Store | No. of Gun Hill & White Plains Rd | |
| Island's Best Custard | 105 City Island Ave | 1960's |
| Izzy's | Nelson & W. 169th St | 1950-56 |
| Izzy Balsam's | Sheridan Ave & Mc Clellan Ave | 1950-75 |
| J & G Nut Shop | 2130 White Plains Rd | 1950's |
| Jack's | Gun Hill Rd & DeKalb Ave | 1940's |
| Jack's | W 231st St | 1940-50's |
| Jack's | Oneida Ave & 233rd St | |
| Jack's | W. 162nd St & Ogden Ave | 1950-60's |
| Jack's Candy Store | Seneca & Bryant Ave | 1950's |
| Jack's Candy Store | Bainbridge Ave & E. 194th St. | 1930-40's |
| Jack's Candy Store | White Plains Rd & Archer St | 1942-1946 |
| Jack's Candy Store | 2153 Starling Ave | 1947-77 |
| Jack's Candy Shop | 744 E 180th St | 1950's |
| Jack's Candy Store | 597 Creston Ave | 1960's |
| Jack & Edie's | Davidson & W Tremont Ave | 1948-65 |

# THE CONFECTION CONNECTION

| | | |
|---|---|---|
| Jack & Milt's Candy Store | Allerton & Wallace Aves | 1960's |
| Jack Bernstein's | E. 168th St & College Ave | |
| Jackson Candy & Cigar | 2419 Westchester Ave | 1950-60's |
| Jackson, W P | 194 Washington Ave | 1950's |
| Jaffe's Luncheonette | E. 170th St & Grand Concourse | |
| Jake's Candy Store | E 141 St between St Ann's Ave & Cypress Ave | 1930's |
| Jake's Place | Castle Hill Ave nr Westchester Ave | 1930-50's |
| Jake/Gussie's | Minerva Pl & Jerome Ave | 1940-60's |
| Jark, Henry | 119 Westchester Square | 1940-60's |
| Jarma's | Tiffany St & E. 167th St | 1940's |
| Jarmin's | Tiffany St & E. 167th St | 1950-60's |
| Jaycee Coffee Shop | Pelham Pkwy N & WP Rd | |
| Jentz, O | 3204 3rd Ave | 1950-60's |
| Jerry's | 2130 Lydig Ave | 1940-50's |
| Jerry's | E. 183rd St & Cambreling | 1940's |
| Jerry's | W Mosholu Pkwy | 1940-50's |
| Jesse's | White Plains Rd & Lydig Ave | 1940-50's |
| Jesse's Sweet Shop | 2130 White Plains Rd | 1960's |
| Jessie & Louis | 271 E 156 St | 1939-42 |
| Jessie's Luncheonette | Creston Ave & E 181st St | 1948-49 |
| Jim & Joe's | Corner Burke Ave & Wallace Ave | 1944-52 |
| Jimmy DeRosa's | 2359 Beaumont Ave & 187th St | 1950-60's |
| Jimmy's | E 172nd St & Commonwealth | 1950's |
| Jimmy's Candy Store | Prospect Ave & E 187 St | 1940's-50's |
| Jippy's | Sedgwick Ave & Fordham Rd | 1960's-70's |
| Joe's Candy | 744 Fox | 1960's |
| Joe's Candy | 1652 Washington Ave | 1960's |
| Joe's Candy Store | Continental & Westchester Ave | |
| Joe's Candy Store | Watson Ave & Olmstead Ave | 1940's-50's |
| Joe's Candy Store | E 184 St & Webster Ave | 1940's-60's |
| Joe's College Luncheonette | Jerome Ave & E 198th St | 1950-60's |
| Joe's Luncheonette | Hunts Point Ave & Seneca | 1940's |
| Joey B's Quick Lunch | 1101 Castle Hill | 1961-67 |
| John's | 653 E 182nd St | |
| John's Candy Store | Cortland Ave bet. E 149 & 150 St | 1931-36 |
| John O'Neill's Candy Store | E 153 St bet. Elton Ave & Melrose | 1920's-30's |
| Johnny's & Rudy's Lucheonette | 632 Cortlandt Ave | 1950's |
| Jonas Candy Store | Fordham Rd. bet. Concourse & Valentine Ave. | 1930's |
| Jonas Candy Store | Cortland Ave. between 149th & E. 150th. | 1930's |
| Jones, Buck | 701 E 160th St | 1950's |
| Jones, J L | 823 Freeman Ave | 1950's |
| Jones, Y | 955 Fox | 1960's |
| Julie's Candy Store | Kingsbridge & W. 238th Street | 1950's |
| Just Right Cigar Company | 933 E 169th St | 1950-60's |
| Kachulis, C | 1249 Ogden Ave | 1950-60's |
| Kackmann, Henry | 4715 White Plains Rd | 1940's |
| Kanaras, L | 2231 Southern Blvd | 1940-60's |
| Kans, F | 724 Allerton Ave | 1940's |
| Kaplan's | Townsend Ave & E 170 St | 1950's |
| Kaplan's | E 167th St & Teller Ave | 1940's-55 |
| Kaplan's Candy Store | Townsend Ave between W 170 St & 171 St | 1948-63 |
| Kaplan's | Gun Hill Rd & Decatur Ave | 1940-50's |
| Kappy's | E. 176th & Walton | 1950-60's |
| Kappy's | E Gun Hill Rd & Hull Ave | 1959-80's |
| Kasten's Candy Store | 1809 Crotona Ave | 1940-50's |
| Katie's | E 153 between Elton & Melrose | 1950-63 |
| Katz P Inc | 1705 Boston Rd | 1940's |
| Katz's Candy Store | Longfellow Ave between Freeman St & 174th St | 1935-42 |
| Kaufman's | E. 183rd St & Walton Ave | 1950-60's |
| Kay-Bee Candy Shop | 3479 Jerome Ave | 1940's |
| Kay-Bee Sugar Bowl | 67 W 183 St | 1940's |
| Kempft & Barner | 2383 Westchester Ave | 1940's |
| Kenig, S | 481 Claremont Pkwy | 1940's |
| Kent Goody Shop | 192 E 167 St | 1940's |
| Kent Luncheonette | E. 167th Street off Concourse | 1951-1969 |
| Kernberg, L | 922 E Tremont Ave | 1960's |
| Kiel's | 1204 Union Ave | 1960's |
| Kines Brothers | 368 E Fordham Rd | 1940's |
| Kitty's Corner Luncheonette | E. 183rd St & Beaumont Ave | 1950-60's |
| Klee, Julius | 310 E 156 St | 1940's |
| Kleinman's Candy Store | Nelson Ave & Featherbed Lane | |
| Kling, Julius | 310 E 156 St | 1940's |
| Klub Kollege | 320 E 148th St | 1960's |
| Klussman, A | 481 St Anns Ave | 1940's |
| Koenig, John | 289 Willis Ave | 1940's |
| Koger Co, The | 966 Freeman | 1940-60's |
| Korman Brothers Inc | 1999 Jerome Ave | 1950's |
| Kornberg's Candy Store | E 184th St & Tiebout Ave | 1945-60 |
| KornBlooms | 1696 Washington Ave, between 173 & 174 St. | 1934-40's |
| Kornfeld's | Brady Ave & White Plains Rd | 1940-49 |
| Kramer's Candy Store | 163 W Tremont Ave | 1950's |
| Kramer's | W 231st St | |
| Kranz's Candy Store | 163rd St & Jackson Ave | 1929-44 |
| Krause's | Beekman Ave & Beech Ter | 1950's |
| Kresse's | Morris Ave & E. 174th St | 1930-46 |
| Krisch, F | 682 Morris Pk Ave | 1940-50's |
| Krum J | 2468 Grand Concourse | 1940-60's |
| Kunkel, Aug | 3027 3rd Ave | 1940's |
| L & B Distributors | 251 E 150 St | 1950-60's |
| L & L Confectionery Store | 1201 White Plains Rd | 1950-60's |
| L& L Confectionery | 1891 Gleason Ave | 1940's-50's |
| L & M Candy Store | 830 Freeman St | 1960's |
| L & V Candy Store | 1356 Boston Rd | 1960's |
| Lande, S | 2201 Jerome Ave | 1940's |
| Landsman | E. 164th St. off Morris Ave | 1935-60's |
| Lantzounis, Pericles | 650 E 163rd St | 1940's |
| Lapin's | E 234 St & E Gun Hill Rd | 1940-50's |
| Lapidos, A | 1030 E 180 St | 1940's |
| Laracuente, I | 949 E 167th St | 1960's |
| Larry's | Gun Hill Rd & Tryon Ave North | 1960's |
| Larry's Luncheonette | 1534 Westchester Ave | 1955-65 |
| Lavin's | | |
| Lebron, D | 1465 Boston Rd | 1960's |
| Lee's | Boston Post Rd & Fish | 1940-78 |
| Leedman's | Westchester Ave & Leland | 1945-60's |
| Leff's | Near Dover Theater | 1950's |
| Leftoff's Cut Rate Candy Store | Jennings St Market | 1930's |
| Lefty Moe's | E. 183rd & Beaumont Ave | 1940's |
| Leiblein Candy Store | Fox St between Westchester Ave & 163rd St | 1940's |
| Leightner's | Kingsbridge Rd & W 231st St | 1950's |
| Lemme (Tony & Anne) | Bronxwood Ave. & E. 213 St. | 1950's |
| Lenetz, Louis | 522 City Island Ave | 1940's |
| Lenore's Sweet Shop | 1863 Westchester Ave | 1950-60's |
| Leo's | Williamsbridge Rd between Mace & Waring Aves | 1950's-60's |

# THE CONFECTION CONNECTION

| | | |
|---|---|---|
| Leo's | E Tremont & Vyse Ave | 1938-42 |
| Leo's Candy Store | Field Place & The Concourse | |
| Leon J | 214 St Arms Ave | 1950-60's |
| Leon's Candy Store | 987 E 178th St | 1960's |
| Leverah's | Woodcrest & W. 165th St | 1940-50's |
| Levinson, I | 1942 Boston Rd | 1940's |
| Leyman, Henry | 734 E 188 St | 1940-60's |
| Libby's | 321 E 166th St | 1928-48 |
| Lieberman, S | 1926 Crotona Parkway | 1940's |
| Lieflander's Candy Store | Honeywell bet E178 St and 179 St | 1950's-60's |
| Liesegang, Karl | 291 E 204th St | 1960's |
| Lifer's | Creston Ave & E 198th St | 1950-60's |
| Lipton, George | 865 E 149th St | 1950's |
| Loft Candy | 72 E Burnside Ave | 1940-50's |
| Loft Candy | 50 E Fordham Rd | 1940-50's |
| Loft Candy | 2443 Grand Concourse | 1940-50's |
| Loft Candy | 1438 Metropolitan Ave | 1940-50's |
| Loft Candy | 885 Prospect Ave | 1940-50's |
| Loft Candy | 1031 Southern Blvd | 1940-50's |
| Loft Candy | 483 E Tremont Ave | 1940-50's |
| Loft Candy | 769 E Tremont Ave | 1940-50's |
| Loft Candy | 1576 Westchester Ave | 1940-50's |
| Loft Candy | 3758 White Plains Rd | 1940-50's |
| Loft Candy | 532 Willis Ave | 1940-50's |
| Loft Candy | 340A E 204th St | 1940-50's |
| Lou's | 3rd Ave & E Tremont Ave | 1947-65 |
| Lou's | Gun Hill Rd & Tryon Ave | 1950's |
| Louie and Ann's | Grand Ave | 1933-55 |
| Louie's | Lydig Ave and Wallace Ave | 1940's-50's |
| Louie's Candy Store | 181st St & Crotona Ave | 1940-60's |
| Louie's Candy Store | Leland & Archer | 1946-49 |
| Luboff | Quimby & Houghton Ave | 1930's |
| Luhrs, J | 1749 University Ave | 1950-60's |
| Lujack's Candy Store | Andrews Ave & W Fordham Rd | 1955-65 |
| Lum & Eddie's | Allerton Ave & Barker | 1940's |
| Luxor Sweet Shop | 210 East 170th Street | 1940-60's |
| Lynch, Susan | 571 East 140th St | 1950's |
| M & M Sweet Shop | 3480 Jerome Ave | 1950's |
| M & N Candy & Nut Shop | 719 E 180th St | 1950's |
| M & S Sweet Shop | 2199 White Plains Rd | 1940's |
| M's | Sedgwick & Van Cortlandt Aves | 1950-60's |
| M's Candy Store | 3891 Sedgwick Ave | 1956-60's |
| Maccaro's Sugar Bowl | 1554 Westchester Ave | 1960's |
| Mac's Luncheonette | 289 Willis Ave | 1950's |
| Madello's Luncheonette | 1647 Crosby Ave | 1950's |
| Mae & Al's | 827 Melrose Ave | 1940-45 |
| Mae's | E. 182nd St & Crotona Ave | 1950-60's |
| Mae's Candy Store | E 182 St & Crotona Park | 1940's-50's |
| Maisonet, A | 1490 Crotona Pk North | 1960's |
| Mannie's | Grand Concourse (E. 150th St.) | 1940-50's |
| Manny's | E.178th St & Bryant Ave | 1940's |
| Manny's Candy Store | Beach Ave & Randall Ave | 1955-64 |
| Marcucci, E | 914 Hoe Ave | 1960's |
| Marshack's | W. 169th & Plimpton Ave. | 1930-40's |
| Martinez, R | 614 E 138th St | 1950's |
| Marty's | Tremont Ave& Anthony Ave | 1950's-60's |
| Mary Ann Candy Store | 1362 Clinton Ave | 1940's |
| Mary's Candy Store | 1155 Intervale Ave | 1960's |
| Matthews Ice Cream | 924 E 163rd St | 1950-60's |
| Matthews, T | 2004 Mohegan Ave | 1950's |
| Max's | 1003 Freeman St | 1945-1951 |

| | | |
|---|---|---|
| Max's | Melrose Ave & E 151st St | 1951-63 |
| Max's Candy Store | E. 182nd St & Prospect Ave | 1938-42 |
| Maxies | Gun Hill Rd & Putnam Pl | 1939-55 |
| Maxie's Candy Store | Melrose & E. 151 St. | 1940's-70's |
| May & Al's Stationery | 827 Melrose Ave | 1950's |
| Mayer, H | 3805 White Plains Rd | 1950's |
| Mayer's | E. 219 St & White Plains Rd | 1960-66 |
| McMahon's | Cypress Ave bet. E. 138th & E. 139th St | |
| Measers | 1661 University Ave | 1940-55 |
| Mejias, M | 1420 Wilkins Ave | 1960's |
| Mellman N & Company | 371 E 146th St | 1940's |
| Mellman N & Company | 361 E 146th St | 1950-60's |
| Melskin, R | 1016 Longwood Ave | 1950's |
| Mendel's | Allerton Ave & White Pl Rd | 1940-50's |
| Menschel's | W. Burnside & Hennessey Pl. | 1933-1943 |
| Mervish, A | 94 E 174th St | 1940's |
| Messer, I | 1589 Bathgate Ave | 1940's |
| Messer, Meyer | 755 Allerton Ave | 1950's |
| Meyer, E | 751 Melrose Ave | 1940-60's |
| Meyers Confectionary | 74 Mt Eden Ave | 1940-50's |
| Meyer's | 121 Mt. Eden Ave | |
| Migden, B | 17 E 182nd St | 1950-60's |
| Mike's Candy Store | W 238th St & Review Pl | 1950-70's |
| Mike's Candy Store | Melrose bet. E 151 & E. 152 St. | 1950-70 |
| Miller's | E. 152nd St & Jackson Ave | 1940's |
| Miller's | E. Tremont & Southern Blvd. | 1920-30's |
| Mills, Samuel | 1062 E Tremont Ave | 1940's |
| Mimi Specialty Company | 279 E 166 St | 1940's |
| Mintz | Allerton Ave & Barker | 1930's |
| Miss Lynn's Candy Store | SW 141st & Alexander Ave | 1925-60's |
| Molina B | 761 Westchester Ave | 1960's |
| Moores Sweet Shop | 789 E 158th St | 1960's |
| Morris' Candy Store | Lafayette & Bryant Aves | 1950's |
| Mr Dee's Candy Store | E 173 St & Boynton Ave | 1953-79 |
| Mr. Di | Bronx River & Boynton Aves | 1950-70's |
| Mr Gordon's | St Anne's Ave & E138th St | 1950-64 |
| Mr Lester | Ogden Ave & Merriam Ave | 1940's |
| Mr. Yellen | E 187th St & Park Ave | 1945-62 |
| Moishe's | Jennings St & Longfellow Ave | 1938-53 |
| Moishe's | Fox St | 1941-45 |
| Molly and Izzy's | W 231st St | 1930's-70's |
| Moskoff's | E 170th St | 1930's |
| Mt Carmel Candy Store | 621 E 187th St | 1950's |
| Mt Eden Candy Store | 3 Mt Eden Ave & Jerome | 1940-50's |
| Mukin's | E. 175th St & Clinton Ave | |
| Muller & Richter | 3805 White Plains Rd | 1960's |
| Mumm's | Layton Ave & Eastern Blvd | 1930's |
| Munoz, F | 882 E 163rd St | 1960's |
| Murphy's Candy Store | 729 East 165th Street | 1930's-40's |
| Murray-Allen Co Inc | 135 E 144th St | 1960's |
| Murray's | Allenon Ave & Barker | 1950's |
| Murray's | Gun Hill Road & Hull Ave | 1950's-80's |
| Music Box Sweet Shop | 1513 Brook Ave | 1960's |
| My Brothers Luncheonette | 749 Astor Ave | 1981-85 |
| Myers F & H | 360 Alexander Ave | 1940-50's |
| N & M Sweet Shop | 3480 Jerome Ave | 1940-60's |
| Nadelberg's Candy Store | W. 169 St. bet. Plimpton & Nelson Ave | 1960's |
| Nathan's Candy Store | E. 174th St & Fulton Ave | 1940-50's |
| Nat's Candy Store | Seneca & Bryant | 1950's |
| Nemeroff's Candy Store | 1565 Wilkins Ave. | 1940's |

| Name | Address | Year |
|---|---|---|
| Ness's Candy Store | Marmion Ave | 1945 |
| Newman's Candy Store | 911 Southern Blvd. | 1920's |
| Newman, Joseph | 1168 Colgate Ave | 1950-60's |
| Nibi, J | 724 Allerton Ave | 1950's |
| Nick's | E. 174th St | 1959-67 |
| NIcky's Candy Store | 896 Melrose Avenue | 1950-60's |
| Nievers, W | 996 Ogden Ave | 1940's |
| Normandy Candy Store | E. 170th St & Walton Ave | 1950-60's |
| Nuts & Butts | Morris & Creston Aves | 1939-48 |
| Olshen's | E. 154th St & Melrose Ave | 1930-40's |
| Ortiz Candy Store | 601 Prospect Ave | 1950's |
| Ottley, Jas | 1430 Washington Ave | 1950's |
| Page & Shaw Chocolates | 572 Westchester Ave | 1950-60's |
| Paley's | Hunt's Point Ave & Faile St | 1940's-50's |
| Pam-Ellen Sweet Shop | 2123 Williamsbridge Rd | 1950-60's |
| Pam & Lee Candy Cupboard | 121 Mt Eden Ave | 1960's |
| Pam & Lee's | 121 Mt Eden Ave | 1960's |
| Paradise Choc Shop | 2425 Grand Concourse | 1940-60's |
| Paramount Sweet Shop | 67 W 183rd St | 1950's |
| Paris, John | 2080 Pitman Ave | 1950's |
| Park Soda Bar | 5989 Broadway | 1950's |
| Parkchester Confectionary | 1861 McGraw Ave | 1940's |
| Patsy's Candy Store | 203rd St off Mosholu | 1935-50 |
| Paula's | W 231 St & Kingsbridge Ave | 1950-70's |
| Peck, I | 403 City Island Ave | 1940-50's |
| Pelotte, M | 1023 Boston Rd | 1950's |
| Penquin Frozen Custard | 785 E Tremont Ave | 1950's |
| Pensky's Candy Store | 1208 Stratford Ave | 1930-40's |
| Peper, C | 4533 3rd Ave | 1940-50's |
| Peppermint Bar | Commonwealth & Beach Ave | 1949-57 |
| Pete's Candy Store | E 167 St between Hoe Ave & West Farms Rd | 1940's-50's |
| Pete's Candy Store | Williamsbridge Rd between Mace Ave & Waring Ave | 1940's-50's |
| Pezzuti, R | 2391 Arthur Ave | 1940's |
| Philips, Spiros | 4030 3rd Ave | 1940's |
| Phil's Candy Store | Creston Ave & East Kingsbridge Rd | 1940's-50's |
| Piccolo, F | 3277 Ampere Ave | 1940-60's |
| Pignone, M | 2481 Belmont Ave | 1940-60's |
| Pinchick's | Boston Rd | 1930's |
| Pippy's Luncheonette | Courtlandt Ave between E 155 St & E 156 St | 1950-52 |
| Plaza Sweet Shop | 1784 University Ave | 1940's |
| Plotkin, N | 1717 University Ave | 1940's |
| PMP Luncheonette | Kingsbridge Rd & Creston | 1940-60's |
| Pollack, A | 1054 Southern Blvd | 1940's |
| Ponza Candy Store | 250 E 151 St | 1940-60's |
| Pope, J C | 1245 Boston Rd | 1940's |
| Pop's | W Brunside Ave & Hennessy Pl | 1940-50's |
| Pop's | 2001 Clinton Ave | 1950's |
| Pop's Candy Store | E. 189th St & Beaumont ave | |
| Pop Sivics' | 162 St near Woodycrest Ave | 1940s-50s |
| Portnoy's | St John's & Southern Blvd | 1940's |
| Prospect-Meyer | 901 Prospect Ave | 1940-60's |
| Prospect Candy/Tobacco | 954 Prospect Ave | 1940-50's |
| Pyramid Candy Company | 1557 Westchester Ave | 1950-60's |
| Quinones, Alicia | 1492 Vyse Ave | 1960's |
| R&T Soda Spa | 1196A Morris Park Ave | 1950's |
| Rabinowitz, A | 155 E 170th St | 1940's |
| Raider's Candy Store | Sheridan Ave. & McClellan St. | 1940-50's |
| Raine's | Allerton Ave & Barker | 1940's |
| Ralph DiBenedetto | Bronx River Ave | 1943-62 |
| Ramirez, L | 840 Tinton Ave | 1950's |
| Ramm, George | 3805 White Plains Rd | 1940's |
| Ramm's Ice Cream Parlor | E 219th St & White Plains Rd | 1900-50's |
| Rand's | 1566 Watson Ave | 1940's |
| R&B Luncheonette | 650 E 233rd St | |
| Rappaports | College Ave & E. 170th St | 1940's |
| Rauch's | St John between Fox & Beck | 1944-50 |
| Rauch's | 973 Avenue St John | |
| Raymond's Sweet Shop | 245 E 167th St | 1940's |
| Reecer Chocolate Shop | 279 E 204th St | 1950-60's |
| Reinah, Sam | 105 E 169th St | 1940's-60's |
| Reiser's | 170th St & Findlay Ave | 1937-57 |
| Reiter, J | 995 Simpson St | 1940's |
| Rendezvous | E. 182nd & Grand Concourse | 1950-73 |
| Rendezvous | Ward Ave & Westchester | 1946-1955 |
| Richard's Candy Store | 1084 Forest Avenue | 1930's-40's |
| Richman | E. 176th St & Anthony Ave | 1938-47 |
| Riggio, Rose | 1975 LaFontaine Ave | 1950's |
| Ritzers | Decatur Ave & Bedford Pk Blvd | 1950's |
| Rockwood Place Candy Store | Walton Ave & Grand Concourse | 1948-58 |
| Rodriquez, R | 1000 Tiffany | 1960's |
| Rogoff's | Corner Lydig Ave & Holland Ave | 1952-56 |
| Rogofsky | Allerton Ave & Barker | 1940's |
| Romeo's Candy Store | Hoffman St bet. E 187 & E 188 St | 1940-48 |
| Ronnie's Sweet Shoppe | 755 Allerton Ave | 1955-65 |
| Rose's | 1793 Montgomery Ave | 1940's |
| Rosie's | 1717 Hoe Ave | 1930-50's |
| Rosie's Sweet Shop | 1185 Morrison Ave | 1960's |
| Rosito, S | 2515 Boston Rd | 1950-60's |
| Roth, I | 1920 Crotona Ave | 1950-60's |
| Rottger, A | 271 E 165th St | 1940's |
| Roy's Candy Store | E. 174th St & Selwyn Ave | 1950's |
| Rubin, D | 2180 White Plains Rd | 1940's |
| Rubin, Sherman | 292 E 166 St | 1940's |
| Rubin's | Corner of Charlotte St & Boston Rd | 1940s-50s |
| Rubin's | E 172 St bet Fteley & Croes | 1940-50's |
| Ruby's | Anthony Ave & Burnside Ave (SE) | 1940s-60s |
| Rudy's | Katonah & E. 235 th St | 1940-50's |
| Rusch, R | 3950 White Plains Rd | 1940's |
| Ruschmeyer, G | 1749 University Ave | 1940's |
| Ruth and Moe's Luncheonette | Gun Hill Road & Putnam Place | 1960s-70s |
| S&W | 1717 University Ave | 1940-55 |
| Sabatelli's | 396 E 154th St | 1940's |
| Saddie's | Corner of Watson & Elder | 1948-55 |
| Sal & Dave's | W 168th St & Nelson Ave | 1940-50's |
| Sal's | Corner of Creston and E 181 St | 1940's-50's |
| Sam and Anna's Candy Store | Coster St and Spofford Ave | 1938-43 |
| Sam and Anne | Teller Ave & 162nd St | 1930-60's |
| Sam & Henry's | 176 St & Jerome Ave | 1940-60's |
| Sam & Lou's | Woodycrest Ave | |
| Sam & Rose's | Boynton & Westchester Ave | 1950's |
| Sam & Sol's | Davidson & W. 184th St | 1940's |
| Sam Chatinsksy Candy Store | Davidson Ave | 1940's |
| Sam's | E. 176th St & Anthony Ave | 1948-60 |
| Sam's Candy Store | 1685 University Ave | 1950-60's |
| Sam's | Katonah Ave & W. 239th St | 1940-50's |
| Sam's | Cor of McGraw & Unionport | |
| Sam's | Woodcrest & W. 165th St. | 1960's |
| Sam's | E. 173rd St & Boston Post Rd | 1950's |
| Sam's | Webster Ave and 205th St | 1940's-70's |

# THE CONFECTION CONNECTION

| | | |
|---|---|---|
| Sam's Candy Store | Astor Ave & Holland Ave | 1960's |
| Sam's Candy Store | E 169th St between Clinton Ave and Franklin Ave | 1933-42 |
| Sam's Candy Store | Boston Rd & 173rd St | 1950's-70's |
| Sam's Luncheonette | W 176th St & University Ave | 1960's |
| Sam & Sadie's Luncheonette | Elder & Watson Aves | 1945-65 |
| Sandra's Candy Store | Zerega & Castle Hill Ave | 1950-60's |
| Sarah & George's | E 193rd St | 1950's |
| Sarah & Izzy's | 197 McClellan St | 1957-80 |
| Sarah & Mike's | Beach & E Tremont Ave | 1944-1966 |
| Sarin's Candy Store | Ogden Ave bet. W 170 St & W 171 St | 1947-66 |
| Saul, J | 35 City Island Ave | 1940's |
| Saxon's Candy Store | 1362 Clinton St | 1960's |
| Scarangella, D | 321 E 166 St | 1950's |
| Schelly Candy Shop | 109 E Burnside Ave | 1940's |
| Scherff, W | 3823 3rd Ave | 1940's |
| Schiff's Candy Store | Astor Place and Holland Ave | 1930's-40's |
| Schillingmann's Confectionery | 56 W Burnside Ave | 1940's |
| Schmid, L | 1191 Castle Hill Ave | 1950-60's |
| Schmidt, A | 403 E 161 St | 1940's |
| Schmidt, W | 3000 Bruckner Blvd | 1940-50's |
| Schmitz, M | 1802 Nereid Ave | 1950's |
| Schneider, F A | 2368 Washington Ave | 1940-60's |
| Schrager Joseph Inc | 936 E Tremont Ave | 1950's |
| Schreiber, E | 197 McClellan Ave | 1950's |
| Schuman, Michael | 1578 Bathgate Ave | 1950-60's |
| Schuman's | 533 E 171 St | 1940's |
| Schwab's | Woodycrest Ave & 167th St | |
| Schwartz | Mohegan Ave & E. 180 St | 1930's |
| Schwartzberg's | 181st St & Creston Ave | 1950-59 |
| Seibel | Mace Avenue & White Plains Rd | 1934-46 |
| Seibel Stationery | 549 E 168th St | 1933-42 |
| Seidenberg & Wishner | 1465 Unionport Rd | 1940's |
| Seidler & Fish | 1858 Jerome Ave | 1940's |
| Seidler, William | 709 E Tremont Ave | 1940-60's |
| Seidler's | 709 E Tremont Ave | 1950's |
| Seidlitz Candy Store | White Plains Rd & Gleason | 1930-40's |
| Semel's | E. 196th St & Briggs Ave | 1920-30's |
| Shakespeare's | Shakespeare Ave & Featherbed Lane | 1950's |
| Shattuck, Frank | 33 E Fordham Rd | 1940-60's |
| Sheinkopf, Morris | 730 Hunts Point Ave | 1940-60's |
| Sheps Candy Store | 180 St. bet. Mohegan & Honeywell | 1940-50's |
| Sheridan's | Willis Ave bet. 144th St & E145th St | 1946-56 |
| Sherry The Tobacconist | 748 E 180th St | 1950's |
| Sheveil, M | 556 Bergen Ave | 1940's |
| Shimowitz, Henry | 972 East 165th St | 1960's |
| Shimowitz, M | 1623 East 172rd St | 1960's |
| Shore's | Belmont Ave & E Tremont Ave | 1940s-60s |
| Sid's Candy Store | 956 E. 174th St | |
| Silver Beach Confectionary | Silver Beach | 1960's |
| Silver Rods | Simpson St & E 165th St | 1940-60's |
| Simon's | West Tremont & Cedar Ave | 1920's-50's |
| Sinnigen, H A | 378 Bedford Pk Blvd | 1940-50's |
| Skippy's Candy Store | West Burnside & Andrews | 1950's |
| Sloppy Sam's | Woodycrest Ave & W 165 St | 1940's-50's |
| Slotnicks Candy Store | Teller bet. E. 161st & E 162nd | 1940's |
| Smith, R M | 1507 Washington Ave | 1950's |
| Smitties | Lydig Ave | 1930-65 |
| Snookies | W. 238th St & Bailey Ave | 1960-70's |
| Snowflake Bake Shop | 2151 White Plains Rd | 1950's |
| Solomon, J | 883 Southern Blvd | 1960's |
| Sol's | E 169th St & Sheridan Ave | 1940-50's |
| Sol's Candy Store | 174th St | 1949-53 |
| Sol & Dave's Candy Store | W. 168th & Nelson Ave. | 1940-50's |
| Sol & Moe's | Kingsbridge & Morris | 1940-50's |
| Sophie & Sam's | E. 178th between Daly & Vyse | 1950's |
| Spa | St. Raymond & Castle Hill | 1950's |
| Spa Luncheonette | 1500 Olmstead Ave | 1950-78 |
| Spector's | Stebbins Ave & E 170th St | 1950's |
| St Murray's Candy Store | Corner of E 161st St | 1960's |
| Stan & Hy's | Walton & 183rd | 1940-50's |
| Stan & Ruby | 1515 Boston Road | 1950's |
| Stegmuller, H | 403 E 161st St | 1950's |
| Steinborn Confectionary | 3216 3rd Ave | 1940's |
| Stellings | 4301 Katonah Ave | 1940's |
| Stephens, B | 1204 Union Ave | 1960's |
| Steve & Eddies | 1811 Southern Blvd | 1940's |
| Stevie's | Mace Ave between Paulding Ave and Colden Ave | 1940's-50's |
| Stiegler, C | 2381 Grand Concourse | 1940's |
| Stubbe, John | 790 E Tremont Ave | 1940's |
| Stube's | E Tremont & Mapes Ave | 1935-42 |
| Stuhls Candy Store | Plimpton & W. 172 St. | 1940-50's |
| Sugarbowl | Claremont Pkwy & 3rd Ave | 1950's |
| Surenko's | Brady Ave and Bronx Park East | 1940's-50's |
| Suther, P | 2381 Grand Concourse | 1940's |
| Sweet Shoppe | Bainbridge Ave and W 198 St | 1940's-60's |
| Sweetland Confectionary | 3216 3rd Ave | 1950's |
| Sweisky's | Vyse & E. 172nd St | 1934-50's |
| Syd's Spa | Holland Ave and Lydig Ave | 1952-62 |
| Taft Sugar Bowl | E. 170th St & Morris Ave | 1940's-60's |
| Takis Brothers | 4196 White Plains Rd | 1940-60's |
| Tares | Corner of 181st St & Morris Ave | 1950-59 |
| Tamburo, L | 601 E 181 St | 1940-50's |
| Tasbirn's | Colgate & Westchester Ave | 1940's |
| Telson, J | 941 E 174th St | 1960's |
| Tempsky Candy Store | Beekman Ave & Oak Ter | 1950's |
| Tess & Tony's Candy Store | E. 183 bet. Hughes & Adams | 1964-1988 |
| Thelma & Sid's | West 169th Street | |
| Three Corners Candy Store | Home St, Longfellow St and West Farms Rd | 1930's-64 |
| Three Sisters Candy Store | 1406 Eilkins Ave | 1960's |
| Tompkins | Gun Hill Rd | |
| Tony's | 178th St & Washington Ave | 1940's |
| Tony's | 182nd St & Hughes Ave | 1960's |
| Tony's Candy & Soda Shop | 1936 Crotona Ave | 1960's |
| Toro, J | 570 E 136th St | 1950's |
| Translateur, E | 4024 3rd Ave | 1950's |
| Trepp, S | 396 E 154th St | 1950-60's |
| Treu, Joseph | 667 Kelly | 1940-60's |
| Turchick, F | 2645 Jerome Ave | 1950's |
| Two Little Streets | Castle Hill Ave & Starling | 1940's-70's |
| Umland, C | 430 E 149th St | 1940-60's |
| Umlands Ice Cream Parlor | 149th St bet Brook & Bergen | 1940's |
| University Confectionery Shoppe | 1601 University Ave | 1960's |
| University Sweet Shoppe | 2362 University Ave | 1960's |
| Uptown Candy Company | 1804 Paulding Ave | 1950-60's |
| Valdakis, E | 2007 Mapes Ave | 1950's |
| Valdes, J | 1022 Stebbens Ave | 1950-60's |
| Vallins, Addle | 1768 Jerome Ave | 1940-50's |
| Vallins, Addle | 67 E 161 St | 1940-60's |
| Vallins, Addle | 103 W Kingsbridge Rd | 1940-50's |

# THE CONFECTION CONNECTION

| | | |
|---|---|---|
| Veeter's | Hoffman St bet E 187 St & E 188 St | 1950's-60's |
| Venus, D | 769 E 156th St | 1950-60's |
| Verdia's Candy Store | 1445 Boston Rd | 1960's |
| Victor's Candy Store | 1421 Minneford Pl | 1960's |
| Victory Sweet & Nut Shop | 23 E 175th St | 1950's |
| Viebrock, D | 459 E Tremont Ave | 1940-60's |
| Viera, J | 1226 Southern Blvd | 1960's |
| Village Green Candy Store and Luncheonette | Concourse Ave and E 181 St | 1950's-75 |
| Vincent's Candy Store | 653 E 182rd St | 1960's |
| Voltmer, F | 632 Courtland Ave | 1940's |
| Wailus Ice Cream Store | Clinton Ave & Boston Rd | 1930's |
| Wally & Joe's | Ogden Ave & W. 165th St | 1946-62 |
| Weber's Bake Shop | 52 W Fordham Rd | 1940's |
| Weinberg's | 181st St & Corner of Daly | 1941-60's |
| Weiner's | E 172nd bet Freley & Croes | 1950-53 |
| Weiner's | Tiffany bet E 167 & E 169th St | |
| Weinsteins | 137 W Tremont Ave | 1954-65 |
| Weiss' Candy Store | Bryant Ave & Lafayette | 1940's-50's |
| West Farms Candy Co | 1030 E 180th St | 1940's |
| Whitestone Confectionary | 1024 Longwood Ave | 1950's |
| Wichern Brothers | 356 Willis Ave | 1940-50's |
| Wilkens, H | 337 E 138th St | 1950-60's |
| Wilkins Ave Candy/Tobacco | 1901 Southern Blvd | 1940-60's |
| Wilkins Sweet Ctr | 1342 Wilkins Ave | 1940-60's |
| Willing, J | Edgewater Camp | 1940's |
| Windeler, G | 3974 White Plains Rd | 1940-60's |
| Wistaria Shop | 343 E Fordham Rd | 1940's |
| Wulpern & Lobman | 3006 Westchester Ave | 1940-50's |
| Yellin's | Brady Ave and White Plains Rd | 1940's-60's |
| Yorkville Candy Company | 2555 Boston Rd | 1940-50's |
| Yuengling, C G | 1051 Westchester Ave | 1940 |
| Zack's Candy Store | Lafayette Ave & Faile St | 1940-50's |
| Zahler's | W Burnside Ave | 1940-50's |
| Zaltzberg, Michael | 388 East 141 St | 1950-60's |
| Zelenko, M | 892 E Tremont Ave | 1940's |
| Zelkins | 205 St. near Concourse | 1940-50's |
| Zico's Fruit & Nut Shop | 192 East 167th St | 1950-60's |
| Ziede's | | 1940's |
| Zimmerman's | Ollinville Ave & Allerton | 1960-80's |
| Zimmerman's | Hoe Ave & E 173rd St. | 1940-53 |
| Zimmy's | Watson & Boynton | 1948-55 |
| Zion Candy Association | 1070 Washington Ave | 1950-60's |
| Zombie's | Faile St | 1950's |
| Zwiebach & Hadman | 1936 Crotona Ave | 1950's |

# note to our readers

The Bronx consists of over 42 square miles or about the size of Paris, France, and therefore it is impossible to cover every area. We recognize that some of you may feel slighted and we are therefore providing you with space to respond, complain, kvetch, and generally tell us what we may have left out.

Attach additional pages as needed. Pictures are always welcomed. We are already planning a revised edition and all correspondence will be carefully considered. For your convenience you may wish to fax us at (914) 592-4893 or e-mail at www.backinthebronx.com or mail to: Back IN THE BRONX, Box 141H, Scarsdale, NY 10583.

**My Name is:**

Last _____ , First _____ Maiden _____

Address: _____

City _____ State _____ Zip _____

e-mail: _____ High School: _____ Yr. Grad: _____

**For your next edition, please consider:**

☐ candy store *(need name, address, approximate years [from-to], description of store, what was sold, etc.)*

☐ neighborhood *(location, special characters, memorable events, etc.)*

☐ high school, junior high, or elementary school *(years you attended, famous or infamous teachers, etc.)*

☐ restaurants *(location, specialties, menus [especially wanted])*

☐ stores *(description of merchandise sold, owner, unique personalities, etc.)*

☐ hang outs *(location, years, special atmosphere)*

☐ Bronx Celebrities *(stories and/or anecdotes)*

☐ How was your life shaped by the Bronx?

☐ Any other thoughts (good or bad) about the Bronx that you'd like us to know about.

# The stories of your life have now been published!

## *All the priceless memories of The Bronx have been bound up for you in this book.*

Now you can really go back in the Bronx… right back to the very first issue and start enjoying every story and article, every moment that we have gathered with over **210 stories** including countless **vintage photographs** about your Bronx in the '30s,'40s, '50s and '60s.

Shop at **Alexander's**, spoon a sundae at **Krum's**. A date in the **Paradise** or a day at **Orchard Beach**. Dancing in **Poe Park** or cheering at **Yankee Stadium**.

This wasn't your life, it IS your life because all those formative years are what made us what we are today. The ups and downs, the hopes and dreams… it's all there for your to keep forever.

You can also locate friends and classmates through our **2000+** classified advertisements.

All these wonderful priceless memories now have a wonderful price. Four years in the making, this finely **bound book** of the complete **18 issues** can now be yours for just $49.95. If you order another for a friend, you'll save $9.90 (shipping and handling) (2 for $99).

*As an extra bonus, the book includes two collector's items: A replica of a 1950's Jahn's menu, plus pictures of the interior of Krum's taken in the '40s-'50s.*

Please be aware that for the most part **this is only available through Back in THE BRONX.** Also, be aware, that though this book makes these wonderful days and memories last, this great offer **will not** because our supply is limited and we know from past experience that the demand will be great.

So don't delay. Fill out the request form or call toll-free **1-800-7BRONX5** to charge your order. And every order comes with a **30 day money-back guarantee.** That's how confident we feel about this offer.

Why is this the deal of a lifetime? *Because it's **your** lifetime.*

Includes Vintage **Jahn's Menu!**

# photo index

Alex & Henry's Restaurant-61
Alexander's Department Store-68,136
Allerton Ave-211
Allerton Avenue Cooperative Housing-115,117
Anna & Tony's Restaurant-81
Art Deco-1-6
Arthur Avenue-59
Ascot Theatre-100,170
Avalon Theatre-104
B.F. Keith Vaudeville-98
Berg, Gertrude-190
Biograph Studios-167
Bobkoff's-67
Borough Hall-118
Boscobel Avenue-81
Botanical Gardens-16
Bronx Zoo-13,14,15
Bronx Beacon Laundry-89
Bronx Borough Hall-118
Bronx Candy Stores-30,203-248
Bronx Terminal Market-6, 12
Burnside Ave-76,102
Burnside Theatre-85,102
Busses-156
Buttons, Red-166
Candy Stores-30,203-281
Castle Hill Pool-12,13
Castle Hill Theatre-103
Charlie's Inn-120
Chester Theatre-104
Churches-160-164
Coliseum-66
Concourse Plaza Hotel-64,116,158,159
Concourse-2-4,159
Coops-115,117
Crawford's Department Store-173
Crest Theatre-90
Crown Drug Store-89
Cushman's Bakery-47
Custard's last Stand-86
D Train-144,145
Daily News-24
Daitch Dairy-42
Davega-47
Davidson Avenue-117

Decatur Ave-83
DiMucci, Dion-174
Dion-174
Dyre Avenue-148
E.L. Grant Hwy-81
Earl Theatre-66
East Tremont Ave-77
Elsmere Theatre-106
Epstein's Delicatessen-37
Fairmount Theatre-101
Featherbed Lane-142,211
Ferraro, Geraldine-181
Fish Building-1,3
Fleetwood Theatre-103
Flynn Edward-121
Fordham Road-35,78,135,138,141
Franklin Theatre-98
Freedomland-49-58
Freeman Theatre-101
Gerard Ave-72
Gino's Restaurant-62
Globe Theatre-106
Goldberg, Molly-190
Gorman's-37,47
Grand Ave-138
Grand Concourse-2-4,159
Grand Theatre-106
Hall of Fame-17
Hearns-47
Highbridge-87-92
Hirsch,Judd-169
Hom & Hom Restaurant-42
Horowitz, David-194
Hub, The-146
IRT Station-143,155
IRT Trains-145,158
Jahn's Ice Cream Parlour-48
Jerome Ave-4
Jewish Center of Highbridge-164
Joe & Joe's Restaurant-63
John's Bargain Store-139,141
Kilmer, Joyce Park-113
Kingsbridge Road-86,138
Klein, Robert-177
Kranepool, Ed-184